# A·N·N·U·A·L E·D·I·T·I·O·N·S

# PSYCHOLOGY
*Thirty-First Edition*

## 01/02

D1245063

**EDITOR**

**Karen G. Duffy**
*SUNY College, Geneseo*

Karen G. Duffy holds a doctorate in psychology from Michigan State University and is currently a professor of psychology at SUNY at Geneseo. She sits on the executive board of the New York State Employees Assistance Program and is a certified community and family mediator. She is a member of the American Psychological Society and the Eastern Psychological Association.

*McGraw-Hill/Dushkin*
530 Old Whitfield Street, Guilford, Connecticut 06437

**Visit us on the Internet**
***http://www.dushkin.com***

# Credits

**1. The Science of Psychology**
Unit photo—© 2000 by PhotoDisc, Inc.

**2. Biological Bases of Behavior**
Unit photo—WHO photo.

**3. Perceptual Processes**
Unit photo—United Nations photo by John Isaac.

**4. Learning and Remembering**
Unit photo—© Cleo Freelance Photography.

**5. Cognitive Processes**
Unit photo—McGraw-Hill/Dushkin photo.

**6. Emotion and Motivation**
Unit photo—United Nations photo by Margot Granitsas.

**7. Development**
Unit photo—© Cleo Freelance Photography.

**8. Personality Processes**
Unit photo—WHO photo by Jean Mohr.

**9. Social Processes**
Unit photo—Florida News Bureau.

**10. Psychological Disorders**
Unit photo—© 2000 by PhotoDisc, Inc.

**11. Psychological Treatments**
Unit photo—Courtesy of Louis P. Raucci.

# Copyright

Cataloging in Publication Data
Main entry under title: Annual Editions: Psychology. 2001/2002.
1. Psychology—Periodicals. I. Duffy, Karen G., comp.II. Title: Psychology.
BF 149.A58    150'    79-180263    ISBN 0-07-243377-9    ISSN 0272-3794

Thirty-First Edition

Cover image © 2001 by PhotoDisc, Inc.

Printed in the United States of America    1234567890BAHBAH54321    Printed on Recycled Paper

# To the Reader

In publishing ANNUAL EDITIONS we recognize the enormous role played by the magazines, newspapers, and journals of the public press in providing current, first-rate educational information in a broad spectrum of interest areas. Many of these articles are appropriate for students, researchers, and professionals seeking accurate, current material to help bridge the gap between principles and theories and the real world. These articles, however, become more useful for study when those of lasting value are carefully collected, organized, indexed, and reproduced in a low-cost format, which provides easy and permanent access when the material is needed. That is the role played by ANNUAL EDITIONS.

Ronnie's parents couldn't understand why he didn't want to be picked up and cuddled as did his older sister when she was a baby. As an infant, Ronnie did not respond to his parents' smiles, words, or attempts to amuse him. By the age of two, Ronnie's parents knew that he was not like other children. He did not speak, was very temperamental, and often rocked himself for hours. Ronnie is autistic. His parents feel that some of Ronnie's behavior may be their fault; they both work long hours as young professionals and leave both children with an older woman during the weekdays. Ronnie's pediatrician assures his parents that their reasoning, while logical, probably holds no merit because the causes of autism are little understood and are likely to be physiological rather than parental. What can we do about children like Ronnie? What is the source of autism? Can it be treated or reversed? Can autism be prevented?

Psychologists attempt to answer these and other questions in a specific way, with scientific methods. Researchers, using carefully planned methods, try to discover the causes of complex human behavior, normal or not. The scientific results of most psychological research are published in professional journals, and therefore may be difficult for the layperson to understand.

*Annual Editions: Psychology 01/02* is designed to meet the needs of lay people and introductory-level students who are curious about psychology. *Annual Editions: Psychology 01/02* provides a vast selection of readable and informative articles primarily from popular magazines and newspapers. These articles are typically written by journalists, but a few are written by psychologists and retain the excitement of the discovery of scientific knowledge.

The particular articles in this volume were chosen to be representative of the most current work in psychology. They were selected because they are accurate in their reporting and provide examples of the types of psychological research that is discussed in most introductory psychology classes.

As in any science, some of the findings discussed in this collection are startling, while others confirm what we already know. Some articles will invite speculation about social and personal issues; others demand careful thought about potential misuse of the applications of research findings. Readers are expected to make the investment of effort and critical reasoning needed to answer such questions and concerns.

I believe that you will find this edition of *Annual Editions: Psychology 01/02* readable and useful. I suggest that students look at the organization of this book and compare it to the organization of their textbook and course syllabus. By examining the *topic guide* that follows the *table of contents,* you can identify the articles that are most appropriate for each particular unit of study in your course.

Your instructor may provide some help in assigning articles to supplement the text. As you read them, try to connect their contents with the principles you are learning from your text and classroom lectures. Some of the articles will help you better understand a specific area of research, while others will help you connect and integrate information from various research areas. Both of these strategies are important in learning about psychology or any other science. It is only through intensive investigation and subsequent integration of the findings from many studies that we are able to discover and apply new knowledge.

Please take time to provide us with feedback to guide the annual revision of this anthology by completing and returning the *article rating form* in the back of the book. With your help, this collection will be even better next year. Thank you.

*Karen Grover Duffy*

Karen Grover Duffy
*Editor*

# Contents

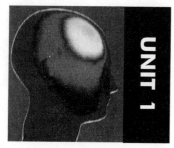

UNIT 1

## The Science of Psychology

Three articles examine psychology
as the science of behavior.

UNIT 2

## Biological Bases of Behavior

Three selections discuss the
biological bases of behavior. Topics
include brain functions and the
brain's control over the body.

The concepts in bold italics are developed in the article. For further expansion please refer to the Topic Guide, the Glossary, and the Index.

## UNIT 3

## Perceptual Processes

Four articles discuss the impact of the senses on human perceptual processes.

## UNIT 4

## Learning and Remembering

Five selections examine how operant conditioning, positive reinforcement, and memory interact during the learning process.

The concepts in bold italics are developed in the article. For further expansion please refer to the Topic Guide, the Glossary, and the Index.

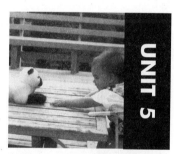

UNIT 5

## Cognitive Processes

Three articles examine how social
skills, common sense, and
intelligence affect human
cognitive processes.

The concepts in bold italics are developed in the article. For further expansion please refer to the Topic Guide, the Glossary, and the Index.

vii

## UNIT 6

## Emotion and Motivation

Four articles discuss the influences of stress, mental states, and emotion on the mental and physical health of the individual.

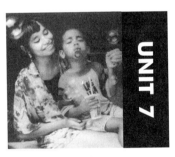

## UNIT 7

## Development

Five articles consider the importance of experience, discipline, familial support, and psychological aging during the normal human development process.

The concepts in bold italics are developed in the article. For further expansion please refer to the Topic Guide, the Glossary, and the Index.

**UNIT 8**

## Personality Processes

Three selections discuss a few of the processes by which personalities are developed. Topics include sex differences, state of mind, and hostility.

The concepts in bold italics are developed in the article. For further expansion please refer to the Topic Guide, the Glossary, and the Index.

## UNIT 9

# Social Processes

Four selections discuss how the individual's social development is affected by genes, stereotypes, prejudice, and self-help.

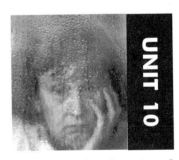

## UNIT 10

# Psychological Disorders

Five articles examine several psychological disorders. Topics include unexpected behavior, the impact of depression on a person's well-being, and physical abuse.

The concepts in bold italics are developed in the article. For further expansion please refer to the Topic Guide, the Glossary, and the Index.

UNIT 11

# Psychological Treatments

Four selections discuss a few
psychological treatments, including
psychoanalysis, psychotherapy
to alleviate depression, self-care,
and the use of drugs.

The concepts in bold italics are developed in the article. For further expansion please refer to the Topic Guide, the Glossary, and the Index.

1

# Topic Guide

This topic guide suggests how the selections in this book relate to the subjects covered in your course.

The Web icon ( ◉ ) under the topic articles easily identifies the relevant Web sites, which are numbered and annotated on the next two pages. By linking the articles and the Web sites by topic, this ANNUAL EDITIONS reader becomes a powerful learning and research tool.

| TOPIC AREA | TREATED IN | TOPIC AREA | TREATED IN |
|---|---|---|---|
| Adolescents | 25. World of Their Own<br>◉ **8, 14, 19, 21, 22, 25** | | 42. Quest for a Cure<br>◉ **25, 26, 27, 30, 31** |
| Aging | 15. Speak, Memory<br>26. Live to 100? No Thanks<br>◉ **22** | Development | 11. Learning Begins Even Before Babies Are Born<br>12. Different Strokes for Different Folks?<br>23. Fetal Psychology<br>24. Four Things You Need to Know About Raising Baby<br>25. World of Their Own<br>26. Live to 100? No Thanks<br>◉ **8, 9, 15, 21, 22** |
| Alzheimer's Disease | 16. Smart Genes?<br>◉ **22** | | |
| Animals | 16. Smart Genes?<br>18. Can Animals Think?<br>◉ **7** | | |
| Athletes | 19. Gold Medal Mind<br>◉ **10, 11, 19** | Drugs/Drug Treatment | 37. Depression: Beyond Serotonin<br>39. Doubting Disease<br>42. Quest for a Cure<br>◉ **31, 32, 33** |
| Brain | 6. Future of the Brain<br>7. Senses<br>8. Vision: A Window on Consciousness<br>◉ **8, 9, 10, 11, 15, 17, 19, 22** | Emotional Intelligence | 22. Emotional Intelligence: Do You Have It?<br>◉ **23** |
| | | Emotions | 21. What's in a Face?<br>22. Emotional Intelligence: Do You Have It?<br>◉ **20, 22, 23** |
| Central Nervous System | 6. Future of the Brain<br>◉ **8, 9, 10, 11, 15** | Faces | 21. What's in a Face?<br>◉ **7, 23** |
| Children | 11. Learning Begins Even Before Babies Are Born<br>12. Different Strokes for Different Folks?<br>23. Fetal Psychology<br>24. Four Things You Need to Know About Raising Baby<br>25. World of Their Own<br>◉ **15, 17, 20, 21, 22** | Fetus | 23. Fetal Psychology |
| | | Genes/Genetics | 4. End of Nature Versus Nurture<br>5. Decoding the Human Body<br>◉ **8, 9, 10, 11, 22, 23** |
| | | Intelligence | 16. Smart Genes?<br>17. Who Owns Intelligence?<br>◉ **15, 16, 17, 18** |
| Cognition | 8. Vision: A Window on Consciousness<br>18. Can Animals Think?<br>◉ **15, 17, 21, 22** | Learning | 11. Learning Begins Even Before Babies Are Born<br>12. Different Strokes for Different Folks?<br>13. What Constitutes "Appropriate" Punishment?<br>◉ **14, 15** |
| Crowding | 32. Coping With Crowding | | |
| Culture | 34. Merits and Perils of Teaching About Other Cultures<br>◉ **4** | Lying | 31. How to Spot a Liar |
| Deafness | 9. Noise<br>◉ **4** | Memory | 14. Lots of Action in the Memory Game<br>15. Speak, Memory<br>◉ **14, 15** |
| Death/Dying | 27. Start the Conversation | | |
| Deception | 3. Psychology's Tangled Web<br>31. How to Spot a Liar<br>◉ **7, 23** | Mental Disorder | 35. Mental Health Gets Noticed<br>36. Mental Disorders Are Not Diseases<br>37. Depression: Beyond Serotonin<br>38. Clustering and Contagion of Suicide |
| Depression | 37. Depression: Beyond Serotonin<br>38. Clustering and Contagion of Suicide | | |

# ● AE: PSYCHOLOGY

The following World Wide Web sites have been carefully researched and selected to support the articles found in this reader. The sites are cross-referenced by number and the Web icon (●) in the topic guide. In addition, it is possible to link directly to these Web sites through our DUSHKIN ONLINE support site at *http://www.dushkin.com/online/*.

**The following sites were available at the time of publication. Visit our Web site—we update DUSHKIN ONLINE regularly to reflect any changes.**

## General Sources

### 1. APA Resources for the Public
*http://www.apa.org/psychnet/*
Use the site map or search engine to access *APA Monitor*, the American Psychological Association newspaper, APA books on a wide range of topics, PsychINFO, an electronic database of abstracts on scholarly journals, and the HelpCenter.

### 2. Mental Help Net
*http://mentalhelp.net*
This comprehensive guide to mental health online features more than 6,300 individual resources. Information on mental disorders and professional resources in psychology, psychiatry, and social work are presented.

### 3. The Psych.com: Internet Psychology Resource
*http://www.thepsych.com*
Thousands of psychology resources are currently indexed at this site. Psychology Disciplines, Conditions & Disorders, Psychiatry, Assistance, and Self-Development are among the most useful.

### 4. School Psychology Resources Online
*http://www.schoolpsychology.net*
Numerous sites on special conditions, disorders, and disabilities, as well as other data ranging from assessment/evaluation to research, are available on this resouce page for psychologists, parents, and educators.

## The Science of Psychology

### 5. Abraham A. Brill Library
*http://plaza.interport.net/nypsan/service.html*
Containing data on over 40,000 books, periodicals, and reprints in psychoanalysis and related fields, the Abraham A. Brill Library's holdings span the literature of psychoanalysis from its beginning to the present day.

### 6. American Psychological Society (APS)
*http://www.psychologicalscience.org/links.html*
The APS is dedicated to advancing the best of scientific psychology in research, application, and the improvement of human conditions. Links to teaching, research, and graduate studies resources are available.

### 7. Psychological Research on the Net
*http://psych.hanover.edu/APS/exponnet.html*
This Net site provides psychologically related experiments. Biological psychology/neuropsychology, clinical psychology, cognition, developmental psychology, emotions, health psychology, personality, sensation/perception, and social psychology are some of the areas covered.

## Biological Bases of Behavior

### 8. Adolescence: Changes and Continuity
*http://www.personal.psu.edu/faculty/n/x/nxd10/biologic2.htm*
A discussion of puberty, sexuality, biological changes, cross-cultural differences, and nutrition for adolescents, including obesity and its effects on adolescent development, is presented here.

### 9. Division of Hereditary Diseases and Family Studies, Indiana University School of Medicine
*http://medgen.iupui.edu/divisions/hereditary/*
The Department of Medical and Molecular Genetics is primarily concerned with determining the genetic basis of disease. It consists of a multifaceted program with a variety of interdisciplinary projects. The areas of twin studies and linkage analysis are also explored.

### 10. Institute for Behavioral Genetics
*http://ibgwww.colorado.edu/index.html*
Dedicated to conducting and facilitating research on the genetic and environmental bases of individual differences in behavior, this organized research unit at the University of Colorado leads to Genetic Sites, Statistical Sites, and the Biology Meta Index, as well as to search engines.

### 11. Serendip
*http://serendip.brynmawr.edu/serendip/*
Serendip, which is organized into five subject areas (brain and behavior, complex systems, genes and behavior, science and culture, and science education), contains interactive exhibits, articles, links to other resources, and a forum area.

## Perceptual Processes

### 12. Psychology Tutorials and Demonstrations
*http://psych.hanover.edu/Krantz/tutor.html*
Interactive tutorials and simulations, primarily in the area of sensation and perception, are available here.

### 13. A Sensory Adventure
*http://illusionworks.com/html/jump_page.html*
This multimedia site on illusions will inform (and perhaps delight) about how we think and perceive.

## Learning and Remembering

### 14. The Opportunity of Adolescence
*http://www.winternet.com/~webpage/adolescencepaper.html*
According to this paper, adolescence is the turning point, after which the future is redirected and confirmed. The opportunities and problems of this period are presented with quotations from Erik Erikson, Jean Piaget, and others.

### 15. Project Zero
*http://pzweb.harvard.edu*
The Harvard Project Zero has investigated the development of learning processes in children and adults for 30 years. Today, Project Zero's mission is to understand and enhance learning, thinking, and creativity in the arts and other disciplines for individuals and institutions.

## Cognitive Processes

### 16. Chess: Kasparov v. Deep Blue: The Rematch
*http://www.chess.ibm.com/home/html/b.html*
Clips from the chess rematch between Garry Kasparov and IBM's supercomputer, Deep Blue, are presented here along with commentaries on chess, computers, artificial intelligence, and what it all means.

### 17. Cognitive Science Article Archive
*http://www.helsinki.fi/hum/kognitiotiede/archive.html*
This excellent Finnish source contains articles on various fields of cognitive science.

### 18. Introduction to Artificial Intelligence (AI)
*http://www-formal.stanford.edu/jmc/aiintro/aiintro.html*
A description of AI is presented here along with links to other AI sites.

## Emotion and Motivation

### 19. CYFERNET-Youth Development
*http://www.cyfernet.mes.umn.edu/youthdev.html*
CYFERNET presents many articles on youth development, including a statement on the concept of normal adolescence and impediments to healthy development.

### 20. Nature vs. Nature: Gergen Dialogue with Winifred Gallagher
*http://www.pbs.org/newshour/gergen/gallagher_5-14.html*
Experience modifies temperament, according to this TV interview. The author of *I.D.: How Heredity and Experience Make You Who You Are* explains a current theory about temperament.

## Development

### 21. American Association for Child and Adolescent Psychiatry
*http://www.aacap.org*
This site is designed to aid in the understanding and treatment of the developmental, behavioral, and mental disorders that could affect children and adolescents. There is a specific link just for families about common childhood problems that may or may not require professional intervention.

### 22. Behavioral Genetics
*http://www.uams.edu/department_of_psychiatry/slides/html/genetics/index.htm*
A slide show on Behavioral Genetics, which includes objectives, methods of genetic investigation, family and twin studies, personality, intelligence, mental disorders, and Alzheimer's Disease, is presented on this Web site.

## Personality Processes

### 23. The Personality Project
*http://personality-project.org/personality.html*
This Personality Project (by William Revelle) is meant to guide those interested in personality theory and research to the current personality research literature.

## Social Processes

### 24. National Clearinghouse for Alcohol and Drug Information
*http://www.health.org*
Information on drug and alcohol facts that might relate to adolescence and the issues of peer pressure and youth culture is presented here. Resources, referrals, research and statistics, databases, and related Net links are available.

## Psychological Disorders

### 25. Anxiety Disorders
*http://www.adaa.org/aboutanxietydisorders/*
Anxiety disorders in children, adolescents, and adults are reviewed by the Anxiety Disorders Association of America (ADAA). A detailed glossary is also included.

### 26. Ask NOAH About: Mental Health
*http://www.noah.cuny.edu/illness/mentalhealth/mental.html*
Information about child and adolescent family problems, mental conditions and disorders, suicide prevention, and much more is available here.

### 27. Mental Health Net: Disorders and Treatments Index
*http://www.mentalhelp.net/dxtx.htm*
Presented on this site are hotlinks to psychological disorders pages, which include anxiety, panic, phobic disorders, schizophrenia, and violent/self-destructive behaviors.

### 28. Mental Health Net: Eating Disorder Resources
*http://www.mentalhelp.net/guide/eating.htm*
This mental health Net site provides a complete list of Web references on eating disorders, including anorexia, bulimia, and obesity.

### 29. National Women's Health Resource Center (NWHRC)
*http://www.healthywomen.org*
NWHRC's site contains links to resources related to women's substance abuse and mental illnesses.

### 30. SA/VE: Suicide Awareness/Voices of Education
*http://www.save.org*
This SA/VE suicide site presents data on suicide prevention. It includes symptoms/danger signs, misconceptions, facts, hospitalization, and other details on depression and suicide.

## Psychological Treatments

### 31. Knowledge Exchange Network (KEN)
*http://www.mentalhealth.org*
Information about mental health (prevention, treatment, and rehabilitation services), is available via toll-free telephone services, an electronic bulletin board, and publications.

### 32. Links to the World of Carl Jung
*http://www.cisnet.com/teacher-ed/jung.html*
Dedicated to the work of Carl Jung, this is a comprehensive resource for Jungian psychology with links to Jung's complete works the Dream Room, reference materials, and the Keirsey Temperament Sorter.

### 33. Sigmund Freud and the Freud Archives
*http://plaza.interport.net/nypsan/freudarc.html*
Internet resources related to Sigmund Freud, which include a collection of libraries, museums, and biographical materials, as well as the Brill Library archives, can be found here.

**We highly recommend that you review our Web site for expandedinformation and our other product lines. We are continually updating and adding links to our Web site in order to offer you the most usable and useful information that will support and expand the value of your Annual Editions. You can reach us at: *http://www.dushkin. com/annualeditions/*.**

www.dushkin.com/online/

# Unit 1

## Unit Selections

1. **Science and Pseudoscience,** *APS Observer*
2. **Research in the Psychological Laboratory: Truth or Triviality?** Craig A. Anderson, James J. Lindsay, and Brad J. Bushman
3. **Psychology's Tangled Web: Deceptive Methods May Backfire on Behavioral Researchers,** Bruce Bower

## Key Points to Consider

❖ Which area of psychology do you think is the most valuable and why? Many people are most aware of clinical psychology by virtue of having watched films and television. Is this the most valuable area of the discipline? About which other areas of psychology do you think the public ought to be informed?

❖ How do you think psychology is related to other scientific disciplines, such as sociology, biology, and human medicine? Are there nonscience disciplines to which psychology might be related, for example, philosophy and mathematics? How so?

❖ Do you think psychologists will ever be able to piece together a single grand theory of human psychology? Do you have your own theory of human behavior? If yes, on what do you base your theory, your own observations? In developing a theory of human behavior, should psychologists rely exclusively on research?

❖ Why is research important to psychology? What kinds of information can be gleaned from psychological research? What is validity? What is external validity? Can you provide an example of each? Why are these concepts important to psychological research? What types of problems are inherent in poorly designed research? How can psychological research be improved? To what general conclusion do Anderson, Lindsay, and Bushman arrive regarding laboratory research? Regarding field research?

❖ Do you think it is ethical to deceive research participants? Under what circumstances do you think participants should be deceived; when should they not be deceived? How frequently do you think deception is used in psychological research? What kinds of research do you think are most likely to utilize deception? Would you ever deceive research participants if you were conducting research?

 **Links**     **www.dushkin.com/online/**

These sites are annotated on pages 4 and 5.

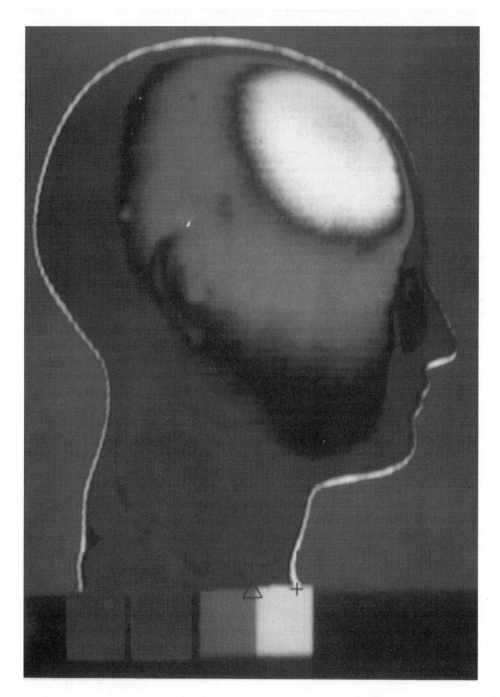

Little did Wilhelm Wundt realize his monumental contribution to science when he opened the first psychological laboratory to examine consciousness in 1879 in Germany. Wundt would barely recognize today's science of psychology as he practiced it.

Contemporary psychology is defined as the science or study of individual mental activity and behavior. This definition reflects the two parent disciplines from which psychology emerged: philosophy and biology. Compared to its parents, psychology is very much a new discipline. Some aspects of modern psychology are particularly biological, such as neuroscience, perception, psychophysics, and behavioral genetics. Other aspects are more philosophical, such as the study of personality, while others approximate sociology, as does social psychology.

Today's psychologists work in a variety of settings. Many psychologists are academics, teaching and researching psychology on university campuses. Others work in applied settings such as hospitals, mental health clinics, industry, and schools. Most psychologists specialize after some graduate training. Industrial psychologists deal with human performance in organizational settings. Clinical psychologists are concerned about the assessment, diagnosis, and treatment of individuals with a variety of mental disorders.

Some psychologists think that psychology is still in its adolescence and that the field is experiencing some growing pains. Since its establishment, the field has expanded to many different areas. As mentioned above, some areas are very applied; other areas emphasize theory and research. The growing pains have resulted in some conflict over what the agenda of the first national psychological association, the American Psychological Association, should be. Because academics perceived this association as mainly serving practitioners, academics and researchers established their own competing association, the American Psychological Society. But despite its varied nature and growing pains, psychology remains a viable and exciting field. The first unit of the book is designed to introduce you to the nature and history of psychology.

In the first article, "Science and Pseudoscience," experts in psychology debate what science really is. They conclude that science has different meanings, depending upon the constituency. Lay people, for example, often embrace as science simple anecdotal observations. Examples of science and anecdote are given.

The next article also pertains to psychological science. The authors ask a cogent question. Is research conducted in psychology, whether in the laboratory or in the field, trivial or worthwhile? The primary question they ask is about validity: Can psychological research in the laboratory, for example, inform us about human behavior in the "real" world? After reviewing a multitude of studies, the authors conclude that psychological research is sound (valid) and that both laboratory and field studies provide useful and parallel information about human behavior.

The third introductory article on psychology is also about psychological research. In some research, psychologists utilize deception. For example, the instructions tell participants that the study is about creativity and that they will write a story after viewing a stimulus. The true nature of the study may really pertain to participants' reactions to sexual stimuli. In other words, the study is not examining creativity at all. The author of the article contends that when psychologists deceive and then debrief research participants about the deception, the participants are changed forever.

# Science and Pseudoscience

**W**hat makes something science? How do we identify what isn't science?

And how do we prevent that pseudoscience from being accepted and promoted as science?

These and other equally loaded questions were taken on at the APS Convention's Presidential Symposium, coordinated this year by then-APS President and current APS Past President Elizabeth Loftus, of the University of Washington.

"We live in a land transformed by science, and yet pseudoscientific ideas are rampant," said Loftus. "Many of these beliefs concern topics that have benefitted from widespread study by psychological scientists. Science and rationality are continually under attack and threatened by a rise of pseudoscience, so I organized this year's Presidential Symposium to illuminate these problems in hopes of fostering critical thinking, educating the public, and ourselves."

Loftus invited several well-known researchers and scholars in the field to help her in her quest, including:

1. Yale University's Robert Steinberg, who spoke on "How more and more research can tell you less and less until finally you know much less than when you started";
2. Carol Tavris, who gave her perspective on "Power, politics, money, and fame: Sources of pseudoscience in research and therapy"; and
3. Ray Hyman, of the University of Oregon, who served as the discussant for these intriguing concepts.

## In the Beginning ...

Loftus kicked off the symposium discussing the tendency of humans, throughout their existence, to find some kind of explanation for the mysteries of the universe, natural events, and life itself. Loftus favorably mentioned and then paraphrased from a book—*Mind Myths: Exploring popular assumptions about the mind and brain,* edited by Sergio Della Sala—that, she said, captured the paradox:

"The changing seasons, growth and decay, storms, floods, droughts, and good and bad fortune, for example, were all attributed to supernatural beings, to famous ancestors, or ancient heroes," she said. "We now have a better understanding of, for instance, thunder and lightning and they don't terrify us as much, but in the absence of this kind of understanding of the mechanisms of the mind, the brain, and the effects of diseases on the mind and brain, we tackle mysteries still by focusing on divine intervention or we take shelter in simplistic superstition."

Loftus then gave a number of examples of how, even today, pseudoscience and misinformation abounds.

"Educated people have been known to recently express beliefs in alien abduction, fire walking, possession, creationism, and even that 90 percent of handicapped people have parents who were not virgins when they married," said Loftus, who then referred to a survey she conducted with her colleagues of non-psychology graduate students that indicated a good percentage of them believed that therapeutic techniques could be used to remember prenatal accounts.

"One problem here is that the books written by believers—full of enchanting anecdotes that are mistaken for science—sell like hot cakes, while books by skeptics trying to debunk these beliefs don't sell as well or at all," she said.

Loftus cited another example of a self-described "personologist" who has written a book on using a person's facial features to determine their personality and nature.

"Why do people persist in believing in impossible or improbable things?" asked Loftus, who turned the podium over the Steinberg, who explored the phenomenon of quasi-science and challenged the assumption that the more data collected about a phenomenon indicates the more we know about that phenomenon.

This assumption is flat out wrong, says Steinberg, who argues that scientists tend to build in certain limited assumptions in collecting data. The results, he says, is that scientists keep getting the same wrong or limited result and then gain confidence in that result so that they eventually become more confident of something that is not true.

"If you misplace your confidence in your quasi-scientific results, you can end up doing more and more research on a topic and know less and less," he said. "In collecting data, we always build in certain limited assumptions. For example, we may limit the participants we test. Or we may limit the kinds of test materials we use. Or we may limit the situations in which we test people."

The result, said Steinberg, is that we keep getting the same wrong, or at least limited, result and gain confidence in it.

"We are thus becoming more and more confident of something that is not true," he said and gave as a case study the example of intelligence. "Hundreds of studies reviewed by Carroll, Jensen, Brand, and others appear to show that there is a general factor. They are right—but only under the assumptions of these studies."

Steinberg presented data that showed that when one expands the range of participants (e.g., to participants in various African and Asian countries, or even culturally diverse populations in the United States), the range of materials used to test intelligence (not just academic-analytical kinds of problems, but creative and practical ones as well), and the kinds of situations in which testing is done (e.g., getting outside classrooms or psychologists' testing rooms), the "G"

factor disappears. Nor do such tests provide very good prediction of real-world performance, he said.

"The punch line is that continued heavy reliance on IQ-based measures, including the SAT, GRE, LSAT, GMAT, and so forth, depends on reliance on a narrow base of assumptions in research," he said. "Because people do not realize they are making these assumptions and because the assumptions often benefit them, they are blind to the assumptions. But these assumptions are there nevertheless, distorting the conclusions that are drawn. We need a broader conception of intelligence and, more generally, we have to be careful to collecting more data does not tell us less rather than more."

## You Know It When You See It

Tavris then presented her perspective on "Power, Politics, Money, and Fame: Sources of pseudoscience in research and therapy" in which she assessed what qualifies as science, what qualifies as pseudoscience, how to tell the difference, and why it matters.

Pseudoscience, said Tavris, is like pornography: we can't define it, but we know it when we see it.

"But what we are arguing about here and what remains a source of confusion for the public is: what is science?" she said. "Philosophers of science have been arguing this for a long time. Some define science by its goal; it is the search for permanent universal laws of behavior. Others define science by its tools; a PET scan is science, an interview is not. Others define it by its subject; a brain is a tangible thing you can study scientifically, whereas love and wisdom and other intangible psychological states are not science. Science for me is one thing: it is an attitude of questioning received wisdom combined with the deepest and most entrenched human cognitive bias—the conformational bias."

Tavris went on to define pseudoscience as the determined pursuit of confirmation of one's beliefs.

"Pseudoscience wears the veneer of science but lacks its central infusing spirit of inquiry and the willingness to come up wrong," she said. "More than ever, I think psychological science has a role to play in counteracting its influence in our culture. Of course, pseudoscience flourishes everywhere in the world and always has. It is a human predilection and not uniquely an American one, however there are two aspects of the American culture that I think foster its particular incarnation in America."

The first aspect, said Tavris, is the American culture's need for certainty. Pseudoscience is popular because it confirms what we believe, she said. The second aspect of our culture that fosters pseudoscience, added Tavris, is the capitalistic quick fix.

"We love instant cures and tonics for what ails us," she said. "From chubbiness to the blues, from serious problems to tragedies. 'We can fix you' is the American credo, and we can fix you especially fast if you take this magic pill or use this magic technology."

These forces, she argues, foster the pseudoscientific effect in research.

"The harmony now between drug researchers and the pharmaceutical industry is stronger and more worrisome than people tend to recognize. Drug companies set up their own research institutes. They sponsor seminars and conferences," she said. "I went to one on new advances in the treatment of depression. All of the advancements were—guess what—antidepressants. So increasingly, biomedical research, even if it is well done, is only giving us part of the story. The public rarely hears the rest—the rest being done by psychological scientists. For example, in the case with the antidepressants, the public rarely hears that upwards of 75 percent of the effectiveness of antidepressants is due to the placebo effect."

Critics of science, said Tavris, are right to remind scientists that they must now assume they have the truth.

"We won't ever have the truth, but, unlike pseudoscience, science give us the ability to be critically demanding," she said. "Demand evidence. Resist the confirmation bias. There are tools that can help us get closer to the answers. Maybe, sometimes, even close enough."

## Science In Another Dimension

Discussant Hyman examined how learned scientists can sometime engage in and fall victim to, pseudoscience.

"I have always been fascinated by the scientist who recognizes good science in one area while at the same time is considered to be doing pseudoscience in another area," he said. "This raises a variety of interesting issues."

Hyman has had extensive experience in debunking pseudoscientific issues. For example, earlier in the decade, he was appointed to a blue ribbon panel to evaluate previously secret programs of psychic spying conducted by the CIA over the past 20 years. In addition, he appears frequently on television shows presenting the skeptical views of various paranormal claims. He is also a founding member of the Committee of Scientific Investigation for the Claims of the Paranormal and serves on the editorial board of the journal the *Skeptic Inquirer.* He conducts an annual workshop titled "The Skeptics Toolbox," that is intended to provide participants with the knowledge and tools to property evaluate paranormal claims.

Hyman used as an example, the case of a recognized astrophysicist who published a book in which he claimed to have proven the existence of the fourth dimension from his investigations of a spiritualistic medium.

"Here we have a person who has earned his credentials and reputation in a recognized field of science," said Hyman. "He then develops and supports a theory that his colleagues categorize as pseudoscience. If this is true, then the same person can practice both science and pseudoscience."

# Research in the Psychological Laboratory: Truth or Triviality?

Craig A. Anderson,[1] James J. Lindsay, and Brad J. Bushman

Department of Psychology, University of Missouri–Columbia, Columbia, Missouri (C.A.A., J.J.L.), and Department of Psychology, Iowa State University, Ames, Iowa (B.J.B.)

## Abstract

This article examines the truism that studies from psychological laboratories are low in external validity. Past rational and empirical explorations of this truism found little support for it. A broader empirical approach was taken for the study reported here; correspondence between lab and field was compared across a broad range of domains, including aggression, helping, leadership style, social loafing, self-efficacy, depression, and memory, among others. Correspondence between lab- and field-based effect sizes of conceptually similar independent and dependent variables was considerable. In brief, the psychological laboratory has generally produced psychological truths, rather than trivialities. These same data suggest that a companion truism about field studies in psychology—that they are generally low on internal validity—is also false.

## Keywords

external validity; metaanalysis; philosophy of science

Are you happy with current rates of violent crime in the United States? How about the U.S. ranking in achievement test scores in science, compared with other industrialized nations? Do recent increases in smoking rates among U.S. teens bother you? Do the continuing problems of high rates of "unsafe sex" practices and the resulting incidence of AIDS seem to cry out for a solution?

Constant attention to the problems of modern U.S. society by the mass media, politicians, and concerned citizens may seem to indicate a generally pessimistic worldview. Paradoxically, though, this focus on problems actually reflects a fundamentally optimistic view that as a society we can and should solve these problems. This same optimism drives modern psychology as well. The whole point of the science of psychology is to learn so that we can improve "things."

## THE DEBATE ABOUT EXTERNAL VALIDITY

This functionalist view gives rise to a long-running and frequently counterproductive debate about the value of theory-oriented laboratory research versus application-oriented field research.

This article addresses a very specific question from this debate: Does the psychological laboratory yield truths or trivialities? Since Campbell (1957) clearly distinguished between *internal* and *external validity,* a common truism has been that laboratory studies are typically high on internal validity but low on external validity.[2] That is, laboratory studies are good at telling whether or not some manipulation of an independent variable causes changes in the dependent variable, but many scholars assume that these results do not generalize to the "real world." Hence, application-oriented scholars sometimes deride the psychological laboratory as a place where only trivial facts are to be found.[3] In essence, the charge is that (some, most, or all) research from the psychological laboratory is externally invalid, and therefore pointless.

One domain where this debate periodically arises concerns aggression (Anderson & Bushman, 1997). Consider obvious differences in surface characteristics between real-world versus laboratory aggression. Assault typically involves two or more people who know each other, arises from an escalating cycle of provocation, and results in serious physical injury. Aggression in the lab, however, typically involves one person (who only thinks that he or she is interacting with an unknown person via computer, or notes, or message boards of one kind or another), in a session that may last only 50 min, and involves the attempted delivery of noxious stimuli such as electric shock or blasts of noise.

But the charge that psychological laboratory research lacks external validity is not unique to the study of aggression. Recent years have seen similar debates in the study of personnel selection (e.g., Schmitt, 1996), leadership (e.g., Wolfe & Roberts, 1993), management (e.g., Griffin & Kacmar, 1991), and human memory (e.g., Banaji & Crowder, 1989; Neisser, 1978). For instance, in one early laboratory study of context-dependent memory. Dallett and Wilcox (1968) asked participants in one condition to study word lists while standing with their heads inside an oddly shaped box that contained flashing lights of several different colors; other participants studied the word lists without putting their heads inside the box. Participants later recalled the lists either with or without the box, and were most successful when the study and recall conditions were the same. As is obvious, these conditions have no counterpart in the "real" world, thus inviting complaints about external validity.

It is easy to see why nonexperts frequently charge that lab studies are trivial, artificial, and pointless, and easy to ignore such complaints as reflections of ignorance. But when the charge comes from experts—other psychological researchers who presumably share goals, training, and perspective—a thoughtful response is required. Such responses have also been forthcoming.

## RESPONSES TO LABORATORY CRITICISMS

### Embracing Invalidity

One particularly elegant response, by Mook (1983), celebrates external *in*validity. He described four cases in which the artificial lab setting is not only acceptable but actually preferred to the real-world setting:

First, we may be asking whether something can happen, rather than whether it typically does happen. Second, our prediction may . . . specify something that ought to happen in the lab. . . . Third, we may demonstrate the power of a phenomenon by showing that it happens even under unnatural conditions that ought to preclude it. Finally, we may use the lab to produce condi-

tions that have no counterpart in real life at all. . . . (p. 382)

Mook's main point is that the goal of most laboratory research is to discover theoretical relations among conceptual variables that are never sufficiently isolated in the real world to allow precise examination.

### What Is Supposed to Generalize?

A second (and related) response is to note that usually researchers are interested in generalization of theoretical relations among conceptual independent and dependent variables, not the specific instantiations of them. The same scandalous joke will mean something different in church than it does in the men's locker room. In one case it may create embarrassment, whereas in the other it may create humor. If one were interested in the effects of humor on thought processes, one would be foolish to use the same joke as an experimental manipulation of "humor" in both settings. The lack of a manipulation's generalizability constitutes an external validity problem only if one intends specific instantiations of conceptual variables to generalize across radically different contexts, but most laboratory research is concerned only with generalizability of the conceptual variables.

### The General Problem With Generalization

A third response begins with the observation that generalization is, generally, risky business. Inductive reasoning, at least in absolute terms, is never wholly justified. Even though every time you have dropped a hammer it has fallen, you cannot know for certain that it will fall the next time. Perhaps the laws of nature will change, or perhaps you will enter a location where your understanding of the laws of nature is revealed to be incomplete. Thus, generalizing from one situation to another, or from one participant population to another, is as problematic for field research as it is for lab research. So, the argument goes, why single out lab research for criticism? At least the lab makes it somewhat easier to satisfy concerns about internal validity, and without internal validity there is nothing to generalize anyway.

But, people do generalize from specific instances to general concepts, then from these general concepts to new situations involving different instances of the general concepts. A justification for such generalization can be readily found both at the level of species survival and at the level of scientific and technological

advances: In both cases, generalization works much of the time.

### Past Empirical Approaches

If what psychologists expect (hope?) to generalize are systematic relations among conceptual variables (i.e., theories), and if we grant that attempting to make generalizations is acceptable as long as it occasionally works, then another response to the external validity challenge becomes feasible. The challenge becomes an empirical question. Three different empirical approaches have been used: single-study tests, single-phenomenon tests, and single-domain tests.

Single-study tests examine a specific laboratory finding in other contexts or with other populations. For example, Godden and Baddeley (1975) successfully generalized the context-dependent memory effect using scuba divers as subjects. Word lists that had been studied underwater were better recalled underwater, whereas lists studied on dry land were better recalled on dry land. Such single-study tests of external validity abound in psychology. Many "work," though of course some do not. Though these tests answer the generalization question for a particular case, they do not adequately answer the broader question concerning the external validity of a given laboratory phenomenon.

Single-phenomenon tests examine the external validity of a whole empirical phenomenon rather than one specific laboratory finding. For example, do laboratory-based effects of anonymity on aggression generalize to field settings? Questions like this can be investigated by using *meta-analytic* techniques. That is, one could statistically average all of the research results from lab and field studies that have tested the relation between anonymity and aggression. We performed such a meta-analysis (Anderson & Bushman, 1997) and found comparable anonymity effects in lab and field settings. Similar tests of the generalizability of a specific laboratory phenomenon can be found in numerous additional areas of psychology. Many of these single-phenomenon tests show comparable effects for the psychological laboratory and field studies. But failures to generalize also occur.

Single-domain tests further broaden the generalizability question to a whole research domain. For example, do most aggression findings from the psychological laboratory generalize to field studies? In other words, do the effects of key independent variables—such as alcohol, anonymity, and media violence—have the same effects in lab and field studies of aggression? If laboratory studies from a given domain are inherently invalid and those from field studies are valid, then lab and field studies in that domain should fail to show any correspondence. We (Anderson & Bushman, 1997; Bushman & Anderson, 1998) used meta-analytic techniques to ask this broad question in the aggression domain, and found considerable correspondence between lab and field.

## A CROSS-DOMAIN EMPIRICAL APPROACH

We extend the single-domain approach by examining the comparability of findings from lab and field across several domains. Basically, we asked whether the effects of the same conceptual independent variables on the same conceptual dependent variables tended to be consistent in lab and field settings across several psychological domains.

### Method

Using the PsycINFO database, we conducted a literature search for the following journals: *Psychological Bulletin, Journal of Applied Psychology, Journal of Personality and Social Psychology,* and *Personality and Social Psychology Bulletin.* We searched with the keyword phrases "meta-analysis" and "quantitative review," and with the combined keyword phrases "meta-analysis" with "field studies" and "meta-analysis" with "laboratory." This selection of journals was intentionally biased toward social psychology because many of the most vociferous criticisms of the psychological laboratory have focused on the social psychological lab. Our search yielded 288 articles.

Many articles were subsequently eliminated because they were methodological in nature, did not include separate tabulations for lab and field settings, or overlapped with a more recent meta-analytic review.[4] The final data set represents 38 pairs of lab and field effects.

### Results and Discussion

We used the standardized mean difference, denoted by *d,* as the indicator of effect size. This index shows the size of the difference between two groups, and does so in terms of the standard deviation. For instance, if Group 1 has a mean of 6 and Group 2 has a mean of 5, and the standard deviation is 2, the effect size *d* would be $(6 - 5)/2 = 0.5$. According to Cohen (1988), a "large" *d* is 0.8, a "medium" d is 0.5, and a "small"

*d* is 0.2. Effect sizes for correlations can easily be converted to *d*s, which we did to allow direct comparisons across different types of studies (Hedges & Olkin 1985). Effect-size averages were weighted by sample size and used pooled standard deviations in most cases, but in a few cases we were unable to determine the weights from the original reports. Table 1 and Figure 1 summarize the results.[5]

Figure 1 plots the value of *d* for the lab and field studies for each domain studied. The figure reveals considerable consistency between laboratory and field effects. That is, across domains, the *d*s for lab and field studies tended to be similar. The correlation, $r = .73$, is considerably higher than the gloomy picture that sometimes emerges from the external validity debate. Some readers might wonder whether the disproportionate number of the data points coming from comparisons of gender effects (6 out of 38) biased the results. However, the plot and correlation look much the same with these 6 data points eliminated ($r = .75$). Similarly, one might wonder about the possible nonindependence of some of the attributional-style data points (the results from Sweeney, Anderson, & Bailey, 1986). Dropping all but the two overall "attribution and depression" effects for positive and negative outcomes again yields essentially the same correlation ($r = .73$). All three of these correlations are considerably larger than Cohen's (1988) conventional value for a large correlation ($r = .5$). Furthermore, an *r* of .73 is equivalent to a *d* of 2.14, a huge effect.

Two complementary questions arise from these results, one asking why the correspondence is so high, the other asking why it is not higher. First, consider some limitations on correspondence between lab and field results. One limitation concerns internal validity problems of field studies. Sometimes field studies "discover" relations between independent and dependent variables that are false, and at other times they fail to discover true relations. Both types of internal invalidity reduce correspondence between field and lab, and hence artificially depress the correlation seen in Figure 1. A second limitation concerns the primary reason for studying psychological phenomena in the lab—to improve one's ability to detect relatively subtle phenomena that are difficult or impossible to isolate in the field. Laboratory studies typically accomplish this by focusing on one or two theoretically interesting independent variables while restricting the action or range of other independent variables. This focus can increase the estimated effect size of experimentally manipulated independent

variables while decreasing the effects of individual difference variables. For example, using only college students as experimental participants restricts the range of individual differences in intelligence and antisocial personality, thereby reducing their effects on dependent variables associated with them. Therefore, reducing the effects of individual differences in the lab also reduces variance due to chance or measurement error and thus increases the estimated effect size of manipulated variables, relative to the estimated effect sizes generated from similar field studies without the (intentional) range restriction on subject variables. Thus, both internal validity problems of field studies and the range restriction of lab studies artificially decrease the lab-field correspondence displayed in Figure 1. Now consider the other question, about factors that helped make the correspondence in Figure 1 so high. First, meta-analytically derived indicators of effect size wash out idiosyncratic effects of individual studies. That is, random or idiosyncratic factors that artificially increase an effect in some studies and decrease it in others tend to balance out when averaged across many studies, in much the way that increasing sample size increases the accuracy of the results in a single study. Second, and perhaps more important, we investigated only research domains that have had sufficient research attention to allow meta-analyses. These would usually be successful research domains, where underlying theories and methods are accurate enough to produce a line of successful studies. Such successful lines of investigation are relatively likely to concern true (internally valid) relations between the key independent and dependent variables.

## CONCLUSIONS

The obvious conclusion from Figure 1 is that the psychological laboratory is doing quite well in terms of external validity; it has been discovering truth, not triviality. Otherwise, correspondence between field and lab effects would be close to zero.

A less obvious conclusion concerns internal validity of field studies. A second part of the broader debate between theory-oriented laboratory researchers and application-oriented field researchers is the truism that field studies generally lack internal validity. If this second truism were accurate, however, the correspondence between lab and field effects could not have been so positive. Thus, field studies in psychology must be doing a pretty

**Table 1.** *Mean effect sizes and confidence intervals for topics studied in the lab and field*

| Source, independent and dependent variables, and setting | Number of samples | Effect size | 95% confidence interval |
|---|---|---|---|
| Ambady and Rosenthal (1992) | | | |
| Observation time and outcoming ratings—lab | 21 | 0.87 | — |
| Observation time and outcome ratings—field | 17 | 0.98 | — |
| Anderson and Bushman (1997) | | | |
| Gendere and physical aggression—lab | 37 | 0.31 | 0.23–0.38 |
| Gender and physical aggression—field | 6 | 0.40 | 0.25–0.55 |
| Gender and verbal aggression—lab | 18 | 0.13 | 0.03–0.24 |
| Gender and verbal aggression—field | 3 | 0.03 | −0.15–0.22 |
| Bushman and Anderson (1998) | | | |
| Anonymity and aggression—lab | 18 | 0.57 | 0.45–0.69 |
| Anonymity and aggression—field | 4 | 0.44 | 0.25–0.63 |
| Trait aggressiveness and aggression—lab | 13 | 0.49 | 0.18–0.29 |
| Trait aggressiveness and aggression—field | 16 | 0.93 | 0.38–0.47 |
| Type A personality and aggression—lab | 9 | 0.34 | 0.18–0.49 |
| Type A personality and aggression—field | 3 | 0.97 | 0.71–1.23 |
| Carlson, Marcus-Newhall, and Miller (1990) | | | |
| Weapons and aggression—lab | 16 | 0.21 | 0.01–0.41 |
| Weapons and aggression—field | 5 | 0.17 | −0.05–0.39 |
| Eagly and Crowley (1986) | | | |
| Gender and helping—lab | 16 | −0.18 | −0.28–0.09 |
| Gender and helping—field (on and off campus) | 36+47= 83 | 0.27 | — |
| Eagly and Johnson (1990) | | | |
| Gender and leadership style—lab | 17 | 0.22 | — |
| Gender and leadership style—organizations | 269 | −0.00 | — |
| Eagly and Karau (1991) | | | |
| Gender and leader emergence—lab | 50 | 0.45 | 0.40–0.51 |
| Gender and leader emergence—natural settings | 24 | 0.10 | 0.02–0.17 |
| Eagly, Karau, and Makhijani (1995) | | | |
| Gender and leader effectiveness—lab | 20 | 0.07 | −0.06–0.20 |
| Gender and leader effectiveness—organizations | 56 | −0.03 | −0.06–0.01 |
| Gordon (1996) | | | |
| Ingratiation and evaluations—university (lab) | 54 | 0.38 | 0.33–0.43 |
| Ingratiation and evaluations—field | 15 | −0.07 | −0.13– −0.00 |
| Karau and Williams (1993) | | | |
| Social loafing—lab | 140 | 0.47 | 0.43–0.51 |
| Social loafing—field | 23 | 0.25 | 0.16–0.35 |
| Kraiger and Ford (1985) | | | |
| Race of ratee and peformance ratings—lab | 10 | 0.07 | −0.41–0.56 |
| Race of ratee and peformance ratings—field | 64 | 0.39 | 0.06–0.75 |
| Kubeck, Delp, Haslett, and McDaniel (1996) | | | |
| Age (continuous) and job-training mastery—lab | 17 | −0.61 | −1.67–0.12 |
| Age (continuous) and job-training mastery—field | 31 | −0.52 | −1.19–0.02 |
| Age and time to finish training—lab | 3 | 0.70 | 0.08–1.58 |
| Age and time to finish training—field | 2 | 1.35 | 1.35–1.35 |
| Age (dichotomous) and job-training mastery—lab | 9 | −0.96 | −1.44– −0.47 |
| Age (dichotomous) and job-training mastery—field | 2 | −0.38 | −0.38– −0.38 |
| Lundeberg and Fox (1991) | | | |
| Expectancies and recall–essay tests—lab | 41 | 0.60 | 0.53–0.67 |
| Expectancies and recall–essay tests—class | 11 | 0.33 | 0.17–0.49 |
| Expectancies and recognition tests—lab | 41 | −0.07 | −0.13– −0.01 |
| Expectancies and recognition tests—class | 14 | 0.28 | 0.14–0.42 |
| Mento, Steel, and Karren (1987) | | | |
| Goal difficulty and performance—lab | 47 | 0.62 | — |
| Goal difficulty and performance—field | 23 | 0.44 | — |
| Mullen and Hu (198) | | | |
| Group membership and similarity of group members—artificially created groups | 2 | 0.43 | 0.04–0.90 |
| Group membership and similarity of group members—real groups | 2 | 0.47 | −0.14–1.16 |
| Narby, Cutler, and Moran (1993) | | | |
| Authoritarianism and trial verdict—video, written, audio trials | 23 | 0.30 | — |
| Authoritarianism and trial verdict—live trials | 3 | 0.49 | — |
| Paik and Comstock (1994) | | | |
| Media violence and aggression—lab | 586 | 0.87 | — |
| Media violence and aggression—field | 556 | 0.42 | — |
| Peters, Hartke, and Pohlman (1985) | | | |
| Leadership style and performance, negative octants—lab | 30 | −0.28 | — |

*(Continued)*

**Table 1.** *(Continued)*

| Source, independent and dependent variables, and setting | Number of samples | Effect size | 95% confidence interval |
|---|---|---|---|
| Leadership style and performance, negative octants—field | 20 | −0.90 | — |
| Leadership style and performance, positive octants—lab | 20 | 0.51 | — |
| Leadership style and performance, positive octants—field | 15 | 0.45 | — |
| Sagie (1994) | | | |
| Decision-making participation and productivity—lab | — | −0.06 | — |
| Decision-making participation and productivity—field | — | −0.02 | — |
| Sweeney, Anderson, and Bailey (1986) | | | |
| Attribution and depression, negative outcomes—lab | 25 | 0.52 | — |
| Attribution and depression, negative outcomes—hospital | 8 | 0.32 | — |
| Attribution and depression, positive outcomes—lab | 16 | −0.24 | — |
| Attribution and depression, positive outcomes—hospital | 5 | −0.28 | — |
| Ability and depression, negative outcomes—lab | 16 | 0.63 | — |
| Ability and depression, negative outcomes—hospital | 3 | 1.15 | — |
| Ability and depression, positive outcomes—lab | 13 | −0.12 | — |
| Ability and depression, positive outcomes—hospital | 3 | −0.12 | — |
| Effort and depression, negative outcomes—lab | 13 | 0.10 | — |
| Effort and depression, negative outcomes—hospital | 2 | 0.49 | — |
| Effort and depression, positive outcomes—lab | 11 | −0.02 | — |
| Effort and depression, positive outcomes—hospital | 2 | −0.04 | — |
| Luck and depression, negative outcomes—lab | 14 | −0.30 | — |
| Luck and depression, negative outcomes—hospital | 3 | −0.61 | — |
| Luck and depression, positive outcomes—lab | 10 | 0.43 | — |
| Luck and depression, positive outcomes—hospital | 3 | 0.63 | — |
| Task difficulty and depression, negative outcomes—lab | 14 | −0.26 | — |
| Task difficulty and depression, negative outcomes—hospital | 2 | −0.14 | — |
| Task difficulty and depression, positive outcomes—lab | 9 | −0.20 | — |
| Task difficulty and depression, positive outcomes—hospital | 2 | 0.61 | — |
| Tubbs (1986) | | | |
| Goal specificity and performance—lab | 34 | 0.57 | 0.14–1.01 |
| Goal specificity and performance—field | 14 | 0.43 | −0.09–0.94 |
| Goal-setting participation and performance—lab | 13 | −0.03 | −0.86–0.80 |
| Goal-setting participation and performance—field | 4 | 0.12 | −0.34–0.59 |

*Note.* All effect-size estimates have been converted to *d*—the average effect size in standard deviation units, weighted by sample size whenever sufficient information was available to do so. If the exact same sampling and methodological procedures were used to gather new data to estimate *d*, and if this were done a large number of times, we should expect that 95% of the time, the new ,ld estimates would fall within the range indicated by the 95% confidence interval.

good job when it comes to internal validity.

In the interests of clarity and space, we have oversimplified the lab-field debate on validity. Obviously, studies in either setting may be high or low on internal and external validity. As long as scholars in both settings keep in mind the complementary pitfalls of too little control over extraneous variables (leading to low internal validity) and of overgeneralizing from the specific features of a specific study (leading to low external validity), we believe the psychological research enterprise will continue to succeed.

Finally, failure to find high correspondence between lab and field studies in a given domain or with a specific phenomenon should not be seen as a failure of the researchers in either setting. Instead, such inconsistencies should be seen as an indicator that further conceptual analysis and additional empirical tests are needed to discover the source of the discrepancy. Perhaps there are psychological processes operating in one context but not the other, or perhaps the relative strength of different causal factors differs in the two contexts (see Anderson & Anderson, 1998, for an example involving the positive relation between uncomfortably hot temperatures and aggressive behavior). In any case, the discrepancy sets the stage for further theoretical and (eventually) practical

advances. And in the end, that's what we all are working for, isn't it?

## Recommended Reading

Anderson, C.A., & Bushman, B.J. (1997). (See References)

Banaji, M.R. & Crowder, R.G. (1989). (See References)

Berkowitz, L., & Donnerstein, E. (1982). External validity is more than skin deep: Some answers to criticism of laboratory experiments. *American Psychologist, 37,* 245–257.

Kruglanski, A.W. (1975). The human subject in the psychology experiment: Fact and artifact. In L. Berkowitz (Ed.), *Advances in*

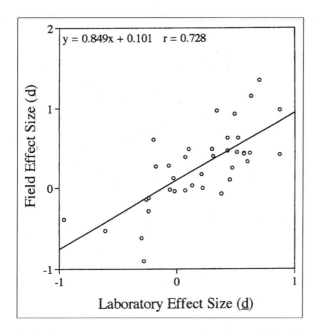

$$y = 0.849x + 0.101 \quad r = 0.728$$

**Fig. 1.** Relation between effect sizes in the laboratory and field. Each point represents the value of *d* for the lab and field studies in a particular meta-analysis.

*experimental social psychology* (Vol. 8, pp. 101–147). New York: Academic Press.

Mook, D.G. (1983). (See References).

**Acknowledgements**—We thank Bruce Bartholomew and Anne Powers for comments on an earlier version. This article is based in part on an invited address delivered by the first author at the May 1998 meeting of the American Psychological Society in Washington, D.C.

## Notes

1. Address correspondence to Craig A. Anderson, Department of Psychology, Iowa State University, W112 Lagomarcino Hall, Ames, IA 50011–3180.

2. Internal validity refers to the degree to which the design, methods, and procedures of a study allow one to conclude that the independent variable caused observable differences in the dependent variable. External validity refers to the degree to which the relationship between the independent and dependent variables found in a study generalizes to other people, places, and times.

3. The companion truism, held by some scholars with a more theoretical orientation, is that field studies on "real" phenomena are so plagued by methodological confounds that they lack internal validity,

and, hence, fail to say anything at all about the phenomenon under study.

4. For example, the Wood, Wong, and Cachere (1991) analysis of the effects of violent media on aggression overlaps with Paik and Comstock's (1994) analysis.

5. Two additional meta-analyses also demonstrated considerable lab–field correspondence, but did not report separate effect sizes. Kraus's (1995) review of the consistency between attitude and behavior and Kluger and DeNisi's (1996) review of the effects of feedback on performance both coded effects by the lab-field distinction, and both reported a nonsignificant relationship between this distinction and effect size.

## References

Ambady, N., & Rosenthal, R. (1992). Thin slices of expressive behavior as predictors of interpersonal consequences: A meta-analysis. *Psychological Bulletin, 111,* 256–274.

Anderson, C.A., & Anderson, K.B. (1998). Temperature and aggression: Paradox, controversy, and a (fairly) clear picture. In R. Green & E. Donnerstein (Eds.), *Human aggression: Theories, research, and implications for social policy* (pp. 247–298). San Diego: Academic Press.

Anderson, C.A., & Bushman, B.). (1997). External validity of "trivial" experiments: The

case of laboratory aggression. *Review of General Psychology, 1,* 19–41.

Banaji, M.R., & Crowder, R.G. (1989). The bankruptcy of everyday memory. *American Psychologist, 44,* 1185–1193.

Bushman, B.J., & Anderson, C.A. (1998). Methodology in the study of aggression: Integrating experimental and nonexperimental findings. In R. Green & E. Donnerstein (Eds.), *Human aggression: Theories, research, and implications for social policy* (pp. 23–48). San Diego: Academic Press.

Campbell, D.T. (1957). Factors relevant to validity of experiments in social settings. *Psychological Bulletin, 54,* 297–312.

Carlson, M., Marcus-Newhall, A., & Miller, N. (1990). Effects of situational aggression cues: A quantitative review. *Journal of Personality and Social Psychology, 58,* 622–633.

Cohen, J. (1988). *Statistical power analysis for the behavioral sciences* (2nd ed.). Hillsdale, NJ: Erlbaum.

Dallett, K., & Wilcox, S.G. (1968). Contextual stimuli and proactive inhibition. *Journal of Experimental Psychology, 78,* 475–480.

Eagly, A.H., & Crowley, M. (1986). Gender and helping behavior: A meta analytic review of the social psychological literature. *Psychological Bulletin, 100,* 283–285.

Eagly, A.H., & Johnson, B.T. (1990). Gender and leadership style: A meta-analysis. *Psychological Bulletin, 108,* 233–256.

Eagly, A.H., & Karau, S.J., (1991). Gender and emergence of leaders: A meta-analysis. *Journal of Personality and Social Psychology, 60,* 685–710.

Eagly, A.H., Karau, 5.J., & Makhijani, M.G. (1995). Gender and the effectiveness of leaders: A meta-analysis. *Psychological Bulletin, 117,* 125–145.

Godden, D., & Baddeley, A. (1975). When does context influence recognition memory? *British Journal of Psychology, 71,* 99–104.

Gordon, R.A. (1996). Impact of ingratiation on judgments and evaluations: A meta-analytic investigation. *Journal of Personality and Social Psychology, 71,* 54–70.

Griffin, R., & Kacmar, M.K. (1991). Laboratory research in management: Misconceptions and missed opportunities. *Journal of Organizational Behavior, 12,* 301–311.

Hedges, L.V., & Olkin, I. (1985). *Statistical methods for meta-analyses.* New York: Academic Press.

Karau, S.J., & Williams, K.D. (1993). Social loafing: A meta-analytic review and theoretical integration. *Journal of Personality and Social Psychology, 65,* 681–706.

Kluger, A.N., & DeNisi, A. (1996). Effects of feedback on performance: A historical review, a meta-analysis, and a preliminary feedback intervention theory. *Psychological Bulletin, 119,* 254–284.

Kraiger, K., & Ford, J.K. (1985). A meta-analysis of ratee race effects in performance ratings. *Journal of Applied Psychology, 70,* 56–75.

Kraus, S.J. (1995). Attitudes and the prediction of behavior: A meta-analysis of the empirical evidence. *Personality and Social Psychology Bulletin, 21,* 58–75.

Kubeck, J.E., Delp, N.D., Haslett, T.K., & McDaniel, M.A. (1996). Does job-related training performance decline with age? *Psychology and Aging, 11,* 92–107.

Lundeberg, M.A., & Fox, P.W. (1991). Do laboratory findings on test expectancy generalize to classroom outcomes? *Review of Educational Research, 61,* 94–106.

Mento, A.J., Steel, R.P., & Karren, R.J. (1987). A meta-analytic study of the effects of goal setting on task performance: 1966–1984. *Organizational Behavior & Human Decision Processes, 39,* 52–83.

Mook, D.G. (1983). In defense of external invalidity. *American Psychologist, 38,* 379–387.

Mullen, B., & Hu, L. (1989). Perceptions of ingroup and outgroup variability: A meta-analytic integration. *Basic and Applied Social Psychology, 10,* 233–252.

Narby, D.J., Cutler, B.L., & Moran, G. (1993). A meta-analysis of the association between authoritarianism and jurors' perceptions of defendant culpability. *Journal of Applied Psychology, 78,* 34–42.

Neisser, U. (1978). Memory: What are the important questions? In M.M. Gruneberg, P.E. Morris, & R.N. Sykes (Eds.), *Practical aspects of memory* (pp. 3–24). London: Academic Press.

Paik, H., & Comstock, G. (1994). The effects of television violence on antisocial behavior: A meta-analysis. *Communication Research, 21,* 516–546.

Peters, L.H., Hartke, D.D., & Pohlman, J.T. (1985). Fiedler's contingency theory of leadership: An application of the meta-analysis procedures of Schmidt & Hunter. *Psychological Bulletin, 97,* 274–285.

Sagie, A. (1994). Participative decision making and performance: A moderator analysis. *Journal of Applied Behavioral Science, 30,* 227–246.

Schmitt, N. (1996). Validity generalization. In R. Barrett (Ed.), *Fair employment strategies in human resource management* (pp. 94–104). Westport, CT: Quorum Books.

Sweeney, P.D., Anderson, K., & Bailey, S. (1986). Attributional style in depression: A meta-analytic review. *Journal of Personality and Social Psychology, 50,* 974–991.

Tubbs, M.E. (1986). Goal setting: A meta-analytic examination of the empirical evidence. *Journal of Applied Psychology, 71,* 474–483.

Wolfe, J., & Roberts, C.R. (1993). A further study of the external validity of business games: Five-year peer group indicators. *Simulation & Gaming, 24,* 21–33.

Wood, W., Wong, F.Y., & Cachere, J.G. (1991). Effects of media violence on viewers' aggression in unconstrained social interaction. *Psychological Bulletin, 109,* 371–383.

# Psychology's Tangled Web

## Deceptive methods may backfire on behavioral researchers

### By BRUCE BOWER

In *Marmion,* Sir Walter Scott describes with memorable succinctness the unanticipated pitfalls of trying to manipulate others: "O, what a tangled web we weave, when first we practice to deceive."

The poet's tangled web aptly symbolizes the situation that some psychological researchers now find themselves struggling with.

Consider a study conducted recently by Kevin M. Taylor and James A. Shepperd, both of the University of Florida in Gainesville. Seven introductory psychology students took part in their pilot investigation, which measured the extent to which performance on a cognitive task was affected by experimenter–provided feedback after each of several attempts. Because of a last-minute cancellation by an eighth study recruit, the researchers asked a graduate student to pose as the final participant.

Only the graduate student knew beforehand that feedback was designed to mislead participants in systematic ways about their successes and failures on the task.

At the conclusion of the trials, an experimenter who had monitored the proceedings briefly left the room. Although they had been warned not to talk to one another, the seven "real" participants began to discuss the experiment and their suspicions about having been given bogus feedback. A brief comparison of the feedback they had received quickly uncovered the researchers' deceptive scheme.

When the experimenter returned, participants acted as though nothing had happened. The experimenter announced that the trials had included

deception and asked students on three separate occasions if they had become suspicious of anything that happened during the laboratory experience. All of them denied having had any misgivings, in interviews as well as on questionnaires, and divulged nothing about their collective revelation.

At that point, the experimenter dismissed the students and expressed confidence that they had provided useful data. The graduate stand-in, who purely by chance had witnessed the participants' secret deliberations, unburdened him of that illusion.

In a letter published in the August 1996 AMERICAN PSYCHOLOGIST, Taylor and Shepperd bravely fessed up to having had the tables turned on them by their own students. In the process, they rekindled a long-running debate about whether psychologists should try to fool research subjects in the name of science.

"Our seven participants do not represent all experimental participants," the Florida investigators concluded. "Nevertheless, their behavior suggests that, even when pressed, participants cannot be counted on to reveal knowledge they may acquire or suspicions they may develop about the deception or experimental hypotheses."

Deceptive techniques have gained prominence in psychological research, and particularly in social psychology, since the 1960s. Moreover, studies that place participants in fabricated situations featuring role-playing confederates of the investigator have attracted widespread attention.

Consider a 1963 investigation conducted by the late Stanley Milgram, which still pervades public consciousness. Although ostensibly recruited for a study of learning and memory, volunteers unwittingly took part in Milgram's exploration of the extent to which people will obey authority figures.

Many volunteers accepted the exhortations of a stern experimenter to deliver increasingly stronger electric shocks to an unseen person in an adjoining room every time that person erred in recalling a list of words. Nearly two-thirds of the participants agreed to deliver powerful shocks to the forgetful individual—a confederate of Milgram's who received no actual shocks but could be heard screaming, pounding the wall, and begging to leave the room.

Milgram's study inspired much debate over the ethics of deceiving experimental subjects and whether data collected in this way offer clear insights into the nature of obedience or anything else. It also heralded a growing acceptance of deceptive practices by social psychologists.

Researchers have tracked this trend by monitoring articles appearing in the JOURNAL OF PERSONALITY AND SOCIAL PSYCHOLOGY, regarded by most as a premier publication. Only 16 percent of empirical studies published there in 1961 used deception. That proportion rose to nearly 47 percent in 1978, dipped to 32 percent in 1986, and returned to 47 percent in 1992. The investigators generally agree that an even larger portion of studies published in other social psychology journals have included deceptive techniques.

Deception still occurs relatively frequently in social psychology studies, although less often than in 1992, holds psychologist James H. Korn of Saint Louis University, who has investigated the prevalence of these practices and written a book titled *Illusions of Reality: A History of Deception in Social Psychology* (1997, State University of New York Press). Dramatic cases of experimental manipulation like Milgram's obedience study rarely appear anymore, he adds.

Instead, deception now usually involves concealing or camouflaging an experiment's true purpose in order to elicit unguarded responses from volunteers. For instance, researchers running a study of the effects of misleading information on memories of a traffic accident presented in a series of slides may simply tell participants that they're conducting an analysis of attention. After completing the study, volunteers get a full explanation of its methods and goals from experimenters in a debriefing session.

In Korn's view, this mellowing of deceptive tactics partly reflects an injunction in the current ethical guidelines of the American Psychological Association that "psychologists never deceive research participants about significant aspects that would affect their willingness to participate, such as physical risks, discomfort, or unpleasant emotional experiences."

Yet, as Taylor and Shepperd's humbling experience demonstrates, even the softer side of deception can have rough edges. In fact, the clandestine knowledge of the Florida recruits underscores the need to do away entirely with deception in psychological research, argue economist Andreas Ortmann of Bowdoin College in Brunswick, Maine, and psychologist Ralph Hertwig of the Max Planck Institute for Human Development in Munich, Germany. Suspicions of being misled may affect subjects' responses and complicate interpretation of the results.

A number of like-minded critics have challenged the ethics of using deceptive techniques, whether or not they generate compelling findings. Ortmann and Hertwig take a more practical stand. They regard deceptive procedures—even in mild forms promulgated by a significant minority—as the equivalent of methodological termites eating away at both the reputation of all psychological researchers and the validity of their findings.

People in general, and the favorite experimental guinea pigs—college undergraduates—in particular, have come to expect that they will be misled in psychology experiments, Ortmann and Hertwig argue. Each new experiment in which participants are deceived and debriefed sets off another round of extracurricular discussions about psychologists' sneaky ruses, they say.

This process transforms interactions between a researcher and a participant into a real-life episode of a repeated prisoner's dilemma game, the researchers contended in the July 1997 AMERICAN PSYCHOLOGIST. In these games, two or more people choose either to cooperate or to pursue self-interest in some task over many trials.

A selfish choice by one person yields a big payoff to that player and virtually nothing for everyone else; cooperation by all players moderately benefits everyone; and multiple selfish moves leave everyone with little or nothing. Cooperation in these games quickly unravels when an identifiable player consistently opts for self-interest (SN: 3/28/98, p. 205). Likewise, participants who have reason to believe that they will somehow be deceived by psychologists are likely to turn uncooperative in the laboratory—and in ways that a researcher may not notice, according to Ortmann and Hertwig.

"Psychologists have good intentions and follow their ethical manual, but they still foster mistrust in their subjects when they use deception," Ortmann says. "This is a question of clean research design, not just ethics."

Most experimental economists avoid using deceptive methods because of concerns about their corrosive effects on the discipline's reputation among potential research participants, the Bowdoin researcher holds. Economics studies depend on highly structured games, such as the prisoner's dilemma, which require volunteers to enact an explicit scenario; investigators monitor changes in behavior over a series of trials. Each participant receives a monetary payment based on his or her overall performance in the experiment.

In contrast, Ortmann and Hertwig assert, psychologists usually do not ask volunteers to assume a specific role or perspective in performing mental tasks, do not conduct multiple trials, and pay participants a flat fee or nothing. Recruits get a poor feel for the purpose of these experiments and are likely to second-guess the scientist's intentions, especially if they suspect that a study includes deception.

Such suspicions flare up all too easily in studies of ongoing social interactions in which one participant secretly plays a fixed role at the researcher's behest, notes psychologist William Ickes of the University of Texas at Arlington. Volunteers who try to talk spontaneously with such a confederate often note an unnatural or bizarre quality to the conversation and become wary of the entire experiment, Ickes says.

The Texas scientist, who studies empathic accuracy (SN: 3/23/96, p. 190), focuses on undirected and unrehearsed encounters between volunteers.

Deception-free methods do not sift out all experimental impurities. Economics research, for instance, places individuals in abstract, potentially confusing situations that may have limited applicability to real-life exchanges of money and goods, Ortmann says. Still, the use of deceptive techniques would stir up mistrust among research subjects and throw the whole enterprise off course, he argues.

Critics of Ortmann and Hertwig's call to outlaw all forms of experimental deception defend its use in judicious moderation. Three psychologists elaborate on this view in the July AMERICAN PSYCHOLOGIST.

"The preponderance of evidence suggests that deceived participants do not become resentful about having been fooled by researchers and that deception does not negatively influence their perceptions about psychology or their attitudes about science in general," states Allan J. Kimmel of the Ecole Supérieure de Commerce de Paris, France.

Several surveys of people who have participated in psychological studies that included deceptive tactics find that, compared to their counterparts in nondeceptive experiments, they report having enjoyed the experience more and having learned more from it, Kimmel says.

Deceptive studies that include careful debriefing sessions preserve psychology's reputation, adds Arndt Bröder of the University of Bonn in Germany. In his own department, Bröder notes, during the debriefing the researchers explain the nature and necessity of experimental deceptions to all participants, most of whom agree to take part in further studies.

Sometimes researchers have no alternative but to hide their intentions from participants, contends Korn. A total ban on deception would obstruct certain types of work, he says, such as explorations of how people form and use ethnic and religious stereotypes.

Positive attitudes expressed on surveys and continued willingness to show up for experiments do not reassure Ortmann and Hertwig that participants accept experimental situations and researchers' directions at face value.

It is not necessarily deception when a researcher fails to tell participants the purpose of an experiment, they say, but it is always deception if a researcher tells falsehoods to participants in the course of an experiment.

At that point, a tangled web of social interactions may begin to trip up scientific progress. Participants who unravel a scientific fib may feel that they should not know more about an experiment than the researcher tells them and that such knowledge may invalidate their responses, maintain Taylor and Shepperd. As a result, perceptive volunteers zip their lips and make nice for the investigator.

All sorts of unspoken inferences by participants can intrude on the best-laid research plans, even if they exclude deception, argues Denis J. Hilton of the Ecole Supérieure des Sciences Economiques et Commerciales in Cergy-Pontoise, France.

In the September 1995 PSYCHOLOGICAL BULLETIN, Hilton analyzed how volunteers' assumptions about the meaning of experimental communications in several areas of psychological research can affect their responses.

For example, participants often read more into response scales than experimenters had intended. In a study noted by Hilton that asked volunteers how often they had felt irritated recently, those given a scale ranging from "several times daily" to "less than once a week" reported relatively minor irritations, such as enduring slow service at a restaurant. Those given a scale ranging from "several times a year" to "less than once every 3 months" cited more extreme incidents, such as a marital fight. The time frame provided by the scales shaped the way in which irritating episodes were defined and tallied.

Further complications in interpreting responses ensue when participants mistrust a researcher's objectives, Ortmann asserts.

"The question of whether deception matters deserves further inquiry," he remarks. "Too often, we as scientists don't think carefully about methodological issues and take for granted our experimental conditions."

## Unit Selections

4. **The End of Nature Versus Nurture,** Frans B. M. de Waal
5. **Decoding the Human Body,** Sharon Begley
6. **The Future of the Brain,** Norbert R. Myslinski

## Key Points to Consider

❖ What do you think contributes most to our psychological make-up and behaviors: the influence of the environment, the expression of genes, or the functioning of the nervous system? Do you believe that perhaps some combination of these factors accounts for psychological characteristics and behaviors? How are these various contributors to behavior studied?

❖ What is genetic research? How is it done? How much of human behavior is influenced by genes? Can you give some examples of the influence of genes on human behavior? How could such research help experts in psychology and medicine predict and treat various disorders? What environmental factors affect genetic expression? Do you have ethical concerns about the human genome project? Or do you believe that the advantages of the project outweigh any concerns?

❖ How does the brain influence human behavior and psychological characteristics? What functions does the brain control? How do we study the brain? What new techniques do we have at our disposal to study the brain? What are the advantages of these techniques? How might these techniques influence how physicians and surgeons now deal with brain disorders or do surgery on the brain? What are some of the types of brain disorders and their symptoms?

❖ What is the spinal cord? Is the spinal cord as important as the brain? How do we study the spine as part of the nervous system? What types of damage can occur to the spinal cord? Where on the spinal cord is damage the most serious? What techniques have scientists developed for dealing with spinal cord damage?

 **Links**          **www.dushkin.com/online/**

8. **Adolescence: Changes and Continuity**
   *http://www.personal.psu.edu/faculty/n/x/nxd10/biologic2.htm*
9. **Division of Hereditary Diseases and Family Studies, Indiana University School of Medicine**
   *http://medgen.iupui.edu/divisions/hereditary/*
10. **Institute for Behavioral Genetics**
    *http://ibgwww.colorado.edu/index.html*
11. **Serendip**
    *http://serendip.brynmawr.edu/serendip/*

These sites are annotated on pages 4 and 5.

As a child, Nancy vowed she did not want to turn out like either of her parents. Nancy's mother was very passive and acquiescent about her father's drinking. When Dad was drunk, Mom always called his boss to report that Dad was "sick" and then acted as if there was nothing wrong at home. Nancy's childhood was a nightmare. Her father's behavior was erratic and unpredictable. If he drank just a little bit, he was happy. If he drank a lot, which was usually the case, he often became belligerent.

Despite vowing not to become like her father, as an adult Nancy found herself in the alcohol rehabilitation unit of a large hospital. Nancy's employer could no longer tolerate her on-the-job mistakes or her unexplained absences from work, and he referred her to the clinic for help. As Nancy pondered her fate, she wondered whether her genes preordained her to follow in her father's inebriated footsteps or whether the stress of her childhood had brought her to this point in her life. After all, being the child of an alcoholic is not easy.

Just as Nancy was, psychologists also are concerned with discovering the causes of human behavior. Once the cause is known, treatments for problematic behaviors can be developed. In fact, certain behaviors might even be prevented when the cause is known. But for Nancy, prevention was too late.

One of the paths to understanding humans is to understand the biological underpinnings of their behavior. Genes and chromosomes, the body's chemistry (as found in hormones, neurotransmitters, and enzymes), and the central nervous system (comprised of the brain, spinal cord, and nerve cells) are all implicated in human behavior. All represent the biological aspects of behavior and ought, therefore, to be worthy of study by psychologists.

Physiological psychologists and psychobiologists are often the ones who examine the role of biology in behavior. The neuroscientist is especially interested in brain functioning; the psychopharmacologist is interested in the effects of various psychopharmacological agents or psychoactive drugs on behavior.

These psychologists often utilize one of three techniques to understand the biology-behavior connection. Animal studies, as reviewed in the first unit, involving manipulation, stimulation, or destruction of certain parts of the brain offer one method of study. A second technique includes the examination of unfortunate individuals whose brains are defective at birth or damaged later by accidents or disease.

We can also use animal models to understand genetics; with animal models we can control reproduction and develop various strains of animals if necessary. Such tactics with humans would be considered extremely unethical. However, the third technique, studying an individual's behavior in comparison to both natural and adoptive parents or studying identical twins reared together or apart, allows psychologists to begin to understand the role of genetics versus environment in human behavior.

This unit is designed to familiarize you with the knowledge psychologists have gleaned by using these techniques to study physiological processes and other mechanisms in human behavior. Each article should interest you and make you more curious about the role of biology in human endeavors.

The first article in this unit reviews almost all aspects of the biological bases of behavior. In "The End of Nature Versus Nurture," Frans B. M. de Waal discusses the nature versus nurture debate, the debate that contests whether genetics or the environment contributes most to our psychological makeup. The author suggests that this debate is often driven not by science but by politics. He argues that the debate is difficult because if a behavior or trait is inherited, it is immutable; in other words, it cannot be changed.

The next selection for this unit examines the role of genes in human behavior. In "Decoding the Human Body," Sharon Begley reviews the human genome project. In this research, scientists are mapping the genetic code for humans. This project is exciting in that it will help us predict who is at risk for various illnesses and other genetically carried factors. The project, however, has caused some controversy in that such information could be misused in the hands of the wrong people.

Genes aren't the only biological underpinnings of human psychology. The next article covers information about the central nervous system, another important biological aspect of human behavior. In "The Future of the Brain," Norbert Myslinki describes new brain imaging techniques. These techniques are helping scientists understand what functions each part of the brain serves. These imaging techniques might also allow physicians to conduct brain surgery in less invasive and therefore less detrimental ways.

# Biological Bases of Behavior

# The End of Nature versus Nurture

## Is human behavior determined by genetics or by environment? It may be time to abandon the dichotomy

### by Frans B. M. de Waal

The defenders of nature and nurture have been at each other's throats for as long as I can remember. Whereas biologists have always believed that genes have something to do with human behavior, social scientists have flocked en masse to the opposite position: that we are fully and entirely our own creation, free from the chains of biology.

I felt the heat of this debate in the 1970s whenever, in lectures for general audiences, I mentioned sex differences in chimpanzees, such as that males are more aggressive and more ambitious than females. There would be howls of protest. Wasn't I projecting my own values onto these poor animals? Why did I even bother to compare the sexes? Did I perhaps have a hidden agenda?

Nowadays the same sort of information makes people yawn! Even direct comparisons between human and ape behavior, something that used to be taboo, fail to get anyone excited. Everyone has heard that men are from Mars and women from Venus. Everyone has seen, in *Time* and *Newsweek*, PET scans of the human brain engaged in various tasks, with different areas lighting up in male and female brains.

This time, however, it is my turn to be troubled. Instead of celebrating the victory of the biological approach, I regard some of the contemporary dichotomies between men and women as gross simplifications rendered politically correct by a fashionable amount of male-bashing (for example, when normal hormonal effects are referred to as "testosterone poisoning"). We remain as far removed as ever from a sophisticated understanding of the interplay between genes and environment. Society has let the pendulum swing wildly back from nurture to nature, leaving behind a number of bewildered social scientists. Yet we still love to phrase everything in terms of one influence or the other, rather than both.

It is impossible to explore where we may be heading 50 years from now without looking back an equal number of years at the charged history of the nature/nurture controversy. The debate is so emotional because any stance one takes comes with serious political implications. Positions have ranged from an unfounded faith in human flexibility by reformists to an obsession with blood and race by conservatives. Each in their own way, these positions have caused incalculable human suffering in the past century.

## Learning and Instinct

Fifty years ago the two dominant schools of thought about animal and human behavior had opposite outlooks. Teaching animals arbitrary actions such as lever-pressing, American behaviorists came to view all behavior as the product of trial-and-error learning. This process was considered so universal that differences among species were irrelevant: learning applied to all animals, including humans. As B.F. Skinner, the founder of behaviorism, bluntly put it: "Pigeon, rat, monkey, which is which? It doesn't matter."

In contrast, the ethological school in Europe focused on naturalistic behavior. Each animal species is born with a number of so-called fixed-action patterns that undergo little modification by the environment. These and other species-specific behaviors represent evolutionary adaptations. Thus, no one needs to teach humans how to laugh or cry; these are innate signals, universally used and understood. Similarly, the spider does not need to learn how to construct a web. She is born with a battery of spinnerets (spinning tubes connected to silk glands) as well as a behavioral program that "instructs" her how to weave threads together.

Because of their simplicity, both views of behavior had enormous appeal. And although

both paid homage to evolution, they sometimes did so in a superficial, arm-waving sort of way. Behaviorists stressed the continuities between humans and other animals, attributing them to evolution. But because for them behavior was learned rather than inborn, they ignored the genetic side, which is really what evolution is all about. While it is true that evolution implies continuity, it also implies diversity: each animal is adapted to a specific way of life in a specific environment. As is evident from Skinner's statement, this point was blithely ignored.

Similarly, some ethologists had rather vague evolutionary notions, emphasizing phylogenetic descent rather than the processes of natural selection. They saw behavioral traits, such as the inhibition of aggression, as good for the species. The argument was that if animals were to kill one another in fights, the species would not survive. This may be true, but animals have perfectly selfish reasons to avoid the escalation of fights that may harm themselves and their relationships. Hence, these ideas have now been replaced by theories about how traits benefit the actor and its kin; effects on the species as a whole are considered a mere by-product.

Behaviorism started losing its grip with the discovery that learning is not the same for all situations and species. For example, a rat normally links actions with effects only if the two immediately follow each other. So it would be very slow to learn to press a bar if a reward followed minutes later. When it comes to food that makes it sick, however, a delay of hours between consumption and the negative sensation still induces food aversion. Apparently, animals are specialized learners, being best at those contingencies that are most important for survival.

At the same time that behaviorists were forced to adopt the premises of evolutionary biology and to consider the world outside the laboratory, ethologists and ecologists were laying the groundwork for the neo-Darwinian revolution of the 1970s. The pioneer here was Dutch ethologist Nikolaas Tinbergen, who conducted ingenious field experiments on the survival value of animal behavior. He understood, for instance, why many birds remove eggshells from the nest after the chicks have hatched. Because the outside of a shell is colored for camouflage but the inside is not, predators such as crows easily locate eggs if broken shells are placed next to them. Throwing out the pieces is an automatic response favored by natural selection because the birds that practice this behavior have more surviving offspring.

Others developed theories to explain behavior that at first sight does not seem to help the actor but someone else. Such "altruism" can be seen in ant soldiers giving their lives in defense of their colony or dolphins lifting a drowning companion to the surface. Biologists assumed that natural selection will allow for assistance among relatives as a means of promoting the same genes. Or, if two animals are unrelated, the favor granted by one must be returned at some future time.

The scientists felt so confident about their explanations of cooperative animal societies that they could not resist extending these ideas to our own species. They saw the hugely cooperative enterprise of human society as based on the same premise of family values and economic tit-for-tat.

It fell to an American expert on ants, Edward O. Wilson, to deliver the news in 1975 that a great deal of human behavior was ripe for the Darwinian perspective and that the social sciences should prepare themselves to work together with biologists on this endeavor. Thus far the two disciplines had led separate lives, but from the perspective of a biologist social science is not much more than the study of animal behavior focused on a single species: ours. Because this is not how social scientists see their work, proposals for a united framework were not kindly received. One of Wilson's outraged opponents even poured cold water over Wilson's head after he gave a lecture. For reasons explained below, his new synthesis, dubbed "sociobiology," was equated with the race policies of the past and ultimately with the Holocaust.

Although the criticism was patently unfair—Wilson was offering evolutionary explanations, not policy suggestions—we shouldn't be surprised that the topic of human biology arouses strong emotions.

## Burdens of the Past

It is generally believed that some human behavior can easily be changed because it is learned, whereas other behavior resists modification because it is part of our biological heritage.

Ideologues of all colors have grasped this division to argue for the innate nature of certain human characteristics (for example, purported race differences in intelligence) and the plasticity of others (such as the ability to overcome gender stereotypes). Thus, Communism was founded on great confidence in human malleability. Because people, unlike social insects, resist submerging individuality for the greater good, some regimes accompanied their revolutions with massive indoctrination efforts. All of this proved in vain, however. Communism went under because of an economic incentive structure that was out of touch with human nature. Unfortunately, it did so only after having caused great misery and death.

Even more disastrous was the embrace of biology by Nazi Germany. Here, too, the collective (*das Volk*) was placed above the individual, but instead of relying on social engineering the method of choice was genetic manipulation. People were classified into "superior" and "inferior" types, the first of which needed to be protected against contamination by the second. In the horrible medical language of the Nazis, a healthy *Volk* required the cutting out of all "cancerous" elements. This idea was followed to its extreme in a manner that Western civilization has vowed never to forget.

Don't think that the underlying selectionist ideology was restricted to this particular time and place, however. In the early part of the 20th century, the eugenics movement—which sought to improve humanity by "breeding from the fitter stocks"—enjoyed widespread appeal among intellectuals in both the U.S. and Great Britain. Based on ideas going back to Plato's *Republic*, sterilization of the mentally handicapped and of criminals was considered perfectly acceptable. And social Darwinism—the idea that in a laissez-faire capitalist economy the strong will outcompete the weak, resulting in general improvement of the population—still inspires political agendas today. In this view, the poor should not be aided in their struggle for existence so as not to upset the natural order.

Given these ideologies, it is understandable why suppressed categories of people, such as minorities and women, fail to see biology as a friend. I would argue, however, that the danger comes from both directions, from biological determinism as well as its opposite, the denial of basic human needs and the belief that we can be everything we want to be. The hippie communes of the 1960s, the Israeli kibbutzim and the feminist revolution all sought to redefine humans. But denial of sexual jealousy, the parent-child bond or gender differences can be carried only so far before a counter-movement will seek to balance cultural trends with evolved human inclinations.

What makes the present era different is that the genocide of World War II is fading into memory while at the same time the evidence for a connection between genes and behavior is mounting. Studies of twins reared apart have reached the status of common knowledge, and almost every week newspapers report a new human gene. There is evidence for genes involved in schizophrenia, epilepsy and Alzheimer's and even in common behavioral traits such as thrill-seeking. We are also learning more about genetic and neurological differences between men and women, as well as between gay and straight men. For example, a small region of the brain in transsexual men (who dress and behave like women) resembles the same region in women's brains.

The list of such scientific advances is getting longer by the day, resulting in a critical mass of evidence that is impossible to ignore. Understandably, academics who have spent their life condemning the idea that biology influences human behavior are reluctant to change course. But they are being overtaken by the general public, which seems to have accepted that genes are involved in just about everything we do and are. Concurrently resistance to comparisons with other animals has dissipated because of a stream of television nature programs that has brought exotic wildlife into our homes while showing animals to be quite a bit smarter and more interesting than people used to believe.

Studies of chimpanzees and bonobos, such as those by Jane Goodall and myself, show that countless human practices and potentials, from politics and child-rearing to violence and even morality, have parallels in the lives of our closest animal relatives. How can we maintain the dualisms of the past—between humans and animals and between body and mind—in the face of all this evidence to the contrary? Current knowledge about our biological background simply doesn't permit a return to the tabula rasa views of the past.

This doesn't solve the problem of ideological abuse, however. If anything, it makes things worse. So long as people have political agendas, they will depict human nature one way or another for their own purposes. Conservatives like to point out that people are naturally selfish, whereas liberals argue that we have evolved to be social and cooperative. The obvious correctness of both influences goes to show what is wrong with simpleminded genetic determinism.

## The Best of Both Worlds

Because genetic language ("a gene for x") plays into our sound-bite culture, there is all the more reason to educate the public that genes, by themselves, are like seeds dropped onto the pavement: powerless to produce anything. When scientists say that a trait is inherited, all they mean is that part of its variability is explained by genetic factors. That the environment usually explains at least as much tends to be forgotten.

As Hans Kummer, a Swiss primatologist, remarked years ago, to try to determine how much of a trait is produced by genes and how much by the environment is as useless as asking whether the drumming that we hear in the distance is made by the percussionist or his instrument. On the other hand, if we pick up distinct sounds on different occasions, we can legitimately ask whether the variation is caused by different drummers or by different drums. This is the only sort of question science addresses when it looks into genetic versus environmental effects.

I foresee a continued mapping of the links between genes and behavior, a much more precise knowledge of how the brain works and a gradual adoption of the evolutionary paradigm in the social sciences. Charles Darwin's portrait will finally decorate the walls of departments of psychology and sociology! But one would hope that all of this will be accompanied by continued assessment of the ethical and political implications of behavioral science.

Traditionally, scientists have acted as if it is none of their business how the information they produce is being used. During some periods they have even actively assisted in political abuse. One notable exception was, of course, Albert Einstein, who may serve as a model of the kind of moral awareness needed in the behavioral and social sciences. If history teaches us anything, it is that it is critical that we remain on the alert against misinterpretations and simplifications. No one is in a better position than the scientists themselves to warn against distortions and to explain the complexities.

In which direction the thinking may develop can perhaps be illustrated with an example from the crossroads between cultural and evolutionary anthropology. Sigmund Freud and many traditional anthropologists, such as Claude Lévi-Strauss, have assumed that the human incest taboo serves to suppress sexual urges between family members. Freud believed that "the earliest sexual excitations of youthful human beings are invariably of an incestuous character." Hence, the incest taboo was seen as the ultimate victory of culture over nature.

In contrast, Edward Westermarck, a Finnish sociologist who lived at about the same time as Freud, hypothesized that early familiarity (such as between mother and child and between siblings) kills sexual desire. Little or no sexual attraction is found, he argued, between individuals who have grown up together. A fervent Darwinian, Westermarck proposed this as an evolved mechanism designed to prevent the deleterious consequences of inbreeding.

In the largest-scale study on this issue to date, Arthur P. Wolf, an anthropologist at Stanford University, examined the marital histories of 14,400 women in a "natural experiment" carried out in Taiwan. Families in this region used to adopt and raise future daughters-in-law, which meant that intended marriage partners grew up together from early childhood. Wolf compared these marriages with those arranged between men and women who did not meet until the wedding day. Using divorce and fertility rates as gauges of marital happiness and sexual activity, respectively, the data strongly supported the Westermarck effect: association in the first years of life appeared to compromise adult marital compatibility. Nonhuman primates are subject to the same mechanism. Many primates prevent inbreeding through migration of one sex or the other at puberty. The migratory sex meets new, unrelated mates, whereas the resident sex gains genetic diversity from the outside. But close kin who stay together also generally avoid sexual intercourse.

Kisaburo Tokuda first observed this in a group of Japanese macaques at the Kyoto zoo in the 1950s. A young adult male that had risen to the top rank made full use of his sexual privileges, mating frequently with all the females except for one: his mother. This was not an isolated case: mother-son matings are strongly suppressed in all primates. Even in bonobos—probably the most sexually active primates on the earth—this is the one partner combination in which sex is extremely rare or absent. Incest avoidance has now been convincingly demonstrated in a host of primates, and the mediating mechanism is thought to be early familiarity.

The Westermarck effect serves as a showcase for Darwinian approaches to human behavior because it so clearly rests on a combination of nature and nurture. The framework includes a developmental component (learned sexual aversion), an innate component (the effect of early familiarity), a cultural component (some cultures raise unrelated children together, others raise siblings of the opposite sex apart, but most have family arrangements that automatically lead to sexual inhibitions among relatives), a sound evolutionary reason (suppression of inbreeding) and direct parallels with animal behavior. On top of this comes the cultural taboo, which is unique to our species. An intriguing question is whether the incest taboo merely serves to formalize and strengthen the Westermarck effect or whether it adds a substantially new dimension.

The unexpected richness of a research program that integrates developmental, genetic, evolutionary and cultural approaches to a well-circumscribed phenomenon demonstrates the power of breaking down old barriers between disciplines. Most likely what will happen in the next millenium is that evolutionary approaches to human behavior will become more and more sophisticated by explicitly taking cultural flexibility into account. Hence, the traditional either/or approach to learning and instinct will be replaced by a more integrated perspective. In the meantime, students of animal behavior will become more interested in environmental effects on behavior and especially—in animals such as primates and marine mammals—the possibility of cultural transmission of information and habits. For example, some chimpanzee communities use stones to crack nuts in the forest, whereas other communities have the same nuts and stones available but don't do anything with them. Such differences are unexplained by genetic variation.

These two developments together will weaken the dichotomies popular today to the point of eliminating them. Rather than looking at culture as the antithesis of nature, we will be gaining a much more profound understanding of human behavior by silently carrying the old nature/nurture debate to its grave.

# FURTHER INFORMATION

SOCIOBIOLOGY: THE NEW SYNTHESIS. Edward O. Wilson. Belknap Press (Harvard University Press), 1975. 25th anniversary edition (in press).

SEXUAL ATTRACTION AND CHILDHOOD ASSOCIATION: A CHINESE BRIEF FOR EDWARD WESTERMARCK. Arthur P. Wolf. Stanford University Press, 1995.

THE MISMEASURE OF MAN. Revised edition. Stephen Jay Gould. W.W. Norton, 1996.

GOOD NATURED: THE ORIGINS OF RIGHT AND WRONG IN HUMANS AND OTHER ANIMALS. Frans de Waal. Harvard University Press, 1997.

**FRANS B. M. DE WAAL** was trained as a zoologist and ethologist in the European tradition in his native country, the Netherlands. He has been in the U.S. since 1981 and is currently director of the Living Links Center at the Yerkes Regional Primate Research Center in Atlanta and is also C.H. Candler Professor of Primate Behavior in the psychology department at Emory University. His research includes social interactions in primates as well as the origins of morality and justice in human society.

# DECODING THE HUMAN BODY

**The secrets of life: It is the most expensive, most ambitious biology mission ever. The Human Genome Project, at $250 million and counting, is biology's moon shot. In the eyes of boosters, it promises to provide no less than the operating instructions for a human body, and will revolutionize the detection, prevention and treatment of conditions from cancer to depression to old age itself. In the eyes of critics, it threatens to undermine privacy and bring on 'genetic discrimination' in insurance and employment. Near the finish line, one effect is indisputable: the genome has reignited the biotech industry. Explaining the genome—and what it means for you.**

BY SHARON BEGLEY

EVERY FRIDAY morning at 11, the directors of the five labs leading the race to decipher the human genome confer by phone to assess their progress. In mid-March, it was clear they were closing in on the next big milestone: reading the 2 billionth chemical "letter" in human DNA. But since some of those letters were redundant, a count of 2 billion would not really tell how close they were to the finish line of 3.2 billion.

Greg Schuler, a molecular biologist turned computer jock at the National Institutes of Health, had just spent the weekend, sitting on the sofa with his laptop in front of his fireplace at home, writing a 674-line program to reanalyze the overlaps. When he sicced it on the redundant sequences, the answer popped out: the Human Genome Project had *already* passed the 2 billion mark, on March 9. It had taken four years to determine the first billion letters in the human genome, but only four months for what Schuler calls "that next odometer moment." The actual chemical letter was—drumroll, please—T.

All right, so it didn't really matter which of the four letters making up DNA claimed position number 2,000,000,000 in the largest, most expensive, most ambitious biology project ever undertaken. But after 13 years and $250 million, through the work of some

1,100 biologists, computer scientists and technicians at 16 (mostly university) labs in 6 countries, the announcement meant that the Human Genome Project was two thirds of the way toward its goal of determining the exact chemical sequence that constitutes the DNA in every cell of every human body. With competitors in the private sector goading them on, scientists in the public project have tripled their pace, sequencing 12,000 letters every minute of every day, 24/7. By last weekend the project, financed by the U.S. government and Britain's Wellcome Trust, had sequenced 2,104,257,000 chemical letters. At this rate, it will complete its "working draft"—90 percent of the genome, with an accuracy of 99.9 percent—in June. And Science will know the blueprint of human life, the code of codes, the holy grail, the source code of *Homo sapiens*. It will know, Harvard University biologist Walter Gilbert says, "what it is to be human."

That knowledge promises to revolutionize medicine and vault the biotech industry into the Wall Street stratosphere. But just as no one foresaw eBay or Amazon when Apple unveiled the first home computer in 1977, so there is no crystal ball clear enough to reveal how knowing the entire human genome will change the way we live and even the way we think about who we are. It is a pretty good bet, though, that doctors will

drip droplets of our genes onto a biochip to figure out if we have the kind of prostate cancer that will kill or not, or to figure out if ours is the kind of leukemia that responds to this drug rather than that one. They will analyze our children's genes to rank their chances of succumbing to heart disease or Alzheimer's. Scientists will learn which genes turn on when a wound heals, when a baby's fingers grow, when a scalp becomes bald or a brow wrinkled, when a song is learned or a memory formed, when hormones surge or stress overwhelms us—and they will learn how to manipulate those genes. Babies will be designed before conception. Employers will take your genetic profile before they offer you a job or withdraw an offer if they don't like the cut of your DNA. The human genome sequence "will be the foundation of biology for decades, centuries or millennia to come," says John Sulston, director of the Sanger Centre, the genome lab near Cambridge, England, where a spiral staircase in the lobby twists upward like the double helix itself.

And all of it will emerge from something like this: ATGCCGCGGCTCCTCC . . . on and on, for about 3.2 billion such letters. Each letter represents a molecule—adenine, cytosine, guanine, thymine. Every cell of every human body, from skin to muscle to liver and everything in between (except red blood cells), contains a copy of the same DNA. The totality of DNA present in the cells of a species is its genome. Although the genetic age has brought incessant reports about genes "for" homosexuality, risk-taking, shyness, anxiety, cancer, Alzheimer's and more, the only thing a gene is actually "for" is a protein. The A's, T's, C's and G's constitute a code. Each triplet of letters instructs special machinery inside a cell to grab onto a particular amino acid. TGG, for instance, snatches the amino acid tryptophan. If you string together enough amino acids, you have a protein—a stomach enzyme that digests food, insulin that metabolizes carbohydrates, a brain chemical that causes depression, a sex hormone that triggers puberty. A gene, then, is an instruction, like the directions in a bead-making kit but written in molecule-ese. Humans have perhaps 80,000 genes, and we are 99.9 percent identical. That is, at only one in 1,000 chemical letters does the genome of, say, Woody Allen differ from that of Stone Cold Steve Austin.

Even at its inception, the creators of the Human Genome Project suspected that it would transform biology, vaulting it past physics as the hot science. But at the moment of its creation, the project was an unwanted child. Charles DeLisi, newly arrived at the Department of Energy, was in charge of research into the biological effects of radiation. In October 1985, he was reading a government report on technologies for detecting heritable mutations, such as those in the survivors of Hiroshima. It hit him: given the slow pace at which biologists were deciphering genes, which you need to do in order to assess mutations, they would finish . . . oh, about when humans had evolved into a new species. "We just weren't going to get there," says DeLisi. So he dashed off memos, ordered up reports, begged scientists to serve on planning committees—and got responses like "I don't want to spin my wheels" on a project that had little chance of happening.

For biologists and the genome, it was far from love at first sight. Critics pointed out that some 97 percent of the human genome—3.1 billion of the 3.2 billion A's, T's, C's and G's—does not spell out a gene. Why bother sequencing this "junk" DNA, whose presence no one can explain, especially when there was no known way to tell what was junk and what was a gene? But when a panel of leading scientists, including skeptics, unanimously endorsed the project in 1988, and it wrested funding from Congress, the Human Genome Project was out of the gate, headed toward a completion date of 2005 at a nice, sedate pace. It didn't last. In May 1998, gene-hunter extraordinaire J. Craig Venter and his newly formed Celera Genomics vowed to trounce the public project by finishing the human genome sequence in just three years. That made Francis Collins, director of the National Human Genome Research Institute, scramble. His

## The Public Genome Team Races . . .

Going public: Collins has led the publicly financed genome project since 1993. This year he rebuffed an offer from the biotech firm Celera to join forces and thus speed up the work: he feared Celera would keep the results private, available only to those who pay, for too long. So the public project goes it alone, posting its discoveries every 24 hours (except weekends) at www.ncbi.nlm.nih.gov/genome/seq.

## . . .The Upstart Master Of the Gene-iverse

**To the swift:** Venter's teams have sequenced the genomes of more organisms than anyone else. His policy of keeping data secret for six months ($5 million buys companies instant access for five years) riles some academics. But Venter's speed means that everyone gets data months sooner.

### What We Know So Far

**Fly boys:** It took 195 scientists to decode *Drosophila's* genome. Why bother? Of 289 human-disease genes, 177 have analogs in the fly, including 68% of cancer genes.

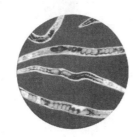

**Almost human?** Half of the known human-disease genes have analogs in the genes of the worm *C. elegans,* raising hopes for the discovery of treatments

**Tiny trailblazer:** *Haemophilus influenzae,* a bacterium, was the first organism whose genome was fully sequenced

Photos by Baylor College of Medicine in Houston; Jones King—Holmes Science Photo Library, Photo Researchers; Oliver Meckes, Photo Researchers (2).

labs had sequenced less than 3 percent of the genome at the original halfway point, so he ordered everyone to forget about the double-checking and the exploring of cool scientific puzzles and just churn out the *#@*ing A's, T's, C's and G's. It worked. In October 1998 Collins announced that his team would have a rough draft in 2001; in March 1999 he pushed it to this spring.

What will it mean to know the complete human genome? Eric Lander of MIT's Whitehead Institute compares it to the discovery of the periodic table of the elements in the late 1800s. "Genomics is now providing biology's periodic table," says Lander. "Scientists will know that every phenome-

non must be explainable in terms of this measly list"—which will fit on a single CD-ROM. Already researchers are extracting DNA from patients, attaching fluorescent molecules and sprinkling the sample on a glass chip whose surface is speckled with 10,000 known genes. A laser reads the fluorescence, which indicates which of the known genes on the chip are in the mystery sample from the patient. In only the last few months such "gene-expression monitoring" has diagnosed a muscle tumor in a boy thought to have leukemia, and distinguished between two kinds of cancer that require very different chemotherapy. Soon, predicts Patrick Brown of Stanford University, ex-

# The Human Parts List

Scientists have identified more than 8,000 human genes, including those linked to breast and colon cancers and Alzheimer's disease. Figuring out how the genes work promises to lead to preventions and treatments. Some of the genes identified:

**Chromo 1**

Each human cell contains DNA organized into 23 pairs of chromosomes. Every chromosome has hundreds to thousands of codes for building proteins.

**GBA**
Gaucher disease
*Absence of fat-breaking enzyme; can lead to jaundice or anemia.*

**HPC1**
Prostate cancer

**GLC1A**
Glaucoma

**PS2 (AD4)**
Alzheimer's disease

**Chromo 2**

**ETM2**
Essential tremor
*A common symptom of neurological disorders such as Parkinson's disease and stroke*

**MSH2**
Colon cancer

**\*CREB**
Memory
*Mice without this gene can't learn simple tasks*

**PAX3**
Waardenburg syndrome
*Associated with deafness and mismatched eye colors*

*PRESUMPTIVE LOCATION

**Chromo 3**

**VHL**
Von Hippel-Lindau
*Abnormal growth of blood vessels. Growth may develop in the retina, in the spinal cord, in certain areas of the brain or in the adrenal glands.*

**SCLC1**
Lung cancer

**MLH1**
Colon cancer
*Some 160,400 Americans died from the disease in 1997*

**ETM1**
Essential tremor

**Chromo 4**

**HD**
Huntington disease
*An inherited degenerative brain disease that leads to dementia*

**EVC**
Ellis-van Creveld syndrome
*Malformation of the wrist bones, partial harelip and prenatal teeth eruption*

**Alpha-synuclein**
Parkinson's disease
*Only recently discovered to be hereditary*

**Chromo 5**

**SRD51A**
Steroid 5-alpha reductase 1
*May lead to baldness and acne*

**\*CSA**
Cockayne syndrome
*Premature aging*

**DTD**
Diastrophic dysplasia
*Malformations in joints*

*PRESUMPTIVE LOCATION

**Chromo 6**

**SCA1**
Spinocerebellar atrophy
*Results in loss of muscle coordination and spasticity*

**IDDM1**
Diabetes
*A chronic disorder that greatly increases the risk of heart disease and kidney failure*

**EPM2A**
Epilepsy

**Chromo 7**

**GCK**
Diabetes

**ELN**
Williams syndrome
*Physical- and mental-development disorder*

**Pendrin**
Pendred syndrome

**CFTR**
Cystic fibrosis

**OB**
Obesity

**Chromo 8**

**WRN**
Werner syndrome
*Premature aging occurring during adolescence*

**MYC**
Burkitt lymphoma
*A rare form of cancer*

**Chromo 9**

**CDKN2**
Malignant melanoma

**ABC1**
Tangier disease

**ABL**
Chronic myeloid leukemia

**TSC1**
Tuberous sclerosis

**Chromo 10**

**PAHX**
Refsum disease
*One symptom is failure of muscle coordination*

**OAT**
Gyrate atrophy
*An error of metabolism known to cause progressive loss of vision*

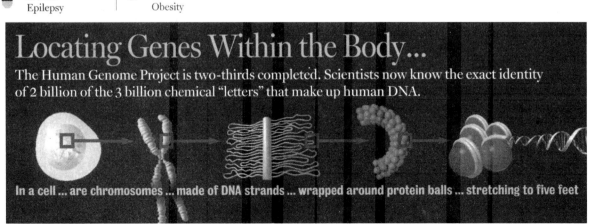

## Locating Genes Within the Body...

The Human Genome Project is two-thirds completed. Scientists now know the exact identity of 2 billion of the 3 billion chemical "letters" that make up human DNA.

In a cell ... are chromosomes ... made of DNA strands ... wrapped around protein balls ... stretching to five feet

Photos by T. Ried–NHGRI–NIH

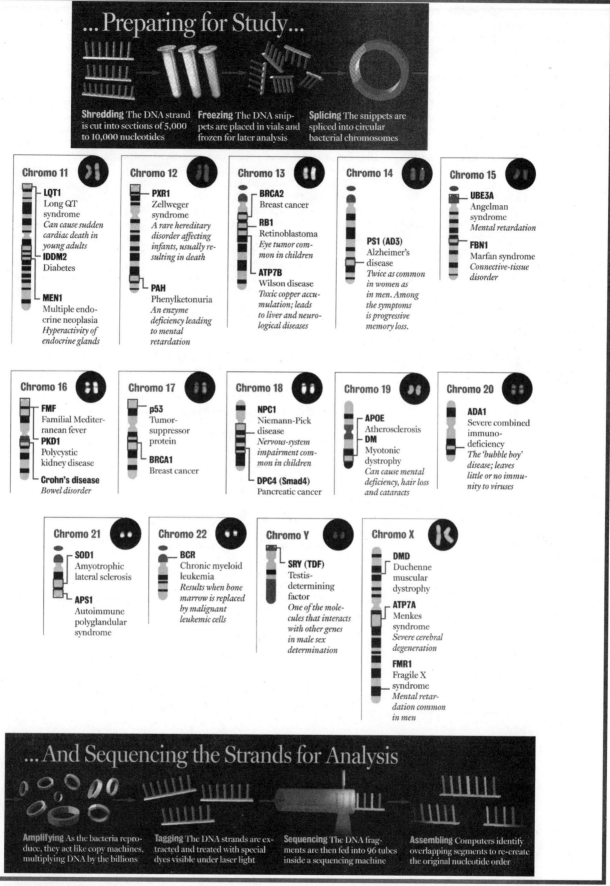

## ... Preparing for Study...

**Shredding** The DNA strand is cut into sections of 5,000 to 10,000 nucleotides

**Freezing** The DNA snippets are placed in vials and frozen for later analysis

**Splicing** The snippets are spliced into circular bacterial chromosomes

### Chromo 11
**LQT1**
Long QT syndrome
*Can cause sudden cardiac death in young adults*
**IDDM2**
Diabetes
**MEN1**
Multiple endocrine neoplasia
*Hyperactivity of endocrine glands*

### Chromo 12
**PXR1**
Zellweger syndrome
*A rare hereditary disorder affecting infants, usually resulting in death*
**PAH**
Phenylketonuria
*An enzyme deficiency leading to mental retardation*

### Chromo 13
**BRCA2**
Breast cancer
**RB1**
Retinoblastoma
*Eye tumor common in children*
**ATP7B**
Wilson disease
*Toxic copper accumulation; leads to liver and neurological diseases*

### Chromo 14
**PS1 (AD3)**
Alzheimer's disease
*Twice as common in women as in men. Among the symptoms is progressive memory loss.*

### Chromo 15
**UBE3A**
Angelman syndrome
*Mental retardation*
**FBN1**
Marfan syndrome
*Connective-tissue disorder*

### Chromo 16
**FMF**
Familial Mediterranean fever
**PKD1**
Polycystic kidney disease
**Crohn's disease**
*Bowel disorder*

### Chromo 17
**p53**
Tumor-suppressor protein
**BRCA1**
Breast cancer

### Chromo 18
**NPC1**
Niemann-Pick disease
*Nervous-system impairment common in children*
**DPC4 (Smad4)**
Pancreatic cancer

### Chromo 19
**APOE**
Atherosclerosis
**DM**
Myotonic dystrophy
*Can cause mental deficiency, hair loss and cataracts*

### Chromo 20
**ADA1**
Severe combined immuno-deficiency
*The 'bubble boy' disease; leaves little or no immunity to viruses*

### Chromo 21
**SOD1**
Amyotrophic lateral sclerosis
**APS1**
Autoimmune polyglandular syndrome

### Chromo 22
**BCR**
Chronic myeloid leukemia
*Results when bone marrow is replaced by malignant leukemic cells*

### Chromo Y
**SRY (TDF)**
Testis-determining factor
*One of the molecules that interacts with other genes in male sex determination*

### Chromo X
**DMD**
Duchenne muscular dystrophy
**ATP7A**
Menkes syndrome
*Severe cerebral degeneration*
**FMR1**
Fragile X syndrome
*Mental retardation common in men*

## ... And Sequencing the Strands for Analysis

**Amplifying** As the bacteria reproduce, they act like copy machines, multiplying DNA by the billions

**Tagging** The DNA strands are extracted and treated with special dyes visible under laser light

**Sequencing** The DNA fragments are then fed into 96 tubes inside a sequencing machine

**Assembling** Computers identify overlapping segments to re-create the original nucleotide order

GRAPHICS ON LAST TWO PAGES: SOURCES: NATIONAL CENTER FOR BIOTECHNOLOGY INFORMATION, NATIONAL LIBRARY OF MEDICINE, NATIONAL INSTITUTES OF HEALTH

RESEARCH BY FE CONWAY AND STEPHEN TOTILO, DESIGN BY BONNIE SCRANTON, GENE-SEQUENCING ILLUSTRATIONS BY CHRISTOPH BLUMRICH—NEWSWEEK.

pression analysis will distinguish prostate cancers that kill from prostate cancers that don't, neurons in a depressed brain from neurons in a normal brain—all on the basis of which genes are active.

Humankind's history is also written in its DNA. "Rare spelling differences in DNA can be used to trace human migrations," says Lander. "Scientists can recognize the descendants of chromosomes that ancient Phoenician traders left behind when they visited Italian seaports." Genetic data support the oral tradition that the Bantu-speaking Lemba of southern Africa are descendants of Jews who migrated from the Middle East 2,700 years ago. And they suggest that 98 percent of the Irish men of Connaught are descended from a single band of hunter-gatherers who reached the Emerald Isle more than 4,000 years ago.

But decoding the book of life poses daunting moral dilemmas. With knowledge of our genetic code will come the power to re-engineer the human species. Biologists will be able to use the genome as a parts list—much as customers scour a list of china to replace broken plates—and may well let prospective parents choose their unborn child's traits. Scientists have solid leads on genes for different temperaments, body builds, statures and cognitive abilities. And if anyone still believes that parents will recoil at playing God, and leave their baby's fate in the hands of nature, recall that couples have already created a frenzied market in eggs from Ivy League women.

Beyond the profound ethical issues are practical concerns. The easier it is to change ourselves and our children, the less society may tolerate those who do not, warns Lori Andrews of Kent College of Law. If genetic tests in utero predict mental dullness, obesity, short stature—or other undesirable traits of the moment—will society disparage children whose parents let them be born with those traits? Already, Andrew finds, some

nurses and doctors blame parents for bringing into the world a child whose birth defect was diagnosable before delivery; how long will it be before the same condemnation applies to cosmetic imperfections? An even greater concern is that well-intentioned choices by millions of individual parents-to-be could add up to unforeseen consequences for all of humankind. It just so happens that some disease genes also confer resistance to disease: carrying a gene for sickle cell anemia, for instance, brings resistance to malaria. Are we smart enough, and wise enough, to know how knocking out "bad" genes will affect our evolution as a species?

From the inception of the genome project, ethicists warned that genetic knowledge would be used against people in insurance and employment. Sorting out whether this is happening is like judging whether HMOs provide quality care. Systematic surveys turn up few problems, but horror stories abound. One man underwent a genetic test and learned that he carried a marker for the blood disorder hemochromatosis. Although he was being successfully treated, his insurer dropped him on the ground that he might stop treatment and develop the disease. Another had a job offer withdrawn for "lying" during a pre-employment physical. He was healthy, but carried a gene for kidney disease. And last December Terri Seargent, 43, was fired from her job as an office manager after she tested positive for the genetic disease that killed her brother. She began receiving preventive treatments. When her self-insured employer got the first bill, she was fired.

So far 39 states prohibit, at least in part, discrimination in health insurance based on genetic tests; 15 have some ban on discrimination in employment. But many of the laws have loopholes. (One of the 15 is North Carolina, where Seargent lives). Employers still, apparently, want genetic information about their workers. A

1999 survey by the American Management Association found that 30 percent of large and midsize firms obtain such information on employees. Seven percent use it in hiring and promotions. "It is still possible to have information about the genome used to take away your health insurance or your job," says Collins. "As yet, we have not seen effective federal legislation [to prevent this]. With genes getting discovered right and left, the opportunities for mischief are on an exponential curve."

Perhaps the greatest unknown is how the completion of the Human Genome Project—not just getting C's, G's, T's and A's, but learning the function of every gene—will shape our views of what we are. There is a great risk of succumbing to a naive biological determinism, ascribing to our genes such qualities as personality, intelligence, even faith. Studies of twins have already claimed (to great criticism, but claimed nonetheless) that genes even shape whether an individual will favor or oppose capital punishment. "We do ascribe some sort of quasi-religious significance to our DNA," says Collins. "We have a tendency to be more deterministic than we should." For now, the power, and the limits, of the genome can only be guessed at. The stage is set. The players are ready. After millions of dollars and millions of hours, the curtain is rising on what our children will surely, looking back in awe, see as the dawn of the century of the genome.

*With* THOMAS HAYDEN, WILLIAM UNDERHILL *in London and* GREGORY BEALS

# The Future of the Brain

*The pairing of innovative technologies with scientific discoveries about the brain opens new ways of handling information, treating diseases, and possibly creating robots with human characteristics.*

*Norbert R. Myslinski*

*For I dipp'd into the future,
far as human eye could see,
Saw the Vision of the world,
and all the wonder that
would be.*

—*Alfred, Lord Tennyson*

An understanding of the brain helps us understand our nature. Over the course of evolution, the brain has acquired greater functions and higher consciousness. The reptilian brain, for instance, exerts control over vegetative functions, such as eating, sleeping, and reproduction. Development of the mammalian brain added the ability to express emotions. The human brain has the additional powers of cognition—such as reasoning, judgment, problem solving, and creativity. The latter functions, which are controlled by an area of the brain called the prefrontal cortex (located behind the forehead), distinguish us from other forms of life and represent the flower of our humanity. They have allowed us to re-create ourselves and decide our destiny.

Besides these long-term changes, our brains undergo short-term modifications during our lifetime. Not only does the brain control behavior, but one's behavior leads to changes in the brain, in terms of both structure and function. Subjective experiences play a major role in brain functions and the manifestation of one's mind, consciousness, and personal values. Thus the brain adapts to each individual's changing world.

Modern society and technology have given us the time, protection, and freedom to focus on the higher powers of the brain. As individual freedoms and the free enterprise system are extended around the world, we will see a continuing rise of innovative ventures and scientific exploration. In addition, our success at eliminating brain diseases and expanding brain functions will depend on the uniquely human characteristics of the brain. Given the finances and technology, we will need vision and creativity.

But modern technology also raises a number of questions about our future. For instance, how will the continuing information explosion challenge the powers of our brains? What does the next century have in store for us regarding memory drugs, brain surgery, brain regeneration, and other treatments for brain disorders? How will the relationships between mind and body or brain and machine evolve? More important, are we prepared to handle such challenges, socially, psychologically, and ethically?

## The Information Explosion

Information technologies have been increasingly successful in helping us acquire and communicate large new areas of knowledge. But the same success challenges the brain's capacity. How will the brain continue to cope with this information explosion? It will probably employ the same techniques it always has: filtering, organizing, and selective forget-

**Our brains allow us to exert such uniquely human powers as reasoning, judgment, problem solving, and creativity—thereby guiding our own development and destiny.**

ting [see "Sherlock Holmes' Lesson," THE WORLD & I, June 2000, p. 316].

Already, the brain filters out more than 99 percent of all sensory input before it reaches consciousness. In the future, it will be even more important to filter out the repetitive, boring, and unnecessary, and retain the novel, relevant, and necessary information. Actually, the brain is not good at remembering isolated facts but is great at organizing and associating thoughts and ideas. This ability will help it handle new information without suffering overload.

Just as important as the biology inside the brain is the technology

This article appeared in the August 2000 issue of *The World & I,* pp. 152-159. *The World & I,* a pubication of The Washington Times Corporation. © 2000.

**As the human genome is mapped, scientists hope to find cures for many genetically linked diseases, including those that affect the brain.**

outside. First with the introduction of books, and now computers, we have become increasingly reliant on artificial means of storing information. Thus the relative need for long-term (storage) memory in the brain and the time span for storage have decreased. As this trend continues, we will make greater use of our working memory and less use of our storage memory [see "Now Where Did I Put Those Keys?" THE WORLD & I, November 1998, p. 160].

Help for our memories may also come in the form of a pill. Research related to Alzheimer's disease has already produced a drug that can improve normal memory in small, healthy animals.

Furthermore, the rate at which we access and share information will most likely continue to accelerate. As a result, our brains will be challenged to think faster and make decisions more quickly. Anything less will be inefficient. Bureaucracy and red tape will be our enemies. We may be compelled to place greater emphasis on intuition and "gut feelings."

## Treating hereditary brain disorders

In living organisms, another type of memory occurs in the form of genetic material known as DNA (deoxyribonucleic acid). It is the blueprint for the body and the chemical memory for traits that are passed down from generation to generation. The DNA representing the human genome (complete set of genetic information) consists of over 3 billion subunits (base pairs) and

contains the coding for anywhere between 40,000 and 100,000 genes.

Scientists are already tackling the ambitious goal of determining the sequence of base pairs and mapping the genes of the entire human genome. Two groups—a publicly funded, international consortium (whose work is known as the Human Genome Project) and the private company Celera Genomics Corporation (based in Rockville, Maryland)—have just recently submitted "working drafts," with the promise of more detailed, high-quality results in the near future.

The human genetic map will help locate biomarkers for the diagnosis and treatment of hereditary disorders, including those affecting the brain. One type of treatment, known as gene therapy, is directed toward replacing defective genes with un-

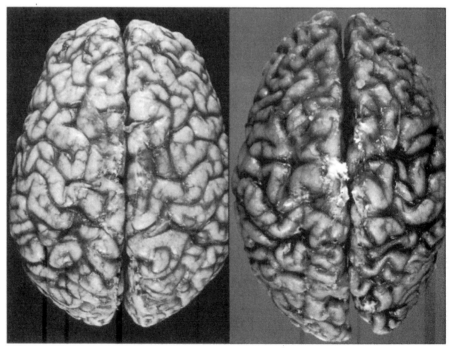

BOTH IMAGES COURTESY OF THE NATIONAL INSTITUTE OF NEUROLOGICAL DISORDERS AND STROKE/NIH

**Convolutions in the brain of an Alzheimer's patient show considerable shrinkage (*right*) compared with those in a normal brain (*left*). Cures for Alzheimer's and other brain diseases may be found through such approaches as genetic engineering or neural cell regeneration.**

damaged ones [see "Doctoring Genes to Beat Disease," THE WORLD & I, December 1997, p. 178]. But the many gene therapy trials conducted over the past 10 years have met with a low success rate, indicating the

need for further refinements to the technique. In the meantime, a promising new strategy called *chimeraplasty*, in which the cell is stimulated to repair its own defective genes, has emerged [see "The Promise of Genetic Cures," THE WORLD & I, May 2000, p. 147]. Either approach may also be used to fight noninherited disorders by increasing the body's production of substances (such as interleukin or interferon) that protect the body.

The genetic information will probably lead to tests performed *in utero* or early in life to detect markers that suggest predispositions to such conditions as obesity and alcoholism, or such diseases as schizophrenia and Alzheimer's. People would then have the opportunity to get genetic counseling and design a lifestyle that integrates medical surveillance to stay healthy. At the same

time, however, we need to improve our system of laws to prevent discrimination against people—particularly in employment and insurance coverage—based on this information. In February this year, President

## Environment and behavior can alter our brains; free will can influence our behavior.

Clinton prohibited federal employers from requiring or requesting genetic tests as a condition of being hired or receiving benefits.

Moreover, knowledge of a person's genotype (gene structure and organization) will not necessarily enable us to predict his phenotype (body structure), which is the manifestation of not only the genetic information but environmental influences and life experiences as well. The phenotype for a brain disease, for example, could range anywhere from no symptoms to total disability. Even identical twins are not 100 percent concordant for most brain disorders. The health and character of the human brain (and the rest of the body) are neither predetermined nor inevitable. Environment and behavior can alter our brains; free will can influence our behavior.

It is also possible that a treatment that alters one gene may affect many traits, even those that we do not wish to change. The same gene linked to a brain disorder might also influence intelligence or creativity. The risk involved in altering a gene is especially great for disorders associated with multiple genes.

### Vaccines, drugs, surgery, and brain regeneration

We have grown up in a world of miracle drugs, but most alleviate just the symptoms. The next century will focus on prevention and cures. Scientists are already working on oral vaccines that would attack the pathological plagues and tangles of Alzheimer's disease, decrease brain damage after a stroke or seizure, and lower the number of seizures in epileptics. We will be able to administer specific substances (called trophic factors) that will stimulate brain cells to multiply and replace cells degenerating because of brain diseases such as Parkinson's and Huntington's.

The trail-and-error method of finding effective drugs is now being replaced by the use of computers to design molecules that will precisely fit into specific receptors for the purpose of treating diseases. In the future, we will also be able to manufacture and use larger quantities of disease-fighting chemicals—such as interleukins, interferon, and brain trophic factors—that occur naturally in the body.

One strategy for making large quantities of specific antibodies is called the monoclonal antibody technique. Antibodies of a particular type are produced in large quantities by fusing the specific antibody-producing cells with tumor cells that grow and proliferate indefinitely. We could even piggyback drugs onto rected at protecting crops and improving their taste and nutritional value. About two dozen companies are now working to enhance the availability and lower the cost of drugs by genetically engineering plants to produce them. Some of the drugs may be ingested by simply eating the plant food.

With the improvement of brain imaging and robotics, brain surgery will improve and become less invasive. The brain is ideally suited for robotic surgery. It is enclosed in a firm skull that's appropriate for mounting instruments and providing fixed reference points by which to navigate the brain. Robotics and microscopic brain imaging will be used for higher precision, fewer mistakes, and minimally invasive surgical techniques.

While pharmacological and surgical treatments improve, another approach that's gaining in importance is the regeneration of neural tissue. This approach has become possible

---

# On Being Human

According to futurist Alvin Toffler, the new millennium will challenge our understanding of what it means to be human. The fusion of computer technology, genetic engineering, and research on the brain will allow us to control our own evolution. For instance, electronic microchips may be placed in our brains to repair lost functions or create new ones. Scientists can now make microchips that are part organic. What about computers that are part protoplasm? When do we stop calling them machines and start calling them life?

There is currently a debate about the ethics of producing human clones or designer babies with "better" abilities. Can we also modify the genes of animals to give them human intelligence? Or can we create robots that take on human characteristics, such as human behavior or even self-replication? If so, should they be considered part human?

Whatever the answers may turn out to be, our differing views of what it means to be human are likely to polarize society because of conflicting causes taken up by political, religious, and scientific groups. We may experience a moral divide that could exceed that seen with slavery or abortion.

—N.R.M.

---

antibodies that target specific parts of the brain, thereby reducing the drug dosage and minimizing side effects.

Another approach currently being pursued is genetically engineering plants to produce pharmaceuticals. Until recently, efforts have been di- because of recent research on stem cells and trophic factors, along with the discovery that adult brain cells can divide and multiply. Neural regeneration is the hope for those who suffer from such disorders as paralysis, Lou Gehrig's disease (amyotrophic lateral sclerosis), Down syndrome, retina degeneration, and Parkinson's disease.

## The mind-body relationship

Charles Schultz, the beloved creator of Charlie Brown and author of the comic strip *Peanuts* for 50 years, died this year on the very day that his farewell strip was published. It was as if he stayed alive just long enough to see it end. Was that just a coincidence?

Warm, loving relationships, as well as isolation, can influence longevity and the will to live. How often have we heard of a person dying soon after his spouse dies? The body is not a biological machine operating independently of the mind. Even Hippocrates proposed that health was a balance of mind and body in the proper environment.

The mind has a powerful effect on our physical health by influencing our immune, cardiovascular, and endocrine systems. It can change the levels of such body substances as cortisol, adrenaline, and natural killer cells. Happy people get sick less often. Angry people have more health problems. Stress, anger, depression, and loneliness suppress the immune system, overexert the heart, raise blood pressure, enhance blood clotting, increase bone loss, harden the arteries, and increase cholesterol and abdominal fat. These factors can increase the incidence and severity of cancer, heart disease, stroke, arthritis, and even the common cold.

Western medicine, however, has underappreciated this mind-body

---

**Robotics and microscopic brain imaging will be used for higher precision, fewer mistakes, and minimally invasive surgical techniques.**

---

# Brain Doctors

Technology will enable drugs to be more selective and surgeries to be more exact. But what about the doctors? How will they change? Their early training will involve greater use of virtual reality and less use of animals. They will emphasize prevention and cure rather than the treatment of symptoms. They will have to be genetic counselors and focus on the whole person rather than symptoms. They must put humanity back into medicine.

Today's neurologists tend to be technicians more than healers. They are trained primarily to diagnose and fix defective brains. Their success is determined by how effective they are at minimizing symptoms, restoring functions, and curing diseases. Although most patients are grateful, many find the doctor's help to be insufficient or lacking. Substituting a side effect for a symptom, or prolonging a life of pain and distress, may not be an improvement in the patient's quality of life.

In addition, the psychological and spiritual needs of the patient often go unattended. Patients need someone to appreciate their distress and relate to them on a human level. Recognizing these needs, medical education is now increasing its emphasis on treating the whole person. Doctors are realizing that the way to a healthy body is through the mind.

—*N.R.M.*

relationship. Now that brain imaging can be used to observe the effect of the mind on the body, we will see the medical establishment embrace this concept as the basis of a legitimate form of therapy. Support groups, meditation, and relaxation therapy will be prescribed to ward off disease and dampen its devastating effects.

Research has shown that people who derive strength and comfort from religion live healthier and longer lives [see "Is Religion Good for Your Health?" THE WORLD & I, February 1996, p. 291]. The benefits of religion go beyond social contact or the encouragement of healthier habits. It can be a mechanism to help cope with life and stressful situations. Faith in a Higher Being has been shown to be an important part of the successful Twelve Steps program of Alcoholics Anonymous—a program that has been extended to treat other addictions, such as gambling and overeating [see "Spirituality in Healing," THE WORLD & I, May 2000, p. 153]. Doctors will use it to increase the compliance of patients with the treatments prescribed for a wide range of acute and chronic medical problems.

People get better because they believe they will. This is called the pla-

cebo effect. A patient's belief that he is receiving effective medicine will alleviate his symptoms. The stronger his belief, the stronger the relief. This effect has been known and used by doctors for many years. It must be taken into account when testing new medicines and therapies.

The placebo effect is based on the brain's ability to anticipate the future and prepare for it. For example, the brain analyzes trajectories of objects in motion and predicts their future location, or it analyzes environmental temperatures and predicts the body's future temperature. Also, our senses are notorious for seeing what we hope to see and tasting what we expect to taste. The brain produces a placebo effect by stimulating cells and releasing hormones that start the healing process in anticipation of getting better.

## The brain-machine connection

Over the past century, we have aided our vision and hearing with lenses and amplifiers. During the next century, we will probably replace eyes and ears with light and sound detectors and computer chips that send signals to the brain.

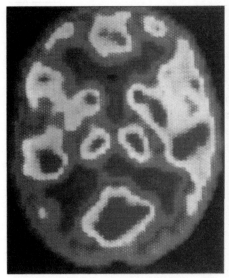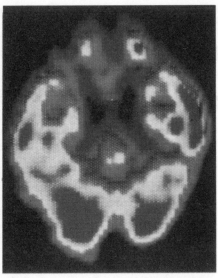

COURTESY OF THE NATIONAL INSTITUTE OF NEUROLOGICAL DISORDERS AND STROKE/NIH

**Just as current PET scans (*above*) reveal general activity in the brain, future techniques may show microscopic details. *Left:* The brain of a young man listening intently to a story uses a great deal of glucose in the auditory cortex (gray areas near the ears). *Right:* An image at a different level of the same brain shows activity in the hippocampus (gray spots at short distances in from the sides), where short-term learning is converted to long-term memory.**

**We need to find ways to understand consciousness and how the brain is involved in the powers of reasoning, creativity, and love.**

Every year, the International NAISO Congress on Information Science Innovations holds a Robot Soccer Competition. Winners are those who create robots that can "see" with greater acuity, "think" more perceptively, and move faster and with greater agility. Software companies are already making advertising claims that their programs can "think." Will molecular electronics and nanotechnology, combined with genetic engineering, give us the power to create sentient robots?

If so, a modern-day Pandora's box is being opened. Unlike scientific breakthroughs of the past, the robots and engineered organisms of the future could have the potential for self-replication. While the uncontrolled replication of mischievous programs on the Internet—as seen with the "Melissa" and "I Love You" viruses—can cause a lot of damage, the uncontrolled replication of senti-

ment robots may pose a threat to our humanity. Will this evolution come suddenly, like the news about cloning the first mammal, or gradually, so that we will get used to it? Or will modern-day Luddites have the courage and foresight to say no and steer us in another direction?

We began the twentieth century looking at the brain's structure through a simple microscope and ended by examining its functions with such techniques as PET (positron emission tomography) and MRI (magnetic resonance imaging). We went through the stages of neuroanatomy, neurophysiology, and neurochemistry. We learned how the brain controls movement and processes sensory information. We scratched the surface in our attempts to clarify intelligence and emotions. Among the challenges of the new century will be to find ways to understand consciousness and how the brain is in-

volved in the powers of reasoning, creativity, and love.

Speculating about the future, however, is daunting, even for experts. In a 1987 survey, medical scientists predicted that by the year 2000 we would probably have a cure for two-thirds of all cancers, AIDS would be eliminated, and coronary bypass surgery would be replaced by less invasive techniques.

Distinguishing between fact and fiction is difficult even today. On the first day of my neuroscience course in graduate school, our instructor told us that half of what he would teach us that semester would eventually prove to be wrong—the problem was, he could not tell which half was wrong. Since then, I have repeatedly witnessed the truth of that statement. Revisions of our knowledge will continue in the twenty-first century. We must keep testing our view of the world, and if it fails, replace it with a better one. We must remain flexible in our beliefs, just as our brains remain flexible in their structure and function.

*Norbert R. Myslinski is associate professor of neuroscience at the University of Maryland and director of Maryland Brain Awareness Week.*

# Unit Selections

# Key Points to Consider

❖ Why are psychologists interested in studying sensations and perceptions? Can you differentiate the two? Isn't sensation the domain of biologists and physicians? Can you rank-order the senses, that is, place them in a hierarchy of importance? Can you justify your rankings?

❖ What role does the brain play in sensation and perception? Can you give specific information about the role of the brain in each sense? Are some senses "distant" senses and some "near" senses in terms of how we perceive a stimulus, whether the stimulus is physical or social? Can you think of other ways to categorize the various senses?

❖ Do you think visual experiences induce consciousness? If not, what is consciousness and what does induce it? From where do you think consciousness originates?

❖ What is deafness? What are some of the causes of deafness? Are Americans at risk for deafness? What are the newest methods for overcoming deafness? What else can be done to reduce noise levels so that they are not detrimental to us?

❖ What is an altered state? What is parapsychology? Do you believe in extrasensory phenomena? If yes, then do you believe in presentiment? Do you believe in it even if there is scientific evidence against this sixth sense? How do psychologists study presentiment? Can you think of any other phenomena that might be considered sixth senses?

 **Links**  **www.dushkin.com/online/**

These sites are annotated on pages 4 and 5.

Susan and her roommate have been friends since freshman year. Because they share so much in common, they decided to become roommates in their sophomore year. They both want to travel abroad one day. Both date men from the same fraternity, are education majors, and want to work with young children after graduation from college. Today they are at the local art museum. As they walk around the galleries, Susan is astonished at her roommate's taste in art. Whatever her roommate likes, Susan hates. The paintings and sculptures that Susan admires are the very ones at which her roommate turns up her nose. "How can their tastes in art be so different?" Susan wonders.

What Susan and her roommate are experiencing is a difference in perception or the interpretation of the sensory stimulation provided by the artwork. Perception and its sister area of psychology, sensation, are the focus of this unit.

For many years in psychology, it was popular to consider sensation and perception as two distinct processes. Sensation was defined in passive terms as the simple event of some stimulus energy (i.e. a sound wave) impinging on the body or on a specific sense organ that then reflexively transmits appropriate information to the central nervous system. Both passivity and simple reflexes were stressed in this concept. Perception, on the other hand, was defined as an integrative and interpretive process that the higher centers of the brain accomplish based on sensory information and available memories for similar events.

The Gestalt psychologists, early German researchers, were convinced that perception was a higher order function compared to sensation. The Gestalt psychologists believed that the whole stimulus was more than the sum of its individual sensory parts; Gestalt psychologists believed this statement was made true by the process of perception.

For example, when you listen to a song, you hear the words, the loudness, and the harmony as well as the main melody. However, you do not really hear each of these separately; what you hear is a whole song. If the song is pleasant to you, you may say that you like the song. If the song is raucous to you, you may say that you do not like it. However, even the songs you do not like on first hearing may become likable after repeated exposure. Hence perception, according to these early Gestalt psychologists, is a more advanced and complicated process than sensation.

This dichotomy of sensation and perception is no longer widely accepted. The revolution came in the mid-1960s when a psychologist published a then-radical treatise in which he reasoned that perceptual processes included all sensory events that he saw as directed by a searching central nervous system. Also, this view provided that certain perceptual patterns, such as recognition of a piece of artwork, may be species-specific. That is, all humans, independent of learning history, should share some of the same

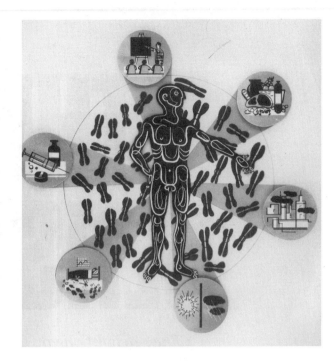

perceptual repertoires. This unit on perceptual processes is designed to further your understanding of these complex and interesting processes.

In the first article, "The Senses," one of the main topics of this unit is introduced to you and reviews many of the dominant senses in the human being. The author concludes that when we understand the senses, we also understand the brain.

The second article in this unit, "Vision: A Window on Consciousness," explores one of the most important senses in humans. The author, Nikos Logothetis, ties together our visual experiences and consciousness. Psychologists have long debated consciousness and tried to define it and find its source. Logothetis strongly suggests that we derive consciousness from our visual experiences. He demonstrates this by showcasing research on visual ambiguity, a situation in which a stimulus appears to be ambiguous to the eyes.

One of the other dominant senses in humans is audition or hearing. In the next article, "Noise," Consumer Reports magazine discloses information about just how much noise Americans are exposed to and why certain noises can be detrimental. With enough exposure to certain sounds, individuals can become deaf. The article also reveals what can be done to save Americans' hearing.

The fourth article in this unit examines another concept related to sensation and perception, paraperception, as studied by parapsychologists. Dean Radin and Colleen Rae ask if there is a sixth sense? The sixth sense to which they allude is presentiment—a reaction to something bad before it occurs. The authors' debate on the existence of this sense is backed by research findings, with each psychologist presenting compelling evidence for or against the existence of presentiment.

# THE SENSES

*They delight, heal, define the boundaries of our world. And they are helping unlock the brain's secrets*

To the 19th-century French poet Charles Baudelaire, there was no such thing as a bad smell. What a squeamish, oversensitive bunch he would have deemed the denizens of 20th-century America, where body odors are taboo, strong aromas are immediately suppressed with air freshener, and perfume—long celebrated for its seductive and healing powers—is banned in some places to protect those with multiple chemical sensitivities.

Indeed, in the years since Baudelaire set pen to paper, civilization has played havoc with the natural state of all the human senses, technology providing the ability not only to tame and to mute but also to tease and overstimulate. Artificial fragrances and flavors trick the nose and tongue. Advertisers dazzle the eyes with rapid-fire images. Wailing sirens vie with the beeping of pagers to challenge the ears' ability to cope.

Yet even as we fiddle with the texture and scope of our sensibilities, science is indicating it might behoove us to show them a bit more respect. Growing evidence documents the surprising consequences of depriving or overwhelming the senses. And failing to

From *U.S. News & World Report,* January 13, 1997, pp. 51-56, 58-59. © 1997 by U.S. News & World Report. Reprinted by permission.

nurture our natural capabilities, researchers are discovering, can affect health, emotions, even intelligence. Hearing, for example, is intimately connected to emotional circuits: When a nursing infant looks up from the breast, muscles in the middle ear reflexively tighten, readying the child for the pitch of a human voice. The touch of massage can relieve pain and improve concentration. And no matter how we spritz or scrub, every human body produces a natural odor as distinctive as the whorls on the fingertips—an aroma that research is showing to be a critical factor in choosing a sexual partner.

Beyond their capacity to heal and delight, the senses have also opened a window on the workings of the human brain. A flood of studies on smell, sight, hearing, touch and taste in the last two decades have upended most of the theories about how the brain functions. Scientists once believed, for example, that the brain was hard-wired at birth, the trillions of connections that made up its neural circuits genetically predetermined. But a huge proportion of neurons in a newborn infant's brain, it turns out, require input from the senses in order to hook up to one another properly.

Similarly, scientific theory until recently held that the sense organs did the lion's share of processing information about the world: The eye detected movement; the nose recognized smells. But researchers now know that ears, eyes and fingers are only way stations, transmitting signals that are then processed centrally. "The nose doesn't smell—the brain does," says Richard Axel, a molecular biologist at Columbia University. Each of our senses shatters experience into fragments, parsing the world like so many nouns and verbs, then leaving the brain to put the pieces back together and make sense of it all.

In labs across the country, researchers are drafting a picture of the senses that promises not only to unravel the mysterious tangle of nerves in the brain but also to offer reasons to revel in sensuous experience. Cradling a baby not only feels marvelous, scientists are finding, but is absolutely vital to a newborn's emotional and cognitive development. And the results of this research are beginning to translate into practical help for people whose senses are impaired: Researchers in Boston last year unveiled a tiny electronic device called a retinal chip that one day may restore sight to people blinded after childhood. Gradually, this new science of the senses is redefining what it means to be a feeling and thinking human being. One day it may lead to an understanding of consciousness itself.

## SIGHT

Seeing is believing, because vision is the body's top intelligence gatherer, at least by the brain's reckoning. A full quarter of the cerebral cortex, the brain's crinkled top

**SIGHT**

## Cells in the retina of the eye are so sensitive they can respond to a single photon, or particle of light.

layer, is devoted to sight, according to a new estimate by neuroscientist David Van Essen of Washington University in St. Louis—almost certainly more than is devoted to any other sense.

It seems fitting, then, that vision has offered scientists their most powerful insights on the brain's structure and operations. Research on sight "has been absolutely fundamental" for understanding the brain, says neurobiologist Semir Zeki of University College in London, in part because the visual system is easier to study than the other senses. The first clues to the workings of the visual system emerged in the 1950s, when Johns Hopkins neurobiologists David Hubel and Torsten Wiesel conducted a series of Nobel Prize–winning experiments. Using hair-thin electrodes implanted in a cat's brain, they recorded the firing of single neurons in the area where vision is processed. When the animal was looking at a diagonal bar of light, one neuron fired. When the bar was at a slightly different angle, a different nerve cell responded.

Hubel and Wiesel's discovery led to a revolutionary idea: While we are perceiving a unified scene, the brain is dissecting the view into many parts, each of which triggers a different set of neurons, called a visual map. One map responds to color and form, another only to motion. There are at least five such maps in the visual system alone, and recent work is showing that other senses are similarly encoded in the brain. In an auditory map, for example, the two sets of neurons that respond to two similar sounds, such as "go" and "ko," are located near each other, while those resonating with the sound "mo" lie at a distance.

Though we think of sensory abilities as independent, researchers are finding that each sense receives help from the others in apprehending the world. In 1995, psycholinguist Michael Tanenhaus of the University of Rochester videotaped people as they listened to sentences about nearby objects. As they listened, the subjects' eyes flicked to the objects. Those movements—so fast the subjects did not realize they'd shifted their gaze—helped them under-

stand the grammar of the sentences, Tanenhaus found. Obviously, vision isn't required to comprehend grammar. But given the chance, the brain integrates visual cues while processing language.

The brain also does much of the heavy lifting for color vision, so much so that some people with brain damage see the world in shades of gray. But the ability to see colors begins with cells in the back of the eyeball called cones. For decades, scientists thought everyone with normal color vision had the same three types of cone cell—for red, green and blue light—and saw the same hues. New research shows, however, that everybody sees a different palette. Last year, Medical College of Wisconsin researchers Maureen Neitz and her husband, Jay, discovered that people have up to nine genes for cones, indicating there may be many kinds of cones. Already, two red cone subtypes have been found. People with one type see red differently from those with the second. Says Maureen Neitz: "That's why people argue about adjusting the color on the TV set."

## HEARING

Hearing is the gateway to language, a uniquely human skill. In a normal child, the ears tune themselves to human sounds soon after birth, cementing the neural connections between language, emotions and intelligence. Even a tiny glitch in the way a child processes sound can unhinge development.

About 7 million American children who have normal hearing and intelligence develop intractable problems with language, reading and writing because they cannot decipher certain parcels of language. Research by Paula Tallal, a Rutgers University neurobiologist, has shown that children with language learning disabilities (LLD) fail to distinguish between the "plosive" consonants, such as *b, t* and *p*. To them, "bug" sounds like "tug" sounds like "pug." The problem, Tallal has long argued, is that for such kids the sounds come too fast. Vowels resonate for 100 milliseconds or more, but

**HEARING**

## At six months, a baby's brain tunes in to the sounds of its native tongue and tunes out other languages.

plosive consonants last for a mere 40 milliseconds—not long enough for some children to process them. "These children hear the sound. It just isn't transmitted to the brain normally," she says.

Two years ago, Tallal teamed up with Michael Merzenich, a neurobiologist at the University of California–San Francisco, to create a set of computer games that have produced stunning gains in 29 children with LLD. With William Jenkins and Steve Miller, the neurobiologists wrote computer programs that elongated the plosive consonants, making them louder—"like making a yellow highlighter for the brain," says Tallal. After a month of daily three-hour sessions, children who were one to three years behind their peers in language and reading had leaped forward a full two years. The researchers have formed a company, Scientific Learning Corp., that could make their system available to teachers and professionals within a few years. (See their Web site: *http://www.scilearn.com* or call 415-296-1470.)

An inability to hear the sounds of human speech properly also may contribute to autism, a disorder that leaves children unable to relate emotionally to other people. According to University of Maryland psychophysiologist Stephen Porges, many autistic children are listening not to the sounds of human speech but instead to frightening noises. He blames the children's fear on a section of the nervous system that controls facial expressions, speech, visceral feelings and the muscles in the middle ear.

These muscles, the tiniest in the body, allow the ear to filter sounds, much the way muscles in the eye focus the eyeball on near or distant objects. In autistic children, the neural system that includes the middle ear is lazy. As a result, these children attend not to the pitch of the human voice but instead to sounds that are much lower: the rumble of traffic, the growl of a vacuum cleaner. In the deep evolutionary past, such noises signaled danger. Porges contends that autistic children feel too anxious to interact emotionally, and the neural system controlling many emotional responses fails to develop.

Porges says that exercising the neural system may help autistic kids gain language and emotional skills. He and his colleagues have begun an experimental treatment consisting of tones and songs altered by computer to filter out low sounds, forcing the middle ear to focus on the pitches of human speech. After five 90-minute sessions, most of the 16 children have made strides that surprised even Porges. Third grader Tomlin Clark, for example, who once spoke only rarely, recently delighted his parents by getting in trouble for talking out of turn in school. And for the first time, he shows a sense of humor. "Listening to sounds seems so simple, doesn't it?" says Porges. "But so does jogging."

## TOUCH

The skin, writes pathologist Marc Lappé, "is both literally and metaphorically 'the body's edge' . . . a boundary against an inimical world." Yet the skin also is the organ that speaks the language of love most clearly—and not just in the erogenous zones. The caress of another person releases hormones that can ease pain and clear the mind. Deprive a child of touch, and his brain and body will stop growing.

This new view of the most intimate sense was sparked a decade ago, when child psychologist Tiffany Field showed that premature infants who were massaged for 15 minutes three times a day gained weight 47 percent faster than preemies given standard intensive care nursery treatment: as little touching as possible. The preemies who were massaged weren't eating more; they just processed food more efficiently, says

TOUCH

# People with "synesthesia" feel colors, see sounds and taste shapes.

Field, now director of the University of Miami's Touch Research Institute. Field found that massaged preemies were more alert and aware of their surroundings when awake, while their sleep was deeper and more restorative. Eight months later, the massaged infants scored better on mental and motor tests.

SIXTH SENSES
# Wish you had that nose?

Folklore abounds with tales of animals possessing exceptional sensory powers, from pigs predicting earthquakes to pets telepathically anticipating their owners' arrival home. In some cases, myth and reality are not so far apart. Nature is full of creatures with superhuman senses: built-in compasses, highly accurate sonar, infrared vision. "Our worldview is limited by our senses," says Dartmouth College psychologist Howard Hughes, "so we are both reluctant to believe that animals can have capabilities beyond ours, and we attribute to them supernatural powers. The truth is somewhere between the two."

In the case of Watson, a Labrador retriever, reality is more impressive than any fiction. For over a year, Watson has reliably pawed his owner, Emily Ramsey, 45 minutes before her epileptic seizures begin, giving her time to move to a safe place. Placed by Canine Partners for Life, Watson has a 97 percent success rate, according to the Ramsey family. No one has formally studied how such dogs can predict seizure onset consistently. But they may smell the chemical changes known to precede epileptic attacks. "Whatever it is," says Harvard University neurologist Steven Schachter, "I think there's something to it."

Scientists have scrutinized other animals for decades, trying to decipher their sensory secrets. Birds, bees, moles and some 80 other creatures are known to sense magnetic fields. But new studies indicate birds have two magnetic detection systems: One seems to translate polarized light into visual patterns that act as a compass; the other is an internal magnet birds use to further orient themselves.

Dolphin sonar so intrigued government researchers that they launched the U.S. Navy marine Mammal Program in 1960, hoping it would lead to more-sophisticated tracking equipment. But the animals still beat the machines, says spokesman Tom LaPuzza. In a murky sea, dolphins can pinpoint a softball two football fields away. A lobe in their forehead focuses their biosonar as a flashlight channels light, beaming 200-decibel clicks.

It took night-vision goggles for humans to replicate the infrared vision snakes come by naturally: A camera-alike device in organs lining their lips lets them see heat patterns made by mammals. And humans can only envy the ability of sharks, skates and rays to feel electric fields through pores in their snouts—perhaps a primordial skill used by Earth's earliest creatures to scout out the new world.

BY ANNA MULRINE

## SMELL

# A woman's sense of smell is keener than a man's. And smell plays a larger role in sexual attraction for women.

Being touched has healing powers throughout life. Massage, researchers have found, can ease the pain of severely burned children and boost the immune systems of AIDS patients. Field recently showed that office workers who received a 15-minute massage began emitting higher levels of brain waves associated with alertness. After their massage, the workers executed a math test in half their previous time with half the errors.

While such findings may sound touchy-feely, an increasing volume of physiological evidence backs them up. In a recent series of experiments, Swedish physiologist Kerstin Uvnas-Moberg found that gentle stroking can stimulate the body to release oxytocin, sometimes called the love hormone because it helps cement the bond between mothers and their young in many species. "There are deep, deep, physiological connections between touching and love," Uvnas-Moberg says. Oxytocin also blunts pain and dampens the hormones release when a person feels anxious or stressed.

For the babies of any species, touch signals that mother—the source of food, warmth and safety—is near. When she is gone, many young animals show physiological signs of stress and shut down their metabolism—an innate response designed to conserve energy until she returns. Without mother, rat pups do not grow, says Saul Schanberg, a Duke University pharmacologist, even when they are fed and kept warm. Stroking them with a brush in a manner that mimics their mother licking them restores the pups to robust health. "You need the right kind of touch in order to grow," says Schanberg, "even more than vitamins."

## SMELL

Long ago in human evolution, smell played a prominent role, signaling who was ready to mate and who ready to fight. But after a while, smell fell into disrepute. Aristotle disparaged it as the most animalistic of the senses, and Immanuel Kant dreamed of losing it. Recent research has restored the nose to some of

its former glory. "Odor plays a far more important role in human behavior and physiology than we realize," says Gary Beauchamp, director of Philadelphia's Monell Chemical Senses Center.

A baby recognizes its mother by her odor soon after birth, and studies show that adults can identify clothing worn by their children or spouses by smell alone. In 1995, Beauchamp and colleagues at Monell reported that a woman's scent—genetically determined—changes in pregnancy to reflect a combination of her odor and that of her fetus.

The sense of smell's most celebrated capacity is its power to stir memory. "Hit a tripwire of smell, and memories explode all at once," writes poet Diane Ackerman. The reason, says Monell psychologist Rachel Herz, is that "smells carry an emotional quality." In her latest experiment, Herz showed people a series of evocative paintings. At the same time, the subjects were exposed to another sensory cue—an orange, for example—in different ways. Some saw an orange. Others were given an orange to touch, heard the word "orange" or smelled the fruit. Two days later, when subjects were given the same cue and were asked to recall the painting that matched it, those exposed to the smell of the orange recalled the painting and produced a flood of emotional responses to it.

Herz and others suspect that an aroma's capacity to spark such vivid remembrances arises out of anatomy. An odor's first way station in the brain is the olfactory bulb, two blueberry-sized lumps of cortex from which neurons extend through the skull into the nose. Smell molecules, those wafting off a cinnamon bun, for example, bind to these olfactory neurons, which fire off their signals first to the olfactory bulb and then to the limbic system—the seat of sexual drive, emotions and memory. Connections between the olfactory bulb and the neocortex, or thinking part of the brain, are secondary roads compared to the highways leading to emotional centers.

Scientists once thought all smells were made up of combinations of seven basic odors. But in an elegant series of experiments, research teams led by Columbia's Axel and Linda Buck of Harvard have shown the mechanics of smell to be much more complicated. In 1991, the scientists discovered a family of at least 1,000 genes corresponding to about 1,000 types of olfactory neurons in the nose. Each of these neuronal types responds to one—and only one—type of odor molecule.

The average person, of course, can detect far more than 1,000 odors. That's because a single scent is made up of more than one type of molecule, perhaps even dozens. A rose might stimulate neurons A, B and C, while jasmine sets off neurons B, C and F. "Theoretically, we can detect an astronomical number of smells," says Axel—the

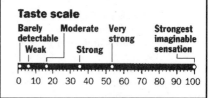
equivalent of 10 to the 23rd power. The brain, however, doesn't have the space to keep track of all those possible combinations of molecules, and so it focuses on smells that were relevant in evolution, like the scent of ripe fruit or a sexually receptive mate—about 10,000 odors in all.

Axel and Buck have now discovered that the olfactory bulb contains a "map," similar to those the brain employs for vision and hearing. By implanting a gene into mice, the researchers dyed blue the nerves leading

## TASTE

# Human beings are genetically hard-wired to crave sweetness; sugar on the lips of a newborn baby will bring a smile.

from the animals' olfactory bulbs to their noses. Tracing the path of these neurons, the researchers discovered that those responsible for detecting a single type of odor molecule all led back to a single point in the olfactory bulb. In other words, the jumble of neurons that exists in the nose is reduced to regimental order in the brain.

Smell maps may one day help anosmics, people who cannot smell. Susan Killorn of Richmond, Va., lost her sense of smell three years ago when she landed on her head while in-line skating and damaged the nerves leading from her nose to her brain. A gourmet cook, Killorn was devastated. "I can remember sitting at the dinner table and begging my husband to describe the meal I'd just cooked," she says. Killorn's ability to detect odors has gradually returned, but nothing smells quite right. One possibility, says Richard Costanzo, a neurophysiologist at Virginia Commonwealth University, is that some of the nerves from her nose have recovered or regenerated but now are hooked up to the wrong spot in her smell map.

Though imperfect, recoveries like Killorn's give researchers hope they may one day be able to stimulate other neurons to regenerate—after a spinal cord injury, for example. Costanzo and others are searching for chemicals made by the body that can act as traffic cops, telling neurons exactly where to grow. In the meantime, Killorn is grateful for every morsel of odor. "I dream at night about onions and garlic," she says, "and they smell like they are supposed to."

## TASTE

Human beings will put almost anything into their mouths and consider it food, from stinging nettles to grubs. Fortunately, evolution armed the human tongue with a

set of sensors to keep venturesome members of the species from dying of malnutrition or poison. The four simple flavors—sweet, salty, bitter and sour—tell human beings what's healthy and what's harmful. But as researchers are finding, the sense of taste does far more than keep us from killing ourselves. Each person tastes food differently, a genetically determined sensitivity that can affect diet, weight and health.

In a quest for novelty, people around the world have developed an affinity for foods that cause a modicum of pain. "Humans have the ability to say, 'Oh, that didn't really hurt me—let me try it again,' " says Barry Green, a psychologist at the John B. Pierce Laboratory in New Haven, Conn. Spicy food, Green has found, gives the impression of being painfully hot by stimulating the nerves in the mouth that sense temperature extremes. The bubbles in soda and champagne feel as if they are popping inside the mouth; in reality, carbon dioxide inside the bubbles irritates nerves that sense pain.

One person's spicy meatball, however, is another's bland and tasteless meal. Researchers have long known that certain people have an inherited inability to taste a mildly bitter substance with a tongue-twisting name: propylthiouracil, or PROP, for short. About a quarter of Caucasians are "nontasters," utterly insensitive to PROP, while the vast majority of Asians and Africans can taste it. Now, researchers at Yale University led by psychologist Linda Bartoshuk have discovered a third group of people called "supertasters." So sensitive are supertasters' tongues that they gag on PROP and can detect the merest hint of other bitter compounds in a host of foods, from chocolate and saccharin to vegetables such as broccoli, "which could explain why George Bush hates it," Bartoshuk says. She has recently discovered that supertasters have twice as many taste buds as nontasters and more of the nerve endings that detect the feel of foods. As a consequence, sweets taste sweeter to supertasters, and cream feels creamier. A spicy dish can send a supertaster through the roof.

In an ongoing study, Bartoshuk's group has found that older women who are nontasters tend to prefer sweets and fatty foods—dishes that some of the supertasters find cloying. Not surprisingly, supertasters also tend to be thinner and have lower cholesterol. In their study, the researchers ask subjects to taste cream mixed with oil, a combination Bartoshuk confesses she finds delicious. "I'm a nontaster, and I'm heavy," she says. "I gobble up the test." But tasting ability is not only a matter of cuisine preference and body weight. Monell's Marcia

| RESULTS OF TASTE TEST ON PREVIOUS PAGE | | |
|---|---|---|
| | SUPER-TASTERS | NON-TASTERS |
| **No. of taste buds** | 25 on average | 10 |
| **Sweet rating** | 56 on average | 32 |
| **Tabasco rating** | 64 on average | 31 |

Average tasters lie in between. Bartoshuk and Lucchina lack the data to rate salt.

Pelchat and a graduate student recently completed a study indicating that nontasters also may be predisposed to alcoholism.

The human senses detect only a fraction of reality: We can't see the ultraviolet markers that guide a honeybee to nectar; we can't hear most of the noises emitted by a dolphin. In this way, the senses define the boundaries of mental awareness. But the brain also defines the limits of what we perceive. Human beings see, feel, taste, touch and smell not the world around them but a version of the world, one their brains have concocted. "People imagine that they're seeing what's really there, but they're not," says neuroscientist John Maunsell of Baylor College of Medicine in Houston. The eyes take in the light reflecting off objects around us, but the brain only pays attention to part of the scene. Looking for a pen on a messy desk, for example, you can scan the surface without noticing the papers scattered across it.

The word "sentience" derives from the Latin verb *sentire,* meaning "to feel." And research on the senses, especially the discovery of sensory mapping, has taken scientists one step further in understanding the state we call consciousness. Yet even this dramatic advance is only a beginning. "In a way, these sexy maps have seduced us," says Michael Shipley, director of neurosciences at the University of Maryland–Baltimore. "We still haven't answered the question of how do you go from visual maps to recognizing faces, or from an auditory map to recognizing a Mozart sonata played by two different pianists." The challenge for the 21st century will be figuring out how the brain, once it has broken the sensory landscape into pieces, puts them together again.

BY SHANNON BROWNLEE
WITH TRACI WATSON

# Vision: A Window on Consciousness

*In their search for the mind, scientists
are focusing on visual perception—
how we interpret what we see*

by Nikos K. Logothetis

When you first look at the center image in the painting by Salvador Dalí, *Old Age, Adolescence, Infancy (The Three Ages)*, what do you see? Most people immediately perceive a man's face, eyes gazing skyward and lips pursed under a bushy mustache. But when you look again, the image rearranges itself into a more complex tableau. The man's nose and white mustache become the mob-cap and cape of a seated woman. The glimmers in the man's eyes reveal themselves as lights in the windows—or glints on the roofs—of two cottages nestled in darkened hillsides. Shadows on the man's cheek emerge as a child in short pants standing beside the seated woman—both of whom, it is now clear, are looking across a lake at the cottages from a hole in a brick wall, a hole we once saw as the outline of the man's face.

In 1940, when he rendered *Old Age, Adolescence, Infancy (The Three Ages)*—which contains three "faces"—Dalí was toying with the capacity of the viewer's mind to interpret two different images from the same set of brushstrokes. More than 50 years later researchers, including my colleagues and I, are using similarly ambiguous visual stimuli to try to identify the brain activity that underlies consciousness. Specifically, we want to know what happens in the brain at the instant when, for example, an observer comprehends that the three faces in Dalí's picture are not really faces at all.

Consciousness is a difficult concept to define, much less to study. Neuroscientists have in recent years made impressive progress toward understanding the complex patterns of activity that occur in nerve cells, or neurons, in the brain. Even so, most people, including many scientists, still find the notion that electrochemical discharges in neurons can explain the mind, and in particular consciousness, challenging.

Yet, as Nobel laureate Francis Crick of the Salk Institute for Biological Studies in San Diego and Christof Koch of the California Institute of Technology have recently argued, the problem of consciousness can be broken down into several separate questions, some of which can be subjected to scientific inquiry [see "The Problem of Consciousness," by Francis Crick and Christof Koch; SCIENTIFIC AMERICAN, September 1992]. For example, rather than worrying about what consciousness is, one can ask: What is the difference between the neural processes that correlated with particular conscious experience and those that do not?

## Now You See It . . .

That is where ambiguous stimuli come in. Perceptual ambiguity is not a whimsical behavior specific to the organization of the visual system. Rather it tells us something about the organization of the entire brain and its way of making us aware of all sensory information. Take, for instance, the meaningless string of French words *pas de lieu Rhône que nous*, cited by the psychologist William James in 1890. You can read this over and over again without recognizing that it sounds just like the phrase "paddle your own canoe." What changes in neural activity occur when the meaningful sentence suddenly reaches consciousness?

JOHNNY JOHNSON

NECKER CUBE can be viewed two different ways, depending on whether you see the "x" on the top front edge of the cube or on its rear face. Sometimes the cube appears superimposed on the circles; other times it seems the circles are holes and the cube floats behind the page.

In our work with ambiguous visual stimuli, we use images that not only give rise to two distinct perceptions but also instigate a continuous alternation between the two. A familiar example is the Necker cube [see illustration at left]. This figure is perceived as a three-dimensional cube, but the apparent perspective of the cube appears to shift every few seconds. Obviously, this alternation must correspond to something happening in the brain.

A skeptic might argue that we sometimes perceive a stimulus without being truly conscious of it, as when, for example, we "automatically" stop at a red light when driving. But the stimuli and the situations that I investigate are actually designed to reach consciousness.

We know that our stimuli reach awareness in human beings, because they can tell us about their experience. But it is not usually possible to study the activity of individual neurons in awake humans, so we perform our experiments with alert monkeys that have been trained to report what they are perceiving by pressing levers or by looking in a particular direction. Monkeys' brains are organized like those of humans, and they respond to such stimuli much as humans do. Consequently, we think the animals are conscious in somewhat the same way as humans are.

We investigate ambiguities that result when two different visual patterns are presented simultaneously to each eye, a phenomenon called binocular rivalry. When people are put in this situation, their brains become

aware of first one perception and then the other, in a slowly alternating sequence.

In the laboratory, we use stereoscopes to create this effect. Trained monkeys exposed to such visual stimulation report that they, too, experience a perception that changes every few seconds. Our experiments have enabled us to trace neural activity that corresponds to these changing reports.

## In the Mind's Eye

Studies of neural activity in animals conducted over several decades have established that visual information leaving the eyes ascends through successive stages of a neural data-processing system. Different modules analyze various attributes of the visual field. In general, the type of processing becomes more specialized the farther the information moves along the visual pathway.

At the start of the pathway, images from the retina at the back of each eye are channeled first to a pair of small structures deep in the brain called the lateral geniculate nuclei (LGN). Individual neurons in the LGN can be activated by visual stimulation from either one eye or the other but not both. They respond to any change of brightness or color in a specific region within an area of view known as the receptive field, which varies among neurons.

From the LGN, visual information moves to the primary visual cortex, which is at the back of the head and conventionally abbreviated as V1. Neurons in V1 behave differently than those in the LGN do. They can usually be activated by either eye, but they are also sensitive to specific attributes, such as the direction of motion of a stimulus placed within their receptive field. Visual information is transmitted from V1 to more than two dozen other distinct cortical regions.

Some information from V1 can be traced as it moves through areas known as V2 and V4 before winding up in regions known as the inferior temporal cortex (ITC), which like all the other structures are bilateral. A large number of investigations, including neurological studies of people who have experienced brain damage, suggest that the ITC is important in perceiving form and recognizing objects. Neurons in V4 are known to respond selectively to aspects of visual stimuli critical to discerning shapes. In the ITC, some neurons behave like V4 cells, but others respond only when entire objects, such as faces, are placed within their very large receptive fields.

Other signals from V1 pass through regions V2, V3 and an area called MT/V5 before eventually reaching a part of the brain called the parietal lobe. Most neurons in MT/V5 respond strongly to items moving in a specific direction. Neurons in other areas of the parietal lobe respond when an animal pays attention to a stimulus or intends to move toward it.

# How to Experience Binocular Rivalry

To simulate binocular rivalry at home, use your right hand to hold the cardboard cylinder from a roll of paper towels (or a piece of paper rolled into a tube) against your right eye. Hold your left hand, palm facing you, roughly four inches in front of your left eye, with the edge of your hand touching the tube.

At first it will appear as though your hand has a hole in it, as your brain concentrates on the stimulus from your right eye. After a few seconds, though, the "hole" will fill in with a fuzzy perception of your whole palm from your left eye. If you keep viewing, the two images will alternate, as your brain selects first the visual stimulus viewed by one eye, then that viewed by the other. The alternation is, however, a bit biased; you will probably perceive the visual stimulus you see through the cylinder more frequently than you will see your palm.

The bias occurs for two reasons. First, your palm is out of focus because it is much closer to your face, and blurred visual stimuli tend to be weaker competitors in binocular rivalry than sharp patterns, such as the surroundings you are viewing through the tube. Second, your palm is a relatively smooth surface with less contrast and fewer contours than your comparatively rich environment has. In the laboratory, we select the patterns viewed by the subjects carefully to eliminate such bias.

—*N.K.L.*

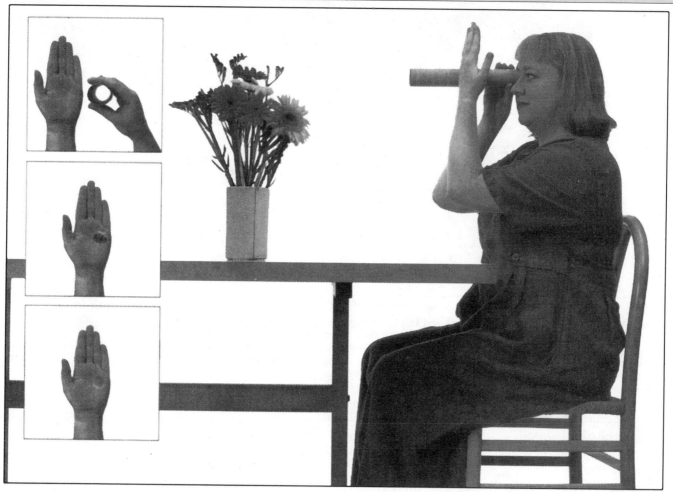

DAN WAGNER

One surprising observation made in early experiments is that many neurons in these visual pathways, both in V1 and in higher levels of the processing hierarchy, still respond with their characteristic selectivity to visual stimuli even in animals that have been completely anesthetized. Clearly, an animal (or a human) is not conscious of all neural activity.

The observation raises the question of whether awareness is the result of the activation of special brain regions or clusters of neurons. The study of binocular rivalry in alert, trained monkeys allows us to approach that question, at least to some extent. In such experiments, a researcher presents each animal with a variety of visual stimuli, usually patterns or figures projected onto a screen. Monkeys can easily be trained to report accurately what stimulus they perceive by means of rewards of fruit juice.

During the experiment, the scientist uses electrodes to record the activity of neurons in the visual-processing

49

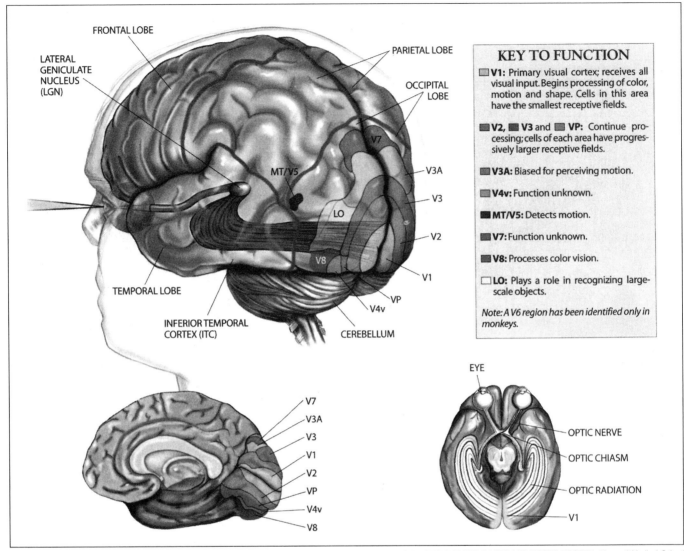

## KEY TO FUNCTION

**V1:** Primary visual cortex; receives all visual input. Begins processing of color, motion and shape. Cells in this area have the smallest receptive fields.

**V2, V3** and **VP:** Continue processing; cells of each area have progressively larger receptive fields.

**V3A:** Biased for perceiving motion.

**V4v:** Function unknown.

**MT/V5:** Detects motion.

**V7:** Function unknown.

**V8:** Processes color vision.

**LO:** Plays a role in recognizing large-scale objects.

*Note: A V6 region has been identified only in monkeys.*

TERESE WINSLOW, WITH ASSISTANCE FROM NOUCHINE HADJIKHANI AND ROGER TOOTELL *Harvard Medical School*

HUMAN VISUAL PATHWAY begins with the eyes and extends through several interior brain structures before ascending to the various regions of the visual cortex (V1, and so on). At the optic chiasm, the optic nerves cross over partially so that each hemisphere of the brain receives input from both eyes. The information is filtered by the lateral geniculate nucleus, which consists of layers of nerve cells that each respond only to stimuli from one eye. The inferior temporal cortex is important for seeing forms. Researchers have found that some cells from each area are active only when a person or monkey becomes conscious of a given stimulus.

pathway. Neurons vary markedly in their responsiveness when identical stimuli are presented to both eyes simultaneously. Stimulus pattern A might provoke activity in one neuron, for instance, whereas stimulus pattern B does not.

Once an experimenter has identified an effective and an ineffective stimulus for a given neuron (by presenting the same stimulus to both eyes at once), the two stimuli can be presented so that a different one is seen by each eye. We expect that, like a human in this situation, the monkey will become aware of the two stimuli in an alternating sequence. And, indeed, that is what the monkeys tell us by their responses when we present them with such rivalrous pairs of stimuli. By recording from neurons during successive presentations of rivalrous pairs, an experimenter can evaluate which neurons change their activity only when the stimuli change and

which neurons alter their rate of firing when the animal reports a changed perception that is not accompanied by a change in the stimuli.

Jeffrey D. Schall, now at Vanderbilt University, and I carried out a version of this experiment in which one eye saw a grating that drifted slowly upward while the other eye saw a downward-moving grating. We recorded from visual area MT/V5, where cells tend to be responsive to motion. We found that about 43 percent of the cells in this area changed their level of activity when the monkey indicated that its perception had changed from up to down, or vice versa. Most of these cells were in the deepest layers of MT/V5.

The percentage we measured was actually a lower proportion than most scientists would have guessed, because almost all neurons in MT/V5 are sensitive to direction of movement. The majority of neurons in MT/V5

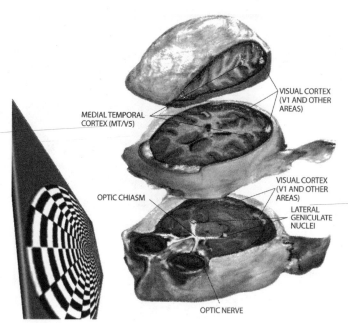

IMAGES OF BRAIN ACTIVITY are from an anesthetized monkey that was presented with a rotating, high-contrast visual stimulus (*lower left*). These views, taken using functional magnetic resonance imaging, show that even though the monkey is unconscious, its vision-processing areas—including the lateral geniculate nuclei (LGN), primary visual cortex (V1) and medial temporal cortex (MT/V5)—are busy.

NIKOS K. LOGOTHETIS

did behave somewhat like those in V1, remaining active when their preferred stimulus was in view of either eye, whether it was being perceived or not.

There were further surprises. Some 11 percent of the neurons examined were excited when the monkey reported perceiving the more effective stimulus of an upward/downward pair for the neuron in question. But a similar proportion of neurons, paradoxically, was most excited when the most effective stimulus was not perceived—even though it was in clear view of one eye. Other neurons could not be categorized as preferring one stimulus over another.

While we were both at Baylor College of Medicine, David A. Leopold and I studied neurons in parts of the brain known to be important in recognizing objects. (Leopold is now with me at the Max Planck Institute for Biological Cybernetics in Tübingen, Germany.) We recorded activity in V4, as well as in V1 and V2, while animals viewed stimuli consisting of lines sloping either to the left or to the right. In V4 the proportion of cells whose activity reflected perception was similar to that which Schall and I had found in MT/V5, around 40 percent. But again, a substantial proportion fired best when their preferred stimulus was not perceived. In V1 and V2, in contrast, fewer than one in 10 of the cells fired exclusively when their more effective stimulus was perceived, and none did so when it was not perceived.

The pattern of activity was entirely different in the ITC. David L. Sheinberg—who also moved with me from Baylor to the Max Planck Institute—and I recorded from

## Keeping Monkeys (and Experimenters) Honest

One possible objection to the experiments described in the main article is that the monkeys might have been inclined to cheat to earn their juice rewards. We are, after all, unable to know directly what a monkey (or a human) thinks or perceives at a given time. Because our monkeys were interested mainly in drinking juice rather than in understanding how consciousness arises from neuronal activity, it is possible that they could have developed a response strategy that appeared to reflect their true perceptions but really did not.

In the training session depicted below, for example, the monkey was being taught to pull the left lever only when it saw a sunburst and the right lever only when it saw a cowboy. We were able to ensure that the monkey continued to report truthfully by interjecting instances in which no rivalrous stimuli were shown (*below*). During these occasions, there was a "right" answer to what was perceived, and if the monkey did not respond correctly, the trial—and thus the opportunity to earn more juice rewards—was immediately ended. Similarly, if the monkey pulled any lever when presented with a jumbled image, in which the sunburst and the cowboy were superimposed (*last panel*), we knew the monkey was lying in an attempt to get more juice.

Our results indicate that monkeys report their experiences accurately. Even more convincing is our observation that monkeys and humans tested with the same apparatus perform at similar levels in different tasks. *N.K.L.*

Sees sunburst
Pulls left lever    **CORRECT=**    **JUICE REWARD**

this area after training monkeys to report their perceptions during rivalry between complex visual patterns, such as images of humans, animals and various man-made objects. We found that almost all neurons, about

Sees sunburst
Pulls left lever **CORRECT=** **JUICE REWARD**

Sees cowboy
Pulls right lever **CORRECT=** **JUICE REWARD**

Sees sunburst
Pulls left lever **CORRECT=** **JUICE REWARD**

Sees a jumble
but wants juice
Pulls any lever **INCORRECT=** **NO JUICE REWARD**

MATT COLLINS

90 percent, responded vigorously when their preferred pattern was perceived, but their activity was profoundly inhibited when this pattern was not being experienced.

So it seems that by the time visual signals reach the ITC, the great majority of neurons are responding in a way that is linked to perception. Frank Tong, Ken Nakayama and Nancy Kanwisher of Harvard University have used a technique called functional magnetic resonance imaging (fMRI)—which yields pictures of brain activity by measuring increases in blood flow in specific areas of the brain—to study people experiencing binocular rivalry. They found that the ITC was particularly active when the subjects reported they were seeing images of faces.

In short, most of the neurons in the earlier stages of the visual pathway responded mainly to whether their preferred visual stimulus was in view or not, although a few showed behavior that could be related to changes in the animal's perception. In the later stages of processing, on the other hand, the proportion whose activity reflected the animal's perception increased until it reached 90 percent.

A critic might object that the changing perceptions that monkeys report during binocular rivalry could be caused by the brain suppressing visual information at the start of the visual pathway, first from one eye, then from the other, so that the brain perceives a single image at any given time. If that were happening, changing neural activity and perceptions would simply represent the result of input switched from one eye to the other and would not be relevant to visual consciousness in other situations. But experimental evidence shows decisively that input from both eyes is continuously processed in the visual system during rivalry.

We know this because it turns out that in humans, binocular rivalry produces its normal slow alternation of perceptions even if the competing stimuli are switched rapidly—several times per second—between the two eyes. If rivalry were merely a question of which eye the brain is paying attention to, the rivalry phenomenon would vanish when stimuli are switched quickly in this way. (The viewer would see, rather, a rapid alternation of the stimuli.) The observed persistence of slowly changing rivalrous perceptions when stimuli are switched strongly suggests that rivalry occurs because alternate stimulus representations compete in the visual pathway. Binocular rivalry thus affords an opportunity to study how the visual system decides what we see even when both eyes see (almost) the same thing.

## A Perceptual Puzzle

What do these findings reveal about visual awareness? First, they show that we are unaware of a great deal of activity in our brains. We have long known that we are mostly unaware of the activity in the brain that maintains the body in a stable state—one of its evolutionarily most ancient tasks. Our experiments show that we are also unaware of much of the neural activity that generates—at least in part—our conscious experiences.

We can say this because many neurons in our brains respond to stimuli that we are not conscious of. Only a tiny fraction of neurons seem to be plausible candidates for what physiologists call the "neural correlate" of conscious perception—that is, they respond in a manner that reliably reflects perception.

We can say more. The small number of neurons whose behavior reflects perception are distributed over the entire visual pathway, rather than being part of a single area in the brain. Even though the ITC clearly has many more neurons that behave this way than those in other regions do, such neurons may be found elsewhere in future experiments. Moreover, other brain regions may be responsible for any decision resulting from whatever stimulus reaches consciousness. Erik D. Lumer and his colleagues at University College London have studied that possibility using fMRI. They showed that in humans the temporal lobe is activated during the conscious experience of a stimulus, as we found in monkeys. But other regions, such as the parietal and the prefrontal cortical areas, are activated precisely at the time at which a subject reports that the stimulus changes.

Learning more about the locations of, and connections between, neurons that correlate with conscious experience will tell us more about how the brain generates awareness. But the findings to date already strongly suggest that visual awareness cannot be thought of as the end product of such a hierarchical series of processing stages. Instead it involves the entire visual pathway as well as the frontal parietal areas, which are involved in higher cognitive processing. The activity of a significant minority of neurons reflects what is consciously seen even in the lowest levels we looked at, V1 and V2; it is only the proportion of active neurons that increases at higher levels in the pathway.

Currently it is not clear whether the activity of neurons in the very early areas is determined by their connections with other neurons in those areas or is the result of top-down, "feedback" connections emanating from the temporal or parietal lobes. Visual information flows from higher levels down to the lower ones as well as in the opposite direction. Theoretical studies indicate that systems with this kind of feedback can exhibit complicated patterns of behavior, including multiple stable states. Different stable states maintained by top-down feedback may correspond to different states of visual consciousness.

One important question is whether the activity of any of the neurons we have identified truly determine an animal's conscious perception. It is, after all, conceivable that these neurons are merely under the control of some other unknown part of the brain that actually determines conscious experience.

Elegant experiments conducted by William T. Newsome and his colleagues at Stanford University suggest that in area MT/V5, at least, neuronal activity can indeed determine directly what a monkey perceives. Newsome first identified neurons that selectively respond to a stimulus moving in a particular direction, then artificially activated them with small electric currents. The monkeys reported perceiving motion corresponding to the artificial activation even when stimuli were not moving in the direction indicated.

It will be interesting to see whether neurons of different types, in the ITC and possibly in lower levels, are also directly implicated in mediating consciousness. If they are, we would expect that stimulating or temporarily inactivating them would change an animal's reported perception during binocular rivalry.

A fuller account of visual awareness will also have to consider results from experiments on other cognitive processes, such as attention or what is termed working memory. Experiments by Robert Desimone and his colleagues at the National Institute of Mental Health reveal a remarkable resemblance between the competitive interactions observed during binocular rivalry and processes implicated in attention. Desimone and his colleagues train monkeys to report when they see stimuli for which they have been given cues in advance. Here, too, many neurons respond in a way that depends on what stimulus the animal expects to see or where it expects to see it. It is of obvious interest to know whether those neurons are the same ones as those firing only when a pattern reaches awareness during binocular rivalry.

The picture of the brain that starts to emerge from these studies is of a system whose processes create states of consciousness in response not only to sensory inputs but also to internal signals representing expectations based on past experiences. In principle, scientists should be able to trace the networks that support these interactions. The task is huge, but our success identifying neurons that reflect consciousness is a good start.

## The Author

NIKOS K. LOGOTHETIS is director of the physiology of cognitive processes division of the Max Planck Institute for Biological Cybernetics in Tübingen, Germany. He received his Ph.D. in human neurobiology in 1984 from Ludwig-Maximillians University in Munich. In 1985 he moved to the brain and cognitive sciences department of the Massachusetts Institute of Technology, where he served as a postdoctoral fellow and research scientist. In 1990 he joined the faculty of the division of neuroscience at Baylor College of Medicine, where he conducted most of the research described in this article. He returned to Germany in 1997.

## Further Reading

A Vision of the Brain. Semir Zeki. Blackwell Scientific Publications, 1993.
The Astonishing Hypothesis: the Scientific Search for the Soul. Francis Crick. Scribner's, 1994.
Eye, Brain and Vision. David H. Hubel. Scientific American Library, 1995.
The Visual Brain in Action. A. David Milner and Melvyn A. Goodale. Oxford University Press, 1996.

# Noise

A RISING RACKET THREATENS OUR HEARING AND
OUR QUALITY OF LIFE.
WHY ISN'T THAT MESSAGE BEING HEARD?

If the world sounds louder these days, it's not your imagination. Air and road traffic are on the rise. Sales of riding mowers and string trimmers are up. We're trading our brooms for shop vacs. Increasingly, noise is used to create excitement and ambience in environments from big-screen movie theaters to exercise studios to video-game parlors. "The old sources of noise are growing," says anti-noise activist Les Blomberg, "and we keep inventing new ones."

In response, anti-noise sentiment is growing. When Echo and other companies started selling new, slightly quieter gas-powered leaf blowers, Los Angeles and other communities could claim a modest victory in their campaigns to ban or limit these notorious noisemakers. But though local noise ordinances are growing more strict, assaults on our ears still get only a fraction of the legislative and regulatory attention given to other forms of pollution. And many consumer products are as noisy as ever, despite technology that could dampen their din.

In this special report, we document how noise can affect your hearing and health. We look at what manufacturers and governments are—and aren't—doing about noise. And we explain what you can do to protect your health and your sanity—including tips on protecting your ears and lists of less-noisy models of products we've tested.

## Loud and louder

Of the estimated 28 million Americans with full or partial hearing loss,

about one-third can partly blame noise for their condition.

To be sure, a large portion are age 60 or older, suffering from what researchers believe may be a natural part of aging. But a growing number are baby boomers such as President Clinton, whose hearing loss is partly attributed to years of exposure to raucous political events. Between 1971 and 1990, hearing problems increased 26 percent among Americans ages 45 to 64, according to the Centers for Disease Control and Prevention.

The louder the sound, the less time you can endure it before it threatens your hearing. In a healthy person, tiny hair cells in the cochlea, the snail-shaped inner ear, convert the mechanical energy of sound into electrical energy used by the brain. The intense energy of a very brief but extremely loud sound, such as the 140-decibel (dBA) report of a rifle, can instantaneously damage or destroy those cells. So can several hours of exposure to very loud sound, as you might experience sitting next to the speakers at a concert. (And not just a hard-rock concert, either; two years ago, Barry Manilow settled a suit brought by an Arizona judge who said his ears were permanently damaged at a Manilow show.)

Regular exposure to sound at lower levels also can take a toll. When you're young, your ears can easily recover from three hours of 110-dBA sound at a typical concert or regularly listening to a walkabout stereo at about 105 dBA (a level some preteens selected in a 1992 test for Zillions, our children's magazine).

But after years of such abuse, the ears begin to tire out. First to go are the hair cells that respond to high frequencies. That's why many people initially lose their ability to hear the "s" and "f" in speech. Some people, including Pete Townshend of The Who, develop tinnitus, which makes you hear a continuous or intermittent ring, hiss, hum, or roar.

Regular activity with sound levels above 100 dBA—including using a chain saw or driving a snowmobile—can pose a threat to your hearing within just 15 minutes (see "How Loud Is Too Loud?").

Most people don't use a chain saw every day or for very long, making it unlikely they'd damage their hearing from that activity alone. But there's evidence that damage from a variety of loud everyday noises—some lasting only for minutes, some for hours—eventually contribute to hearing loss.

In 1994 Elliott Berger, a scientist working for E.A.R., a maker of hearing protection, compared six studies of noise encountered by average people. Over a 24-hour period, subjects endured an average of 78 decibels. That's high enough to contribute to long-term hearing loss, according to the Environmental Protection Agency. (The 78-dBA average included quiet time but also very loud experiences, including practicing the trumpet and attending an Omnimax movie.)

The rising din may be affecting even very young Americans. A 1992 study of California schoolchildren found a tripling of high-frequency hearing loss among second-graders and a quadrupling among eighth-graders, compared with

## How loud is too loud?

Use these recommendations for ear protection when operating the products or participating in the noisy activities listed at right. Susceptibility to hearing loss varies among individuals. But since you can't predict your own vulnerability, err on the side of caution. Except where noted, products are placed in the category where the noisiest models would likely fall. Advice is based on findings by the National Institute on Deafness and Other Communication Disorders.

### DANGEROUS
### (about 110 dBA and up)

- *Always use ear protection*

Firearms
Fireworks and jet engines
   at close range
Loud concerts or music clubs

### HARMFUL
### (about 100 to 110 dBA)

- *Protect ears when exposure
  exceeds 15 minutes*

Chain saw
Snowmobile
Loud aerobics class

### POTENTIALLY HARMFUL
### (about 85 to 100 dBA)

- *Ear protection recommended,
  especially for regular, lengthy exposure*

Circular saw
Loud string trimmer or power blower
Motorcycle at high speed
Loud wedding reception
Loud mower, typical lawn tractor or
   riding mower
Loud vacuum cleaner

### RELATIVELY SAFE
### (about 85 dBA or less)

- *Ear protection not needed*

City traffic noise
Hair dryer
Electric string trimmer or mower
Quiet vacuum cleaner
Noisy dishwasher
Noisy air conditioner

hearing loss in similar groups studied a decade earlier. The study, co-authored by audiologist Sharon Fujikawa, points to noise as a possible culprit.

Even when it's not loud enough to threaten hearing, constant noise can diminish other aspects of life. In 1997 Gary Evans, a Cornell University environmental psychologist, found that children assaulted by frequent aircraft noise at school didn't learn to read as well as peers in quieter environments. Other studies show that excessive noise endured for many hours raises blood pressure and stress-related cortisol levels and increases irritability and fatigue.

### Noise and the law

While many people may not be aware of the health hazards of noise, they're well aware of the annoyance. Throughout the country, individuals have successfully campaigned to strengthen laws against racetracks, amphitheaters, car stereos, and even barking dogs—and the anti-noise momentum appears to be growing. Blomberg, who established the Noise Pollution Clearinghouse three years ago, says he receives 100 calls a week from people nationwide seeking help with noise-abatement activities.

Mary Ann Anderson is an example of the trend. In July 1995, fed up with the roar of personal watercraft (also known as Jet Skis), the resident of Friday Harbor, Wash., led a successful effort to have the vehicles banned from the pristine San Juan Islands of Puget Sound. The push started with a petition drive, developed into a local ordinance, and ended last summer when the state Supreme Court upheld the new law.

Across the country, municipalities large and small are strengthening their noise ordinances and upping penalties. New York City's regulations, updated two years ago, now mandate fines as high as $525 for a barking dog and $4,200 for a noisy air conditioner.

Most control over noise from railroads, highways, and airports lies not at home but in Washington. While the federal government has launched some anti-noise initiatives—like installing noise barriers along highways and mandating a gradual reduction in sound levels for commercial airliners—activists say they're often pre-empted by federal law. "Many municipalities want to stop railroad or road noise and can't," says Eric Zwerling, director of the Rutgers Noise Technical Assistance Center in New Brunswick, N.J.

Even in the workplace, where occupational noise can pose significant threats to health, federal regulation falls

short. Exposure to workplace noise is regulated by the Occupational Safety and Health Administration (OSHA). In general, it requires that hearing protection be worn by workers exposed to 90 dBA over an eight-hour period each day. But agriculture isn't an occupation covered under the law, leaving many workers at risk.

Moreover, OSHA inspectors don't regularly visit sites employing ten or fewer people. So millions of workers may remain unprotected in small factories, aerobics centers, video parlors, music clubs, and other sites where the decibel levels can be dangerous. And patrons have no protection at all.

In the past those problems might have been addressed by the federal Office of Noise Abatement and Control (ONAC), created in 1972 as an arm of the Environmental Protection Agency. But ONAC, which had begun the work of monitoring noise in certain environments, promulgating product standards, and aiding states and municipalities in passing stronger noise ordinances, lost its funding in 1982.

### Are manufacturers listening?

Some companies that make noisy products are muting them somewhat, as our tests have confirmed in recent years. But other companies appear to be resisting designs that could make consumer products less noisy.

The quietest examples of some products we've tested in recent years have likely benefited from good engineering. And while none were among the cheapest, many quiet models were about average in price and were fine performers.

Those findings contradict the claims of some manufacturers that designing for quiet drives up price or compromises

---

*See me, hear me*, The Who's Pete Townshend is among the hearing-impaired rock stars who are encouraging younger musicians, through educational videos and other media, to protect their ears when performing.

**"Most companies could make a product quieter if they wanted to," says Steve Orfield, president of a Minneapolis-based lab that consults on acoustics and other sensory issues. "They've simply decided it's not valuable."**

basic performance. The Hoover Co., for instance, has found that good performance correlates with higher noise, according to Charles DeGraff, vice president of engineering. "Certainly, noise is an issue," he says, "but people do not want to give up cleaning performance in favor of low noise."

DeGraff says Hoover's *WindTunnel,* $300, is among his company's least noisy household models. But in our most recent report, we found that several vacuums costing less performed just as well overall and were notably quieter.

Some manufacturers, it's clear, make low noise more of a priority than others and more vigorously pursue ways to achieve that goal affordably. Bennett Brooks, president of Brooks Acoustics, a consulting firm in Vernon, Conn., says that "there are some low-cost, clever things that can be done" to make a product less noisy.

For example, Brooks says, changing the design of the motor housing on a blender can reduce noise at little or no cost. Echo says its new, quieter backpack power blowers are priced only a few dollars higher than their noisier predecessors.

### The foreign edge in noise

Aside from companies that are forced by public outcry to change, many manufacturers committed to making products quieter have done so to sell abroad. In many parts of the world, homes are smaller and often closer together. More people live in apartments, and walls may be thin.

"You couldn't sell an American-made dishwasher in Europe, because it's so noisy," says Bill Lang, president of the International Institute of Noise Control Engineering.

Indeed, the anti-noise bias is so strong abroad that many governments have passed sweeping product-noise directives. In Europe, consumers are entitled to sound-level information on loud household appliances. "Pass by" requirements—how loud a truck can sound to a pedestrian—are far more strict than corresponding U.S. regulations.

Some of the most innovative product-noise research in the U.S. has been done in an effort to sell abroad. To meet European noise standards, American motorcycle maker Harley-Davidson recently spent $35 million to redesign its engines to be half as noisy yet maintain their distinctive roar. (The project yielded an unexpected dividend: higher horsepower.)

In contrast to Europe, the U.S. sets few noise standards for products. With the exception of a mandatory standard for cap guns, for example, there are no limits placed on toy noise. Ken Giles, a Consumer Product Safety Commission spokesman, says the agency investigates only products whose decibel level and duration of use could be demonstrated to cause hearing loss—something that's not easy to prove.

Nor are most products labeled for noise levels—as, for example, appliances are for energy consumption. In the late 1970s and early 1980s, ONAC did attempt to institute noise labeling, starting with lawn mowers. Lobbyists instead forged a compromise that allowed the lawn-mower manufacturers to voluntarily create their own labels. But they were unclear and inconsistent, according to Ken Feith, former director of ONAC's department of standards and regulations. In the 1980s, after ONAC lost its funding and its effective enforcement power, the labels, says Feith, "just faded into the night."

There's a perception among some manufacturers that American customers care little about noise. Tom Fedorka, senior manager of technology development at Matsushita, says his company, based in Japan, has pushed for noise abatement in its vacuum cleaners sold here, even though he has observed a disinterest among American consumers. Quieter products, he says, are "not something the customer is demanding at this point in time."

In a 1995 CONSUMER REPORTS survey, however, noise was the leading consumer complaint about full-sized canister vacuums and the third-ranked gripe about uprights.

With the drive toward products that can be sold around the world, it's likely that quieter products created for Europe and Japan will result in quieter products for the U.S., too. In the meantime, perhaps only by purchasing quieter products—and complaining about noisy ones—will people convince manufacturers that noise matters.

## Protecting your ears

Soft foam earplugs and acoustic earmuffs are among the most effective hearing protectors, according to the National Institute for Occupational Safety and Health. Plugs are less conspicuous and generally more comfortable, but earmuffs are easier to put on and remove. The packaging of all hearing protectors sports a noise reduction rating (NRR) estimating how many decibels they eliminate. But experts suggest that you simply wear protection that's comfortable and learn to fit it correctly. If sound fidelity is important to you, consider special "musician" or "hi-fi" plugs (starting at less than $20) that claim to reduce noise uniformly across all frequencies. It's wise to wear both both plugs and earmuffs for extremely loud activities—running a chain saw, for example.

*Plugging it*
*Tightly roll a soft foam earplug, then pull the ear upward and outward while inserting it.*

Illustrations by Trevor Johnston

*Muffing it*
*A pair of earmuffs costs about $15 and up.*

## Recommendations

The world could be quieter. Here's what you can do to help:

**Learn when proper ear protection is needed, and use it.** (See "How Loud Is Too Loud?" and "Protecting Your Ears".) Get into the habit of carrying a set of earplugs, just as you'd carry sunglasses to protect your eyes.

**Educate your kids about noise.** This can be daunting if your kids are teens, but help is available. Not-for-profit organizations with material for young people include Hearing Education and Awareness for Rockers (*www.hearingeducation.com*), the National Hearing Conservation Association (*www.hearingconservation.org*), and the League for the Hard of Hearing in New York (*www.lhh.org*).

**Choose quieter models.** When we test autos, major appliances, power equipment, and other products, we include noise measurements in the evaluation. Our tests show you may pay more or sacrifice performance when choosing a quieter model of a product, but that isn't always the case.

**Organize citizens' action.** The Vermont-based Noise Pollution Clearinghouse (*www.nonoise.org*) is ground zero for anti-noise grassroots groups. The group provides news on a variety of noise issues, links to the web sites of successful anti-noise groups, and examples of effective noise ordinances.

**Press for government action.** Sen. Robert Torricelli (D-N.J.) and Rep. Nita Lowey (D-N.Y.) are leading efforts to revitalize noise control and prevention efforts at the Environmental Protection Agency. Torricelli's proposal includes a $30 million health impact study. CU believes such action is long overdue.

**Tell people to turn it down.** Like the anti-smoking campaign begun in the 1980s, making loud noise socially unacceptable may be the best way to protect your hearing—and to get some peace and quiet.

# IS THERE A SIXTH SENSE?

**Ever have a hunch, an instinct or an intuition? Research psychologist Dean Radin, Ph.D., claims that hunches might actually foretell the future. The University of Oregon's Ray Hyman, Ph.D., however, isn't so sure.**

DEAN RADIN, PH.D, WITH COLLEEN RAE

Alex, a university colleague, was cleaning his double-action, six-shot revolver in preparation for a hunting trip later in the month. In this pistol, when the trigger is pulled the hammer is cocked, the cylinder revolves, and the hammer falls on the next chamber, all in one smooth motion. For safety's sake, Alex normally kept five bullets in the revolver, with the hammer resting on the sixth, empty chamber.

Before cleaning the gun, he later told me, he removed the five bullets and set them aside. When finished cleaning, he began to put the bullets back in the cylinder. When he arrived at the fifth and final bullet, he suddenly got a distinct sense of dread. It had something to do with that bullet.

Alex was bothered about the odd feeling because nothing like it had ever happened to him before. He decided to trust his gut, so he put the bullet aside and positioned the pistol's hammer as usual over the sixth chamber. The chamber next to it, which normally held the fifth bullet, was now also empty.

Two weeks later, Alex was at a hunting lodge with his fiancée and her parents. That evening, unexpectedly, a violent argument broke out between the parents. Alex tried to calm them down, but the father, in an insane rage, grabbed Alex's gun, which had been in a drawer, and pointed it at his wife.

Alex tried to intervene by jumping between the gun and the woman, but he was too late—the trigger was already being pulled. For a horrifying split second, Alex knew that he was about to get shot at point-blank range. But instead of a sudden, gruesome death, the pistol went "click." The cylinder had revolved to an empty chamber—the very chamber that would have contained the fifth bullet if Alex had not set it aside two weeks earlier.

Had Alex actually predicted the future, or was this just an extraordinary coincidence? There are several possible explanations for why such "intuitive hunches" sometimes play out. One is that on a subconscious level, we are always thinking and coming to conclusions, but that these register only as hunches to our conscious mind. Another is that we pick up telling cues from body language, subliminal sounds or peripheral vision without being consciously aware of doing so. A third is that for each amazing coincidence we remember, we forget all the times we had a hunch and it didn't pan out. A fourth possibility is that we modify our memories for our own convenience, creating a connection where it may not have existed. And so on. These sorts of prosaic explanations probably account for many intuitive hunches. But they don't explain them all.

As in the case of Alex's intuition, a series of carefully documented case studies raises the possibility that some intuitions are due to a genuine sixth sense. But to confirm that those stories are what they appear to be, we must turn to controlled laboratory tests.

In a pilot study and in three follow-up experiments, I have observed that many people respond unconsciously to something bad—even before it happens. Take the prototypical case of a well-known editor of a popular magazine. When she asks the question, "Is there a sixth sense?" I don't answer directly. I ask if she'd like to participate in an experiment that uses pictures randomly selected by computer, and she agrees.

I have her sit before a blank computer screen. All I've told her is that she's about to see a series of digitized photographs. Some will be calm, like a placid lake, and others will be emotional, like a big spider. On two fingers of her left hand, I attach electrodes that measure tiny

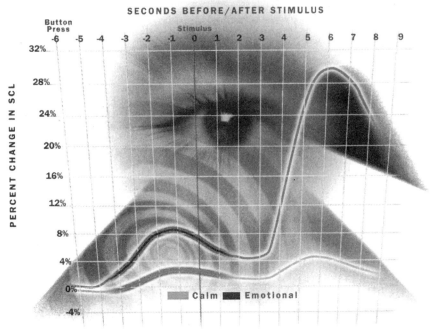

SECONDS BEFORE/AFTER STIMULUS

INIFOGRAPHIC: ANDY CHRISTIE

The dynamic top line you see demonstrates, according to parapsychologist Dean Radin, Ph.D., the heightened reaction his test subjects experienced in unconscious anticipation of an "emotional" picture about to be displayed on a computer screen. The bottom lines represent their subdued reaction before seeing the calmer pictures.

changes in her skin resistance. On a third finger I place an electrode that monitors blood flow. I explain that all she has to do is press the button on the mouse when she's ready to begin, and then look at the pictures.

I leave the room, she relaxes, and then she presses the button. For five seconds, the screen remains blank, and then the computer randomly selects one picture out of a large pool of photos—some calming and some provocative. The picture is displayed for three seconds, and then the screen goes blank for eight seconds. Finally, a message appears announcing that she can start the next trial whenever she's ready.

She repeats this sequence 40 times. At the end of the experiment, I analyze the data recorded by the electrodes and prepare two summary graphs. Each graph shows average changes in her skin resistance and blood flow before, during and after she saw either calm or emotional pictures. What she immediately notices is that after she viewed the emotional pictures, both her skin resistance and fingertip blood flow dramatically changed. And after she viewed calm pictures, her physiology hardly changed at all.

"So I responded emotionally when I saw something emotional, and I remained calm when I saw something calm," she says. "How does that demonstrate a sixth sense?"

I direct her attention to the segment of the graph showing her responses before the computer selected the pictures. "This bump shows that your body responded to emotional pictures before the computer selected them. And this flat line," I say, pointing to the other line,

"shows that your body did not respond before calm pictures were shown. You see? Your body was responding to your future emotion before the computer randomly selected an emotional or calm picture."

As this sinks in, I add, "We can now demonstrate in the laboratory what at some level we've known all along: Many people literally get a gut feeling before something bad happens. Our viscera warn us of danger even if our conscious mind doesn't always get the message."

Our editor's body showed signs of what I call presentiment, an unconscious form of "psi" perception. Psi is a neutral term for psychic experiences, and though it sounds like fodder for an episode of the "X-Files," scientists around the world have studied the subject in the laboratory for over a century. The scientific evidence is now stronger than ever for commonly reported experiences such as telepathy (mind-to-mind communication), clairvoyance (information received from a distant place) and precognition (information received from a distant time). Studies suggest that we have ways of gaining information that bypass the ordinary senses. The sixth sense and similar terms, like second sight and extrasensory perception (ESP), refer to perceptual experiences that transcend the usual boundaries of space and time.

## If the sixth sense truly exists, it could help detect an airplane crash seconds before it happens, potentially saving the lives of everyone on board.

In trying to take these findings further, I realized that we have to dig deeper than what's detectable at the conscious level. While ESP and psi generally refer to conscious psychic experiences, I've always thought that asking people to consciously report subtle psi impressions was a shot in the dark. What would happen if we bypassed the psychological defense mechanisms that filter our perceptions and censor our conscious awareness? Would we find psi experiences that people weren't aware of?

A handful of colleagues have paved the way for this type of investigation. In the mid-1960s, psychologist Charles Tart, Ph.D., of the University of California at Davis, measured skin conductance, blood volume, heart

# Where's the Science in Psi? by Ray Hyman, Ph.D.

Dean Radin asks, "Do our experiments prove without question that the sixth sense exists?" He then answers, "Not yet," correctly recognizing that we need further successful experiments, by independent investigators, to prove that such a sixth sense is real.

But even that's not so simple. The independent investigators must do more than duplicate Radin's findings. They must do so using different apparatus, measurements and randomizing procedures than he did to avoid replicating any errors he may have made inadvertently, otherwise they're just perpetuating faulty findings.

I can already spot some potential errors in his methods. For example, Radin's claim that people in his presentiment experiments unconsciously anticipated emotional pictures—based on his observation of changes in their skin resistance—violates some basic principles of cause and effect in science. That's because the case for presentiment rests on comparing changes in physiological states, and different methods of calculating such changes can yield wildly different results.

For example, many years ago, a student was doing research to show that blinded rats are better than sighted rats at transferring their learning to a new task. The trouble was, a previous researcher had found just the opposite effect. The difference between the two studies? How they measured change. The earlier researcher had calculated the simple difference between the number of errors the rats made on the first task and the number of errors they made on the second task; the student, meanwhile, had measured the changes in terms of percentages. This seemingly innocuous difference led to completely opposite findings! When we used the same measuring technique on both studies, they yielded uniform results.

In addition to the potential pitfalls of choosing a measuring method, researchers must also account for the great degree of variability of physiological changes, which Radin does not do convincingly. Skin resistance, like other physiological measures, varies greatly from person to person and over short and long periods. It also reacts to many aspects of the test subjects' internal and external environment, which is why investigators use a number of adjustments to remove unwanted variation so they can focus only on the changes in which they are interested.

While to his credit, Radin does try to reduce some unwanted variability, his efforts seem to be indirect and arbitrary at best, especially when the process can be very tricky. Radin measured the change in physiological states by subtracting the very first sample of skin resistance on each trial from all the remaining samples of skin resistance for that trial. The evidence for presentiment, he says, is the fact that the averages of the change in skin resistance are larger before viewing emotional pictures than before calm pictures. That seems to make sense. But the first samples of skin readings taken in the trial set the baseline against which the results of all future trials will be compared and computed. So if, for some reason, the first samples of the trials involving emotional targets happen to have a somewhat lower value of skin resistance than the first samples of the calm trials, this alone would yield, perhaps falsely, a bigger "change score" for the emotional trials.

To see this problem in action, assume that the average raw score level for both calm and emotional trials is 20. If the baseline for the calm trials is 15, then the change score for the calm trials would be 20–15=5. If the baseline for the emotional trials is 10, then the change score for the emotional trials would be 20–10=10. Thus, the scoring procedure produces a bigger change in the emotional trials, all because of the differences in baselines. As you can see, the simple choice of method can greatly influence the findings. The devil, as they say, is in the details.

So how de we know which measure to trust when each gives a different outcome? The solution is clear only when we have a detailed theory of the underlying process being studied. But that's a key problem here: There is a general lack of a positive theory of ESP or psi. What kind of a process is it? How does it behave? Indeed, as many parapsychologists recognize, ESP is, at present, defined negatively, in terms of what it is not; the experimenter claims she has found psi when she has eliminated all normal scientific explanations for the outcome. Given this hazy state of affairs, there is no principled way to state what the correct measurement procedure should be. This would not be too serious if different methods produced the same outcome. But we do not know if this is the case in Radin's experiments.

If I am investigating changes in the firings of nerve impulses in the optic nerve, for example, we have both extensive theory and data to inform us of the appropriate measures to use: We know the underlying distribution of such firings and we know how to appropriately transform them so that the measures of change make sense in terms of what we know about nerves and nerve impulses. In the case of the presentiment hypothesis, however, we do not have a detailed theory and sufficient data to know what sorts of transformations and measures of change make sense. So before we can believe that the physiological changes show that the subject is anticipating the emotional picture, we need to show, at the least, that different ways of measuring the physiological changes will yield the same outcome. We also would need to collect the physiological measures under more varied circumstances and over longer time periods.

The history of attempts to investigate scientifically psychical phenomena goes back 150 years, and is replete with examples of psychical researchers claiming they finally proved the existence of the paranormal. In each instance, subsequent generations of parapsychologists have had to discard as badly flawed what had seemed to the previous generation to be irrefutable proof of psi, or psychic phenomena.

A case in point is the study cited by Radin of the "significant correlations in brain waves between isolated identical twins." This study was reported in the journal *Science* in 1965 by Duane and Behrendt. These investigators took advantage of the fact that alpha brain waves can be induced by simply closing one's eyes. The researchers put two members of a pair of twins in separate rooms and connected them to electrodes to measure their brain waves. They instructed one of the twins to shut her eyes at predetermined times. This produced the expected alpha rhythms in her brain waves, and supposedly caused the other twin's brain waves to show alpha rhythms at the same time. If this is indeed what had happened, it would be evidence for ESP. But there were many methodological problems. First, the isolation of the twins was not very convincing since they were in adjacent rooms. Second, the evidence for the correlation of the brain waves was based solely on subjective, visual inspection of the brain wave recordings. As psychologists know, people are very poor at determining correlations subjectively, which is why experimenters trust only correlations tabulated by computers.

Duane and Behrendt later admitted, among other things, that because the twins were not in shielded rooms, they could conceivably have sent coded signals to one another. "In retrospect, the biggest defect in our experimental procedure was that we did not rule out completely conventional forms of communication between the twins, and we did not perform a statistical analysis to eliminate spontaneous alpha rhythms." While they continued to seek the "hard, quantitative data" they said would prove or refute the hypothesis, neither these authors or anyone else has succeeded, during the intervening 35 years, in replicating these results under scientific conditions.

In his book *The Conscious Universe* (Harper*Edge*, 1997), Dean Radin remains optimistic that, correctly interpreted, the experimental outcomes of parapsychological experiment conclusively demonstrate the existence of psi or ESP.

But if the century and a half of psychical research has taught us anything, then the next generation will likely not be able to replicate Radin's presentiment results and will begin to search elsewhere for their elusive quarry. On the other hand, if history ceases to repeat itself, future parapsychologists may very well find ways to help us develop our intuitive powers. It remains to be seen whether Radin's research will pave the way.

*Ray Hyman, Ph.D., is a professor of psychology at the University of Oregon.*

---

rate, and verbal reports between two people, called a sender-receiver pair. He, as the sender, received random electrical shocks to see if remote receivers could detect those events. Tart found that while they weren't consciously aware of anything out of the ordinary, the distant receivers' physiology registered significant reactions to the shocks he experienced.

In other, independent experiments, engineer Douglas Dean at the Newark College of Engineering; psychologist Jean Barry, Ph.D., in France; and psychologist Erlendur Haraldsson, Ph.D., at the University of Utrecht, all observed significant changes in receivers' finger blood volume when a sender, located thousands of miles away, directed emotional thoughts toward them. The journal *Science* also published a study by two physiologists who reported finding significant correlations in brain waves between isolated identical twins. These sorts of studies came to be known as Distant Mental Intention on Living Systems (DMILS).

The idea for studying intuitive hunches came to me in 1993, while I was a research fellow in the psychology department at the University of Edinburgh in Scotland. I was investigating the "feeling of being stared at." In the laboratory, I separated two people, placing them in rooms that were 100 feet away from each another. Then I monitored person #1's electrodermal activity while person #2 stared at person #1 over a one-way closed-circuit video system. Although the stared-at person could have no conscious idea when the "starer" was doing the looking, since the two were in different rooms and the staring occurred at random times, I did observe small changes in the skin resistance of the person being stared at over closed-circuit television.

In thinking about this result, I realized that (for relativistic reasons) this sort of "nonlocal" connection across space implied a complementary connection across time. If we were seeing a genuine space-separated effect between people, then the same thing ought to work as a time-separated effect within one person. I called this proposed effect "presentiment" because the term suggests a response to a future emotional event.

I soon discovered that even the staunchest skeptics, those ready to swear on a stack of scientific journals that psi was impossible, were somewhat less critical of intuitive hunches. That's because most people have had at least one.

I myself hardly believed the results of the studies I conducted on the magazine editor and others. But I couldn't find any mistakes in the study design or analysis of the results. Some months later, Dick Bierman, Ph.D., a professor at the University of Amsterdam, learned of my studies and couldn't believe them either. So he repeated the experiment in his lab and found the same results. Since then, two students of psychologist Robert Morris, Ph.D., at the University of Edinburgh, have also repeated the study, and again found similar results. More replication attempts are now under way in several other laboratories.

Do our experiments prove without question that the sixth sense exists? Not yet. What we have are three independent labs reporting similar effects based on data from more than 200 participants. The proof of the pudding will rest upon many more labs getting the same results. Still, our studies, combined with the outcomes of many other types of tests by dozens of investigators on precognition and other classes of psi phenomena, have caused even highly skeptical scientists to ponder what was previously unthinkable—the possibility of a genuine sixth sense.

In 1995, for example, no less an arch-skeptic than the late astronomer Carl Sagan rendered his lifelong opinion that all psi effects were impossible. But in one of his last books, *The Demon-Haunted World: Science as a Candle in the Dark,* he wrote, "At the time of writing there are three claims in the ESP field which, in my opinion, deserve serious study: (1) that by thought alone humans can (barely) affect random number generators in computers; (2) that people under mild sensory deprivation can receive thoughts or images "projected" at them; and (3) that young children sometimes report the details of a previous life, which upon checking turn out to be accurate and which they could not have known about in any other way than reincarnation."

If scientists eventually agree that a sixth sense exists, how might this change society? On one hand, it may change nothing; we may learn that genuine psi abilities are rare and only weakly predictive, and thus inconsequential for most practical purposes.

On the other hand, it's possible that the study of the sixth sense will revolutionize our understanding of causality and have radically new applications. For example, in the January issue of *Alternative Therapies,* psychologist William Braud, Ph.D., professor and research director at the Institute of Transpersonal Psychology and co-director of the Institute's William James Center for Consciousness Studies, discusses the concept of "retroactive intentional influence" as applied to healing. He poses the idea that in cases where serious illnesses disappear virtually overnight, perhaps a healer went back in time to jumpstart the healing process.

Braud is well aware of the mind-bending nature of this hypothesis, but it is not purely fantastical. In his article, he reviews several hundred experiments examining a wide range of retrocausal phenomena, from mental influence of random numbers generated by electronic circuits, to guessing picture targets selected in the future, to studies examining the "feeling of being stared at," to presentiment experiments. He concludes that this sizable but not well-known body of carefully controlled research indicates that some form of retroactive intentional influence is indeed possible, and may have important consequences for healing.

A less radical application might be for early warning systems. Imagine that on a future aircraft all the members of the flight crew are connected to an onboard computer system. The system is designed to continuously monitor heart rate, electrical activity in the skin, and blood flow. Before the crew comes aboard, each person is calibrated to see how he or she responds before, during and after different kinds of emotional and calm events. Each person's idiosyncratic responses are used to create a person-unique emotional "response template," which is fed into the computer.

While the plane is in the air, the computer monitors each crew member's body to assess their emotional level. If the computer detects that all crew members are about to have an emotional response (and the aircraft is otherwise operating normally), then the computer could alert the pilot. Sometimes even a few seconds of advance warning in an aircraft can save the lives of everyone on board.

Very likely, some intuitive hunches do indicate the presence of a sixth sense. But for whom? Probably everyone, to a degree. But just as some people have poor vision, it is also quite likely that some people are effectively "psi-blind." I suspect that in the future, with a little assistance from specialized technologies, the same way a hearing aid can improve poor hearing, it may become possible to boost our weak sixth sense.

---

*Dean Radin, Ph.D., a parapsychologist, is president of the Boundary Institute in Los Altos, California. Colleen Rae is a freelance writer in Chapel Hill, North Carolina.*

## READ MORE ABOUT IT

*The Consscious Universe: The Scientific Truth Of Psychic Phenomena,* Dean Radin, Ph.D. (Harper*Edge,* 1997).

*Parapsychology: The Controversial Science,* Richard S. Broughton (Ballantine, 1992).

## Unit Selections

## Key Points to Consider

❖ What is learning? What is memory? How are the two linked? Are they necessarily always linked to each other?

❖ Can fetuses learn? If yes, what is it that they learn? By what mechanisms would unborn children learn? Is this type of learning important? Do you think the types of learning they do are different from the learning older children experience?

❖ What are learning styles? Can you provide a concrete example of a learning style? Why are learning styles important? Does everyone have the same learning style? Should teachers try to match each child's style to the materials or to the teaching method? What does research suggest about the success of matching?

❖ What is operant conditioning? What principles of learning have we gleaned from the study of operant conditioning and other forms of simple learning? What is reinforcement? What is punishment? Why is it better to reinforce than punish behaviors? How can operant principles be practiced or put into effect in everyday life?

❖ Why is memory important? What is forgetting? Why do psychologists want to know about mechanisms that underlie learning and remembering? To what use can we put this information? Do we learn and remember like a computer does? Why do we forget? Are there methods we can use that can improve memory? What are they and can you give an example of each? What types of memory lapses are normal? What memory lapses signal problems? How do memory lapses normally unfold with age?

 **Links**    # www.dushkin.com/online/

These sites are annotated on pages 4 and 5.

Do you remember your first week of classes at college? There were so many new buildings to recognize and people's names to remember. And you had to recall accurately where all your classes were as well as your professors' names. Just remembering your class schedule was problematic enough. For those of you who lived in residence halls, the difficulties multiplied. You had to remember where your residence was, recall the names of individuals living on your floor, and learn how to navigate from your room to other places on campus, such as the dining halls and library. Then came examination time. Did you ever think you would survive college exams? The material in terms of difficulty level and amount was perhaps more than you thought you could manage.

What a stressful time you experienced when you first came to campus! Much of what created the stress was the strain on your learning and memory systems, two complicated processes. Still, most of you survived just fine and with your memories, learning strategies, and mental health intact.

The processes you depended on when beginning college were learning and memory, two of the processes studied the longest by psychologists. Today, with their sophisticated experimental techniques, psychologists have detected several types of memory processes and have discovered what makes learning more complete so that subsequent memory is more accurate. We also discovered that humans aren't the only organisms capable of these processes; all types of animals can learn, even an organism as simple as an earthworm or an amoeba.

Psychologists know, too, that rote learning and practice are not the only forms of learning. For instance, at this point in time in your introductory psychology class, you might be studying operant and classical conditioning, two simple but nonetheless important forms of learning of which both humans and simple organisms are capable. Both types of conditioning can occur without our awareness or active participation in them. The processes of learning and remembering (or its reciprocal, forgetting) are examined here in some detail.

The unit begins with a look at learning even before life begins. In "Learning Begins Even Before Babies Are Born, Scientists Show," Beth Azar discovers that the fetus can indeed learn about sounds and flavors. Such learning comes from experiences of the mothers. Researchers have, with difficulty, discovered clever methods for studying fetal learning in utero.

The second article looks at learning styles, a subject that has long interested psychologists. Teachers today are often told that they should discover a child's learning style and then match

teaching methods to it. In "Different Strokes for Different Folks?" Steven Stahl examines this recommendation after first defining learning style.

In the third article, "What Constitutes 'Appropriate' Punishment?" Paul DeVito and Ralph Hyatt examine one simple form of learning, operant conditioning or behavior modification. The authors differentiate punishment from reinforcement and then describe when and how punishment, if used, needs to be dispensed. The authors conclude, by the way, that reinforcement of positive behaviors is far preferable over punishment of negative behaviors.

The last two articles in this unit pertain to memory. George Johnson's article reports on new experiments on memory. In "Speak, Memory," Emily Mitchell first discusses common memory problems, some relating to aging, then proceeds to elucidate several memory techniques from which we can all benefit, even if we don't have serious memory disorders such as Alzheimer's disease.

# Learning and Remembering

# Learning begins even before babies are born, scientists show

## The prenatal environment

The fetus learns to interpret sounds, flavors and vibrations, studies have found.

By Beth Azar
*Monitor staff*

The old metaphor of children as blocks of unmolded clay has lost its relevance over the decades. Research reveals not only that newborns have many genetically based preferences, but some of those preferences may also be the result of fetal learning.

Newborns remember certain aspects of their fetal environment, researchers argue. And research in animals and humans finds that the fetus is capable of rudimentary forms of learning.

This is not to say that parents should start trying to teach their children prenatally, say researchers. Rather, it confirms the importance of prenatal care during a time when the human fetus is developing not only physically but also cognitively. The research may also provide clinicians with a measure they can use to evaluate infant health prenatally.

### A memory for sounds

There's no evidence that playing Mozart to an unborn child will encourage musical aptitude, but research does confirm that newborns enter the world with a preference for certain sounds from the fetal world. That world is dominated by two sounds: the mother's heartbeat and her voice. According to research by Columbia University psychologist William Fifer, PhD, and his colleagues, newborns prefer their mother's voice to the voice of other women. They also prefer her voice when it's electronically altered to sound as it did in the uterus, compared with her voice outside the uterus.

In contrast, infants don't prefer their father's voice over the voices of other men, indicating that they have a particular preference for prenatal sounds, not just familiar sounds, says Fifer.

It's likely that it is the cadences, and not the specific words, that the newborns recognize, he adds. One study found that newborns recognize the cadences of rhymes that they heard their mother say repeatedly during the last few weeks of pregnancy, but not the specific words themselves.

"These studies show that there is a mechanism for longterm memory available to the fetus," says Fifer.

The fetus may also have the capacity to remember food flavors available in utero, says Julie Mennella, PhD, of the Monell Chemical Senses Center in Philadelphia. She's found that the fetus has access to flavors, such as garlic, that become present in the amniotic fluid. This flavor transfer from mother to infant can continue after birth as many flavors from the mother's diet are integrated into her breast milk. These early experiences with flavors may form the basis of some food preferences as the child ages, says Mennella, who is beginning experiments to test that theory.

### Habituation

Further evidence of fetal learning comes from studies of habituation—the process through which an animal learns, over repeated episodes of stimulation, to give less attention to an increasingly familiar stimulus. To test habituation in the human fetus, researchers apply a stimulus—often a vibrating device—to a pregnant woman's abdomen. By 26 weeks of gestation, a human fetus will reliably move in response to such a stimulus, researchers find. And, after repeated stimulation, a fetus will stop responding, having habituated to the stimulus. However, if a new stimulus is used, the fetus will once again respond.

**There's no evidence that playing Mozart to an unborn child will encourage musical aptitude, but research does confirm that newborns enter the world with a preference for certain sounds from the fetal world.**

Some researchers argue that habituation is a measure of learning that can predict later cognitive abilities, says psychologist Eugene K. Emory of Emory University.

In particular, Leo Leader, PhD, believes that clinicians can use fetal habituation to evaluate the health and development of the fetus. He's conducted several studies that correlate habituation with later development. Other researchers aren't convinced it's time to start making predictions, but they don't rule out the possibility in the near future.

The National Institute on Child Health and Human Development, which funds much of the fetal research, has hosted two meetings of fetal researchers to discuss the possibility of using data from basic research to begin to inform clinicians.

### Fetal learning

Animal researchers can study more specific forms of learning because they can manipulate the fetus in ways impossible to attempt in humans. In rats, researchers can remove an individual pup from its mother's uterus and, keeping it attached to the umbilical cord, keep it alive in small dishes filled with a temperature-regulated water bath that mimics amniotic fluid. The pups can be kept inside the amniotic sac or removed.

Binghamton University psychologist William T. Smotherman, PhD, has taken the lead in fetal learning studies. He's designed a standard conditioned-learning paradigm that he can manipulate to examine specific questions about fetal learning, including the molecular mechanisms that control it. The paradigm involves one aspect of feeding behavior—learning to respond to a nipple in a way to promote feeding, a behavior we assume is instinctive but that may partly involve learning. Smotherman places an artificial nipple close to the fetus' mouth, and if the fetus grasps the nipple, it receives a squirt of mother's milk into its mouth.

He finds that by around 21 days gestation—equivalent to early in the ninth month of a human pregnancy—the fetuses easily and quickly learn to respond to the nipple as if they were going to receive milk from it.

When researchers examine this response at the molecular level, they find that the milk triggers the release of certain neuropeptides in the brain of the rat fetus, which work to reinforce early feeding behaviors such as suckling. For example, the milk triggers a release of opiates into the fetuses' brains, which reinforces the pups' behavior. When Smotherman and his colleagues block this opiate release, the fetuses no longer become conditioned to the artificial nipple, indicating that the chemicals are necessary for learning.

He's also found that if he exposes fetuses to the nipple and the milk, but not paired in time, they don't become conditioned to respond to the nipple. They have the equivalent amount of experience with the crucial stimuli—the milk and the nipple—but because the two stimuli aren't coupled in time, learning doesn't occur.

This may have implications for premature infants who are fed either intravenously or through a feeding tube. Like the rat fetuses that receive the milk without access to the nipple, these infants may not learn to associate eating with suckling. It may be helpful to pair feeding with some type of non-nutritive suckling, says Smotherman.

### Working for warmth

Indiana University psychologist Jeffery Alberts, PhD, agrees that fetal experiences and early newborn experiences help shape early development. Research by him and research scientist April Ronca, PhD, finds that the physical pressures put on the fetus just before and during labor are critical for developmental success and that, after birth, environment can shape early learning.

In one study, the Indiana researchers found that day-old rat pups will work to gain access to heat. Postdoctoral fellow Cynthia Hoffman, PhD, designed an operant conditioning paradigm, taking advantage of the fact that young, immobile pups periodically move their heads from side to side. When the pups in the experiment randomly turned their heads to the left, Hoffman rewarded them with 20 seconds of belly warming—she ran warm water under the plates the pups were lying on. They quickly learned to turn their heads to the left to elicit the belly warming, says Alberts.

"This research shows us how environmental factors, like warmth, can quickly shape behavior very early in life," he says.

## Further reading

"Fetal Development: A Psychobiological Perspective," by J. P. Lecanuet, W. Fifer, N. A. Krasnegor, W. Smotherman (Lawrence Erlbaum Associates, Inc., 1995).

# DIFFERENT STROKES FOR DIFFERENT FOLKS?

## A Critique of Learning Styles

By Steven A. Stahl

I WORK WITH a lot of different schools and listen to a lot of teachers talk. Nowhere have I seen a greater conflict between "craft knowledge" or what teachers know (or at least think they know) and "academic knowledge" or what researchers know (or at least think they know) than in the area of learning styles. Over the years, my experience has told me to trust teachers; it has also taught me that teachers' craft knowledge is generally on target. I don't mean to say that teachers are always right, but they have learned a great deal from their thousands of observations of children learning in classrooms. So, when teachers talk about the need to take into account children's learning styles when teaching, and researchers roll their eyes at the sound of the term "learning styles," there is more to it than meets the eye.

The whole notion seems fairly intuitive. People are different. Certainly different people might learn differently from each other. It makes sense. Consider the following from the Web site of the National Reading Styles Institute, a major proponent of the application of learning styles to the teaching of reading:

> We all have personal styles that influence the way we work, play, and make decisions. Some people are very analytical, and they think in a logical, sequential way. Some students are visual or auditory learners; they learn best by seeing or hearing. These students are likely to conform well to traditional methods of study.
>
> Some people (we call them "global learners") need an idea of the whole picture before they can understand it, while "analytic learners" proceed more easily from the parts to the whole. Global learners also tend to learn best when they can touch what they are learning or move around while they learn. We call these styles of learning "tactile" and "kinesthetic." In a strictly traditional classroom, these students are often a problem for the teacher. She has trouble keeping them still or quiet. They seem unable to learn to read. (http://www.nrsi.com/about.html)

This all seems reasonable, but it isn't.

## Research and Learning Styles

The reason researchers roll their eyes at learning styles is the utter failure to find that assessing children's learning styles and matching to instructional methods has any effect on their learning. The area

*Steven A. Stahl is professor of reading education at the University of Georgia and co-director of the Center for Improvement of Early Reading Achievement. His research interests are in beginning reading and vocabulary instruction.*

From *American Educator,* Fall 1999, pp. 27-31. Reprinted with permission of the author and *American Educator,* the quarterly journal of American Federation of Teachers.

ILLUSTRATED BY BRU ASSOCIATES

[The assumption that one can improve instruction by matching materials to children's modality strengths] appears to lack even minimal empirical support.[2]

Kampwirth and Bates, in 1980, found 24 studies that looked at this issue. Again, they concluded:

Matching children's modality strengths to reading materials has not been found to be effective.[3]

In 1987, Kavale and Forness reviewed 39 studies using a meta-analysis technique that would be more sensitive to these effects. They found that matching children by reading styles had nearly no effect on achievement. They concluded:

Although the presumption of matching instruction strategies to individual modality preferences has great intuitive appeal, little empirical support for this proposition was found. . . . Neither modality testing nor modality teaching were shown to be [effective].[4]

A fifth review, in 1992, by Snider found difficulties in reliably assessing learning styles and a lack of convincing research that such assessment leads to improvement in reading.

Recognition of individuals' strengths and weaknesses is good practice; using this information, however, to categorize children and prescribe methods can be detrimental to low-performing students. Although the idea of reading style is superficially appealing, critical examination should cause educators to be skeptical of this current educational fad.[5]

These five research reviews, all published in well-regarded journals, found the same thing: One cannot reliably measure children's reading styles and even if one could, matching children to reading programs by learning styles does not improve their learning. In other words, it is difficult to accurately identify children who are "global" and "analytic." So-called global children do not do better in whole language programs than they would in more phonics-based programs. And so-called analytic children do not do better in phonics programs than they do in whole language programs. In short, time after time, this notion of reading styles does not work.

This is an area that has been well researched. Many other approaches to matching teaching approaches to learning styles have not been well researched, if at all. I could not find studies in refereed journals, for example, documenting whether the use of Howard Gardner's Multiple Intelligences Model[6] improved

with the most research has been the global and analytic styles referred to in the NRSI blurb above. Over the past 30 years, the names of these styles have changed—from "visual" to "global" and from "auditory" to "analytic"—but the research results have not changed.

In 1978, Tarver and Dawson reviewed 15 studies that matched visual learners to sight word approaches and auditory learners to phonics. Thirteen of the studies failed to find an effect, and the two that found the effect used unusual methodology. They concluded:

Modality preference has not been demonstrated to interact significantly with the method of teaching reading.[1]

One year later, Arter and Jenkins reviewed 14 studies (some of these are overlapping), all of which failed to find that matching children to reading methods by preferred modalities did any good. They concluded:

instruction. This does not mean, of course, that the use of the model does not improve achievement, only that I could not find studies validating its use. The same is true of other learning style models.

One cannot prove a negative. Even if all of these studies failed to find that matching children by learning styles helps them read better, it is always possible that another study or another measure or another something will find that matching children to their preferred learning modality will produce results. But in the meantime, we have other things that we *know* will improve children's reading achievement. We should look elsewhere for solutions to reading problems.

Yet, the notion of reading styles (or learning styles) lingers on. This is true not only in my talks with teachers, but also in the literature that teachers read. The most recent issue of *Educational Leadership* included, as part of a themed issue on innovations, several articles on learning styles. *Phi Delta Kappan* also regularly contains articles on learning styles, as do other publications intended for teachers.

## Research into Learning Styles

Among others, Marie Carbo claims that her learning styles work is based on research. [I discuss Carbo because she publishes extensively on her model and is very prominent on the workshop circuit. In the references for this article, I cite a few examples of her numerous writings on the topic.[7]] But given the overwhelmingly negative findings in the published research, I wondered what she was citing, and about a decade ago, I thought it would be interesting to take a look. Reviewing her articles, I found that out of 17 studies she had cited, only one was published.[8] Fifteen were doctoral dissertations and 13 of these came out of one university—St. John's University in New York, Carbo's alma mater. None of these had been in a peer-refereed journal. When I looked closely at the dissertations and other materials, I found that 13 of the 17 studies that supposedly support her claim had to do with learning styles based on something other than modality. In 1997, I found 11 additional citations. None of these was published, eight were dissertations, and six of these came from St. John's. In short, the research cited would not cause anyone to change his or her mind about learning styles.

## What Do People Mean by Learning Styles?

Modality refers to one of the main avenues of sensation such as vision and hearing. I have only talked about modality-based reading styles because these are both the best researched and the most heavily promoted. The National Reading Styles Institute claims that it has worked with "over 150,000 teachers," and its advertisements seem to be everywhere. Furthermore, these notions of "visual" and "auditory" learners or "global" and "analytic" learners have been around for a long time and have found their way into a number of different programs, not just the NRSI programs.

There are other ways of looking at learning styles. People have proposed that children vary not only in perceptual styles, but on a host of different dimensions. To name a few, people have suggested that children are either two-dimensional/three-dimensional, simultaneous/sequential, connecting/compartmentalizing, inventing/reproducing, reflective/impulsive, field dependent/field independent, and so on.

Some of these are *learning preferences*, or how an individual chooses to work. These might include whether a person prefers to work in silence or with music playing, in bright light or dim light, with a partner or alone, in a warm room or a cool room, etc.

Some of these are *cognitive styles*, such as whether a person tends to reflect before making a choice or makes it impulsively, or whether a person tends to focus on details or sees the big picture.

Some of these are *personality types*, such as whether a person is introverted or extroverted.

Some of these are *aptitudes*, like many of Howard Gardner's multiple intelligences. Gardner suggests that people vary along at least seven different dimensions—*linguistic* or the ability to use language, *logico-mathematical* or the ability to use reasoning especially in mathematics, *spatial* or the ability to use images or pictures, *bodily-kinesthetic* or the ability to control movement, *musical, interpersonal* or the ability to work with people, and *intrapersonal* or the thinking done inside oneself. The last two are more like personality types, rather than aptitudes or even learning styles. The others are Gardner's attempt to expand the notion of what we think is intelligent behavior to people who are skilled in music, or dance, or even in interpersonal relations. In contrast to the traditional vision of learning styles as either/or categories (either a person is visual or he or she is auditory), multiple intelligences are put forth by Gardner as separate abilities. A child may be strong in a few of these areas, or none of these areas.

What is a teacher to do with all this? If there are children who prefer to work with music, then the teacher might either provide Walkmans for those who prefer music or play music openly and provide earplugs for those who don't. If there are children who prefer to work in bright light, the teacher might seat those children over by the window. Children who like to snack while reading can be allowed to eat during class (healthy foods, of course). It would be easy to see how accommodating all of these preferences in a class could lead to chaos. How would a teacher lecture, give assignments, or even call to order a class in which a sizable proportion of the students was wearing earplugs? Or how does one regulate the temperature so part of the room is warm and part cool?

Others have used learning styles theory as a way of making sure that all the needs of diverse learners are being met. Marguerite Radenich used Gardner's model to examine literature study guides.[9] Her ideal was one that incorporated all of these ways of knowing into an integrated whole to be used to study adolescent literature. Thus, Gardner's model was used here to create more multidimensional instruction. This is very different from using these different styles to segregate children into groups where they would receive fairly one-dimensional instruction.

Thoughtful educators have tried to make this work, and perhaps it is workable, but trying to meet all of the preferences of a group of children would seem to take energy that would be better spent on other things. This is especially true since no one has proven that it works.

## Learning Styles and Fortune Telling

Why does the notion of "learning styles" have such enduring popularity—despite the lack of supporting evidence? I believe that this phenomenon has a lot in common with fortune telling.

You go to see a fortune teller at a circus. She looks you over and makes some quick judgments—how young or old you are, how nicely you are dressed, whether you appear anxious or sad or lonely—and based on these judgments, tells your fortune. The fortune she tells may be full of simple and ambiguous statements—"you will be successful at your next venture," "you will be lucky at love," or may be more complex—"you are successful at home, but someone is jealous; make sure you watch yourself." Either way, the statements are specific enough so that they sound predictive, but ambiguous enough that they could apply to a number of situations.

When we read the statements on a Learning Style Inventory, they sound enough like us that we have a flash of recognition. These inventories typically consist of a series of forced choices, such as these from Marie Carbo's *Reading Style Inventory, Intermediate,* 1995.[10]

A) I always like to be told exactly how I should do my reading work.
B) Sometimes I like to be told exactly how I should do my reading work.
C) I like to decide how to do my reading work by myself.

Or

A) I like to read in the morning.
B) I don't like to read in the morning.

A) I like to read after lunch.

B) I don't like to read after lunch.

A) I like to read at night.
B) I don't like to read at night.

Or

A) I read best where it's quiet with no music playing.
B) I read best where there is music playing.
C) I read about the same where it's quiet or where there is music playing.

Since all of us have some preferences (my experience is that adults have clear preferences about music during reading, especially), these items tend to ring true. Like the fortunes told by the fortune teller, these statements at first light seem specific enough to capture real distinctions among people. But the problem with choices like these is that people tend to make the same choices. Nearly everybody would prefer a demonstration in science class to an uninterrupted lecture. This does not mean that such individuals have a visual style, but that good science teaching involves demonstrations. Similarly, nearly everybody would agree that one learns more about playing tennis from playing than from watching someone else play. Again, this does not mean that people are tactile/kinesthetic, but that this is how one learns to play sports. Many of these "learning styles" are not really choices, since common sense would suggest that there would not be much variance among people. In the class sample provided with the Reading Style Inventory above, for example, 96 percent of the fifth-graders assessed preferred quiet to working while other people were talking, 88 percent preferred quiet to music, 79 percent picked at least two times a day when they preferred to work, 71 percent had no preference about temperature, and so on. Virtually all of the questions had one answer preferred by a majority of the students.

The questions are just specific enough to sound like they mean something, but vague enough to allow different interpretations. For example, does "music" refer to Mozart or Rap? Obviously, one's choices would be different for different types of music. A more serious question would arise over the "teacher direction" item. Doesn't the amount of teacher direction needed depend on the difficulty of the assignment? There are some assignments that are self evident and do not need much teacher direction, but when work gets complex, students need more direction. This is not a matter of preference.

The other major problem with these inventories is that there are no questions about a child's reading ability. So children with reading problems are given the same measure as children who are doing well in reading. This has two effects. First, there is a bias on some items for children with different abilities. Consider these two items, also from the Carbo inventory:

A) It's easy for me to remember rules about sounding out words.
B) It's hard for me to remember rules about sounding out words.

Or

A) When I write words, I sometimes mix up the letters.
B) When I write words, I almost never mix up the letters.

Children with reading problems are more likely to answer that they do not remember phonics rules and that they sometimes mix up the letters. According to the learning styles research reports, such children are likely to be considered as having a global (or visual) preference.[11] Actually, this may not be a preference at all, but a reflection of the child's current level of reading ability. The potential for harm occurs when children with reading problems are classified as "global" (visual) learners and thereby miss out on important instruction in decoding, or are classified as "analytic" (auditory) learners and miss out on opportunities to practice reading in connected text.

Not including information about reading ability also leads to some strange prescriptions. Adults attending learning styles workshops often get prescriptions for beginning reading instruction methods, such as the language experience approach or phonics/linguistic approaches, certainly not needed by competent readers. And for children, too, some of the approaches may be inappropriate. The language experience approach, for example, is best suited for children at the emergent literacy stage, when they need to learn about basic print concepts, one-to-one matching, letter identification, and so on.[12] For a second-grader, or even a newly literate adult, language experience may be appropriate (if they still have not mastered basic print concepts) or highly inappropriate (if they are already reading fluently). It depends on the readers' skill, not their learning styles.

## Reliability

If you are to use a test, even an inventory like the one cited above, it should be reliable. If a test is reliable, that means you are going to get the same (or close to the same) results every time you administer it. If a test is 100 percent reliable (or has a reliability coefficient of 1.0), then a person will score exactly the same on Thursday as on Tuesday. Perfection is tough to come by, so we generally want a reliability coefficient to be .90 or higher.[13] If a test is not reliable, or trustworthy, then it is difficult to believe the results.

This is a problem, not only with inventories, but with any measure that asks subjects to report about themselves.

Reliabilities of these measures are relatively low. The self-reported reliabilities of Carbo's Reading Style Inventory and Dunn and Dunn's Learning Style Inventories are moderate, especially for a measure of this kind—in the neighborhood of the .60s and the .70s. Similar reliabilities are reported for the Myers-Briggs Inventory, another learning styles assessment.[14] These are lower than one would want for a diagnostic measure. And, these scores are inflated, since for many items there is generally one answer that nearly everybody chooses. This would tend to make the reliabilities higher.

The vagueness in the items may tend to make the reliabilities low. Again, how a child interprets each item will influence how it is answered, as with the "teacher direction" and "music" examples discussed earlier.

Test-retest reliabilities are particularly important for a measure of learning styles. These moderate reliabilities could be interpreted in two ways. The test itself may not be a reliable measure of what it is supposed to measure—that is, a person has a stable learning style, but the test is not getting at it. If the test is not reliable, then the information it gives is not trustworthy.

The other possibility is that learning styles may change, from month to month, or even week to week. This is also problematic. If we are talking about matching a person to a situation using this instrument, this is a relatively long-term (semester or academic year) matching. If a person's style changes, then one either must measure learning styles frequently, or allow for more flexible assignments.

## How Reading Develops

The Learning Style model assumes that different children need different approaches to learn to read. Children are different. They come to us with different personalties, preferences, ways of doing things. However, the research so far shows that this has little to do with how successful they will be as readers and writers. Children also come to us with different amounts of exposure to written text, with different skills and abilities, with different exposure to oral language. The research shows that these differences *are* important.

Rather than different methods being appropriate for different children, we ought to think about different methods being appropriate for children at different stages in their development. Children differ in their phonemic abilities, in their ability to recognize words automatically, in their ability to comprehend and learn from text, and in their motivation and appreciation of literature.[15] Different methods are appropriate for different goals. For example, approaches that involve the children in reading books of their own choice are important to develop motivated readers.[16] But whole language approaches, which rely largely on children to choose the materials they read, tend not to be as effective as more teacher-directed approaches for developing children's word recognition or comprehension.[17]

A language experience approach may be appropriate to help a kindergarten child learn basic print concepts. The child may learn some words using visual cues, such as might be taught through a whole word method. With some degree of phonological awareness, the child is ready to learn letters and sounds, as through a phonic approach. Learning about letters and sounds, in combination with practice with increasingly challenging texts, will develop children's ability to use phonetic cues in reading, and to cross-check using context. With additional practice in wide reading, children will develop fluent and automatic word recognition. None of this has anything to do with learning styles; it has to do with the children's current abilities and the demands of the task they have to master next.

## What Do Teachers Get out of Learning Styles Workshops?

I have interviewed a number of teachers who have attended learning styles workshops. These were meetings of 200 to 300 teachers and principles, who paid $129 or so to attend a one-day workshop or up to $500 to attend a longer conference. They have found them to be pleasant experiences with professional presenters. The teachers also feel that they learned something from the workshops. After I pressed them, what it seemed that they learned is a wide variety of reading methods, a respect for individual differences among children, and a sense of possibilities of how to teach reading. This is no small thing. However, the same information, and much more, can be gotten from a graduate class in the teaching of reading.

These teachers have another thing in common—after one year, they had all stopped trying to match children by learning styles.

## REFERENCES

1. Tarver, Sara, and M. M. Dawson. 1978. Modality preference and the teaching of reading. *Journal of Learning Disabilities* 11: 17–29.
2. Arter, J. A., and Joseph A. Jenkins. 1979. Differential diagnosis-prescriptive teaching: A critical appraisal. *Review of Educational Research* 49: 517–555.
3. Kampwirth, T. J., and M. Bates. 1980. Modality preference and teaching method. A review of the research. *Academic Therapy* 15: 597–605.
4. Kavale, Kenneth, A., and Steven R. Forness. 1987. Substance over style: Assessing the efficacy of modality testing and teaching. *Exceptional Children* 54: 228–239.
5. Snider, Vicki. E. 1992. Learning styles and learning to read: A critique. *Remedial and Special Education* 13: 6–18.
6. Gardner, Howard. 1993. *Frames of mind: The theory of multiple intelligences.* New York: Basic Books.
7. For example, Carbo, Marie. 1997. Reading styles times twenty. *Educational Leadership* 54 (6): 38–42; Carbo, Marie, Rita Dunn, and Kenneth Dunn. 1986. *Teaching students to read through their individual learning styles.* Englewood Cliffs, N.J.: Prentice-Hall.
8. See Stahl, Steven A. 1988. Is there evidence to support matching reading styles and initial reading methods? A reply to Carbo. *Phi Delta Kappan* 70 (4): 317–322.
9. Radenich, Marguerite Cogorno. 1997. Separating the wheat from the chaff in middle school literature study guides. *Journal of Adolescent and Adult Literacy* 41 (1): 46–57.
10. All examples are from Carbo, Marie. 1995. *Reading Style Inventory Intermediate (RSI-I);* Author.
11. Carbo, M. 1988. Debunking the great phonics myth. *Phi Delta Kappan* 70: 226–240.
12. Stahl, Steven A., and Patricia D. Miller. 1989. Whole language and language experience approaches for beginning reading: A quantitative research synthesis. *Review of Educational Research* 59 (1): 87–116.
13. Harris, Albert J., and Edward Sipay. 1990. *How to increase reading ability.* 10th ed. White Plains, N.Y.: Longman.
14. Pittenger, David, J. 1993. The utility of the Myers-Briggs Type Indicator. *Review of Educational Research* 63: 467–488.
15. Stahl, Steven A. 1998. Understanding shifts in reading and its instruction, *Peabody Journal of Education* 73 (3–4): 31–67.
16. Morrow, Lesley M., and Diane Tracey. 1998. Motivating contexts for young children's literacy development: Implications for word recognition development. In *Word recognition in beginning literacy,* edited by J. Metsala and L. Ehri. Mahwah, N.J.: Erlbaum; Turner, Julianne, and Scott G. Paris. 1995. How literacy tasks influence children's motivation for literacy. *The Reading Teacher* 48: 662–673.
17. Stahl and Miller, op. cit., Stahl, Steven A., C. William Suttles, and Joan R. Pagnucco. 1996. The effects of traditional and process literacy instruction on first-graders' reading and writing achievement and orientation toward reading. *Journal of Educational Research.* 89: 131–144.

# What Constitutes "APPROPRIATE" PUNISHMENT?

*Although Americans insist that anti-social behavior must be controlled, they are ambivalent about methods to do so.*

## Paul L. DeVito and Ralph Hyatt

TAKE A FEW moments to test your philosophy of punishment. Read each of the following situations and write out your responses to the questions that follow them.

• Poverty-stricken teenagers Joey and Art had been dreaming about the rock concert for months, and now that it was in town they only could continue to dream, for they did not have the entrance fee. In desperation, Art sneaked into the kitchen and snatched several dollars from his mother's hiding place in the cupboard. That evening, Joey's father cracked him across the face and accused him of stealing the money. Art, his supposed friend, had lied to his parents and implicated Joey. Art's father complained to Joey's father about the felony. After Joey screamed out the truth, Joey's father angrily approached Art, grasped him around the throat, and quickly got a confession. Art was confined to his room for a week by his parents.

a) Did Joey deserve his whacking?
b) Should Art have been choked?
c) Were Art's parents too lenient?

• Pennsylvania has a unit called "super-max" in its maximum security prisons. This unit houses chronic troublemakers, who totally are segregated from the other inmates. They are given one hour daily of isolated exercise out of their small cells. Many have spent years in super-max.

a) Is it humane to isolate troublesome maximum security prisoners? For such long periods of time?
b) Is this program consistent with rehabilitation?
c) Does the death penalty make more sense?

• Autistic children, although often quite intelligent, do not develop in expected ways. They may be overly active, speech can be delayed, and they do not establish normal human attachments. Many gesture in strange ways and do not make good eye contact. At times, they can be destructive to themselves and others. Some professionals believe that physical restraint is necessary to get their attention as well as a means of helping them to release their pent-up anger. Aversion therapy, a group of methods for treating such individuals, includes paddling and mild electric shock. This mode of treatment also has been used with some success with drug addicts, sexual deviants, and people demonstrating extremely violent behavior.

*Dr. DeVito is chairman, Department of Psychology, Saint Joseph's University, Philadelphia, Pa. Dr. Hyatt, Psychology Editor of USA Today, is professor emeritus of psychology, Saint Joseph's University.*

a) Should aversion therapy be used as a form of treatment or banned by law?

b) How about physical restraint?

These situations and questions were given to a variety of people on an informal, non-scientific basis. It is safe to say that your particular response—or any of them—is included among those of the group. Respondents replied with a yes, no, and everything in-between to each question. Those at the extremes invariably qualified their answers if additional conditions were to exist. This should come as no surprise since those interviewees who were psychologists, attorneys, correctional employees, and school counselors also had no pat answers.

Recent events bear out the uncertainties people have about meting out punishment, some praying for mercy and forgiveness, others demanding justice—and often blood. Take the caning of Michael Fay, the 18-year-old American visiting Singapore, who was accused of spray-painting and tossing eggs at automobiles, among other acts of vandalism. Prior to his punishment of four cane strokes, which was "mercifully" reduced from six, American sentiment, as revealed by a series of polls, was pro-caning by a large majority. Even Fay's emotional denials of any wrong-doings other than removing some street signs did not soften their hearts.

Americans, it was hypothesized, had had it up to their eyeballs with teenage social irresponsibility, lack of respect, and gun toting crime. "He deserves it" and "He should have known better" generally expressed their exasperation. Yet, in his hometown in Ohio, 90 days of incarceration and a $750 fine would have taken care of the matter.

It is worth recalling that, in the 1960s, flogging was a form of legal punishment in Delaware. The whipping post still was being used there in 1952. American colonists brought with them and promulgated their array of European penalties—imprisonment, banishment, mutilation, branding, flogging, and execution—despite the forbiddance of "cruel and unusual punishment" in the Constitution!

Many who advocate the death penalty maintain that it could terminate concerns about too few prisons, the cost of incarceration, and the entire mess of rehabilitation and what that means. Yet, the fact is that the death penalty never has succeeded as a deterrent to heinous acts, nor have stiffer sentences.

"The increased severity of the penalties has not reduced crime, it has only increased the prison population," writes former Common Pleas Court judge Lois G. Forer in her book, *A Rage to Punish.* Her non-mandatory sentencing approach runs head-on into Pres. Clinton's "Three strikes and you're out" solution, which throws away the key after a felon's third violent crime. She argues that the crime rate "has

not risen materially since 1980 while the prison population and numbers of inmates on death row have soared." She believes in the full use of restitution, fines, education, and counseling. Prior to O.J. Simpson's trial, Americans were in disagreement regarding the appropriateness of the death penalty for him. This occurs in a society that presumes innocence unless proven guilty beyond reasonable doubt.

## Defining wrongdoing and setting penalties

There is little wonder that everyone has opinions about punishment. People are subjected to it from the moment they slide out of the womb into a new environment full of strange sounds, temperatures, and pressures. Painful feelings continue from that experience onward: delay in feeding when hungry, soaked diapers, restraint when dressed, scraped knees, sibling rivalry, etc. We are not sure an infant perceives these events as punishment (although "Why is all this happening to me?" may be going through his or her mind), but the concept develops quickly when something like a hot stove is touched: Do the wrong thing and a penalty (pain) follows. Confusion occurs, research has shown, when a penalty does not directly follow wrongdoing or follows it erratically.

The conceptual riddle begins when we try to define "wrong" and "penalty." Wrongdoing, in the first place, may be real or perceived. Someone may believe you did something wrong when, actually, you didn't. Or he or she may accuse you of wrongdoing just to do you in. Also, one can wrong people, property, and God.

Penalties are no less universally agreed upon. There are tongue-lashing, restriction of freedoms, and corporal and capital punishment, not to omit condemnation to hell of sinners. Depending on the occasion, and given a choice, the offender may rather have one form than the other. For example, a kid may prefer to have his rear end smacked in public than hear his mother scream, "Do it again and I'll tell everyone you're a bed-wetter!" Then there is the judgment of how little is little and how big is big. One person's "little" smack is another's "big" one. Is a judge's verdict of one to three years incarceration short or long? What quantity of penalty does a child's "big mouth" deserve? What type of penalty, if any, is suitable for an infant? For doing how much of what?

Insights do not become any less confusing by remembering Proverbs: 13-2: "He that spareth the rod hateth his own son." If one can assume that autistic behaviors such as inattention, aggression, and destructiveness can be improved or eradicated by the use of corporal punishment, should it be permissible? Suppose parents

strongly request such "teaching" or "therapeutic" procedures for their autistic child?

Psychologist B.F. Skinner, who condemned the overutilization of punishment, wrote about this issue: "If brief and harmless aversive stimuli, made precisely contingent over self-destructive behavior, suppress the behavior and leave the children free to develop in other ways, I believe it can be justified. When taken out of context, such stimuli may seem less than humane, but they are not to be distinguished from the much more painful stimuli sometimes needed in dentistry and various medical practices. To remain satisfied with punishment without exploring non-punitive alternations is the real mistake."

There is something about punishment that relates it to evil. Do wrong and you get punished; do right and you don't. Does that principle apply to God? Rabbi Harold Kushner's best-seller, *Why Bad Things Happen to Good People,* grapples with that question from a theological perspective. He argues that much of what happens to us—the good and the bad—occurs purely by chance. God does not manage our each and every action, punishing some and rewarding others.

Thomas Hobbes, the 17th-century philosopher, believed that humans are basically solitary, selfish, and practical. They accept socialization primarily to satisfy their needs for safety and protection; otherwise, they wantonly would murder, rape, and pillage. Given the condition of today's world—most prominently in Rwanda, Serbia, and Chechnya, to name a few trouble spots—one is hard put to wave away this negative view, which squarely places Homo sapiens among all other creatures in the universe. Naturalist Charles Darwin, in *Origin of the Species,* espoused the evolutionary theory that solidly links human emotions to lowly organisms.

Sigmund Freud's id theory postulates a self-seeking pleasure instinct in everyone. The superego, an internalized conscience which evolves from early parental scolding and spanking, continually battles the id in order to keep people socialized. Thus, evils lurk inside and outside of individuals, and must be tamed by punishment of some sort.

There are, of course, philosophies and research which deem that humans are basically good. Psychologists have found, for instance, that effective nurturing and love are products of healthy, well-adjusted individuals, not those who are bestial. Kind and helpful children are popular with their peers and self-confident, not isolated and fearful. However, few philosophers, if any, deny the potential malevolence in all people. The enduring question is: What are the most effective methods for socializing humans?

Skinner noted, "We have not yet discovered adequate non-punitive practices to replace the aversive part of our genetic endowment. For example, we are far from abandoning the use of force in international relations or in maintaining domestic order. People living closely together, and that includes teachers and students, therapists and clients, can seldom avoid all forms of punishment."

According to contemporary psychological theory, punishment is included under the domain of behavior modification. Psychologists define it as any procedure that reduces or suppresses an undesirable behavior. The behavior is *not* eradicated or forgotten—just not expressed as it was before. There are both positive and negative forms. "Positive punishment," popularly known as corporal punishment, is exemplified by a child receiving a hand slap after biting his mother's leg. "Negative punishment" is applied, for instance, when a teenager who receives a poor report card is grounded for three weeks. The U.S. criminal justice system largely is based on this form—that is, when one is guilty of some crime, punishment usually is a monetary fine or incarceration. Something painful is applied in positive punishment, whereas something attractive is taken away in negative punishment. Both can have the effect of suppressing an unwanted response.

The alternative is known as reinforcement, where the objective is to increase the likelihood of some desired behavior. As with punishment, there are positive and negative approaches. When Johnny mows the lawn and is told "What a great job!" that is positive reinforcement. He probably will be less resistant to mowing the lawn again. A classic example of negative reinforcement is nagging. When you nag so much that your spouse yields in order to shut you up, that is negative reinforcement. Skinner was a champion of positive reinforcement, and his students coined the phrase "Spare the rod, use behavior mod!"

Experimental studies of positive and negative punishment, with both human and animal subjects, unequivocally demonstrate the effectiveness of these procedures in eliminating unacceptable behaviors. A serious problem, though, is that, in addition to suppressing the behavior, negative punishment often produces undesirable side effects. In a 1953 study, hungry spider monkeys were trained to press a switch for food. Once this response was learned, the experimenters placed a snake in the monkeys' cage whenever they reached for food. This was certain punishment since monkeys are terrified of snakes. After a few such experiences, the monkeys completely stopped pressing the switch for food. However, numerous side effects soon became apparent, including disturbances in eating behavior (loss of 15–25% of body weight), sexual disorders, and a breakdown in social relationships. Most of the monkeys began to develop classic human neurotic and psychotic symptoms, including asthma, facial and muscular tics, and hallucinations.

Do you know a parent who has not experienced a temper tantrum from his or her child? To stop such shenanigans, children have been restricted to their rooms, had cold water thrown in their faces, been yelled at, slapped, ignored, and exposed to countless other "creative" remedies. In a newspaper column, pediatrician T. Berry Brazelton counseled: "Parents are likely to feel manipulated by this kind of behavior, but they miss the purpose of these episodes if they feel they must either eliminate them or punish the child for them. Tantrums are expressions of the child's inner struggle for self-control. It is up to the child to work it out—not the parent." What if the child is throwing hard metal toys against the dining room furniture, though? Or hitting the parents with a stick? Or kicking out the window in the kitchen door? Should he or she be allowed to "work it out"?

The last few decades have shown a rise of disobedience along with violence among children and adolescents. In their vernacular, they seem to be "losing it." Psychologists have become more sensitive to this acting out, and label it "loss of impulse control" when it becomes extreme. One way or another, anti-social behavior must be curbed.

Confusion about punishment reigns in part because of semantics. "Abuse" means unwarranted, inhuman punishment. Child sexual abuse probably has few dissenters in terms of definition, but that is not to say that differences of opinion do not exist. Unless there is a sadomasochistic relationship, spouse abuse also presents relatively few problems in definition. Prisoner abuse, no matter how severe, probably would elicit the fewest disagreements. Discipline, on the other hand, typically evokes multiple meanings and the greatest debates—even between parents.

Are physical restriction, isolation to a room, and being screamed at forms of punishment? Is the current popular technique of "time out," when a child must sit quietly in some corner of the room for an unspecified time, not to be considered punishment? Does anything change when the procedure is described as a lesson in listening? Suppose the child refuses to go into time out, what then? Is the prisoner in super-max being punished or disciplined?

A recent op-ed column in a large city newspaper espoused corporal punishment in the classroom because "using the rod early can help keep some youths from more serious trouble later." The writer continued: "Of course, people warped by the Benjamin Spock school hyperventilate at the slightest mention of paddling. They still believe the Socratic method can be applied to youthful Al Capones. The object lesson for kids is that as they approach adulthood, violation of others' property or property rights results in punishments much worse than minor taps on the tush."

Children should not grow up with a set of models—parents, teachers, etc.—who are abusive. There is absolutely no argument with that. It is known that the abused tend to become abusers, in turn. The major objective is never to hurt or uncontrollably release anger, but, rather, to curb unacceptable behavior and teach methods of altering it. Infants must *never* be given corporal punishment. Toddlers should be distracted by showing them attractive toys and objects or playing simple games, not slapped.

No matter what it is called—discipline or punishment—good judgment is required. By definition, however, judgment is an opinion, an estimate. It can not be measured or weighed with any scientific accuracy. The hope is· that judges, teachers, parents, and others in authority will have sufficient information and self-control to make judgments that are fair, proper, and good. Ordinarily, assessment of their judgments is made after the fact, often when it is too late to alter. Society's task is to make adequate provisions for the training and education of those who are given the responsibility to judge.

## Dispensing discipline effectively

Although the following guidelines denote parent-child relationships, the principles apply to all situations: employer-employee, correctional officer-inmate, teacher-student, etc.

• Accentuate the positives. Youngsters should learn behaviors that are acceptable, rather than constantly being told what to avoid. Example: Rather than "Stop yelling," say "Please use a quiet voice."

• Do not label your child. Eliminate name-calling and generalizations. Be specific. Behavior is undesirable, not people. Example: Rather than "You're a liar," say "If you do not tell the truth about going to the movies, your brother no longer will trust you."

• Discipline should follow the unacceptable behavior as closely as possible. *Each* spouse has equal responsibility for disciplining his or her child.

• Setting reasonable limits reflects your values and love. Limits provide the basis of your offspring's self-confidence throughout his or her lifetime.

• When setting limits, ask yourself the following questions:

a) Are they understood? Ask the youngster to state the limit and why it was set.

b) Are they appropriate in this situation?

c) Have too many been set lately?

d) Is the child confused by mixed messages, sometimes having a limit set for a particular misbehavior; at other times, not?

e) Are you ready to enforce a violation of the limit reasonably?

• Discipline is a learning process, never purely a coercive experience to prove your mastery and control.

# LOTS OF ACTION IN THE
# MEMORY GAME

New experiments are prompting scientists to rethink
their old ideas about how memories form—
and why the process sometimes falters

## By GEORGE JOHNSON

SCIENTISTS HAVE LONG BELIEVED that constructing memories is like playing with neurological Tinkertoys. Exposed to a barrage of sensations from the outside world, we snap together brain cells to form new patterns of electrical connections that stand for images, smells, touches and sounds.

The most unshakable part of this belief is that the neurons used to build these memory circuits are a depletable resource, like petroleum or gold. We are each bequeathed a finite number of cellular building blocks, and the supply gets smaller each year. That is certainly how it feels as memories blur with middle age and it gets harder and harder to learn new things. But like so many absolutes, this time-honored notion may have to be forgotten—or at least radically revised.

In the past year, a series of puzzling experiments has forced scientists to rethink this and other cherished assumptions about how memory works, reminding them how much they have to learn about one of the last great mysteries—how the brain keeps a record of our individual passage through life, allowing us to carry the past inside our head.

"The number of things we know now that we didn't know 10 years ago is not very large," laments Charles Stevens, a memory researcher at the Salk Institute in La Jolla, Calif. "In fact, in some ways we know less."

This much seems clear: the traces of memory—or engrams, as neuroscientists call them—are first forged deep inside the brain in an area called the hippocampus (after the Latin word for seahorse because of its arching shape). Acting as a kind of neurological scratch pad, the hippocampus stores the engrams temporarily until they are transferred somehow (perhaps during sleep) to permanent storage sites throughout the cerebral cortex. This area, located behind the forehead, is often described as the center of intelligence and perception. Here, as in the hippocampus, the information is thought to reside in the form of neurological scribbles, clusters of connected cells.

It has been considered almost gospel that these patterns are constructed from the supply of neurons that have been in place since birth. New memories, the story goes, don't require new neurons—just new ways of stringing the old ones together. Retrieving a memory is a matter of activating one of these circuits, coaxing the original stimulus back to life.

The picture appears eminently sensible. The billions of neurons in a single brain can be arranged in countless combinations, providing more than enough clusters to record even the richest life. If adult brains were cranking out new neurons as easily as skin and bone grow new cells, it would serve only to scramble memory's delicate filigree.

Studies with adult monkeys in the mid-1960s seemed to support the belief that the supply of neurons is fixed at birth. Hence the surprise when Elizabeth Gould and Charles Gross of Princeton University reported last year that the monkeys they studied seemed to be minting thousands of new neurons a day in the hippocampus of their brain. Even more jarring, Gould and Cross found evidence that a steady stream of the fresh cells may be continually migrating to the cerebral cortex.

No one is quite sure what to make of these findings. There had already been hints that spawning of brain cells, a process called neurogenesis, occurs in animals with more primitive nervous systems. For years, Fernando Nottebohm of Rockefeller University has been showing that canaries create a new batch of neurons every time they learn a song, then slough them off when it's time to change tunes.

But it was widely assumed that in mammals and especially primates (including the subset *Homo sapiens*), this wholesale manufacture of new brain parts had long ago been phased out by evolution. With a greater need

# CAPTURING MOMENTS...

MUSTARD OR KETCHUP? The memory of a Mark McGwire home run is likely to last longer than what you piled on your hot dog. Uncertain exactly how the brain creates and keeps memories, researchers do know it involves the hippocampus, which ultimately feeds memories to the cerebral cortex.

## Touch

The sun's heat activates sensory nerves, sending data to the cortex's **somato-sensory** area for processing

## Sound

The ear detects the roar of the crowd and relays it to the **primary auditory cortex** in the temporal lobe

## Sight

The eye encodes the image of McGwire as nerve impulses and sends them to the **primary visual cortex**

## Taste and Smell

Receptors in the nose pick up the flavor of the mustard and relay it to the **olfactory cortex**

# ...TO LAST A LIFETIME

## Immediate memory
### LESS THAN ONE MINUTE

Consisting of a brief flash of raw stimuli corresponding to the senses, it creates an image containing almost an exact replica of each stimulus. Unless transferred to short-term memory, however, the mental snapshot is quickly lost

## Short-term memory
### A FEW HOURS TO A WEEK

All the sensory information is then sent to the hippocampus where it is coordinated and organized. Over the next day, some parts of the snapshot begin to blur, while the more important details are moved to permanent storage

## Long-term memory
### PERMANENT

Some theorize that organization and repetition of the information cause it to be transferred and held in storage sites throughout the cerebral cortex. What is finally remembered is only a fraction of the original picture

---

to store memories for the long haul, these creatures would need to ensure that the engrams weren't disrupted by interloping new cells.

Not everyone found this argument convincing. (Surely birds had important things to remember too.) When neurogenesis was found to occur in people, the rationalizations began to take the tone of special pleading: there was no evidence that the new brain cells had anything to do with memory or that they did anything at all.

That may yet turn out to be the case with the neurons found by the Princeton lab. The mechanism Gould and her colleagues uncovered in macaque monkeys could be nothing more than a useless evolutionary leftover, a kind of neurological appendix. But if, as many suspect, the new neurons turn out to be actively involved with inscribing memories, the old paradigm is in for at least a minor tune-up—and maybe a complete overhaul.

It is telling that the spawning ground for the neurons is the hippocampus, which is indisputably crucial to memory. Patients with hippocampal injuries lose their ability to acquire new facts, though they can still recall impressions laid down in the years before the damage occurred. Maybe, Gould speculates, the newly generated hippocampal neurons are especially agile in forming connections with one another. As in the canaries, the new cells would readily join hands to encode a new memory. Then, when they were no longer needed, they would be flushed from the system, and the engram would be transferred elsewhere for safekeeping.

That explanation fits pretty well with the old theories. More puzzling, though, is

another of the study's findings: the steady migration of new neurons from the hippocampus to the cerebral cortex. Could these neurons be somehow involved in ferrying information into permanent storage—storing short-term memories for the long term?

Perhaps, Gould and her colleagues ventured in a recent paper, this purported transport mechanism provides a means of time-stamping memories, helping us keep track of when we learned what. Older memories would be somehow associated with older neurons. No one is even guessing how this might work. But if memories are indeed flowing through the brain in rivulets of new neurons, then all the old ideas will have to be reconsidered.

The brain is so complex and neuroscientific experiments are so difficult to interpret that this whole picture could change in a year. Whatever happens with neurogenesis, the fundamental notion that engrams are made by stringing together neurons—whether new ones or old ones or a combination of the two—is likely to survive in some form.

In the meantime, other laboratories are trying to refine their understanding of just how neurons forge these connections. Here, too, many long established assumptions don't seem so solid anymore.

For the past 20 years, neuroscientists have been piecing together a story in which the key to linking neurons is a kind of molecular switch called an NMDA receptor. (The letters stand for the polysyllabic name of a chemical used to identify these molecules in experiments.) The mechanism is thought to work like this: if one neuron repeatedly

sends signals to a second neuron, its NMDA receptors respond by unleashing a cascade of chemical reactions that strengthen the bond between the two cells. Just how this occurs remains a matter of almost religious debate. But somehow the "volume" of the connection is turned up. In some cases, entirely new connections may be formed.

It has been known for years that mice whose NMDA receptors have been chemically blocked have trouble learning their way around a maze. In the most dramatic demonstration of the power of the idea, Joseph Tsien, another Princeton researcher, developed a genetically engineered breed of "smart mice" with souped-up NMDA receptors and showed that the rodents had enhanced powers of memory.

But just as the pieces were starting to fall together, Tsien's lab did another experiment that complicated matters. Mice were bred with no NMDA receptors in a region of the hippocampus known to be especially crucial to memory. As expected, these mice showed seriously diminished memory power. But when they were exposed to a stimulating environment full of toys and exercise wheels, they got their memory back. When the scientists examined the mice's hippocampal tissue with an electron microscope, they found that new neural connections had been formed without the aid of the seemingly crucial NMDA memory switches. "That was really surprising," Tsien says.

There are a couple of plausible explanations. Neurons in the hippocampus might be making new connections using some entirely different means that has escaped researchers' attention. Or the connections normally forged in the hippocampus were being formed instead in the cortex, where the mice's NMDA receptors remained intact. Brains are so amazingly resilient that it's common for functions lost in one area to be taken over by another. In any case, the neat lines of the old picture have been fuzzed up again.

Zeroing in on the mechanism of imprinting engrams and determining whether or not neurogenesis is involved will be just the first steps in a long progression toward understanding how we remember. If memories are indeed stored as configurations of connected cells, then what do these patterns look like? How many neurons does it take to represent the image of your pet cat, and how is that pattern connected to the patterns that represent the abstract categories of cats, pets, mammals and living things?

And when you read a book, how are the neurons stitched together to record the memorable passages? How are they filed so you know the memory came from a book and not from your own experience? And while you are scanning the pages, how do you call up the patterns that represent the definitions of the words and their sounds, and the rules for unpacking meaning from a sentence?

A half-century ago, the neuroscientist Karl Lashley wrote a paper called "In Search of the Engram," describing his frustrating attempt to find the cluster of neurons in which a rat stored its memory of a maze. After training the animal to negotiate the labyrinth, he snipped away at the brain bit by bit. While the animal became increasingly sluggish and confused, Lashley was never able to find a single location where the memory was inscribed. "I sometimes feel," Lashley ruefully wrote, "that the necessary conclusion is that learning just is not possible."

Fifty years later, memory researchers find themselves with the same mix of confusion and awe. But for all their puzzlement, they hold out hope that experiment by experiment, they are deepening their knowledge of how memory works—and inching toward a day when they can repair it when it falters.

---

*George Johnson, a New York Times writer, is the author of* In the Palaces of Memory. *His most recent book is* Strange Beauty: Murray Gell-Mann and the Revolution in 20th-Century Physics

---

**TELLTALE SIGNALS**

# When to Start Fretting About Forgetfulness

You forget where you put your keys, often misplace your glasses and certainly can't remember names as well as you used to. At bedtime, you stare haplessly into the bathroom mirror, wondering whether you've already brushed your teeth. Once you showed up for a dinner date at the wrong restaurant. What's happening? Should you regard these lapses as a sign of more serious memory problems, maybe even Alzheimer's?

Forget it. Mental slips like these are a normal part of midlife. Even teenagers, capable of reeling off entire CDs of rock lyrics, occasionally blank out—though one might be suspicious of instances involving chores requested by parents or teachers. Unless your forgetfulness is accompanied by deeper failures in reasoning and logic, it's nothing to fret about. After all, if being absentminded were a sign of mental disar-

ray, you'd have to write off Einstein, who bungled simple arithmetic even while working on relativity.

You *should* feel concern if memory loss becomes a consistent pattern—forgetting what you've just said or done, repeatedly missing appointments, telling old jokes again and again or unwittingly making phone calls to the same people about the same subjects. Or if these flubs are followed by changes in behavior, such as irritability, depression or irrational suspicions (your house has been broken into, your spouse is cheating on you, people are out to get you).

Even then, don't jump to hasty conclusions. In middle age, many things can cause memory loss or mental fuzziness, to say nothing of confused thinking—menopause, for example, whose effects can be eased with estrogen-replacement therapy. Also, keep in mind (remember?)

that age takes a very normal toll on what psychologists call processing speed—the rapidity with which you can summon up the names of people and places. Our brains, in any case, have evolved with a certain built-in forgetfulness, lest they become hopelessly cluttered with useless information.

In older people too, memory problems may be the result of poor diet, vitamin deficiencies or glandular imbalances (all reversible with treatment) rather than the classic types of dementia associated with old age. Even if a physician ultimately diagnoses Alzheimer's disease—which is done by eliminating other possibilities rather than by a direct test, because none is available other than a brain biopsy—the news needn't be as bleak as it once might have seemed.

The mind-robbing disease is still incurable, and the

drugs that are currently available only ease certain symptoms like anxiety, confusion and insomnia or slightly slow down its relentless progression. Still, Alzheimer's assault on the brain varies enormously from person to person. Even five or 10 years after a diagnosis, some people have only modest memory loss while retaining old skills like the ability to play golf or sail a boat—or, for that matter to recall long-ago happenings. Alzheimer's, moreover, is one of the hottest areas of scientific research. Already scientists have identified some of the genes involved in the growth of the nerve-cell-killing plaques in the brain that are widely suspected to be at the root of the disease. These discoveries make it quite likely that we'll start seeing the first effective therapies for Alzheimer's in the next few years. —*By Frederic Golden*

## THE MIND

# SPEAK, MEMORY

## As we age, remembering often is harder work than it once was. Here are some ways to improve your sense of recall

By EMILY MITCHELL

MEMORY MAKES US WHO WE ARE. And because it is our identity, we worry about it, fretting if we can't remember the name of someone we just met—or know well—getting upset when we can't recall where we put our keys or left the car in the parking lot or whether we mailed the phone bill. We walk into a room and halt in midstride, the purpose forgotten. These annoying things happen to most of us eventually, and for a simple reason. Just as the body changes over time, so does the brain. "On any intelligence or memory test," says University of Chicago gerontologist Michael Roizen, "we lose, on average, 5% of our capability for every decade after 30."

As scientists discover more about the mysterious workings of the brain, it is encouraging to learn that many age-related changes can be slowed, including the decline of memory. The first step is to understand how memory works. Our head doesn't have a separate, identifiable system for remembering. A single memory is made of tiny pieces of information accumulated and stored over time. Those bits are held in a complex network of some 100 billion neurons, or nerve cells, that can make thousands of connections with other cells in the brain. Subsystems within the cortex handle specific things like names, sounds, textures, faces and smells. Say the word dog, and the busy brain fires up a host of images, sensory impressions and emotions, then reconstructs a specific, unique memory.

The connections between neurons—the synapses—are formed on branchlike structures called dendrites. In a normal, healthy person, these can gradually shrink over time, slowing the process of recalling information and leading to those familiar lapses called "senior moments." Memory gridlock is both-ersome, but, says Johns Hopkins neurologist Barry Gordon, "what most people complain about is not that serious at all. They're probably not going to get Alzheimer's; they just care more about forgetfulness as they get older."

## ATTENTION MUST BE PAID

When adults concerned about their memory come to the Pisgah Institute for Psychiatry and Education in Asheville, N.C., psychologist Ed Hamlin gives them standard tests for visual and verbal memory, delayed recall and delay in attention and concentration. For most, the results are reassuring: their memory is not only good, it exceeds the average for their age.

But what about those times when they experience a total blank? Says Hamlin: "A number of problems are not problems with memory at all. They are really problems with your attention." There are three basic steps in memory: registration, retention and retrieval. They occur sequentially; if new information isn't taken in (registered), it can't be stored. Focusing on incoming material, whether heard, seen or read, helps implant it in memory. Psychologist Cynthia Green advises students in her memory classes at New York City's Mount Sinai Medical Center that "often what we think we forgot we really didn't 'get' in the beginning."

Sorting and storing the multitude of information available in the modern world takes work. Just look at a teenager listening to music and chatting on a cell phone while simultaneously tapping out commands on a computer. For many older men and women, such sensory overload makes focusing more difficult. Eliminating unnecessary sounds and other distractions, experts suggest, makes it easier to concentrate on exactly what you want to remember.

> "Anything that uses all your senses to do something forms associations that make the brain more fit and agile."
>
> —Lawrence Katz

Attention can be reinforced by repeating new information or making associations to link it to other memories. When introduced to someone new, for example, repeat the person's name, ask how it's spelled or make some other comment that will help fix it in your mind. Professor Arthur Wingfield, director of Brandeis University's Memory and Cognition Laboratory, explains: "What you are trying to do is get yourself to pay attention and encode it. Younger people can do this faster; older people have to work harder."

From *Time*, February 28, 2000, pp. G1-G3. © 2000 by Time Inc. Reprinted by permission.

## THE HARDER YOU TRY

If there's a golden rule for remembering, it's this: the best way is not to try. In a memory-enhancement course Hamlin teaches at the University of North Carolina's College for Seniors, he emphasizes that when something previously known is truly forgotten, the struggle to recall it defeats the purpose. "Anxiety about your memory," he maintains, "is actually harming it." People sometimes stew for hours trying to dredge up the name of a movie star from a past era. It seems right on the tip of the tongue. The face floats up before the eyes, co-stars' names and titles of past movies spring to mind, but the name, ah, remains elusive until you awake in the middle of the night, saying "Mona Freeman" or "Louis Jourdan" with satisfaction.

Why this frustrating delay? In the view of some scientists, the brain is working on recall, but the other names are interfering. Don't try to think about the names that are blocking it. Brandeis' Wingfield says, "They will dissipate, and you will be able to retrieve it." Or divert the mind by thinking about something else, and the name will frequently pop up.

Older people simply have more to remember. Says Professor Albert Rizzo of the University of Southern California's School of Gerontology: "After you have lived a rich, full life, you have a larger amount of 'books' in your brain, thousands of them, as opposed to the hundred when you were younger. You have to sift through more, like a librarian." Re-creating the original stimulus can often prompt recall. If the reason for entering a room seems to have temporarily vanished, retrace your footsteps. Rizzo explains, "This re-energizes the brain and brings it back to where you were 'mentally' beforehand, and—bong!—you remember."

## GET SHARP WITH STRATEGIES

One key to sharpening memory skills, Rizzo tells students in his eight-week memory seminars, is to become "your own personal scientist." You have to figure out where the fault lines are and then apply various strategies and techniques. Organization won't necessarily improve memory, but it will help reduce the number of things you have to remember. Deciding on a specific place for everyday items is a good way to avoid having to play hide-and-seek with them. Making lists, keeping track of appointments in a calendar or daily diary or using sticky notes as quick reminders help free the mind.

Billie Stewart, 64, of Asheville keeps a sticky pad in her car, and when she thinks of an errand that needs to be done, she jots it down. "If I write down bakery," she says, "I can let go of it and don't have to clog up my memory." Written reminders aren't cheat-

ing. Far from it. They make it easier for the brain to handle a larger quantity of information. Technology gives us an increasing number of things to remember—PIN numbers, passwords, all those pesky dotcom names—but at the same time provides excellent aids to jog the memory. Some people leave daily reminders on their own answering machines or send themselves e-mail messages.

Try memorizing the country code, city code and phone number for someone outside the U.S. as one string of digits and see how difficult it is. Breaking unwieldy pieces of information into smaller pieces makes them easier to remember. The process is called "chunking," and that's why we can remember Social Security and telephone numbers. Large unbroken sets of numbers, such as driver's licenses, can be artificially divided into chunks for easier recall. "Clustering" is another effective technique. Seven, according to experts, is the magic number for short-term, or working, memory. That's roughly how many things we can consciously hold in the mind at one time. But we can trick it into holding more by inventing seven or so main categories and then grouping several things under each.

## WAKE UP, BRAIN!

Until a few years ago, it was thought that everyone was born with a finite number of brain cells. Then in the 1990s—designated by Congress as the Decade of the Brain—scientists raised the possibility that the miraculous organ inside our head is capable of creating new cells. Just as important, they

found it can grow additional dendrites, those spiky branches on each cell that help communication with other cells.

The brain never stops learning, and forcing it to absorb new information or figure out a different way of doing a routine task stimulates it to make new dendritic connections that help offset some of the normal, age-related loss. The brain is essentially lazy, and when asked to do something over and over, it invariably finds the easiest way. Doing things differently challenges the brain. Brush your teeth with the nondominant hand or take a shower with your eyes closed, and suddenly you're not on automatic pilot.

The more robust the brain, the better the chance that memory can be improved. Says Duke University neurobiologist Lawrence Katz: "Anything that uses all your senses to do something forms associations that make the brain more fit and agile." Katz and co-author Manning Rubin came up with 83 "neurobic" exercises for their book *Keep Your Brain Alive*. Sample different food, they suggest, reposition your furniture, travel by a different route, learn a language—try anything that will alter the brain's neural pathways. Certain activities, like gardening and fishing, are beneficial because they involve so many senses. Your lifestyle shapes how your brain will be as you get older.

Everyday life can excel as a brain gym where you are your own personal trainer. At 72, Harold Gallay of Clearwater, Fla., has a memory as keen as that of a man half his age, rattling off sports statistics and regularly besting his four grown children at Trivial Pursuit. For years, he and his wife Leona, 71, have played bridge, done daily crossword puzzles, read newspapers cover to cover and discussed current news.

## VALUE THE MATURE MIND

Though everyone hopes for a long life, most fear old age and the decline of body and brain. "The mind does change," says Hamlin, "but it is not inferior. It is different." Each of us needs to appreciate our mind as it is instead of as it once was. Teens who can talk, listen to music and surf the Web at the same time are admirably adept at taking in many bits of information, but they may not connect them in meaningful ways. Speed, after all, isn't everything. Though less swift, the older person continues to absorb new material, comparing it with knowledge and insights gleaned over a lifetime. The process becomes less reflexive and more reflective. And the word for that is wisdom.

**—With reporting by Dee Gill/St. Petersburg, Erik Gunn/Chicago, Anne Moffett/Washington, Adrianne Navon/New York and Jacqueline Savaiano/Los Angeles**

## Unit Selections

## Key Points to Consider

❖ Why study cognition? Why study the development of cognitive abilities; why would this be of interest to psychologists? What exact role does the brain play in cognitive abilities, for example language processing? What role does experience play in cognitive development? Does culture play a role in cognition? How so? What aspects of culture most influence how we process incoming information about our world?

❖ What is intelligence? Are learning and thinking central to our concepts of intelligence? How so? How can we improve intelligence, at least according to research on mice? Why would we want to improve intelligence? Do you have any ethical concerns about genetically tampering with intelligence levels?

❖ What are the various types of intelligence described by Howard Gardner? Why, then, is traditional IQ testing controversial? Can you think of people whom you would call "bright" by standards other than the traditional definitions of intelligence? What are some of the myths (and are they true) surrounding the theory of multiple intelligences? How can intelligence be enhanced by education? Should the concept of intelligence spread beyond the area of cognition?

❖ Do you believe that animals can think? Can you offer anecdotal evidence? Can you offer scientific evidence? If animals think, how is their thinking similar to that of humans? How is it different?

 **Links**   **www.dushkin.com/online/**

These sites are annotated on pages 4 and 5.

As Rashad watches his 4-month old, he is convinced that the baby possesses a degree of understanding of the world around her. In fact, Rashad is sure he has one of the smartest babies in the neighborhood. Although he is indeed a proud father, he keeps these thoughts to himself so as not to alienate his neighbors whom he perceives as having less intelligent babies.

Jack lives in the same neighborhood as Rashad. However, Jack doesn't have any children, but he does own two fox terriers. Despite Jack's most concerted efforts, the dogs never come to him when he calls them. In fact, the dogs have been known to run the opposite way on occasion. Instead of being furious, Jack accepts his dogs' disobedience because he is sure the dogs are just dumb beasts and don't know any better.

Both of these vignettes illustrate important and interesting ideas about cognition or thought processes. In the first vignette, Rashad ascribes cognitive abilities and high intelligence to his child; in fact, Rashad perhaps ascribes too much cognitive ability to his 4-month old. On the other hand, Jack assumes that his dogs are incapable of thought, more specifically, incapable of premeditated disobedience, and therefore he forgives them.

Few adults would deny the existence of their cognitive abilities. Some adults, in fact, think about thinking, something which psychologists call metacognition. Cognition is critical to our survival as adults. But are there differences in mentation in adults? And what about other organisms? Can young children—infants for example—think? If they can, do they think like adults? And what about animals; can they think and solve problems? These and other questions are related to cognitive psychology and cognitive science, which is showcased in this unit.

Cognitive psychology has grown faster than most other specialties in psychology in the past 20 years. Much of this has occurred in response to new computer technology as well as to the growth of psycholinguistics. Computer technology has prompted an interest in artificial intelligence, the mimicking of human intelligence by machines. Similarly the study of psycholinguistics has prompted the examination of the influence of language on thought and vice versa.

While interest in these two developments has eclipsed interest in more traditional areas of cognition such as intelligence, we cannot ignore these traditional areas in this anthology. With regard to intelligence, one persistent problem has been the difficulty of defining just what intelligence is. David Wechsler, author of several of the most popular intelligence tests in current clinical use, defines intelligence as the global capacity of the individual to act purposefully, to think rationally, and to deal effectively with the environment. Other psychologists have proposed more complex definitions. The definitional problem arises when we try to develop tests that validly and reliably measure such concepts. Edward Boring once suggested that we define intelligence as whatever it is that an intelligence test measures.

The first article in this unit offers the reader an introduction to the complex relationship between cognition and genetics. Specifically, this article describes research with mice who have been genetically altered to make them more intelligent. This enhanced intelligence improves the learning and memory abilities of the altered mice. The author claims that research along this line may well help us find treatments for genetic memory disorders.

The discussion of intelligence continues in the next article, which takes a new and broader approach to intelligence. Howard Gardner writes about his theory of multiple intelligences. Gardner suggests that the traditional definition of intelligence is too narrow and should be expanded to include other measures. Gardner is highly critical, however, about the misuse of his theory and the attempts to expand the concept of intelligence too far.

The final article in the unit asks whether animals can think. The conclusion of the research that is alluded to is, yes, animals can think, but their thought processes certainly are not as rich or as complex as those of humans. Vivid examples are provided.

Cognitive Processes

# SMART GENES?

## A new study sheds light on HOW MEMORY WORKS and raises questions about whether we should use genetics to make people brainier

**BY MICHAEL D. LEMONICK**

THE SMALL, BROWN, FURRY CREAture inside a cage in Princeton University's molecular-biology department looks for all the world like an ordinary mouse. It sniffs around, climbs the bars, burrows into wood shavings on the floor, eats, eliminates, sleeps. But put the animal through its paces in a testing lab, and it quickly becomes evident that this mouse is anything but ordinary. One after another, it knocks off a variety of tasks designed to test a rodent's mental capacities—and almost invariably learns more quickly, remembers what it learns for a longer time and adapts to changes in its environment more flexibly than a normal mouse.

This is a supermouse, no doubt about it, though it didn't get its better brain by coming from another world. It was engineered by scientists at Princeton, M.I.T. and Washington University, who cleverly altered its DNA—or, more precisely, that of its genetic forebears—in ways that changed the reactions between neurons deep within its tiny cranium. The result, say its creators, is a strain of mouse (which they nicknamed "Doogie," after the precocious lead character of the old TV show *Doogie Howser, M.D.*) that is smarter than his dim-witted cousins. Not only that, the scientists wrote in last week's issue of the journal *Nature,* "our results suggest that the genetic enhancement of mental and cognitive attributes such as intelligence and memory in mammals is feasible."

Their audacious use of the *I* word triggered an avalanche of criticism from many of their colleagues, who called their conclusions unwarranted and farfetched. And it's easy to understand why. The idea that intelligence is rooted in the genes has long been an inflammatory notion—witness the charges of racism put to Richard Herrnstein and Charles Murray, authors of *The Bell Curve,* their controversial study of IQ and race. Beyond that, the very concept of intelligence is slippery. It involves many qualities—some of them elusive, like creativity, others more clear-cut like the ability to solve problems. "This is a very important study," says Eric Kandel, of the Howard Hughes Medical Institute at Columbia University, but he goes on to sound a polite note of caution. "Intelligence involves many genes, many features," he adds. "There are many things that go into it."

Yet even if Doogie isn't the Einstein of the order Rodentia, as some headline writers have portrayed him, most psychologists and neurobiologists are convinced that its memory and learning ability have indeed been enhanced. That has important implications. It suggests that even though the gulf between mice and men is continent-wide, this sort of research may eventually lead to practical medical results for humans, such as therapies to treat learning and memory disorders, including Alzheimer's disease, a condition likely to afflict more and more people in an increasingly aging population. In fact, the Princeton scientists are talking to drug companies about commercializing their work.

And the research inevitably raises the possibility that healthy people will try to boost their performance or, even more likely, that of their children—a prospect that has bioethicists ruminating feverishly.

Therapeutic promise is only one key implication of the new research. More immediate, and for now more important, is that the work gives neurobiologists further evidence about what memory is and how it works—a mystery whose secrets have been slowly unfolding for decades.

One thing has become clear to scientists: memory is absolutely crucial to our consciousness. Says Janellen Huttenlocher, a professor of psychology at the University of Chicago: "There's almost nothing you do, from perception to thinking, that doesn't draw continuously on your memory."

It can't be otherwise, since there's really no such thing as the present. As you read

# THE I.Q. GENE?
# HOW BUILDING A BETTER MOUSE COULD POTENTIALLY BENEFIT PEOPLE

## Adding more of a single gene...

The gene NR2B helps build a protein called NMDA, which acts as a receptor for specific chemical signals. These chemical signals train brain cells to fire in repeating patterns; the patterns are what we experience as memories

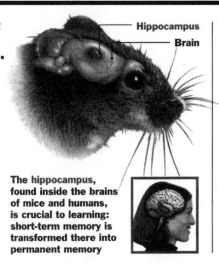

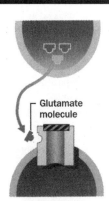

The hippocampus, found inside the brains of mice and humans, is crucial to learning: short-term memory is transformed there into permanent memory

## ...opens lots of tiny gates...

The NR2B part of NMDA receptors is plentiful in the hippocampus of young mice but drops off drastically after sexual maturity. Scientists believe that by genetically boosting NR2B in adults, they can give mature animals the learning skills of youngsters

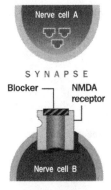

**1 Without two independent signals, the NMDA receptor remains blocked**

**2 One signal is a glutamate molecule, released by a neighboring cell**

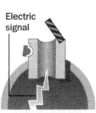

**3 The other is a change in electric potential, triggered within the cell**

**4 Unblocked by the signals, calcium flows in, helping to form a memory**

## ...that make mice "smarter"...

Genetically altered mice consistently outperformed control mice in six tests of learning and memory; their brain cells also showed increased sensitivity to new stimuli

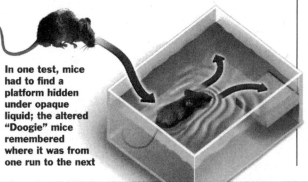

**In one test, mice had to find a platform hidden under opaque liquid; the altered "Doogie" mice remembered where it was from one run to the next**

## ...and may help humans someday

While no one is yet proposing to alter the human NR2B gene, scientists are studying the idea of creating drugs to boost its activity. That could mean new therapies for learning disabilities and memory problems, perhaps even helping Alzheimer's patients

TIME Graphic by Ed Gabel and Joe Zeff

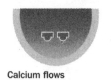

this sentence, the sentence that went before is already a second or two in the past; the first line of this story went by minutes ago. Yet without a memory of what's been said, none of what you are now reading makes the slightest sense. The same is true for our lives as a whole. Memory provides personal context, a sense of self and a sense of familiarity with people and surroundings, a past and present and a frame for the future.

But even as psychologists and brain researchers have learned to appreciate memory's central role in our mental lives, they have come to realize that memory is not a single phenomenon. "We do not have a

memory system in the brain," says James McGaugh, director of the Center for the Neurobiology of Learning and Memory at the University of California, Irvine. "We have memory *systems,* each playing a different role."

When everything is going right, these different systems work together seamlessly. If you're taking a bicycle ride, for example, the memory of how to operate the bike comes from one set of neurons; the memory of how to get from here to the other side of town comes from another; the nervous feeling you have left over from taking a bad spill last time out comes from still another. Yet you

are never aware that your mental experience has been assembled, bit by bit, like some invisible edifice inside your brain.

And brain researchers might never have picked up on the fragmentary nature of memory without their studies of people whose memory has been damaged by illness or injury. The most celebrated such individual is H.M. In 1953, when he was 27, he had drastic brain surgery to cure severe epilepsy. The operation cured his epilepsy, but removing parts of his brain's temporal lobes, including a structure called the hippocampus, destroyed his ability to form new memories. H.M., who is still alive, has a reasonably good short-term memory. Once introduced to a visitor, he will remember the person's name and other information while a conversation lasts. But if the visitor leaves and returns, H.M. has no memory whatsoever of having met the person. In fact, H.M. has no permanent memory of anything that happened after his surgery. As far as he's concerned, it's still 1953, and that old man looking back at him from the mirror bears only a passing resemblance to the young man he knows himself to be.

That sort of impairment has convinced scientists that the medial temporal lobe and hippocampus are key in transforming short-term memories into permanent ones, and also that permanent memories are stored somewhere else; otherwise, H.M. would have lost them too.

But a remarkable experiment performed in 1962 by Canadian psychologist Brenda Milner proved that H.M. *can* form new memories of a very specific sort. For many days running, she asked him to trace a design while looking in a mirror. As far as H.M. knew, the task was a brand-new one each time he confronted it. Yet as the days wore on, his performance improved. Some part of his brain was retaining a memory of an earlier practice session, a so-called implicit—rather than explicit, or consciously remembered—memory. People who suffer from Alzheimer's disease exhibit the same sort of behavior—and it's the medial temporal lobe that is first affected by this devastating disease.

In patients with Huntington's disease, it's the part of the brain called the basal ganglia that's destroyed. While these victims have perfectly intact explicit memory systems, they can't learn new motor skills. An Alzheimer's patient can learn to draw in a mirror but can't remember doing it; a Huntington's patient can't do it but can remember trying to learn. Yet another region of the brain, an almond-size knot of neural tissue known as the amygdala, seems to be crucial in forming and triggering the recall of a special subclass of memories that is tied to strong emotion, especially fear. The hippocampus allows us to remember having been afraid; the amygdala evidently calls up the goosebumps that go along with each such memory.

These are just some of the major divisions. Within the category of implicit (a.k.a. nondeclarative) memory, for example, lie the subcategories of associative memory—the phenomenon that famously led Pavlov's dogs to salivate at the sound of a bell, which they had learned to associate with food—and of habituation, in which we unconsciously file away unchanging features of the environment so we can pay closer attention to what's new and different upon encountering a new experience.

Within explicit, or declarative, memory, on the other hand, there are specific subsystems that handle shapes, textures, sounds,

faces, names—even distinct systems to remember nouns vs. verbs. All of these different types of memory are ultimately stored in the brain's cortex, within its deeply furrowed outer layer—a component of the brain dauntingly more complex than comparable parts in lesser species. Experts in brain imaging are only beginning to understand what goes where, and how the parts are reassembled into a coherent whole.

WHAT SEEMS TO BE A SINgle memory is actually a complex construction. Think of a hammer, and your brain hurriedly retrieves the tool's name, its appearance, its function, its heft and the sound of its clang, each extracted from a different region of the brain. Fail to connect a person's name with his or her face, and you experience the breakdown of that assembly process that many of us begin to experience in our 20s—and that becomes downright worrisome when we reach our 50s.

It was this weakening of memory and the parallel loss of ability to learn new things easily that led Princeton molecular biologist Joe Tsien to the experiments reported last week. "This age-dependent loss of function," he says, "appears in many animals, and it begins with the onset of sexual maturity."

What's happening when the brain forms memories—and what fails with aging, injury and disease—involves a phenomenon known as "plasticity." It's obvious that something in the brain changes as we learn and remember new things, but it's equally obvious that the organ doesn't change its overall structure or grow new nerve cells wholesale. Instead, it's the connections between new cells—and particularly the strength of these connections—that are altered by experience. Hear a word over and over, and the repeated firing of certain cells in a certain order makes it easier to repeat the firing pattern later on. It is the pattern that represents each specific memory.

How this reinforcement happens was a puzzle for much of this century, until 1949, when Canadian psychologist Donald Hebb came up with a related notion: since most memories consist of a group of disparate elements coming together—the hammer again—something more must be happening than just an electrical signal in one brain cell setting off a response in another. Something in the brain must be acting as a "coincidence detector," taking biochemical note that two nerve cells are firing simultaneously and coordinating two different sets of information.

Over the past decade or so, neurophysiologists have been focusing in on a particular molecule they believe could well be at least one version of Hebb's coincidence detector. Called N-methyl D-aspartate, or NMDA, this substance sits at the ends of the dendrites, the branchlike projections that protrude from nerve and brain cells, waiting

to respond to incoming signals. Like other receptor molecules, NMDA reacts to a chemical cue—in the case of learning and memory formation, glutamate—emitted by the axon from a neighboring cell.

But unlike other receptors, NMDA doesn't find this signal sufficient. It must also receive an electrical discharge from its own cell. Only when both cells are talking at once does the NMDA receptor turn on. It then permits calcium ions to flow into the host cell, which somehow—no one knows the details yet—makes the cell easier to turn on next time around. This phenomenon, known as long-term potentiation, is believed to be the essence of one type of memory formation.

NMDA's role in learning and memory isn't just theoretical. It has been known for years that blocking NMDA receptors with drugs, or knocking them out completely at the genetic level, makes animals learning-disabled, even amnesiac. Administering drugs that stimulate the receptor, conversely, tends to improve memory.

Tsien and his team took the next logical step. "A decade ago," says Stanford neuropsychiatrist Dr. Robert Malenka, "if you had asked, Would it be possible to manipulate a higher cognitive function like learning and memory by changing a single molecule? most scientists would have looked at you as if you were crazy."

Yet that's just what Tsien & Co. did, focusing not just on the NMDA receptor but on a particular component of it. Called NR2B, it's very active in young animals (which happen to be good at learning), less active in adults (who aren't), and is found mostly in the forebrain and hippocampus (where explicit, long-term memories are formed). The researchers spliced the gene that creates NR2B into the DNA of ordinary mouse embryos to create the strain they called Doogie. Then they ran the mice through a series of standardized tests—sort of a rodent SAT. In one, the mice were given a paw shock while in a box; after a few rounds, they showed signs of fear from just being in the box, having learned that a shock was likely to follow. They learned in similar fashion to be afraid when a bell sounded—a variation on Pavlov's dog experiments. In each case, the Doogies learned faster than normal mice. The same happened with a novel-object test: after becoming familiar with two plastic toys, the Doogies would show special interest when one was replaced; normal mice tended to be equally curious about a familiar object and a new one.

The altered mice grow up looking and acting just like ordinary mice, with no evidence of seizures or convulsions, according to Tsien. That's critical. The NMDA receptor shows up throughout the brain, and though calcium is crucial to learning and memory, too much of it can lead to cell death. That's what happens during a stroke: when brain cells are deprived of oxygen, they release huge amounts of glutamate, which over-stimulates nearby NMDA receptors and kills their host cells. Nature may have designed NR2B-based receptors to taper off in adult brains for a reason. Some scientists fear that the altered mice may be prone to strokes. "You might worry about what happens when these animals get old," says neuroscientist Larry Squire of the University of California, San Diego.

Premature cell death isn't the only possible complication. Stanford's Robert Malenka has shown that the NMDA receptor is involved in sensitizing the brain to drugs like cocaine, heroin and amphetamines, and others are investigating its role in triggering chronic pain—two more indications that it may not be wise to try to fool Mother Nature.

It will be a while before such dangers arise, though, and—as cancer researchers have discovered all too often—it isn't even certain that what works in mice will work in people. Tsien and his colleagues believe it's not unreasonable to think it will. "The NMDA receptor in humans is nearly identical to the receptor in mice, rats, cats and other

animals," he says. "We believe it's highly likely that it plays a similar role in humans."

Even so, Tsien has no plan to try tinkering with human genes—nor could he under current ethical guidelines. Drugs that can boost the action of the NR2B molecule, however, are not only ethical but already being contemplated. "Princeton has applied for a use patent for this gene," says Tsien, acknowledging his contacts with drugmakers, "although we wouldn't try to patent the gene itself."

There remains the nagging question of what it means precisely to say that Tsien & Co. have created a smarter mouse. "What is it that is being tested?" asks Gerald Fischbach, director of the National Institute of Neurological Disorders and Stroke. "That's the problem with mouse behavior. It's not clear that we're talking about the same thing when we talk about learning in a rodent and learning in a human."

Tsien concedes that using the emotive word intelligence in the paper was sure to generate controversy. "We really don't mean to suggest," he explains, "that human intelligence is the same as animal intelligence.

But I would argue that problem solving is clearly part of intelligence, and learning and memory are crucial to problem solving. And these mice are better learners, with better memories, than other mice."

But Tsien doesn't claim that he and his colleagues have found the unique genetic key to intelligence or even to memory. "It's likely that brain plasticity involves many molecules," he says. "This is just one of them." On the other hand, he asserts—and his critics would not disagree—that "intelligence *does* arise out of biology, at least in part." How much remains the great question. Whatever the answer, little Doogie surely represents an important step in unraveling what role our genes play in constructing not just memory but all the other attributes of the human mind. And clearly he won't be the last.

*—With reporting by David Bjerklie and Alice Park/New York, J. Madeleine Nash/ Chicago and Dick Thompson/Washington*

# Who Owns Intelligence?

## by HOWARD GARDNER

Three unresolved issues will dominate the discussion of intelligence:
whether intelligence is one thing or many things; whether intelligence is inherited;
and whether any of its elements can accurately be measured. The debate,
a prominent psychologist argues, is really over proprietary
rights to a fundamental concept of our age

ALMOST a century ago Alfred Binet, a gifted psychologist, was asked by the French Ministry of Education to help determine who would experience difficulty in school. Given the influx of provincials to the capital, along with immigrants of uncertain stock, Parisian officials believed they needed to know who might not advance smoothly through the system. Proceeding in an empirical manner, Binet posed many questions to youngsters of different ages. He ascertained which questions when answered correctly predicted success in school, and which questions when answered incorrectly foretold school difficulties. The items that discriminated most clearly between the two groups became, in effect, the first test of intelligence.

Binet is a hero to many psychologists. He was a keen observer, a careful scholar, an inventive technologist. Perhaps even more important for his followers, he devised the instrument that is often considered psychology's greatest success story. Millions of people who have never heard Binet's name have had aspects of their fate influenced by instrumentation that the French psychologist inspired. And thousands of psychometricians—specialists in the measurement of psychological variables—earn their living courtesy of Binet's invention.

Although it has prevailed over the long run, the psychologists' version of intelligence is now facing its biggest threat. Many scholars and observers—and even some iconoclastic

**Howard Gardner** teaches human development at the Harvard Graduate School of Education. Among his books are *Multiple Intelligences* (1993), *Extraordinary Minds* (1997), and *The Disciplined Mind.*

psychologists—feel that intelligence is too important to be left to the psychometricians. Experts are extending the breadth of the concept—proposing many intelligences, including emo-

tional intelligence and moral intelligence. They are experimenting with new methods of ascertaining intelligence, including some that avoid tests altogether in favor of direct measures of brain activity. They are forcing citizens everywhere to confront a number of questions: What is intelligence? How ought it to be assessed? And how do our notions of intelligence fit with what we value about human beings? In short, experts are competing for the "ownership" of intelligence in the next century.

THE outline of the psychometricians' success story is well known. Binet's colleagues in England and Germany contributed to the conceptualization and instrumentation of intelligence testing—which soon became known as IQ tests. (An IQ, or intelligence quotient, designates the ratio between mental age and chronological age. Clearly we'd prefer that a child in our care have an IQ of 120, being smarter than average for his or her years, than an IQ of 80, being older than average for his or her intelligence). Like other Parisian fashions of the period, the intelligence test migrated easily to the United States. First used to determine who was "feeble-minded," it was soon used to assess "normal" children, to identify the "gifted," and to determine who was fit to serve in the Army. By the 1920s the intelligence test had become a fixture in

 From *The Atlantic Monthly*, February 1999, pp. 67-76. © 1999 by Howard Gardner. Reprinted by permission.

educational practice in the United States and much of Western Europe.

Early intelligence tests were not without their critics. Many enduring concerns were first raised by the influential journalist Walter Lippmann, in a series of published debates with Lewis Terman, of Stanford University, the father of IQ testing in America. Lippmann pointed out the superficiality of the questions, their possible cultural biases, and the risks of trying to determine a person's intellectual potential with a brief oral or paper-and-pencil measure.

Perhaps surprisingly, the conceptualization of intelligence did not advance much in the decades following Binet's and Terman's pioneering contributions. Intelligence tests came to be seen, rightly or wrongly, as primarily a tool for selecting people to fill academic or vocational niches. In one of the most famous—if irritating—remarks about intelligence testing, the influential Harvard psychologist E. G. Boring declared, "Intelligence is what the tests test." So long as these tests did what they were supposed to do (that is, give some indication of school success), it did not seem necessary or prudent to probe too deeply into their meaning or to explore alternative views of the human intellect.

Psychologists who study intelligence have argued chiefly about three questions. The first: Is intelligence singular, or does it consist of various more or less independent intellectual faculties? The purists— ranging from the turn-of-the-century English psychologist Charles Spearman to his latter-day disciples Richard J. Herrnstein and Charles Murray (of *The Bell Curve* fame)—defend the notion of a single overarching "g," or general intelligence. The pluralists—ranging from L. L. Thurstone, of the University of Chicago, who posited seven vectors of the mind, to J. P. Guilford, of the University of Southern California, who discerned 150 factors of the intellect—construe intelligence as composed of some or even many dissociable components. In his much cited *The Mismeasure of Man* (1981) the paleontologist Stephen Jay Gould argued that the conflicting conclusions reached on this issue reflect alternative assumptions about statistical procedures rather than the way the mind is. Still, psychologists continue the debate, with a majority sympathetic to the general-intelligence perspective.

The public is more interested in the second question: Is intelligence (or are intelligences) largely inherited? This is by and large a Western question. In the Confucian societies of East Asia individual differences in endowment are assumed to be modest, and differences in achievement are thought to be due largely to effort. In the West, however, many students of the subject sympathize with the view—defended within psychology by Lewis Terman, among others—that intelligence is inborn and one can do little to alter one's intellectual birthright.

Studies of identical twins reared apart provide surprisingly strong support for the "heritability" of psychometric intelligence. That is, if one wants to predict someone's score on an intelligence test, the scores of the biological parents (even if the child has not had appreciable contact with them) are more likely to prove relevant than the scores of the adoptive parents. By the same token, the IQs of identical twins are more similar than the IQs of fraternal twins. And, contrary to common sense (and political correctness), the IQs of biologically related people grow closer in the later years of life. Still, because of the intricacies of behavioral genetics and the difficulties of conducting valid experiments with human child-rearing, a few defend the proposition that intelligence is largely environmental rather than heritable, and some believe that we cannot answer the question at all.

Most scholars agree that even if psychometric intelligence is largely inherited, it is not possible to pinpoint the sources of differences in average IQ between groups, such as the fifteen-point difference typically observed between African-American and white populations. That is because in our society the contemporary—let alone the historical—experiences of these two groups cannot be equated. One could ferret out the differences (if any) between black and white populations only in a society that was truly color-blind.

One other question has intrigued laypeople and psychologists: Are intelligence tests biased? Cultural assumptions are evident in early intelligence tests. Some class biases are obvious—who except the wealthy could readily answer a question about polo? Others are more subtle. Suppose the question is what one should do with money found on the street. Although ordinarily one might turn it over to the police, what if one had a hungry child? Or what if the police force were known to be hostile to members of one's ethnic group? Only the canonical response to such a question would be scored as correct.

Psychometricians have striven to remove the obviously biased items from such measures. But biases that are built into the test situation itself are far more difficult to deal with. For example, a person's background affects his or her reaction to being placed in an unfamiliar locale, being instructed by someone dressed in a certain way, and having a printed test booklet thrust into his or her hands. And as the psychologist Claude M. Steele has argued in these pages (see "Race and the Schooling of Black Americans," April, 1992), the biases

> **For the first time in many years the intelligence establishment is clearly on the defensive—and the new century seems likely to usher in quite different ways of thinking about intelligence.**

prove even more acute when people know that their academic potential is being measured and that their racial or ethnic group is widely considered to be less intelligent than the dominant social group.

The idea of bias touches on the common assumption that tests in general, and intelligence tests in particular, are inherently conservative instruments—tools of the establishment. It is therefore worth noting that many testing pioneers thought of themselves as progressives in the social sphere. They were devising instruments that could reveal people of talent even if those people came from "remote and apparently inferior backgrounds," to quote from a college catalogue of the 1950s. And occasionally the tests did discover intellectual diamonds in the rough. More often, however, they picked out the privileged. The still unresolved question of the causal relationship between IQ and social privilege has stimulated many a dissertation across the social sciences.

Paradoxically, one of the clearest signs of the success of intelligence tests is that they are no longer widely administered. In the wake of legal cases about the propriety of making consequential decisions about education on the basis of IQ scores, many public school officials have become test-shy. By and large, the testing of IQ in the schools is restricted to cases involving a recognized problem (such as a learning disability) or a selection procedure (determining eligibility for a program that serves gifted children).

Despite this apparent setback, intelligence testing and the line of thinking that underlies it have actually triumphed. Many widely used scholastic measures, chief among them the SAT (renamed the Scholastic Assessment Test a few years ago), are thinly disguised intelligence tests that correlate highly with scores on standard psychometric instruments. Virtually no one raised in the developed world today has gone untouched by Binet's seemingly simple invention of a century ago.

## Multiple Intelligences

THE concept of intelligence has in recent years undergone its most robust challenge since the days of Walter Lippmann. Some who are informed by psychology but not bound by the assumptions of the psychometricians have invaded this formerly sacrosanct territory. They have put forth their own ideas of what intelligence is, how (and whether) it should be measured, and which values should be invoked in considerations of the human intellect. For the first time in many years the intelligence establishment is clearly on the defensive—and the new century seems likely to usher in quite different ways of thinking about intelligence.

One evident factor in the rethinking of intelligence is the perspective introduced by scholars who are not psychologists. Anthropologists have commented on the parochialism of the Western view of intelligence. Some cultures do not even have a concept called intelligence, and others define intelligence in terms of traits that we in the West might consider odd—obedience, good listening skills, or moral fiber, for example. Neuroscientists are skeptical that the highly differentiated and modular structure of the brain is consistent with a unitary form of intelligence. Computer scientists have devised programs deemed intelligent; these programs often go about problem-solving in ways quite different from those embraced by human beings or other animals.

Even within the field of psychology the natives have been getting restless. Probably the most restless is the Yale psychologist Robert J. Sternberg. A prodigious scholar, Sternberg, who is forty-nine, has written dozens of books and hundreds of articles, the majority of them focusing in one or another way on intelligence. Sternberg began with the strategic goal of understanding the actual mental processes mobilized by standard test items, such as the solving of analogies. But he soon went beyond standard intelligence testing by insisting on two hitherto neglected forms of intelligence: the "practical" ability to adapt to varying contexts (as we all must in these days of divorcing and downsizing), and the capacity to automate familiar activities so that we can deal effectively with novelty and display "creative" intelligence.

Sternberg has gone to greater pains than many other critics of standard intelligence testing to measure these forms of intelligence with the paper-and-pencil laboratory methods favored by the profession. And he has found that a person's ability to adapt to diverse contexts or to deal with novel information can be differentiated from success at standard IQ-test problems. His efforts to create a new intelligence test have not been crowned with easy victory. Most psychometricians are conservative—they like the tests that have been in use for decades, and if new ones are to be marketed, these must correlate well with existing instruments. So much for openness to novelty within psychometrics.

Others in the field seem less bound by its strictures. The psychologist and journalist Daniel Goleman has achieved worldwide success with his book *Emotional Intelligence* (1995). Contending that this new concept (sometimes nicknamed EQ) may matter as much as or more than IQ, Goleman draws attention to such pivotal human abilities as controlling one's emotional reactions and "reading" the signals of others. In the view of the noted psychiatrist Robert Coles, author of *The Moral Intelligence of Children* (1997), among many other books, we should prize character over intellect. He decries the amorality of our families, hence our children; he shows how we might cultivate human beings with a strong sense of right and wrong, who are willing to act on that sense even when it runs counter to self-interest. Other, frankly popular accounts deal with leadership intelligence (LQ), executive intelligence (EQ or ExQ), and even financial intelligence.

Like Coles's and Goleman's efforts, my work on "multiple intelligences" eschews the psychologists' credo of operationalization and test-making. I began by asking two questions: How did the human mind and brain evolve over millions of years? and How can we account for the diversity of skills and capacities that are or have been valued in different communities around the world?

Armed with these questions and a set of eight criteria, I have concluded that all human beings possess at least eight intelligences: linguistic and logical-mathematical (the two most prized in school and the ones central to success on standard intelligence tests), musical, spatial, bodily-kinesthetic, naturalist, interpersonal, and intrapersonal.

I make two complementary claims about intelligence. The first is universal. We all possess these eight intelligences—and possibly more. Indeed, rather than seeing us as "rational animals," I offer a new definition of what it means to be a human being, cognitively speaking: *Homo sapiens sapiens* is the animal that possesses these eight forms of mental representation.

My second claim concerns individual differences. Owing to the accidents of heredity, environment, and their interactions, no two of us exhibit the same intelligences in precisely the same proportions. Our "profiles of intelligence" differ from one another. This fact poses intriguing challenges and opportunities for our education system. We can ignore these differences and pretend that we are all the same; historically, that is what most education systems have done. Or we can fashion an education system that tries to exploit these differences, individualizing instruction and assessment as much as possible.

> **Interest in the subject of intelligence is likely to be fed by the creation of machines that display intelligence and by the possibility that we can genetically engineer organisms of a specific intelligence or intelligences.**

## *Intelligence and Morality*

As the century of Binet and his successors draws to a close, we'd be wise to take stock of, and to anticipate, the course of thinking about intelligence. Although my crystal ball is no clearer than anyone else's (the species may lack "future intelligence"), it seems safe to predict that interest in intelligence will not go away.

To begin with, the psychometric community has scarcely laid down its arms. New versions of the standard tests continue to be created, and occasionally new tests surface as well. Researchers in the psychometric tradition churn out fresh evidence of the predictive power of their instruments and the correlations between measured intelligence and one's life chances. And some in the psychometric tradition are searching for the biological basis of intelligence: the gene or complex of genes that may affect intelligence, the neural structures that

are crucial for intelligence, or telltale brain-wave patterns that distinguish the bright from the less bright.

Beyond various psychometric twists, interest in intelligence is likely to grow in other ways. It will be fed by the creation of machines that display intelligence and by the specific intelligence or intelligences. Moreover, observers as diverse as Richard Herrnstein and Robert B. Reich, President Clinton's first Secretary of Labor, have agreed that in coming years a large proportion of society's rewards will go to those people who are skilled symbol analysts—who can sit at a computer screen (or its technological successor), manipulate numbers and other kinds of symbols, and use the results of their operations to contrive plans, tactics, and strategies for enterprises ranging from business to science to war games. These people may well color how intelligence is conceived in decades to come—just as the need to provide good middle-level bureaucrats to run an empire served as a primary molder of intelligence tests in the early years of the century.

Surveying the landscape of intelligence, I discern three struggles between opposing forces. The extent to which, and the manner in which, these various struggles are resolved will influence the lives of millions of people. I believe that the three struggles are interrelated; that the first struggle provides the key to the other two; and that the ensemble of struggles can be resolved in an optimal way.

The first struggle concerns the breadth of our definition of intelligence. One camp consists of the purists, who believe in a single form of intelligence—one that basically predicts success in school and in school-like activities. Arrayed against the purists are the progressive pluralists, who believe that many forms of intelligence exist. Some of these pluralists would like to broaden the definition of intelligence considerably, to include the abilities to create, to lead, and to stand out in terms of emotional sensitivity or moral excellence.

The second struggle concerns the assessment of intelligence. Again, one readily encounters a traditional position. Once chiefly concerned with paper-and-pencil tests, the traditionally oriented practitioner is now likely to use computers to provide the same information more quickly and more accurately. But other positions abound. Purists disdain psychological tasks of any complexity, preferring to look instead at reaction time, brain waves, and other physiological measures of intellect. In contrast, simulators favor measures closely resembling the actual abilities that are prized. And skeptics warn against the continued expansion of testing. They emphasize the damage often done to individual life chances and self-esteem by a regimen of psychological testing, and call for less technocratic, more humane methods—ranging from self-assessment to the examination of portfolios of student work to selection in the service of social equity.

The final struggle concerns the relationship between intelligence and the qualities we value in human beings. Although no one would baldly equate intellect and human worth, nuanced positions have emerged on this issue. Some (in the *Bell Curve* mold) see intelligence as closely related to a person's ethics and values; they believe that brighter people are more likely to appreciate moral complexity and to behave judiciously. Some call for a sharp distinction between the realm of intellect on the one hand, and character, morality, or ethics on the other. Society's ambivalence on this issue can be discerned in the figures that become the culture's heroes. For every Albert Einstein or Bobby Fischer who is celebrated for his intellect, there is a Forrest Gump or a Chauncey Gardiner who is celebrated for human—and humane—traits that would never be captured on any kind of intelligence test.

Thanks to the work of the past decade or two, the stranglehold of the psychometricians has at last been broken. This is a beneficent development. Yet now that the psychometricians have been overcome, we risk deciding that anything goes—that emotions, morality, creativity, must all be absorbed into the "new (or even the New Age) intelligence." The challenge is to chart a concept of intelligence that reflects new insights and discoveries and yet can withstand rigorous scrutiny.

An analogy may help. One can think of the scope of intelligence as represented by an elastic band. For many years the definition of intelligence went unchallenged, and the band seemed to have lost its elasticity. Some of the new definitions expand the band, so that it has become taut and resilient; and yet earlier work on intelligence is still germane. Other definitions so expand the band that it is likely finally to snap—and the earlier work on intelligence will no longer be of use.

Until now the term "intelligence" has been limited largely to certain kinds of problem-solving involving language and logic—the skills at a premium in the bureaucrat or the law professor. However, human beings are able to deal with numerous kinds of content besides words, numbers, and logical relations—for example, space, music, the psyches of other human beings. Like the elastic band, definitions of intelligence need to be expanded to include human skill in dealing with these diverse contents. And we must not restrict attention to solving problems that have been posed by others; we must consider equally the capacity of indi-

viduals to fashion products—scientific experiments, effective organizations—that draw on one or more human intelligences. The elastic band can accommodate such broadening as well.

So long as intelligences are restricted to the processing of contents in the world, we avoid epistemological problems—as we should. "Intelligence" should not be expanded to include personality, motivation, will, attention, character, creativity, and other important and significant human capacities. Such stretching is likely to snap the band.

Let's see what happens when one crosses one of these lines—for example, when one attempts to conflate intelligence and creativity. Beginning with a definition, we extend the descriptor "creative" to those people (or works or institutions) who meet two criteria: they are innovative, and their innovations are eventually accepted by a relevant community.

No one denies that creativity is important—and, indeed, it may prove even more important in the future, when nearly all standard (algorithmic) procedures will be carried out by computers. Yet creativity should not be equated with intelligence. An expert may be intelligent in one or more domains but not necessarily inclined toward, or successful in, innovation. Similarly, although it is clear that the ability to innovate requires a certain degree of intelligence, we don't find a significant correlation between measures of intellect and of creativity. Indeed, creativity seems more dependent on a certain kind of temperament and personality—risk-taking, tough-skinned, persevering, above all having a lust to alter the status quo and leave a mark on society—than on efficiency in processing various kinds of information. By collapsing these categories together, we risk missing dimensions that are important but separate; and we may think that we are training (or selecting) one when we are actually training (or selecting) the other.

> **The concept of "intelligence" should not be expanded to include personality, motivation, will, character, creativity, and other important and significant human capacities. Such stretching is likely to snap the band.**

Next consider what happens when one stretches the idea of intelligence to include attitudes and behaviors—and thus confronts human values within a culture. A few values can be expressed generically enough that they command universal respect: the Golden Rule is one promising candidate. Most values, however, turn out to be specific to certain cultures or subcultures—even such seemingly unproblematic ones as the unacceptability of killing or lying. Once one conflates morality and intelligence, one needs to deal with widely divergent views of what is good or bad and why. Moreover, one must confront the fact that people who score high on tests of moral reasoning may act immorally outside the test situation—even as courageous and self-sacrificing people may turn out to be unremarkable on formal tests of moral reasoning or intelligence. It is far preferable to construe intelligence itself as morally neutral and then decide whether a given use of intelligence qualifies as moral, immoral, or amoral in context.

As I see it, no intelligence is moral or immoral in itself. One can be gifted in language and use that gift to write great verse, as did Johann Wolfgang von Goethe, or to foment hatred, as did Joseph Goebbels. Mother Teresa and Lyndon Johnson, Mohandas Gandhi and Niccolò Machiavelli, may have had equivalent degrees of interpersonal intelligence, but they put their skills to widely divergent uses.

Perhaps there is a form of intelligence that determines whether or not a situation harbors moral considerations or consequences. But the term "moral intelligence" carries little force. After all, Adolf Hitler and Joseph Stalin may well have had an exquisite sense of which situations contained moral considerations. However, either they did not care or they embraced their own peculiar morality, according to which eliminating Jews was the moral thing to do in quest of a pure Aryan society, or wiping out a generation was necessary in the quest to establish a communist state.

## *The Borders of Intelligence*

**W**RITING as a scholar rather than as a layperson, I see two problems with the notion of emotional intelligence. First, unlike language or space, the emotions are not contents to be processed; rather, cognition has evolved so that we can make sense of human beings (self and others) that possess and experience emotions. Emotions are part and parcel of all cognition, though they may well prove more salient at certain times or under certain circumstances: they accompany our interactions with others, our listening to great music, our feelings when we solve—or fail to solve—a difficult mathematical problem. If one calls some intelligences emotional, one suggests that other intelligences are not—and that implication flies in the face of experience and empirical data.

The second problem is the conflation of emotional intelligence and a certain preferred pattern of behavior. This is the trap that Daniel Goleman sometimes falls into in his otherwise admirable *Emotional Intelligence*. Goleman singles out as

> I question
> the wisdom
> of searching
> for a "pure"
> intelligence. I do
> not believe that
> such alchemical
> intellectual essences
> actually exist;
> they are a product
> of our penchant
> for creating
> terminology.

emotionally intelligent those people who use their understanding of emotions to make others feel better, to solve conflicts, or to cooperate in home or work situations. No one would dispute that such people are wanted. However, people who understand emotion may not necessarily use their skills for the benefit of society.

For this reason I prefer the term "emotional sensitivity"—a term (encompassing my interpersonal and intrapersonal intelligences) that could apply to people who are sensitive to emotions in themselves and in others. Presumably, clinicians and salespeople excel in sensitivity to others, poets and mystics in sensitivity to themselves. And some autistic or psychopathological people seem completely insensitive to the emotional realm. I would insist, however, on a strict distinction between emotional sensitivity and being a "good" or "moral" person. A person may be sensitive to the emotions of others but use that sensitivity to manipulate or to deceive them, or to create hatred.

I call, then, for a delineation of intelligence that includes the full range of contents to which human beings are sensitive, but at the same time designates as off limits such valued but separate human traits as creativity, morality, and emotional appropriateness. I believe that such a delineation makes scientific and epistemological sense. It reinvigorates the elastic band without stretching it to the breaking point. It helps to resolve the two remaining struggles: how to assess, and what kinds of human beings to admire.

Once we decide to restrict intelligence to human information-processing and product-making capacities, we can make use of the established technology of assessment. That is, we can continue to use paper-and-pencil or computer-adapted testing techniques while looking at a broader range of capacities, such as musical sensitivity and empathy with others. And we can avoid ticklish and possibly unresolvable questions about the assessment of values and morality that may well be restricted to a particular culture and that may well change over time.

Still, even with a limited perspective on intelligence, important questions remain about which assessment path to follow—that of the purist, the simulator, or the skeptic. Here I have strong views. I question the wisdom of searching for a "pure" intelligence—be it general intelligence, musical intelligence, or interpersonal intelligence. I do not believe that such alchemical intellectual essences actually exist; they are a product of our penchant for creating terminology rather than determinable and measurable entities. Moreover, the correlations that have thus far been found between supposedly pure measures and the skills that we actually value in the world are too modest to be useful.

What does exist is the use of intelligences, individually and in concert, to carry out tasks that are valued by a society. Accordingly, we should be assessing the extent to which human beings succeed in carrying out tasks of consequence that presumably involve certain intelligences. To be concrete, we should not test musical intelligence by looking at the ability to discriminate between two tones or timbres; rather, we should be teaching people to sing songs or play instruments or transform melodies and seeing how readily they master such feats. At the same time, we should abjure a search for pure emotional sensitivity—for example, a test that matches facial expressions to galvanic skin response. Rather, we should place (or observe) people in situations that call for them to be sensitive to the aspirations and motives of others. For example, we could see how they handle a situation in which they and colleagues have to break up a fight between two teenagers, or persuade a boss to change a policy of which they do not approve.

Here powerful new simulations can be invoked. We are now in a position to draw on technologies that can deliver realistic situations or problems and also record the success of subjects in dealing with them. A student can be presented with an unfamiliar tune on a computer and asked to learn that tune, transpose it, orchestrate it, and the like. Such exercises would reveal much about the student's intelligence in musical matters.

Turning to the social (or human, if you prefer) realm, subjects can be presented with simulated interactions and asked to judge the shifting motivations of each actor. Or they can be asked to work in an interactive hypermedia production with unfamiliar people who are trying to accomplish some sort of goal, and to respond to their various moves and countermoves. The program can alter responses in light of the moves of the subject. Like a high-stakes poker game, such a measure should reveal much about the interpersonal or emotional sensitivity of a subject.

A significant increase in the breadth—the elasticity—of our concept of intelligence, then, should open the possibility for innovative forms of assessment far more realistic than the classic short-answer examinations. Why settle for an IQ or an SAT test, in which the items are at best remote proxies for the ability to design experiments, write essays, critique musical performances, and so forth? Why not instead ask people actually (or virtually) to carry out such tasks? And yet by not opening up the Pandora's box of values and subjectivity, one can continue to make judicious use of the insights and technologies achieved by those who have devoted decades to perfecting mental measurement.

To be sure, one can create a psychometric instrument for any conceivable human virtue, including morality, creativity, and emotional intelligence in its several senses. Indeed, since the publication of Daniel Goleman's book dozens of efforts have been made to create tests for emotional intelligence. The resulting instruments are not, however, necessarily useful. Such instruments are far more likely to satisfy the test maker's desire for reliability (a subject gets roughly the same score on two separate administrations of the test) than the need for validity (the test measures the trait that it purports to measure).

Such instruments-on-demand prove dubious for two reasons. First, beyond some platitudes, few can agree on what it means to be moral, ethical, a good person: consider the differing values of Jesse Helms and Jesse Jackson, Margaret Thatcher and Margaret Mead. Second, scores on such tests are much more likely to reveal test-taking savvy (skills in language and logic) than fundamental character.

In speaking about character, I turn to a final concern: the relationship between intelligence and what I will call virtue—those qualities that we admire and wish to hold up as examples for our children. No doubt the desire to expand intelligence to encompass ethics and character represents a direct response to the general feeling that our society is lacking in these dimensions; the expansionist view of intelligence reflects the hope that if we transmit the technology of intelligence to these virtues, we might in the end secure a more virtuous population.

I have already indicated my strong reservations about trying to make the word "intelligence" all things to all people—the psychometric equivalent of the true, the beautiful, and the good. Yet the problem remains: how, in a post-Aristotelian, post-Confucian era in which psychometrics looms large, do we think about the virtuous human being?

My analysis suggests one promising approach. We should recognize that intelligences, creativity, and morality—to mention just three desiderata—are separate. Each may require its own form of measurement or assessment, and some will prove far easier to assess objectively than others. Indeed, with respect to creativity and morality, we are more likely to rely on overall judgments by experts than on any putative test battery. At the same time, nothing prevents us from looking for people who combine several of these attributes—who have musical and interpersonal intelligence, who are psychometrically intelligent and creative in the arts, who combine emotional sensitivity and a high standard of moral conduct.

Let me introduce another analogy at this point. In college admissions much attention is paid to scholastic performance, as measured by College Board examinations and grades. However, other features are also weighed, and sometimes a person with lower test scores is admitted if he or she proves exemplary in terms of citizenship or athletics or motivation. Admissions officers do not confound these virtues (indeed, they may use different scales and issue different grades), but they recognize the attractiveness of candidates who exemplify two or more desirable traits.

We have left the Eden of classical times, in which various intellectual and ethical values necessarily commingled, and we are unlikely ever to re-create it. We should recognize that these virtues can be separate and will often prove to be remote from one another. When we attempt to aggregate them, through phrases like "emotional intelligence," "creative intelligence," and "moral intelligence," we should realize that we are expressing a wish rather than denoting a necessary or even a likely coupling.

We have an aid in converting this wish to reality: the existence of powerful examples—people who succeed in exemplifying two or more cardinal human virtues. To name names is risky—particularly when one generation's heroes can become the subject of the next generation's pathographies. Even so, I can without apology mention Niels Bohr, George C. Marshall, Rachel Carson, Arthur Ashe, Louis Armstrong, Pablo Casals, Ella Fitzgerald.

In studying the lives of such people, we discover human possibilities. Young human beings learn primarily from the examples of powerful adults around them—those who are admirable and also those who are simply glamorous. Sustained attention to admirable examples may well increase the future incidence of people who actually do yoke capacities that are scientifically and epistemologically separate.

In one of the most evocative phrases of the century the British novelist E. M. Forster counseled us, "Only connect." I believe that some expansionists in the territory of intelligence, though well motivated, have prematurely asserted connections that do not exist. But I also believe that as human beings, we can help to forge connections that may be important for our physical and psychic survival.

Just how the precise borders of intelligence are drawn is a question we can leave to scholars. But the imperative to broaden our definition of intelligence in a responsible way goes well beyond the academy. Who "owns" intelligence promises to be an issue even more critical in the next century than it has been in this era of the IQ test.

# Can Animals Think?

In *The Parrot's Lament*, Eugene Linden reveals how animals demonstrate aspects of intelligence as they escape from, cheat and outfox humans

## BY EUGENE LINDEN

THE FIRST TIME FU MANCHU BROKE OUT, ZOO-keepers chalked it up to human error. On a balmy day, the orangutans at the Omaha Zoo had been playing in their big outdoor enclosure. Not long thereafter, shocked keepers looked up and saw Fu and his family hanging out in some trees near the elephant barn. Later investigation revealed that the door that connects the furnace room to the orangutan enclosure was open. Head keeper Jerry Stones chewed out his staff, and the incident was forgotten. But the next time the weather was nice, Fu Manchu escaped again. Fuming, Stones recalls, "I was getting ready to fire someone."

The next nice day, alerted by keepers desperate to keep their jobs, Stones finally managed to catch Fu Manchu in the act. First, the young ape climbed down some airvent louvers into a dry moat. Then, taking hold of the bottom of the furnace door, he used brute force to pull it back just far enough to slide a wire into the gap, slip a latch and pop the door open. The next day, Stones noticed something shiny sticking out of Fu's mouth. It was the wire lock pick, bent to fit between his lip and gum and stowed there between escapes.

Fu Manchu's jailbreaks made headlines in 1968, but his clever tricks didn't make a big impression on the scientists who specialize in looking for signs of higher mental processes in animals. At the time, much of the action in animal intelligence was focused on efforts to teach apes to use human languages. No researcher cared much about ape escape artists.

And neither did I. In 1970, I began following studies of animal intelligence, particularly the early reports of chimpanzees who learned how to use human words. The big breakthrough in these experiments came when two psychologists, R. Allen and Beatrice Gardner, realized their chimps were having trouble forming wordlike sounds and decided to teach a young female named Washoe sign language instead. Washoe eventually learned more than 130 words from the language of the deaf called American Sign Language.

Washoe's success spurred more language studies and created such ape celebrities as Koko the gorilla and Chantek the orangutan. The work also set off a fierce debate in scientific circles about the nature of animal intelligence—one that continues to this day. Indeed, it has been easier to defeat commu-

nism than to get scientists to agree on what Washoe meant three decades ago when she saw a swan on a pond and made the signs for "water bird." Was she inventing a phrase to describe waterfowl, or merely generating signs vaguely associated with the scene in front of her?

Over the years I have written several articles and two books on animal-intelligence experiments and the controversy that surrounds them. I have witnessed at close range the problems scientists encounter when they

---

## CHIMPS

**WHAT THE SKEPTICS SAY** Most feats of chimp "intelligence" can be explained as the learning of simple rules motivated by the desire for treats

**WHAT CHIMPS DO** In captivity, they have shown that they know when others have been misinformed—or can be fooled. Awareness of mental states is a key part of consciousness

---

## DOLPHINS

**WHAT THE SKEPTICS SAY** The marie mammals may have big brains, but they're used to navigate, not cogitate

**WHAT DOLPHINS CAN DO** Marineland's Zippy would pick up objects before pool-cleaning divers saw them, then drop them behind the humans. The ruse suggests Zippy was not only playful but also keenly aware of human abilities and habits

---

## BEES

**WHAT THE SKEPTICS SAY** The insect may work hard, but it's essentially brainless

**WHAT BEES DO** They not only dance to tell others where to find pollen; there is also evidence that bees somehow realize when they are given a bum steer. When scientists fooled bee scouts by taking them to flowers in a boat in the middle of a lake, few bees flew out over water after the scouts danced

## LEOPARDS

**WHAT THE SKEPTICS SAY** Why should a leopard be smart? It's already perfect

**WHAT LEOPARDS DO** An orphaned cat that was returned to the wild in India moved her cubs from the jungle to her former house when floods neared. Later, she returned one cub to her den across a still swollen river. To ferry the second cub, she hopped in the prow of the owner's canoe and waited for him to take them across

mals that hoodwink or manipulate their keepers, stories about wheeling and dealing, stories of understanding and trust across the vast gulf that separates different species. And, if the keepers have had a few drinks, they will tell stories about escape.

Each of these narratives reveals another facet of what I have become convinced is a new window on animal intelligence: the kind of mental feats they perform when dealing with captivity and the dominant species on the planet—humanity.

## What Do You Want for That Banana?

CAPTIVE ANIMALS OFTEN BECOME STUDENTS of the humans who control their lives. The great apes in particular are alert to situations that might temporarily give them the upper hand—for example, when something useful or valuable rolls into their exhibit or is left behind. The more worldly animals recognize the concept of value as meaning "something I have that you want," and they are not above exploiting such opportunities for all they are worth.

Consider the time that Charlene Jendry was in her office at the Columbus Zoo and word came to her that a male gorilla named Colo was clutching a suspicious object. Arriving on the scene, Charlene offered Colo some peanuts, only to be met with a blank stare. Realizing that they were negotiating, Charlene upped the ante and offered a piece of pineapple. At this point, without making eye contact with Charlene, Colo opened his hand and revealed that he was holding a key chain, much in the manner that a fence might furtively show a potential customer stolen goods on the street. Relieved that it was not anything dangerous or valuable, Charlene gave Colo the piece of pineapple. Astute bargainer that he was, Colo then broke the key chain and gave Charlene a link, perhaps figuring, "Why give her the whole thing if I can get a bit of pineapple for each piece?"

try to examine phenomena as elusive as language and idea formation. Do animals really have thoughts, what we call consciousness? The very question offends some philosophers and scientists, since it cuts so close to what separates men from beasts. Yet, notes Harvard's Donald Griffin, to rule out the study of animal consciousness handicaps our understanding of other species. "If consciousness is important to us and it exists in other creatures," says Griffin, "then it is probably important to them."

Frustrated with what seemed like an endless and barren ideological debate, I began to wonder whether there might be better windows on animal minds than experiments designed to teach them human signs and symbols. When I heard about Fu Manchu, I realized what to me now seems obvious: if animals can think, they will probably do their best thinking when it serves their purposes, not when some scientist asks them to.

And so I started exploring the world of animal intelligence from the other side. I started talking to people who deal with animals professionally: veterinarians, animal researchers, zookeepers—people like Jerry Stones. Most are not studying animal intelligence per se, but they encounter it, and the lack of it, every day.

Get a bunch of keepers together and they will start telling stories about how their charges try to outsmart, beguile or otherwise astonish humans. They tell stories about ani-

If an animal can show some skill in the barter business, why not in handling money? One ape, an orangutan named Chantek, did just that during his years as part of a study of sign language undertaken by psychologist Lyn Miles at the University of Tennessee. Chantek learned more than 150 words, but that wasn't all. He also figured out that if he did chores such as cleaning up his room, he could earn coins that he could later spend on treats and rides in Lyn's car.

Chantek's understanding of money seems to have extended far beyond simple transactions to such sophisticated concepts as inflation and counterfeiting. Lyn first used poker chips as the coin of the realm, but Chantek decided that he could expand the money supply by breaking the chips in two. When Lyn switched to using washers, Chantek found pieces of aluminum foil and tried to make imitation washers that he could pass off as the real thing. Lyn also tried to teach Chantek more virtuous habits such as saving, sharing and charity.

When I caught up with the orangutan at Zoo Atlanta, where he now lives, I did not see evidence of charity, but I did see an example of sharing that a robber baron might envy. When Lyn gave Chantek some grapes and asked him to share them with her, Chantek promptly ate all the fruit. Then, seemingly remembering that he'd been asked to share, handed Lyn the bare stem.

## The Parrot's Lament

CAN ANIMALS HAVE A sense of humor? Sally Blanchard, publisher of a newsletter called the *Pet Bird Report,* thinks a pet parrot may have pulled her leg. That's one explanation for the time her African gray parrot, named Bongo Marie, seemed to feign distress at the possible de-

mise of an Amazon parrot named Paco.

It happened one day when Blanchard was making Cornish game hen for dinner. As Blanchard lifted her knife, the African gray threw back its head and said, "Oh, no! Paco!" Trying not to laugh, Blanchard said, "That's not Paco," and showed Bongo

Marie that the Amazon was alive and well. Mimicking a disappointed tone, Bongo Marie said, "Oh, no," and launched into a raucous laugh.

Was the parrot joking when it seemed to believe the other bird was a goner? Did Bongo Marie comprehend Blanchard's response? Studies of African grays have shown that they

can understand the meaning of words—for example, that red refers to a color, not just a particular red object. Parrots also enjoy getting a reaction out of humans, and so, whether or not Bongo Marie's crocodile tears were intentional, the episode was thoroughly satisfying from the parrot's point of view.

What does this tell us? We have been equipped by nature for tasks like juggling numbers and assigning value to things, but these signal human abilities may also be present in more limited form in our closest relatives. Chimps engage in sharing, trading and gift giving in the wild, and they more than hold their own in the primitive bazaar of the zoo.

## Lend a Helping Tail

WHY WOULD AN ANIMAL WANT TO COOPERATE with a human? The behaviorist would say that animals cooperate when, through reinforcement, they learn it is in their interest to cooperate. This is true as far as it goes, but I don't think it goes far enough. Certainly with humans, the intangible reinforcement that comes with respect, dignity and accomplishment can be far more motivating than material rewards.

Gail Laule, a consultant on animal behavior with Active Environments Inc., uses rewards to encourage an animal to do something, but also recognizes that animals are more than wind-up toys that blindly respond to tempting treats. "It's much easier to work with a dolphin if you assume that it is intelligent . . .That was certainly the case with Orky," says Laule, referring to her work with one of the giant dolphins called orcas or killer whales. "Of all the animals I've worked with, Orky was the most intelligent . . . He would assess a situation and then do something based on the judgments he made."

Like the time he helped save a member of the family. Orky's mate Corky gave birth in the late 1970s, but the baby did not thrive at first, and the keepers took the little killer whale out of the tank by stretcher for emergency care and feeding. Things began to go awry when they returned the orca to the tank. The boom operator halted the stretcher when it was still a few feet above the water. Suddenly the baby began throwing up, through both its mouth and its blowhole. The keepers feared it would aspirate some vomit, which could bring on a fatal case of pneumonia, but they could not reach the baby dangling above.

Orky had been watching the procedure, and, apparently sizing up the problem, he swam under the stretcher and allowed one of the men to stand on his head. This was remarkable, says Tim, since Orky had never been trained to carry people on his head like Sea World's Shamu. Then, using the amazing power of his tail flukes to keep steady, Orky provided a platform that allowed the keeper to reach up and release the bridle so that the 420-lb. baby could slide into the water within reach of help.

## The Keeper Always Falls for That One

A SAD FACT OF LIFE IS THAT IT IS EASIER TO spot evidence of intelligence in devious behavior than in acts of cooperation or love. Sophisticated acts of deception involve the conscious planting of false beliefs in others, which in turn implies awareness that others have mental states that can be manipulated. British psychologist Andrew Whiten of the University of St. Andrews in Scotland says this ability is a "mental Rubicon" dividing humans and at least the other great apes from the rest of the animal kingdom.

While psychologists have studied various forms of animal deception, zookeepers are its targets every day. Helen Shewman, of the Woodland Park Zoo in Seattle, Wash., recalls that one day she dropped an orange through a feeding porthole for Meladi, one of the female orangutans. Instead of moving away, Meladi looked Helen in the eye and held out her hand. Thinking that the orange must have rolled off somewhere inaccessible, Helen gave her another one. When Meladi shuffled off Helen noticed that she had hidden the original orange in her other hand.

Tawan, the colony's dominant male, watched this whole charade, and the next day he too looked Helen in the eye and pretended that he had not yet received an orange. "Are you sure you don't have one?" Helen asked. He continued to hold her gaze and held out his hand. Relenting, she gave him another, then noticed that he had been hiding his orange under his foot.

## We Gotta Get Outta This Place

WHILE ALL SORTS OF ANIMALS HAVE TRIED TO break out of captivity, orangutans are the master escape artists of the menagerie. Besides picking locks, orangs have been known to make insulating mitts out of straw in order to climb over electric fences. Indeed, orangs have become design consultants: some zookeepers have used them to test new enclosures on the theory that if an orang can't find a way out, no other species of ape will. How do the orangs do it? One ingredient of

success may be a patient, observing temperament. Zoologist Ben Beck once noted that if you give a screwdriver to a chimpanzee, it will try to use it for everything except its intended purpose. Give one to a gorilla, and it will first rear back in horror—"Oh, my God, it's going to hurt me!"—then try to eat it, and ultimately forget about it. Give it to an orangutan, however, and the ape will first hide it and then, once you have gone, use it to dismantle the cage.

Along with Fu Manchu's crafty getaways, the most memorable orang escapes include a breakout at the Topeka Zoo. Jonathan, a young male, had been temporarily isolated in a holding area and resented it mightily. Keepers were not particularly worried because his cage was secured with an elaborate "guillotine" door that opened vertically and was remotely controlled by pneumatic pressure. When the door was closed, its top fit between two plates. As an extra precaution, a keeper would insert a pin through keyhole-like apertures in the plates and in the top of the door. The 5-in. pin would then be flopped over so that it could not be withdrawn without being flipped into the proper position. Taken together, these redundant security systems should have been able to contain most humans, much less an ape.

Nonetheless, a volunteer who regularly came to play with an infant orang in a neighboring cage began reporting that she could see Jonathan fiddling with something at the top of his cage. Geoff Creswell, a keeper, investigated, but when he looked in on the orang, Jonathan was always sitting quietly in a corner. Always, that is, until the day Creswell had a sudden, heart-stopping encounter with the big male outside his cage in a corridor of the holding area. After Jonathan had been put back behind bars, the keepers discovered that he had used a piece of cardboard to flip the pin into position so that it could be pushed out.

Jonathan's escape offered evidence of a panoply of higher mental abilities. He concealed his efforts from the humans in charge of him (but seemed not to realize that the person visiting the next cage might snitch on him); he figured out the workings of the locking mechanism and then fashioned a tool that enabled him to pick the lock. Perhaps most impressive was the planning and perseverance that went into this feat.

Sally Boysen, a psychologist at Ohio State University, probed the degree to which a chimp's ability to reason is subservient to the animal's desires. Her experiment involved two female chimps, Sheba and Sarah, and centered on a game in which Sheba would be shown two dishes filled with different amounts of treats. The first dish Sheba pointed to would be given to Sarah, meaning that Sheba had to think smaller to get larger. When she could actually see the treats, Sheba invariably pointed to the larger

---

## ELEPHANTS

**WHAT THE SKEPTICS SAY** Elephant communication consists of simple calls

**WHAT ELEPHANTS DO** At the Bronx Zoo, two elephants will take turns eating treats to foil keepers trying to lure them in for the night. The scheme requires the waiting elephant to trust the other not to eat the goodies

amount, only to see them given to Sarah. However, when tokens were substituted for real food, Sheba quickly realized that pointing to the smaller amount would get her the larger amount. It would seem that in the presence of real food, Sheba's appetites persistently overcame her ability to reason. When temptation was removed, Sheba could bring her cognitive abilities to bear and achieve her desired, albeit selfish, goal.

The same experiment was conducted with children. Four-year-olds realize that if they point to a smaller amount of food, they will be rewarded with more. Three-year-olds don't. This suggests that sometime during human maturation, children's cognitive abilities develop to the point that they realize

they can be rewarded for restraint. The evidence also suggests that Sheba and other chimps are right on the cusp of that threshold. "In the course of an afternoon, we could toggle between Sheba reacting like a three-year-old and a four-year-old simply by switching what she was looking at," says Boysen.

Even if intelligence is shackled in animals, we can see it break out in flashes of brilliance. Countless creatures draw on their abilities not only to secure food and compete with their peers, but also to deal with, deceive and beguile the humans they encounter. Every so often, they do something extraordinary, and we gain insight into our own abilities, and what it's like to be an orangutan or an orca.

What is intelligence anyway? If life is about perpetuation of a species, and intelligence is meant to serve that perpetuation, then we can't hold a candle to pea-brained sea turtles who predated us and survived the asteroid impact that killed off the dinosaurs. As human history has shown, once minds break free of religious, cultural and physical controls, they burn hot and fast, consuming and altering everything around them. Perhaps this is why higher mental abilities, though present in other creatures, are more circumscribed. Still, it is comforting to realize that other species besides our own can stand back and appraise the world around them, even if their horizons are more constrained than the heady, perilous perspective that is our blessing and curse.

## Unit Selections

## Key Points to Consider

❖ What is motivation? What is an emotion? How are the two related to each other?

❖ What makes great athletes different from the rest of us? Are they just more athletically inclined? Do you think if you altered your focus or your motivational level, you would be a better athlete? A better student? Explain why.

❖ Why do people gain weight? What motivates them to eat and eat, or to eat the wrong foods? What motivates individuals to lose weight? Why, in general, are Americans some of the most overweight people on the face of the earth? What can we do to lose weight and to maintain a healthy weight?

❖ From where do emotions originate, nature or nurture? Why did you give the answer you did? Do you think a person's level of emotionality or overall personality can change with time or is it somehow fixed early in life?

❖ Why is the face the key to understanding others' emotions? Are there any universally expressed facial emotions? What are the problems with studying universal emotions; in other words, does culture play a role in emotional expression? Are adult emotions similar to or different from emotions of younger individuals? How so?

❖ Are various emotions controlled by different factors? For example, is one emotion controlled by the brain while others are controlled by the situation? What are some positive emotions? What are some examples of negative emotions?

❖ What is emotional intelligence? Why are individuals who are high in emotional intelligence successful? Can EQ be cultivated? Emotional intelligence is important on the job. Where else might emotional intelligence come in handy? Explain.

 **Links** **www.dushkin.com/online/**

These sites are annotated on pages 4 and 5.

Jasmine's sister was a working mother and always reminded Jasmine about how exciting her life was. Jasmine chose to stay home with her children, 2-year old Min, 4-year-old Chi'Ming, and newborn Mi-may. One day, Jasmine was having a difficult time with the children. The baby, Mi-may, had been crying all day from colic. The other two children had been bickering over their toys. Jasmine, realizing that it was already 5:15 and her husband would be home any minute, frantically started preparing dinner. She wanted to fix a nice dinner so that she and her husband could eat after the children went to bed, then relax together.

This was not to be. Jasmine sat waiting for her no-show husband. When he finally walked in the door at 10:15, she was furious. His excuse, that his boss had invited the whole office for dinner, didn't reduce Jasmine's ire. She reasoned that her husband could have called, could have taken 5 minutes to do that. Jasmine berated her husband. Her face was taut and red with rage and her voice wavered. Suddenly, bursting into tears, she ran into the living room. Her husband retreated to the safety of their bedroom.

Exhausted and disappointed, Jasmine sat alone and pondered why she was so angry with her husband. Was she just tired? Was she frustrated by negotiating with young children all day and did she simply want another adult around once in a while? Was she secretly worried and jealous that her husband was seeing another woman and had lied about his whereabouts? Was she combative because her husband's and her sister's lives seemed so much fuller than her own? Jasmine was unsure just how she felt and why she exploded in such rage at her husband, someone she loved dearly.

This story, while sad and gender-stereotyped, is not necessarily unrealistic when it comes to emotions. There are times when we are moved to deep emotion. On other occasions, we expect waterfalls of tears but find that our eyes are dry or simply a little misty. What are these strange things we call emotions? What motivates us to rage at someone we love?

These questions and others have inspired psychologists to study emotions and motivation. The above episode about Jasmine, besides introducing these topics to you, also illustrates why these two

topics are usually interrelated in psychology. Some emotions, such as love, pride, and joy, are pleasant, so pleasant that we are motivated to keep them going. Other emotions, such as anger, grief, and jealousy, are terribly draining and oppressive, so negative that we hope they will be over as soon as possible. Emotions and motivation and their relationship to each other are the focus of this unit.

The first two articles in this unit relate to motivation; the last two pertain to emotions. In "The Gold Medal Mind," James Bauman questions what motivates great athletes. He notes that the best athletes are different from the rest of us. After careful consideration he concludes that great athletes have certain mental abilities that motivate them to focus more on their performance.

In "Why We're Fat," author Stacey Schultz ponders a perennial question for Americans. Why are so many Americans overweight? Are we more motivated to eat than we are to stay healthy? Schultz helps us understand why we gain weight and what we can do to lose weight.

Two articles on emotions follow. The first, "What's in a Face?" offers a fascinating insight into emotional expressiveness. Beth Azar, a regular writer for the *APA Monitor*, discusses whether the face indeed mirrors our emotional states. She also argues that the face is important to social interactions because it tells us so much about another person's emotions and moods.

The final article on emotional intelligence (EQ) offers a description of this relatively new concept. EQ is the ability to recognize one's own or another's emotional states. Those high in EQ tend to be very successful regardless of their intelligence level and other abilities. Work sites are important places to be high in EQ.

# THE GOLD MEDAL **MIND**

ANY COMPETITIVE ATHLETE WILL TELL YOU THAT WHAT SEPARATES THE GREAT HOPEFULS FROM THE GREAT ACHIEVERS IS THE KNOWLEDGE AND APPLICATION OF MENTAL SKILLS. HERE, U.S. OLYMPIC TRAINING CENTER SPORT PSYCHOLOGIST **JAMES BAUMAN, PH.D.,** REVEALS JUST WHAT IT WILL TAKE TO SUCCEED IN SYDNEY THIS SUMMER— OR AT LEAST JUST IMPRESS EVERYONE AT THE GYM.

The day before Jonathan Jordan was to compete in the 1996 NCAA Track and Field Indoor Championships in Bakersfield, he got food poisoning and had to be rushed to the hospital. His coach tried to convince him to withdraw from the next day's race, but with the championship on the line, Jordan refused to quit.

The next morning, the 26-year-old triple and long jumper from suburban Chicago focused all his energy on the one good jump he knew he had to make. "I put everything into it," he said. "I was more relaxed than I ever was." When the jump measured an expansive 23 feet, a surprised Jordan said, "Oh my God." He had placed first, in spite of his weakened condition.

"In such situations I have found myself asking: 'How can I compete now?' But you concentrate and dig for something you didn't know you had," says Jordan, who will head for the Olympic Trials in Sacramento this summer.

A computer with all the gigabytes in the world is useless without the software to make it run. And so it is with the Olympian, whose mind is the software controlling that collection of hardware known as flesh and bone and muscle. Aside from their astounding physical prowess, it is the Olympians' mental muscles—and how they flex them—that really sets them apart from everyday athletes.

"The difference between you and the guy next to you is almost completely mental," says Curt R. Clausen, 32, the six-foot-one former public administrator whose newly shaved head will stand out in the 50-kilometer Olympic race walk in Sydney. "At the highest level," says Clausen, who is ranked No. 1 in the United States and fourth in the world, "that's what makes the difference."

In my more than 10 years of working with hundreds of athletes, as the sport psychologist at Washington State University and one of four sports psychologists for the Sport Science and Technology Division of the U.S. Olympic Committee, I have seen how "mental management" contributes to an athlete's performance. Some Olympians even say it accounts for 90% of their success. While it's difficult to quantify percentages, we do know from years of research and hundreds of studies just how important psychological preparation is to optimum athletic performance.

It can even conquer the worst of distractions, as it did for Kathy Ann Colin, who overcame physical injuries, the distraction of college and a family disaster before becoming the No. 1 kayaker in the U.S.

Colin has had her eyes on the Olympics since she was 6, thinking she'd get there through gymnastics. But after tearing a ligament in her right knee when she was 12, she turned to kayaking. She had to give that up, too, when she left her hometown of Kailua, Hawaii, to attend the University of Washington. But after graduating from college and landing a good job with Boeing, Colin knew that if she were ever to compete in the Olympics, she had to train full time. Three years ago, she moved to the U.S. ARCO Olympic Training Center in Chula Vista, California, to work out with the national team.

 Reprinted with permission from *Psychology Today*, June 2000, pp. 62-69, 87. © 2000 by Sussex Publishers, Inc.

When finally, last summer, the day came for her to qualify for the 2000 Olympics, tragedy struck. Colin's parents, who had flown all the way from Hawaii, were robbed at the airport and left with nothing but the clothes on their backs.

"I spent the whole day crying and rounding up clothes from teammates," the athlete recalls.

On top of that, she and kayak pair teammate Tamara Jenkins were having trouble balancing, and their warm-ups were "awful." When experts predicted that the race would be the fastest anyone had seen in 20 years, the pair was distracted, nervous and excited—all at once.

"I knew what I had to do," says Colin. "I had put too much time and effort into this." So with all the tenacity her five-foot-eight, 145-pound body could muster, she turned to Jenkins and said: "We can do this. Focus and relax and don't worry about anything else. Just do what we do."

And they did. Colin and Jenkins will be paddling for the gold in the K-2 in Sydney this summer.

Numerous studies over the years confirm that successful athletes are better able than the rest of us to deal with distractions. Olympic athletes in particular find ways to remain focused on an event to the exclusion of negative influences such as unruly crowds, inclement weather, even family problems. In his 1986 comparative study, Stanford University's Albert Bandura, Ph.D., internationally known for his work in personality and social learning theory, showed that while the vast majority of us spend lots of time worrying about things we can't control, successful athletes attend primarily to those cues or stimuli that are relevant, or within their control.

And where mental ability counts most is in preparation.

In addition to the intense concentration or focus of a Jordan, Clausen or Colin, "mental management" in-volves a number of techniques, including imaging, comparing performances, positive self-talk, mental relaxation, and achieving what athletes call "flow." And you don't have to be Olympic material to benefit from them. While the rest of us may lack the dream or the gift to compete in Sydney this summer, we can still use our minds to improve our sports performance.

MENTAL REHEARSAL is when athletes not only picture their movements but imagine feeling them as well. In 1988, Canadian sport psychologists Terry Orlick, Ph.D., and John Partington, Ph.D., found that 99% of the 235 athletes they surveyed rely on this technique to prepare for a high stakes race. Studies by the U.S. Olympic Training Center show that 94% of coaches use mental rehearsal for training and competition.

Colin describes how she glides through the waters in her mind as she lies in bed at night: "I focus on the feel of the boat and on my paddling. I am in the race. I get nervous energy. My muscles are triggered as I simulate a stroke in my mind. The boat is picking up; it's gliding and I'm gliding with it."

During warm-ups on the water, Colin's visualizations are key: "I'll hold a stop watch and imagine the start. My strategy is to figure out the number of strokes I need to win. I tell myself I want to get 152—and then I make the plan. I know exactly where I'll be when I stop, and I'll be within a second of my goal. So when the race comes, there's nothing new."

It's not as easy to mind-map a four-hour race. But Curt Clausen has his own way of visualizing the 50-kilometer race walk.

"I start by saying, 'I want to win this race.' Then I make a detailed plan with contingencies, strategies and coping methods. I take that plan, visualize the whole

# TAKING IT TO THE GYM

You may not have the physical attributes to perform at the level of an Olympian, but you can get the most out of whatever you do to stay in shape by adapting the same mental techniques athletes use.

• *Set realistic goals.* Be specific about what you want to accomplish, whether it's walking five miles or biking once a week. Devise steps to achieve the goal and commit to a start-date.
• *Build self-confidence* by maintaining a clear and honest inventory of your skills. You're obviously not going to shoot a curl first thing in the morning if you haven't been on a surfboard in 10 years. But you *can* build on what you have accomplished before and believe in the untapped potential that is yours.
• *Relax.* There are a lot of ways to do it. Think about things that put you at ease. Breathe easily and fully. Picture the muscles in your body as being loose and limber.

Conjure up soothing images—scenes that make you feel genuinely good.
• *Imagine your performance.* Rehearse in your mind what it will look like and how you will feel as you break that sweat, run that extra half-mile, curl 10 more pounds. See yourself doing it; then do it.
• *Positive self-talk your way to success.* First, stop berating yourself for a less than stellar performance. Instead, tell yourself that you will accomplish your goal because you do have the skills to do it. Keep coaxing yourself. And, above all, listen to your self-talk.
• *Control distractions* by making a quick checklist of everything that might derail you from accomplishing your goal. Eliminate the things you can't control, like the weather, and focus on those you can, like having the proper shoes or equipment for your sport. Then concentrate on the here and now, because what you do right now and how you do it are the only true parameters of performance.

thing and then enter the race with it so that it's running through my head over and over."

An academic All-American with a bachelor's degree in criminal justice and a master's degree in forensic science, Jonathan Jordan talks to elementary school children about the importance of education as well as the preparation needed to become an Olympic athlete.

He begins his visualization two days before an event, he tells them. "I see myself on the runway. Then, I'm taking off on the board. From there, I'm holding my phases, and then I'm landing. If I get prepared like that beforehand," he explains, "then when I get there I don't worry about it. That's something I've been doing for 10 years."

By now he even does it subconsciously. While walking through his hometown shopping mall, Jordan has startled himself by suddenly leaping in the air. "I caught myself doing that one day. I was doing it for quite a bit of time before I realized."

According to Brent Rushall, Ph.D., in his 1991 book *Imagery Training in Sports: A Handbook for Athletes, Coaches and Sport Psychologists,* effective performance imagery involves the ability to:

- Focus on the most desirable aspects of the performance;
- Emphasize the feeling of the activity by including all senses that come into play;
- Conjure the image several times;
- Envision the whole environment, including the arena;
- Incorporate competition strategies into the image.

"Each successful imagery trial should be followed by covert positive reinforcement," Rushall wrote. "The combination of trials and reinforcement is critical for the mental skill to work."

COMPARING PERFORMANCES with competitors of the same caliber helps athletes build confidence.

"I try to match my mental abilities with the best in the world," said Andrew Hermann, 29, who will compete in his first Olympic games in the 50-kilometer race walk this summer in Sydney. Hermann ran distance and cross-country at Willamette College in Oregon before turning to race walking, competing in both 20- and 50-kilometer events. He placed second in the Olympic Trials in February.

Right before that, he took a number of tests to gauge his performance against other champions in his field. Afterward, he thought: "I'm just as tough as the best. Why can't I compete and put on a world-class performance?

Kathy Ann Colin was already a top-ranked junior kayaking champion when she went to the U.S. Nationals in Sacramento eight years ago, but it wasn't until she competed in the Olympic trials for the first time in 1996 that she had a true measure of her abilities.

"I remember driving to the airport. Everyone thought I did well, but I was upset because I knew I could do better," she said. "Up to that point, I was just having fun. But then when I was there, I was jealous because I knew I could do it." A year later, she began training full time at the ARCO Olympic Training Center.

When Jonathan Jordan first compared himself with others, the prognosis wasn't good. But when he tried out for the U.S. track and field team in 1996 and didn't make it, the failure strengthened his resolve.

"I had never gone up against guys who had competed for the U.S. for so many years," recalls Jordan. "I said, 'Man, am I supposed to be here?' " Now he knows what to expect. "With a field like that, you either jump well or, you don't. I know I'm going to jump well because I know the competition."

POSITIVE SELF-TALK is another self-esteem builder. This internal dialogue, while not the stuff of Hamlet or Macbeth, helps athletes assess their performance; they use it to monitor, instruct and encourage.

"Sometimes I'm having problems with focus, where I'm just not up to it," says Colin. "So, I say, 'Come on. Just do it.' " She urges herself on, saying "ten strokes for power," then "ten for rhythm," then "ten for legs." At one point during the race she'll be thinking, "Legs, legs, legs" with such ferocity that she'll blurt it out, much to the chagrin of teammate Jenkins.

During a race, Curt Clausen carries on conversations with himself about his splits, his heart rate, the effort he's making, how fast he's going, how hard he can push. "More importantly," he says, "I repeat key words: relax, smile, low arms—all little techniques."

Based on their comprehensive study of Olympic gymnasts, Michael Mahoney, Ph.D., and M. Avener, Ph.D., reported in the *Canadian Journal of Sport Sciences* in 1992 that the more positive the self-talk, the easier it is for athletes to excel. In a separate study, published in *Cognitive Therapy and Research* in 1977, they found that athletes who made the U.S. men's gymnastics team used more positive self-talk than those who didn't.

Negative self-talk, on the other hand, is worse than no talk at all. In 1987, pioneering psychologist and founder of rational emotive therapy Albert Ellis, Ph.D., identified general irrational beliefs that can interfere with athletes reaching their potential. They include statements such as: "If I don't do well, I'm an incompetent person," or "I must do well to gain the approval of others." This can result in emotional distraction and decreased performance.

"It's a battle with yourself," says Jordan. "I tell myself, 'Jonathan, you trained too hard for this. That's why you're going to win it.' It's not being arrogant. It's just a statement of fact."

RELAXATION is especially important when even the slightest deviation from the norm can throw Olympians off. "The worst part about a race is the stress," says Clausen. "You tend to turn that into muscular tension, which detracts from your performance. I do deep breathing to trigger relaxation throughout my entire body."

Race-walker Andrew Hermann relaxes by visualizing a soothing blue liquid running through his body, from his head to his toes. "If I'm really in a jam," he says, "I picture brown sugar and pouring water over it. I see it dissolve and it makes the tensions dissolve wherever they are."

Von Ware, 24, ranked No. 3 in the United States in the triple jump, will prepare for his Olympic trials in Sacramento this July as he has prepared for past meets, by listening to music, strumming his guitar, tapping on a set of drums or fiddling with his laptop. A self-described "computer graphics nut," he hopes to own his own software company someday. Right now, though, he has his eyes on the prize—Olympic victory.

"The triple jump is structured. It's very technical, very rhythmic," says Ware. "And relaxation definitely helps."

Ware's abilities to jump, climb, run and perform a variety of athletic moves were recognized at an early age, especially after he broke the high school long jump record of 51 feet in 1994. At that point, Ware abandoned football, his sport of choice, and began to make the Olympics more than a dream.

What makes him happiest, he says, is seeing his mother smiling in the stands as he competes.

"For me," he says, "that's total bliss."

"FLOW" sums up the feelings of bliss, euphoria and contentment that athletes feel when they're on a roll, when the physical and mental aspects of performance are completely synchronized. In that state, nothing else, not even the crowd in the stands, matters.

"For me, it's almost an out-of-body experience," says Ware. "It's as if you can't feel your arms or legs or anything. I see nothing but the runway and pit, and my body just responds."

According to 1999 studies by Susan Jackson, Ph.D., of the Queensland University of Technology in Australia, and Mihaly Csikszentmihalyi, Ph.D., of Claremont Graduate University in California, the relationship between an athlete's confidence and the challenge being faced is a main factor in determining whether or not the athlete experiences competitive flow.

Jackson, in a 1992 study published in the *Journal of Applied Sport Psychology,* interviewed 28 elite athletes across seven different sports and found that the key factors contributing to flow are confidence, focus, how the performance felt and progressed, optimal motivation and arousal levels. She also found that athletes perceived the flow state to be within their control.

Flow is "a relaxed, fluid feeling, where my technique is better than anyone's," says Clausen. "I'm smiling. I'm scanning my competitors. I'm saying, 'I got these guys here today.' This is fun. Until this season, I was unable to do that."

---

*James Bauman, Ph.D., is a sports psychologist at the U.S. Olympic Training Center in Chula Vista, California.*

### READ MORE ABOUT IT

*In Pursuit of Excellence: How to Win in Sport and Life Through Mental Training, Third Ed.,* Terry Orlick, Ph.D. (Human Kinetics, 2000).
*Flow In Sports,* Susan Jackson, Ph.D., and Mihaly Csikszentmihalyi, Ph.D. (Human Kinetics, 1999).

# Why we're fat

## Gender and age matter more than you may realize

**BY STACEY SCHULTZ**

Isn't it just like a man? Although his 56-year-old wife, Maureen, had been counting calories since her teens, Tom Javaux ate what he wanted and remained trim well into middle age. When the 62-year-old retired bricklayer finally developed a paunch and went on the same diet as his wife, he dropped more weight and lost it faster than she did—50 pounds to her 35.

Another injustice between the sexes? You bet. The latest obesity research shows that men and women differ in almost every respect when it comes to weight over the course of a lifetime: when they gain it, where they gain it, and at what rate. In women, sex hormones wreak havoc on the ability to control appetite, energy expenditure, and fat storage. In men, it is the slowing down of physical activity that tends to add pounds. But overweight men, because of *where* they carry their weight, can be at higher risk than women for heart disease and other serious health problems.

Despite the differences, the body shapes of both sexes share one alarming similarity: Both men and women are getting fat in epidemic proportions. Well over half of all American adults—about 63 percent of men and 55 percent of

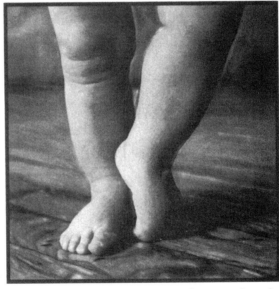

PHOTOGRAPHS BY BARBARA COLE

women age 25 and older—are overweight. Last week, in a special issue devoted entirely to obesity, the *Journal of the American Medical Association* reported new statistics that are nothing short of astonishing for a nation seemingly so obsessed with health and fitness: The rate of obesity—18 percent—has soared from 12 percent just seven years ago, making the United States now secure in its position as the fattest nation in the developed world.

"This rate is shocking," says Jeffrey Koplan, director of the Centers for Dis-

ease Control and Prevention, "and it means that we have a huge public-health problem." Indeed, depending on weight and age, obesity significantly increases the risk of high blood pressure and high cholesterol, diabetes, and gallbladder disease.

Obesity is determined by a measure called the body mass index, or BMI, which tallies weight adjusted for height. A BMI of 18 to 24.9 is considered normal, 25 to 29.9 is overweight, and 30 or higher is obese. A woman 5 feet, 5 inches tall who weighs 162 pounds is considered overweight; if she weighs 186 pounds she is obese. A 5-foot, 10-inch man who weighs 188 pounds is overweight; if he weighs 216 pounds he is obese. Both the overweight man and the overweight woman have BMIs of 27; the obese pair have BMIs of 31.

The prevalence of obesity may be troubling, but it shouldn't be all that surprising. As a species, humans have evolved with instincts to seek and store fat. Easy fat storage is crucial for survival in times of famine, yet for decades Americans have been seated at a veritable feast. Says Tom Wadden, director of the Weight and Eating Disorders Program at the University of Pennsylvania, "Now it has become a maladaptive trait

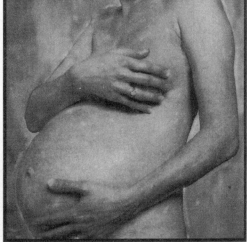
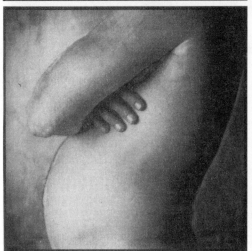
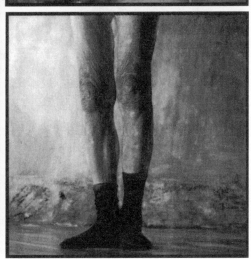

## The years take shape

*How and where we gain weight have to do with age and sex.*

**CHILDHOOD.** Lessons learned young can be hard to break. Poor eating habits have caused a huge surge in kids' rate of obesity.

**PUBERTY.** Teenage girls obsess about their weight with good reason. They change from 12 percent fat to 25 percent fat virtually overnight.

**PREGNANCY.** Weight gained early in pregnancy may be harder to take off later. And men get fatter just by being married.

**MIDDLE AGE.** These are the danger years, especially for men. Weight carried around the middle is more dangerous than weight on arms and thighs.

**OLD AGE.** Both men and women lose muscle and bone mass. Appetite wanes, and hormonal protections disappear. Limbs get skinny.

PHOTOGRAPHS BY BARBARA COLE

because we are living in times when we have a surplus of food." As a result, he says, "we are all getting obese."

The good news is that if men and women know when they are most likely to fatten up—and why—they can take steps to avoid the extra pounds.

## Tubby teens

For women, the lifelong battle against the scale starts in the teen years. Sex hormones kick into gear, preparing girls to nurture babies by causing an explosion of fat on the hips, buttocks, and chest. Teenage girls are notoriously conscious of their weight, says Wadden—and, as it turns out, for good reason. Before adolescence, girls have no more than 12 percent body fat. Afterward, they have as much as 25 percent. That's the average amount for an adult female who is not overweight, but the change

often comes faster than girls can emotionally adjust.

By contrast, late-adolescent boys, whose hormones are geared more toward muscle development, have only about 15 percent body fat. They can eat three helpings of dinner seemingly without effect, because muscle burns more calories than fat. "Boys are a different kind of engine," Wadden says.

Teen boys tend to be more physically active than teen girls. But a decrease in physical activity among both sexes is contributing to a recent 70 percent increase in the rate of obesity among young adults. Only 25 percent of U.S. high schools offered daily physical education classes in 1995, down from 42 percent in 1991. Girls, who tend to see exercise in terms of weight management, are less active than boys, who participate more for the joy of competition.

School lunches aren't helping. Though federal guidelines instruct public schools to limit fat to a third of the total calories

in their lunch programs, many districts offer fast-food carts, with fries and burgers, because students clamor for them. Moreover, even though Americans have decreased fat consumption from 42 percent to 34 percent of their diet over the past 30 years, they still eat too much sugar and processed carbohydrates. And the weight added by all that white bread and pasta takes its toll immediately: The average 20-year-old, says David Ludwig, director of the obesity program at Children's Hospital in Boston, already shows signs of hardening of the arteries.

## The marriage penalty

The reproductive years, from the 20s to the 40s, are belt-loosening times for both sexes but for different reasons. Just being married causes men to gain weight, but not women. "We found that married men were significantly fatter than men who had never been or were previously married," says Jeffery Sobal, a nutritional sociologist at Cornell University who conducted the study. Men eat more when they are married, the study showed, and they spend less time playing organized sports. (On the whole, though, men get a tremendous health boost from being married, Sobal says. They drink less, often quit smoking, use fewer drugs, and, in general, engage in less risky behavior.)

For women in this age bracket, pregnancy is of course the main cause of excess poundage. But new research shows that *when* those extra pounds are gained may determine whether the weight stays or goes after baby arrives. Weight gained in the first 20 weeks of pregnancy hangs on six months postpartum, says Jennifer Lovejoy, associate professor with the Pennington Biomedical Research Center in Baton Rouge, La. The weight put on after 20 weeks contributes to the weight of the baby and is less likely to stick around, Lovejoy says. One study found that those women who retained weight post-pregnancy had gained twice as much in the first 20 weeks as the women who did not retain weight, even though both groups gained the same amount over the nine months. This doesn't mean women should be dieting in the early stages of pregnancy, but at the same time, pregnancy is not an invitation to raid the refrigerator. Eating healthily while staying within the recommended guideline for weight gain

## Heavyweight states

*States with high percentages of overweight\* people tend to be those lightest in their wallets. It may be that fresh fruits and vegetables are harder to find in less affluent areas.*

| THE HEAVIEST | | THE THINNEST | |
|---|---|---|---|
| West Virginia | 37.8 | Arizona | 22.5 |
| Mississippi | 37.5 | Massachusetts | 26.9 |
| Alaska | 36.2 | Nevada | 27.0 |
| Louisiana | 36.1 | Colorado | 27.2 |
| Alabama | 35.8 | Connecticut | 27.4 |
| Kentucky | 35.8 | Vermont | 27.4 |

*People with a body mass index between 25 and 30, taken from U.S. Department of Health and Human Services data

(roughly 30 pounds for a woman of normal weight, less for overweight women), is the way to go.

Women are also at a disadvantage after giving birth, says Wadden of the University of Pennsylvania, simply because they spend more time than men do around food. "[Women] tend to be grazers, and over the course of a day they can easily pick up an extra 500 calories." African-American women need to be particularly careful, notes a study in this week's *Journal of the American College of Cardiology.* Just the slightest weight gain, researchers found, puts them at higher risk of hypertension and heart failure.

Exercise can help, but here again women have a harder time than men. Tracy Horton, at the University of Colorado's Center for Human Nutrition, found that men and women use up fat at different rates during exercise. Women tend to burn relatively more fat. But in the hours after a workout, that may come back to haunt them, Horton says. Women's bodies can detect the fat deficit and so try to replenish fat stores as soon as possible by putting fat from meals right back on their thighs and hips. Men, on the other hand, burn more carbohydrates, so their bodies are more likely to hold on to new carbos and less likely to hang on to the fat. It may not

HORMONE RESEARCH
# Leptin's uncertain promise

**B**rain met belly last week, in a rendezvous scientists have been trying to arrange for years. A hormone that affect the brain's appetite-control centers knocked an average of 4 pounds off people in a month, researchers announced, without their resorting to crash diets or Ironman exercise plans.

When the substance, called leptin, was discovered five years ago drug companies drooled at the prospect of turning it into a weight-loss drug. A study by obesity experts and published in the *Journal of the American*

*Medical Association* last week revealed one of the first signs that leptin works in people, albeit variously. Some strains of mice given leptin injections lose their appetite, but the human response to leptin is more complex. In overweight individuals, the hormone sometimes barely works at all.

**Genes.** On occasion, though, leptin has dramatic effects. A family in Britain struggled with two extremely obese children—one a 65-pound 3-year-old. Then a physician found that the youngsters shared a rare genetic defect that made it im-

possible for them to produce leptin. Given injections of the hormone, the 3-year-old's appetite plunged 80 percent, and his 10-year-old cousin shed a startling 25 percent of her body weight.

But people get fat for myriad reasons; dozens of genes govern how much they eat and how much of that food they burn up. That's why scientists are developing drugs that tackle fat in different ways. Meridia and Xenical are the two hottest weight-loss drugs now on the market. Meridia acts on brain chemicals that blunt appetite,

while Xenical blocks the intestine from absorbing some fat. But because obesity arises for all different reasons, the same drug cannot work for everyone. Still, the leptin report indicates that scientists are making headway. Art Campfield, an obesity researcher at the University of Colorado's Center for Human Nutrition in Denver, expects that promising obesity drugs will be tested in humans beginning sometime next year.

*—Jennifer Couzin*

Paris last summer astounded Dennis Styne. But his astonishment had less to do with the City of Lights than with the city's light meals. "Actually it was the kids' menus," says Styne. "These were ordinary, middle-class restaurants, and for about $6 the kids got a lamb chop and green beans." A pediatric endocrinologist at the University of California-Davis, Styne couldn't help but compare the Parisian lunch, with less than 200 calories, with a 1,300-calorie fast-food lunch in the United States: double cheeseburger, fries, and a shake.

Despite years of warnings that plump children grow into sicker adults, today 1 in every 5 U.S. children is overweight. That's double the rate of two decades ago. Last week, however, brought some good news: Simply ungluing kids from the television set, researchers reported, can reduce weight. And family-oriented weight control programs have shown real success in keeping the pounds down.

**Warning signs.** Children grow unevenly so weight problems can be hard to spot. But if 85 percent of a child's peers are thinner than he is, it's a warning sign, as is weight carried in the middle of the body and a family history of obesity.

All three mean that it's time to take action. Literally. In the TV-reduction study, Stanford University researchers found that six months of limiting elementary-school children to seven hours of television and video games a week led to a small but noticeable drop in body fat.

But as Styne says, "You can't work off a bad diet." Laurel Mellin of the University of California-San Francisco, who developed a program called Shapedown, says parents need to nurture emotional resilience in kids, so they don't turn to food to make bad feelings go away. (Pressure without support, she warns, can lead to eating disorders such as anorexia.)

Jacqueline Clemente, who dropped 20 pounds from her 260-pound frame in this program—and nearly an additional 30 in the succeeding seven months—says it was important to know her family was with her. "It helped me feel comfortable with myself *and* understand how to eat right," says the 15-year-old from San Mateo, Calif. She says she felt unhappy and isolated before the program. On this day, however, she was rushing off to meet friends at her high school's football game. —*J.F.*

be fair, but ultimately, women simply have to restrain their intake of food more than do men.

## The danger zone

As if wrinkles and gray hair weren't enough, men and women in their 50s are more likely to be obese than at any other time of their lives. And where that fat sits on the body matters. The potbelly that men often grow in their middle years is not just unattractive, it's dangerous—considerably more so than the fat that women typically carry on their hips, thighs, and arms.

The midlife paunch, which doctors call "visceral fat," poses a risk because it surrounds the internal organs. It releases fatty acids that make their way into the liver, diminishing the organ's ability to process the hormone insulin, eventually causing diabetes. The fat also affects how the kidneys process insulin, a factor that scientists say may lead to high blood pressure. For every 10 percent increase over normal weight, men and women have about a 20 percent jump in risk for heart disease.

For women, these middle years can be a double whammy. In menopause, when women stop producing estrogen, gravity pulls down on hips, thighs, and

buttocks, but abdominal fat often starts creeping upward. "This may be why, after menopause, the rate of heart disease in women equals that of men," says Aviva Must of Tufts University School of Medicine. Before that the rate of heart disease in women is significantly lower than that of men. Fortunately, hormone replacement therapy can minimize this abdominal weight gain.

## Senior slimming

As men and women reach their 60s and beyond, their body weight typically starts to decline. "As we get older we lose lean tissue, or muscle mass," Must says. "We have less body mass and less caloric need, so we gradually lose weight." Chronic diseases and medications can also interfere with appetite, as can depression and a diminished sense of taste. Weight-bearing exercises will help maintain muscle mass and keep the body strong. Weightlifting is especially important for women because it can stave off osteoporosis by maintaining bone density—and because women have less muscle to lose to begin with. "If a woman loses a significant portion of her muscle mass, she will be far weaker than a man who loses the same amount," Must says.

Ultimately, being overweight is likely to lead to premature death. People who are severely overweight are four times as likely to die before their expected lifespan, and people who are moderately overweight are twice as likely to die early. So the Javauxs take to the track together, walking a mile twice a week. She is slower than he, and she says most people on the track pass her by. But, she says, "We really want to succeed. I'm doing it for him, and he's doing it for me." It just may take her a little longer, and she may have to work a little harder to get there.

*With Josh Fischman*

# What's in a face?

**Do facial expressions reflect inner feelings?**
**Or are they social devices for influencing others?**

BY BETH AZAR
*Monitor* staff

After 30 years of renewed interest in facial expression as a key clue to human emotions, frowns are appearing on critics' faces. The face, they say, isn't the mirror to emotions it's been held out to be.

The use of facial expression for measuring people's emotions has dominated psychology since the late 1960s when Paul Ekman, PhD, of the University of California, San Francisco and Carroll Izard, PhD, of the University of Delaware, reawakened the study of emotion by linking expressions to a group of basic emotions.

Many took that work to imply that facial expressions provided the key to people's feelings. But in recent years the psychology literature has been sprinkled with hotly worded attacks by detractors who claim that there is no one-to-one correspondence between facial expressions and emotions. In fact, they argue, there's no evidence to support a link between what appears on someone's face and how they feel inside.

But this conflict masks some major areas of agreement, says Joseph Campos, PhD, of the University of California at Berkeley. Indeed, he says, "there is profound agreement that the face, along with the voice, body posture and hand gestures, forecast to outside observers what people will do next."

The point of contention remains in whether the face also says something about a person's internal state. Some, such as Izard, say, "Absolutely." Detractors, such as Alan Fridlund, PhD, of the University of California, Santa Barbara, say an adamant "No." And others, including Campos and Ekman, land somewhere in the middle. The face surely can provide important information about emotion, but it is only one of many tools and should never be used as a "gold standard" of emotion as some researchers, particularly those studying children, have tended to do.

"The face is a component [of emotion]," says Campos. "But to make it the center of study of the human being experiencing an emotion is like saying the only thing you need to study in a car is the transmission. Not that the transmission is unimportant, but it's only part of an entire system."

## WHERE IT ALL BEGAN

Based on findings that people label photos of prototypical facial expressions with words that represent the same basic emotions—a smile represents joy, a scowl represents anger—Ekman and Izard pioneered the idea that by carefully measuring facial expression, they could evaluate people's true emotions. In fact, since the 1970s, Ekman and his colleague Wallace Friesen, PhD, have dominated the field of emotion research with their theory that when an emotion occurs, a cascade of electrical impulses, emanating from emotion centers in the brain, trigger specific facial expressions and other physiological changes—such as increased or decreased heart rate or heightened blood pressure.

If the emotion comes on slowly, or is rather weak, the theory states, the impulse might not be strong enough to trigger the expression. This would explain in part why there can sometimes be emotion without expression,

> "The face is like a switch on a railroad track. It affects the trajectory of the social interaction the way the switch would affect the path of the train."
>
> *Alan Fridlund*
> *University of California, Santa Barbara*

they argue. In addition, cultural "display rules"—which determine when and whether people of certain cultures display emotional expressions—can derail this otherwise automatic process, the theory states. Facial expressions evolved in humans as signals to others about how they feel, says Ekman.

"At times it may be uncomfortable or inconvenient for others to know how we feel," he says. "But in the long run, over the course of evolution, it was useful to us as signalers. So, when you see an angry look on my face, you know that I may be preparing to respond in an angry fashion, which means that I may attack or abruptly withdraw."

## THE FACE IS LIKE A SWITCH

Although Fridlund strongly disagrees with Ekman in his writings, arguing that expressions carry no inherent meaning, the two basically agree that facial expressions forecast people's future actions. But instead of describing expressions from the point of view of the expresser, as Ekman tends to do, Fridlund thinks more in terms of people who perceive the expressions.

Expressions evolved to elicit behaviors from others, says Fridlund. So, a smile may encourage people to approach while a scowl may impel them to stay clear, and a pout may elicit words of sympathy and reassurance. And, he contends, expressions are inherently social. Even when people are alone they are holding an internal dialogue with another person, or imagining themselves in a social situation.

"The face is like a switch on a railroad track," says Fridlund. "It affects the trajectory of the social interaction the way the switch would affect the path of the train."

Thinking of facial expressions as tools for influencing social interactions provides an opportunity to begin predicting when certain facial expressions will occur and will allow more precise theories about social interactions, says Fridlund. Studies by him and others find that expressions occur most often during pivotal points in social interactions—during greetings, social crisis or times of appeasement, for example.

"At these pivotal points, where there's an approach, or proximity, or more intimacy, the face as well as the gestures form a kind of switching sta-

tion for the possibilities of social interactions," says Fridlund.

The University of Amsterdam's Nico Frijda, PhD, agrees that expressions are a means to influence others. They also, he believes, occur when people prepare to take some kind of action whether there are others present or not. For example, if you're scared and want to protect yourself, you frown and draw your brows in preparation—what Ekman would call a "fear" expression. But there is no one-to-one correspondence between the face and specific emotions, Frijda contends.

"There is some affinity between certain emotions and certain expressions," he says, "if only because some emotions imply a desire for vigorous action, and some facial expressions manifest just that."

## NOT A 'GOLD STANDARD'

Herein lies the major point of contention within the facial expression community, says Berkeley's Campos.

"All sides agree that the face—and voice and posture, for that matter—forecast what a person will do next," he says. "But over and above that, is feeling involved?"

Although much work in the emotion literature relies on a link between facial expression and emotions, there's a paucity of evidence supporting it.

"There's some sense in which faces express emotion, but only in the sense that everything expresses emotion," says psychologist James Russell, PhD, of the University of British Columbia, a long-time critic of the expression-emotion link. "Music does, posture does, words do, tone of voice does, your behavior does. The real question is, 'Is there anything special about faces?' And there we really don't know much."

What's more likely, argues Russell, is that facial expressions tell others something about the overall character of a person's mood—whether it's positive or negative—and context then provides details about specific emotions.

Others, including Ekman and Campos, contend that the face can display information about emotions. But, they admit, it is by no means a "gold standard." The face is only one of many measures researchers can use to infer emotion. And those who only examine faces when trying to study emotion will jump to false conclusions.

"There is a link between facial expression and emotion," explains developmental psychologist Linda Camras, PhD, of DePaul University. "But it's not a one-to-one kind of relationship as many once thought. There are many situations where emotion is experienced, yet no prototypic facial expression is displayed. And there are times when a facial expression appears with no corresponding emotion."

In a classic set of experiments with infants, Camras found that some facial expressions can occur in the absence of the emotions they supposedly represent.

"An emotion has to be plausible [for the situation you're examining]," she says. "You can't do blind coding of facial expression and necessarily be on the right track, even for infants."

But to say, as Fridlund does, that there's no connection between some facial expressions and some emotions is simply wrong, says Ekman. When we look at people's expressions, he says, we don't receive direct information about their heart rate or other physiological changes that accompany emotions. We might even think, "He's going to whack me" rather than "He's angry," says Ekman.

"But these signals—facial expressions and physiological changes associated with internal emotions—can't exist independently," he contends.

## FURTHER REFERENCE

Ekman, P., & Rosenberg, E. (1997). *What the Face Reveals.* New York: Oxford University Press.

Fridlund, A. (1994). *Human Facial Expression: An Evolutionary View.* San Diego, CA: Academic Press.

Russell, J., & Fernandez-Dols, J. M. (Eds.) (1997). *The Psychology of Facial Expression.* New York: Cambridge University Press.

# Emotional Intelligence:

## Do You Have It?

**Are your employees making you angry? What if it's not what they are doing wrong, but rather your reaction to the problem? Here's how you can become emotionally intelligent.**

by Phillip M. Perry

**Fran bristles** when you ask if a job is getting done. David sabotages projects when you criticize his work. And Oliver snaps when you pile on too many assignments.

You must deal with these employees, but how?

You've gotten where you are today because of your cognitive intelligence, technical competence, and analytical skills. But you're starting to get a funny feeling that those capabilities are not enough. Why don't they work when you try to turn around these problem individuals?

Worse yet: Why are you starting to feel angry toward these employees? You're tempted to just up and yell at them.

Well, here's some good news. You have already made a great start toward resolving these knotty workplace problems, because you recognize how you feel. That's the first step toward achieving a new set of skills that business psychologists now say are required to deal with today's workplace problems.

Taken as a group, the new skills comprise "emotional intelligence." That's the ability to recognize your emotions and those of the people around you, and the competence to work with those emotions to resolve employee problems.

 From *Floral Management*, October 1998, pp. 24-29. © 1998 by Phillip M. Perry. Reprinted by permission.

Ignore this new intelligence at your own risk. "There is a cost to the bottom line from low levels of emotional intelligence on the job," says Daniel P. Goleman, author of *Emotional Intelligence,* the best-seller that recently got people buzzing about the topic. Goleman says that success at work is 20 percent dependent on intellectual ability, and 80 percent dependent on emotional intelligence.

Odd thing is, we've had a clue to the importance of this knowledge for many years. We've known all along that customers buy for emotional reasons. They purchase to fill an inner need, then they rationalize it later. Up until now, though, we haven't recognized that employees act from similar motives. At work, people behave in ways that express their inner feelings. Later, they justify their actions.

This explains why some employees stubbornly resist your logical exhortations to change. When your directives do not address individuals' emotions, you are destined to fail. That's why it's vital to learn these new skills today.

Here's what business psychologists say to do to resolve common workplace situations.

## Fran the Foot-dragger

Despite Fran's enthusiasm, skills and intelligence, she's slogging through molasses as she works on that project that you need done in two days. The task seems simple enough: Give a facelift to the drieds and permanent botanicals section. She makes attempt after attempt, then has to start over. And she constantly comes to you with small questions. You start screaming inside: "Why doesn't she just get the job done?" The last straw comes when she asks if she can start over again using the ancient Chinese Feng Shui philosophy of space and energy. You explode: "Get back to the sales floor and get it done! I need it done now!"

# Listen Up

Good listening skills are key to a productive work environment. Sharpen yours by using a procedure called RECE, developed by Toni Bernay, a clinical psychologist and executive coach in Beverly Hills, Calif.

Here are the elements of RECE, which stands for **R**ecognize, **E**ngage, **C**ollaborate, and **E**mpower, and how to use them in response to the "Fran the Foot dragger" situation.

**1. Recognize the employee.** When an individual enters your work area, stop what you are doing and look directly at the person. Act as though you are glad to see the individual, not as though you are being distracted from your work.

**2. Engage the employee.** Communicate well by listening to the individual's words and responding appropriately. Here's how you might respond to Fran:

"Gosh, that's a creative solution. My problem is that I am very familiar with conventional merchandising and not with Feng Shui, and I am the one who has to deal with the merchandising and display throughout this and our other stores. Let's try Feng Shui next month, so I can get prepared for it. Right now I am under the gun and would appreciate if you would use conventional display techniques.

**3. Collaborate.** Work with the employee to solve the current problem and plan ahead so the problem does not occur again. With Fran, try having her work with an experienced display co-worker. Ask Fran to set an appointment with you to discuss how your shop can migrate to Feng Shui.

**4. Empower.** Encourage the employee to take the initiative, and reward any creative solutions. Fran already feels empowered because you have acknowledged her initiative, and you have asked her to make an appointment with you so you can learn more about the newer merchandising method.

—*P. P.*

Barking orders at a subordinate may get the task accomplished, but at tremendous cost. Employee self-image and morale plummet. Your employees will hesitate to approach you again. Bottom line: The work ends up being sub-par.

So what to do? Toni Bernay, a clinical psychologist and executive coach in Beverly Hills, Calif., suggests the classic two-stepped approach of emotional intelligence:

**1. Become aware of your own emotions.** In this case, there is likely a combination of emotions. There is anger grown from frustration. There is fear that a critical task will not get done and you will look ineffective to your own supervisor.

**2. Develop an action plan** to resolve those troubling emotions. "Perhaps you have not learned the skills of delegation well," offers Bernay. "Or perhaps you have not learned to slow down and work with people closely when you launch a project." Further, perhaps you have not communicated well with Fran during the first stages of the project when she was sending you signals that not all was well. "Maybe you need to take stock and work on listening skills," says Dr. Bernay. (For more on listening skills, see sidebar, right.)

## David, the Chronic Saboteur

Fran was a one-shot. Now, how about David, who has been simmering on the back burner for many months? While David has been a valuable worker, he seems to have developed a prima donna complex lately. Any slight criticism seems to set him off: He starts making demands that other departments cannot meet. When he doesn't get his way he always seems to find some "good excuse" why his tasks don't

## Anger in the Workplace: Good or Bad?

Suppose you are a manager for whom anger is a driving force through the day. Are you being destructive by expressing anger in the workplace?

Not necessarily, says John Mayer, a University of New Hampshire psychologist who was one of the original formulators of the emotional intelligence concept.

"There are fair ways to exhibit temper," says Mayer. "Be sure to be angry at what happened rather than at the individual. Be angry that a job didn't get done or that an employee jeopardized his own future."

Make sure the employee understands the target of your anger by expressing yourself in terms such as "I'm angry that this job did not get done."

get done. Things have finally reached a head. You're furious. What to do?

**Don't take it personally.** Don't call a meeting right away, suggests John Mayer, a University of New Hampshire psychologist who was one of the original formulators of the emotional intelligence concept. "First, figure out what is making you angry ahead of time. Then call the meeting when you calm down."

Ask yourself why you have become angry at David. Because he makes you look like a bad manager? Because you lost a company competition due to poor performance? Because you feel David is targeting you personally?

"Try to separate the employee's actions from what you do," says Mayer. "Understand that you were a good supervisor and this person did not live up to it. You can at least realize that whatever is going on is not a direct reflection on you. This

will help calm you down." Then you can approach David with the same rational questions as you did with Fran (see sidebar, above).

**Start a dialog.** In this case, start early by keeping a work diary of the specific actions David has taken, including his unreasonable demands and the late work, or tasks that have fallen through the cracks. Then, ask David what you can do to help keep this pattern from repeating.

In recalling a specific outburst from David, you might say something like, "It seems to me you must have been feeling frustrated that you did not have the tools you asked for to get the job done."

Notice that the "seems to me" statement does not attempt to say with certainty how David was feeling. And just as important, you are not agreeing that he needed the tools to get his work done. But you are starting a dialog. Now, encourage David to open up and talk with you about what steps the two of you can take together to resolve the continuing problem.

**Don't psychoanalyze.** What if you sense that David has built up lots of resentments, and you want to encourage him to express them? Mayer cautions against going too far when dealing with sources of emotions. The employee may be experiencing problems at home that may be causing angry outbursts in the office, for example, but he may not want to share this information with you.

"The manager does not have a contract to psychoanalyze the employee," cautions Mayer. "Be sensitive enough that you do not create emotional turmoil that gets in the way of progress, but avoid going so far as to intrude on what may be none of your business. Figure out the boundary."

### Overworked Oliver Has an Outburst

You've been piling on the work, thanks to an unforeseen barrage of

weddings. You know your employees are under stress. Then something snaps. Oliver bursts into your office and yells at you: "How can you tell us to do all of this extra work? There's just no time to get it all done. Don't you know how to manage?"

How you respond in the next five to 10 seconds is critical, according to David R. Caruso, a consultant with Harris McCully Associates, a New York-based human resources firm. Caruso suggests the following steps:

**1. Identify feelings.** "First, you need to calm down and control your feelings," says Caruso. "Don't assume this is an attack on you personally."

Then identify the feelings of the employee. "Read the emotions expressed in the face, the body language and tone of voice," says Caruso. "It's probably not pure anger. It's frustration. There may be some fear of not being effective."

**2. Deal with the problem.** If you have time to deal with the problem on the spot, invite the employee to sit down, then close the door. Don't take any interruptions, or answer the phone. Say, "I have a few minutes if you want to talk about it."

Let the person talk for the first minute or so, says Caruso. "Then always reflect on what the individual has said." Caruso suggests language such as this:

"Well, you have said that the workload is way too much. You said that you are feeling stressed out, and that the quality of the work is going to suffer. I appreciate your telling me these things. It's difficult for people to deliver bad news, and as a manager I cannot be effective without information, so I want to thank you first. I don't know what I can do now, but we need to spend time together and figure out what is happening and what can be done. I cannot promise an easy solution and maybe there is no solution. But it's certainly worth trying to come up with one."

You have echoed and interpreted what the individual has said. It is important not to deny emotions by ignoring them. But once again, don't tell people how they are feeling: "You're really angry." This will just make them angrier because your easy interpretation seems to belittle the complex emotions they have. Instead tell them how it "seems to you" they are feeling.

You use this initial meeting to buy time rather than to solve the problem on the spot. Make an appointment with a time frame so it does not fall through the cracks, causing further frustration. Say something like: "This is a serious enough issue that I want to discuss it in detail. Do you have time later today when we can go through all of your concerns?"

You have calmed down the person, taken them seriously and given them hope. Before your next meeting, do your research. Talk with other employees and get a sense of what the staff is feeling. Then you will be prepared with possible solutions when you meet with the employee.

## Don't Miss the Boat

There is no one perfect solution to any problem. Emotional intelligence is a learned process rather than a preordained set of steps. Some managers say they don't want to spend time calming down employees or becoming "amateur psychologists." These managers are missing the boat in a changing world where technical skills are no longer sufficient for success. Says Caruso: "Managers become successful when they start to view themselves as managers of people, not just as technicians."

---

*Phillip M. Perry is a freelance writer based in New York City and a regular contributor to* Floral Management.

# Unit 7

## Key Points to Consider

❖ Why is embryonic life so important? How do the experiences of the fetus affect the child after it is born? What factors deter the fetus from achieving its full potential?

❖ Do parents matter or do you think that child development is mostly dictated by genes? Do you think that both nature and nurture affect development? Do you think one of these factors is more important than the other? Which one and why? Do you think it is important for both parents to be present during their child's formative years? Do you think fathers and mothers differ in their interactions with their children? How so?

❖ What is puberty? What is adolescence? How are today's teens different from teens in the past, for example their parents' generation? What societal factors are influencing teens today? If you had to rank these factors, which are most influential, which are least influential?

❖ Why do we age? Can we stay younger longer? What do Americans say is more important—a high quality but shorter life or a poorer quality and longer life? Why do you think they answered the way they did? How would you answer and why? Would you want to live to 100? Explain why or why not.

❖ Why is death a stigmatized topic in America? Do you think people should discuss it more often and more openly? Do you think they ever will? How can we make dying easier for the dying person and for those close to the dying person? What can be done to help those with terminal illnesses?

 **Links** | **www.dushkin.com/online/**

These sites are annotated on pages 4 and 5.

The Garcias and the Szubas are parents of newborns. Both sets of parents wander down to the hospital's neonatal nursery where both babies, José Garcia and Kimberly Szuba, are cared for by pediatric nurses when the babies are not in their mothers' rooms. Kimberly is alert, active, and often crying and squirming when her parents watch her. On the other hand, José is quiet, often asleep, and less attentive to external stimuli when his parents watch him.

Why are these babies so different? Are the differences gender-related? Will these differences disappear as the children develop or will the differences become exaggerated? What does the future hold for each child? Will Kimberly excel at sports and José excel at English? Can Kimberly overcome her parents' poverty and succeed in a professional career? Will José become a doctor like his mother or a pharmacist like his father? Will both of these children escape childhood disease, abuse, and the other misfortunes sometimes visited upon children?

Developmental psychologists are concerned with all of the Kimberlys and Josés of our world. Developmental psychologists study age-related changes in language, motor and social skills, cognition, and physical health. They are interested in the common skills shared by all children as well as the differences between children and the events that create these differences.

In general, developmental psychologists are concerned with the forces that guide and direct development. Some developmental theorists argue that the forces that shape a child are found in the environment in such factors as social class, quality of available stimulation, parenting style, and so on. Other theorists insist that genetics and related physiological factors, such as hormones, underlie the development of humans. A third set of psychologists—in fact many—believe that some combination or interaction of both factors, physiology and environment (or nature and nurture), is responsible for development.

In this unit, we are going to look at issues of development in a chronological fashion. The first selection pertains to fetal development, which is crucial to the development of the child after it is born. Various environmental factors can deter development of or even damage the fetus. Janet Hopson reviews these in "Fetal Psychology."

In "Four Things You Need to Know About Raising Baby," author Joanna Lipari highlights research on infants that demonstrates that babies are active learners and therefore need certain stimulation and experiences to assist them to be fully functioning. The article alludes to some well-known myths about infants (such as, infants are nonlearners) and the research that is disproving them.

We move next to some information about adolescence. In "A World of Their Own," Sharon Begley suggests that teens today are very different from teens of past generations. While their peers are still very influential, there are a number of other societal influences that were not experienced by past teens. The Internet, for example, is a new phenomenon and is a powerful influence on today's teens. Begley interviewed teens and reveals what they think and say about these societal changes and the impacts on their own lives.

The next article is about adulthood and aging. The American Association for Retired People conducted a recent poll to determine whether quality of life or quantity (age) is more important to its members. Most elderly opted for a shorter life with better quality rather than a longer life with poor quality.

The final article in this series looks at the ultimate stage in development—death. Death is stigmatized in America; few people openly discuss it. There is much information contained in the article about issues surrounding death, such as hospice care, how to be with a dying person, and so forth. The article claims that we ought to be more open and is therefore designed to stimulate dialogue on this topic.

**Development**

# pFsEYTcAHLOLOGY

Behaviorally speaking, there's little difference between a newborn baby and a 32-week-old fetus. A new wave of research suggests that the fetus can feel, dream, even enjoy *The Cat in the Hat*. **The abortion debate may never be the same.**

By Janet L. Hopson

The scene never fails to give goose bumps: the baby, just seconds old and still dewy from the womb, is lifted into the arms of its exhausted but blissful parents. They gaze adoringly as their new child stretches and squirms, scrunches its mouth and opens its eyes. To anyone watching this tender vignette, the message is unmistakable. Birth is the beginning of it all, ground zero, the moment from which the clock starts ticking. Not so, declares Janet DiPietro. Birth may be a grand occasion, says the Johns Hopkins University psychologist, but "it is a trivial event in development. Nothing neurologically interesting happens."

Armed with highly sensitive and sophisticated monitoring gear, DiPietro and other researchers today are discovering that the real action starts weeks earlier. At 32 weeks of gestation—two months before a baby is considered fully prepared for the world, or "at term"—a fetus is behaving almost exactly as a newborn. And it continues to do so for the next 12 weeks.

As if overturning the common conception of infancy weren't enough, scientists are creating a startling new picture of intelligent life in the womb. Among the revelations:

• By nine weeks, a developing fetus can hiccup and react to loud noises. By the end of the second trimester it can hear.

• Just as adults do, the fetus experiences the rapid eye movement (REM) sleep of dreams.

• The fetus savors its mother's meals, first picking up the food tastes of a culture in the womb.

**A fetus spends hours in the rapid eye movement sleep of dreams.**

Reprinted with permission from *Psychology Today*, September/October 1998, pp. 44-48, 76. © 1998 by Sussex Publishers, Inc.

• Among other mental feats, the fetus can distinguish between the voice of Mom and that of a stranger, and respond to a familiar story read to it.

• Even a premature baby is aware, feels, responds, and adapts to its environment.

• Just because the fetus is responsive to certain stimuli doesn't mean that it should be the target of efforts to enhance development. Sensory stimulation of the fetus can in fact lead to bizarre patterns of adaptation later on.

The roots of human behavior, researchers now know, begin to develop early—just weeks after conception, in fact. Well before a woman typically knows she is pregnant, her embryo's brain has already begun to bulge. By five weeks, the organ that looks like a lumpy inchworm has already embarked on the most spectacular feat of human development: the creation of the deeply creased and convoluted cerebral cortex, the part of the brain that will eventually allow the growing person to move, think, speak, plan, and create in a human way.

At nine weeks, the embryo's ballooning brain allows it to bend its body, hiccup, and react to loud sounds. At week ten, it moves its arms, "breathes" amniotic fluid in and out, opens its jaw, and stretches. Before the first trimester is over, it yawns, sucks, and swallows as well as feels and smells. By the end of the second trimester, it can hear; toward the end of pregnancy, it can see.

## FETAL ALERTNESS

Scientists who follow the fetus' daily life find that it spends most of its time not exercising these new abilities but sleeping. At 32 weeks, it drowses 90 to 95% of the day. Some of these hours are spent in deep sleep, some in REM sleep, and some in an indeterminate state, a product of the fetus' immature brain that is different from sleep in a baby, child, or adult. During REM sleep, the fetus' eyes move back and forth just as an adult's eyes do, and many researchers believe that it is dreaming. DiPietro speculates that fetuses dream about what they know—the sensations they feel in the womb.

Closer to birth, the fetus sleeps 85 to 90% of the time, the same as a newborn. Between its frequent naps, the fetus seems to have "something like an awake alert period," according to developmental psychologist William Fifer, Ph.D., who with his Columbia University colleagues is monitoring these sleep and wakefulness cycles in order to identify patterns of normal and abnormal brain development, including potential predictors of

sudden infant death syndrome. Says Fifer, "We are, in effect, asking the fetus: 'Are you paying attention? Is your nervous system behaving in the appropriate way?'"

## FETAL MOVEMENT

Awake or asleep, the human fetus moves 50 times or more each hour, flexing and extending its body, moving its head, face, and limbs and exploring its warm wet compartment by touch. Heidelise Als, Ph.D., a developmental psychologist at Harvard Medical School, is fascinated by the amount of tactile stimulation a fetus gives itself. "It touches a hand to the face, one hand to the other hand, clasps its feet, touches its foot to its leg, its hand to its umbilical cord," she reports.

Als believes there is a mismatch between the environment given to preemies in hospitals and the environment they would have had in the womb. She has been working for years to change the care given to preemies so that they can curl up, bring their knees together, and touch things with their hands as they would have for weeks in the womb.

Along with such common movements, DiPietro has also noted some odder fetal activities, including "licking the uterine wall and literally walking around the womb by pushing off with its feet." Laterborns may have more room in the womb for such maneuvers than first babies. After the initial pregnancy, a woman's uterus is bigger and the umbilical cord longer, allowing more freedom of movement. "Second and subsequent children may develop more motor experience in utero and so may become more active infants," DiPietro speculates.

Fetuses react sharply to their mother's actions. "When we're watching the fetus on ultrasound and the mother starts to laugh, we can see the fetus, floating upside down in the womb, bounce up and down on its head, bum-bum-bum, like it's bouncing on a trampoline," says DiPietro. "When mothers watch this on the screen, they laugh harder, and the fetus goes up and down even faster. We've wondered whether this is why people grow up liking roller coasters."

## FETAL TASTE

Why people grow up liking hot chilies or spicy curries may also have something to do with the fetal environment. By 13 to 15 weeks a fetus' taste buds already look like a mature adult's, and doctors know that the amniotic fluid that surrounds it can smell strongly of curry, cumin,

**By 15 weeks, a fetus has an adult's taste buds and may be able to savor its mother's meals.**

# What's the Impact on Abortion?

Though research in fetal psychology focuses on the last trimester, when most abortions are illegal, the thought of a fetus dreaming, listening and responding to its mother's voice is sure to add new complexity to the debate. The new findings undoubtedly will strengthen the convictions of right-to-lifers—and they may shake the certainty of pro-choice proponents who believe that mental life begins at birth.

Many of the scientists engaged in studying the fetus, however, remain detached from the abortion controversy, insisting that their work is completely irrelevant to the debate.

"I don't think that fetal research informs the issue at all," contends psychologist Janet DiPietro of Johns Hopkins University. "The essence of the abortion debate is: When does life begin? Some people believe it begins at conception, the other extreme believes that it begins after the baby is born, and there's a group in the middle that believes it begins at around 24 or 25 weeks, when a fetus can live outside of the womb, though it needs a lot of help to do so.

"Up to about 25 weeks, whether or not it's sucking its thumb or has personality or all that, the fetus cannot survive outside of its mother. So is that life, or not? That is a moral, ethical, and religious question, not one for science. Things

can behave and not be alive. Right-to-lifers may say that this research proves that a fetus is alive, but it does not. It cannot."

"Fetal research only changes the abortion debate for people who think that life starts at some magical point," maintains Heidelise Als, a psychologist at Harvard University. "If you believe that life begins at conception, then you don't need the proof of fetal behavior." For others, however, abortion is a very complex issue and involves far more than whether research shows that a fetus hiccups. "Your circumstances and personal beliefs have much more impact on the decision," she observes.

Like DiPietro, Als realizes that "people may use this research as an emotional way to draw people to the pro-life side, but it should not be used by belligerent activists." Instead, she believes, it should be applied to helping mothers have the healthiest pregnancy possible and preparing them to best parent their child. Columbia University psychologist William Fifer, Ph.D., agrees. "The research is much more relevant for issues regarding viable fetuses—preemies."

Simply put, say the three, their work is intended to help the babies that live—not to decide whether fetuses should.—*Camille Chatterjee*

---

garlic, onion and other essences from a mother's diet. Whether fetuses can taste these flavors isn't yet known, but scientists have found that a 33-week-old preemie will suck harder on a sweetened nipple than on a plain rubber one.

"During the last trimester, the fetus is swallowing up to a liter a day" of amniotic fluid, notes Julie Mennella, Ph.D., a biopsychologist at the Monell Chemical Senses Center in Philadelphia. She thinks the fluid may act as a "flavor bridge" to breast milk, which also carries food flavors from the mother's diet.

## FETAL HEARING

Whether or not a fetus can taste, there's little question that it can hear. A very premature baby entering the world at 24 to 25 weeks responds to the sounds around it, observes Als, so its auditory apparatus must already have been functioning in the womb. Many pregnant women report a fetal jerk or sudden kick just after a door slams or a car backfires.

Even without such intrusions, the womb is not a silent place. Researchers who have inserted a hydrophone into the uterus of a pregnant woman have picked up a noise level "akin to the background noise in an apartment," according to DiPietro. Sounds include the whooshing of blood in the mother's vessels, the gurgling and rumbling of her stomach and intestines, as well as the tones of her voice filtered through tissues, bones, and fluid, and the

voices of other people coming through the amniotic wall. Fifer has found that fetal heart rate slows when the mother is speaking, suggesting that the fetus not only hears and recognizes the sound, but is calmed by it.

## FETAL VISION

Vision is the last sense to develop. A very premature infant can see light and shape; researchers presume that a fetus has the same ability. Just as the womb isn't completely quiet, it isn't utterly dark, either. Says Fifer: "There may be just enough visual stimulation filtered through the mother's tissues that a fetus can respond when the mother is in bright light," such as when she is sunbathing.

Japanese scientists have even reported a distinct fetal reaction to flashes of light shined on the mother's belly. However, other researchers warn that exposing fetuses (or premature infants) to bright light before they are ready can be dangerous. In fact, Harvard's Als believes that retinal damage in premature infants, which has long been ascribed to high concentrations of oxygen, may actually be due to overexposure to light at the wrong time in development.

A six-month fetus, born about 14 weeks too early, has a brain that is neither prepared for nor expecting signals from the eyes to be transmitted into the brain's visual cortex, and from there into the executive-branch frontal lobes, where information is integrated. When the fetus

A fetus prefers hearing Mom's voice over a stranger's—speaking in her native, not a foreign tongue—and being read aloud familiar tales rather than new stories.

is forced to see too much too soon, says Als, the accelerated stimulation may lead to aberrations of brain development.

## FETAL LEARNING

Along with the ability to feel, see, and hear comes the capacity to learn and remember. These activities can be rudimentary, automatic, even biochemical. For example, a fetus, after an initial reaction of alarm, eventually stops responding to a repeated loud noise. The fetus displays the same kind of primitive learning, known as habituation, in response to its mother's voice, Fifer has found.

But the fetus has shown itself capable of far more. In the 1980s, psychology professor Anthony James DeCasper, Ph.D., and colleagues at the University of North Carolina at Greensboro, devised a feeding contraption that allows a baby to suck faster to hear one set of sounds through headphones and to suck slower to hear a different set. With this technique, DeCasper discovered that within hours of birth, a baby already prefers its mother's voice to a stranger's, suggesting it must have learned and remembered the voice, albeit not necessarily consciously, from its last months in the womb. More recently, he's found that a newborn prefers a story read to it repeatedly in the womb—in this case, *The Cat in the Hat*—over a new story introduced soon after birth.

DeCasper and others have uncovered more mental feats. Newborns can not only distinguish their mother from a stranger speaking, but would rather hear Mom's voice, especially the way it sounds filtered through amniotic fluid rather than through air. They're xenophobes, too: they prefer to hear Mom speaking in her native language than to hear her or someone else speaking in a foreign tongue.

By monitoring changes in fetal heart rate, psychologist Jean-Pierre Lecanuet, Ph.D., and his colleagues in Paris have found that fetuses can even tell strangers' voices apart. They also seem to like certain stories more than others. The fetal heartbeat will slow down when a familiar French fairy tale such as *"La Poulette"* ("The Chick") or *"Le Petit Crapaud"* ("The Little Toad"), is read near the mother's belly. When the same reader delivers another unfamiliar story, the fetal heartbeat stays steady.

The fetus is likely responding to the cadence of voices and stories, not their actual words, observes Fifer, but the conclusion is the same: the fetus can listen, learn, and remember at some level, and, as with most babies

and children, it likes the comfort and reassurance of the familiar.

## FETAL PERSONALITY

It's no secret that babies are born with distinct differences and patterns of activity that suggest individual temperament. Just when and how the behavioral traits originate in the womb is now the subject of intense scrutiny.

In the first formal study of fetal temperament in 1996, DiPietro and her colleagues recorded the heart rate and movements of 31 fetuses six times before birth and compared them to readings taken twice after birth. (They've since extended their study to include 100 more fetuses.) Their findings: fetuses that are very active in the womb tend to be more irritable infants. Those with irregular sleep/wake patterns in the womb sleep more poorly as young infants. And fetuses with high heart rates become unpredictable, inactive babies.

"Behavior doesn't begin at birth," declares DiPietro. "It begins before and develops in predictable ways." One of the most important influences on development is the fetal environment. As Harvard's Als observes, "The fetus gets an enormous amount of 'hormonal bathing' through the mother, so its chronobiological rhythms are influenced by the mother's sleep/wake cycles, her eating patterns, her movements."

The hormones a mother puts out in response to stress also appear critical. DiPietro finds that highly pressured mothers-to-be tend to have more active fetuses—and more irritable infants. "The most stressed are working pregnant women," says DiPietro. "These days, women tend to work up to the day they deliver, even though the implications for pregnancy aren't entirely clear yet. That's our cultural norm, but I think it's insane."

Als agrees that working can be an enormous stress, but emphasizes that pregnancy hormones help to buffer both mother and fetus. Individual reactions to stress also matter. "The pregnant woman who chooses to work is a different woman already from the one who chooses not to work," she explains.

She's also different from the woman who has no choice but to work. DiPietro's studies show that the fetuses of poor women are distinct neurobehaviorally—less active, with a less variable heart rate—from the fetuses of middle-class women. Yet "poor women rate themselves as less stressed than do working middle-class women," she notes. DiPietro suspects that inadequate nutrition and exposure to pollutants may significantly affect the fetuses of poor women.

Stress, diet, and toxins may combine to have a harmful effect on intelligence. A recent study by biostatistician Bernie Devlin, Ph.D., of the University of Pittsburgh, suggests that genes may have less impact on IQ than previously thought and that the environment of the womb may account for much more. "Our old notion of nature influencing the fetus before birth and nurture after birth needs an update," DiPietro insists. "There is an antenatal environment, too, that is provided by the mother."

Parents-to-be who want to further their unborn child's mental development should start by assuring that the antenatal environment is well-nourished, low-stress, drug-free. Various authors and "experts" also have suggested poking the fetus at regular intervals, speaking to it through a paper tube or "pregaphone," piping in classical music, even flashing lights at the mother's abdomen.

Does such stimulation work? More importantly: Is it safe? Some who use these methods swear their children are smarter, more verbally and musically inclined, more physically coordinated and socially adept than average. Scientists, however, are skeptical.

"There has been no defended research anywhere that shows any enduring effect from these stimulations," asserts Fifer. "Since no one can even say for certain when a fetus is awake, poking them or sticking speakers on the mother's abdomen may be changing their natural sleep patterns. No one would consider poking or prodding a newborn baby in her bassinet or putting a speaker next to her ear, so why would you do such a thing with a fetus?"

Als is more emphatic: "My bet is that poking, shaking, or otherwise deliberately stimulating the fetus might alter its developmental sequence, and anything that affects the development of the brain comes at a cost."

Gently talking to the fetus, however, seems to pose little risk. Fifer suggests that this kind of activity may help parents as much as the fetus. "Thinking about your fetus, talking to it, having your spouse talk to it, will all help prepare you for this new creature that's going to jump into your life and turn it upside down," he says— once it finally makes its anti-climactic entrance.

# FOUR THINGS
## YOU NEED TO KNOW
## ABOUT RAISING BABY

*New thinking about the newborn's brain, feelings
and behavior are changing the way we look at parenting*

BY JOANNA LIPARI, M.A.

**B**ookstore shelves are crammed with titles purporting to help you make your baby smarter, happier, healthier, stronger, better-behaved and everything else you can imagine, in what I call a shopping-cart approach to infant development. But experts are now beginning to look more broadly, in an integrated fashion, at the first few months of a baby's life. And so should you.

Psychological theorists are moving away from focusing on single areas such as physical development, genetic inheritance, cognitive skills or emotional attachment, which give at best a limited view of how babies develop. Instead, they are attempting to synthesize and integrate all the separate pieces of the infant-development puzzle. The results so far have been enlightening, and are beginning to suggest new ways of parenting.

The most important of the emerging revelations is that the key to stimulating emotional and intellectual growth in your child is your own behavior—what you do, what you don't do, how you scold, how you reward and how you show affection. If the baby's brain is the hardware, then you, the parents, provide the software. When you understand the hardware (your baby's brain), you will be better able to design the software (your own behavior) to promote baby's well-being.

The first two years of life are critical in this regard because that's when your baby is building the mental foundation that will dictate his or her behavior through adulthood. In the first year alone, your baby's brain grows from about 400g to a stupendous 1000g. While this growth and development is in part predetermined by genetic force, exactly how the brain grows is dependent upon emotional interaction, and that involves you. "The human cerebral cortex adds about 70% of its final DNA content after birth," reports Allan N. Schore, Ph.D., assistant clinical professor of psychiatry and biobehavioral sciences at UCLA Medical School, "and this expanding brain is directly influenced by early environmental enrichment and social experiences."

Failure to provide this enrichment during the first two years can lead to a lifetime of emotional disability, according to attachment theorists. We are talking about the need to create a relationship and environment that allows your child to grow up with an openness to learning and the ability to process, understand and experience emotion with compassion, intelligence and resilience. These are the basic building blocks of emotional success.

Following are comparisons of researchers' "old thinking" and "new thinking." They highlight the four new insights changing the way we view infant development. The sections on "What To Do" then explain how to apply that new information.

**1** **FEELINGS TRUMP THOUGHTS**
It is the emotional quality of the relationship you have with your baby that will stimulate his or her brain for optimum emotional and intellectual growth.

**OLD THINKING:** In this country, far too much emphasis is placed on developing babies' cognitive abilities. Some of this push came out of the promising results of the Head Start program. Middle-class families reasoned that if a little stimulation in an underendowed home environment is beneficial, wouldn't "more" be better? And the race to create the "superbaby" was on.

Gone are the days when parents just wished their child were "normal" and could "fit in" with other kids. Competition for selective schools and the social pressure it generates has made parents feel their child needs to be "gifted." Learning exercises, videos and educational toys are pushed on parents to use in play with their children. "Make it fun," the experts say. The emphasis is on developing baby's cognitive skills by using the emotional reward of parental attention as a behavior-training tool.

**THE NEW THINKING:** Flying in the face of all those "smarter" baby books are studies suggesting that pushing baby to learn words, numbers, colors and shapes too early forces the child to use lower-level thinking processes, rather than develop his or her learning ability. It's like a pony trick at the circus: When the pony paws the ground to "count" to three, it's really not counting; it's simply performing a stunt. Such "tricks" are not only not helpful to baby's learning process, they are potentially harmful. Tufts University child psychologist David Elkind, Ph.D., makes it clear that putting pressure on a child to learn information sends the message that he or she needs to "perform" to gain the parents' acceptance, and it can dampen natural curiosity.

Instead, focus on building baby's emotional skills. "Emotional development is not just the foundation for important capacities such as intimacy and trust," says Stanley Greenspan, M.D., clinical professor of psychiatry and pediatrics at George Washington University Medical School and author of the new comprehensive book *Building Healthy Minds.* "It is also the foundation of intelligence and a wide variety of cognitive skills. At each stage of development, emotions lead the way, and learning facts and skills follow. Even math skills, which appear [to be] strictly an impersonal cognition, are initially learned through the emotions: 'A lot' to a 2-year-old, for example, is more than he would expect, whereas 'a little' is less than he wants."

It makes sense: Consider how well you learn when you are passionate about a subject, compared to when you are simply required to learn it. That passion is the emotional fuel driving the cognitive process. So the question then becomes not "what toys and games should I use to make my baby smarter?" but "how should I interact with my baby to make him 'passionate' about the world around him?"

**WHAT TO DO:** When you read the baby "milestone" books or cognitive development guides, keep in mind that the central issue is your baby's *emotional* development. As Greenspan advises, "Synthesize this information about milestones and see them with emotional development as the central issue. This is like a basketball team, with the coach being our old friend, emotions. Because emotions tell the child what he wants to do—move his arm, make a sound, smile or frown. As you look at the various 'milestone components'—motor, social and cognitive skills—look to see how the whole mental team is working together."

Not only will this give you more concrete clues as to how to strengthen your emotional relationship, but it will also serve to alert you to any "players" on the team that are weak or injured, i.e., a muscle problem in the legs, or a sight and hearing difficulty.

## 2 NOT JUST A SCREAMING MEATLOAF: BIRTH TO TWO MONTHS
It's still largely unknown how well infants understand their world at birth, but new theories are challenging the traditional perspectives.

**OLD THINKING:** Until now, development experts thought infants occupied some kind of presocial, precognitive, preorganized life phase that stretched from birth to two months. They viewed newborns' needs as mainly physiological—with sleep-wake, day-night and hunger-satiation cycles, even calling the first month of life "the normal autism" phase, or as a friend calls it, the "screaming meatloaf" phase. Certainly, the newborn has emotional needs, but researchers thought they were only in response to basic sensory drives like taste, touch, etc.

**THE NEW THINKING:** In his revolutionary book, *The Interpersonal World of the Infant,* psychiatrist Daniel Stern, Ph.D., challenged the conventional wisdom on infant development by proposing that babies come into this world as social beings. In research experiments, newborns consistently demonstrate that they actively seek sensory stimulation, have distinct preferences and, from birth, tend to form hypotheses about what is occurring in the world around them. Their preferences are emotional ones. In fact, parents would be unable to establish the physiological cycles like wake-sleep without the aid of such sensory, emotional activities as rocking, touching, soothing, talking and singing. In turn, these interactions stimulate the child's brain to make the neuronal connections she needs in order to process the sensory information provided.

**WHAT TO DO:** "Take note of your baby's own special biological makeup and interactive style," Greenspan advises. You need to see your baby for the special individual he is at birth. Then, "you can deliberately introduce the world to him in a way that maximizes his delight and minimizes his frustrations." This is also the time to learn how to help your baby regulate his emotions, for example, by offering an emotionally overloaded baby some soothing sounds or rocking to help him calm down.

## 3 THE LOVE LOOP: BEGINNING AT TWO MONTHS
At approximately eight weeks, a miraculous thing occurs—your baby's vision improves and for the first time, she can fully see you and can make direct eye contact. These beginning visual experiences of your baby play an important role in social and emotional development. "In particular, the mother's emotionally expressive face is, by far, the most potent visual stimulus in the infant's environment," points out UCLA's Alan Schore, "and the child's intense interest in her face, especially in her eyes, leads him/her to track it in space to engage in periods of intense mutual gaze." The result: Endorphin levels rise in the baby's brain, causing pleasurable feelings of joy and excitement. But the key is for this joy to be interactive.

**OLD THINKING:** The mother pumps information and affection into the child, who participates only as an empty receptacle.

**THE NEW THINKING:** We now know that the baby's participation is crucial to creating a solid attachment bond. The loving gaze of parents to child is reciprocated by the baby with a loving gaze back to the parents, causing their endorphin levels to rise, thus completing a closed emotional circuit, a sort of "love loop." Now, mother (or father) and baby are truly in a dynamic, interactive system. "In essence, we are talking less about what the mother is doing to the baby and more about how the mother is being with the baby and how the baby is learning to be with the mother," says Schore.

The final aspect of this developing interactive system between mother and child is the mother's development of an "emotional synchronization" with her child. Schore defines this as the mother's ability to tune into the baby's internal states and respond accordingly. For example: Your baby is quietly lying on the floor, happy to take in the sights and sounds of the environment. As you notice the baby looking for stimulation, you respond with a game of "peek-a-boo." As you play with your child and she responds with shrieks of glee, you escalate the emotion with bigger and bigger gestures and facial expressions. Shortly thereafter, you notice the baby turns away. The input has reached its maximum and you sense your child needs you to back off for awhile as she goes back to a state of calm and restful inactivity. "The synchronization between the two is more than between their behavior and thoughts; the synchronization is on a biological level—their brains and nervous systems are linked together," points out Schore. "In this process, the mother is teaching and learning at the same time. As a result of this moment-by-moment matching of emotion, both partners increase their emotional connection to one another. In addition, the more the mother fine-tunes her activity level to the infant during periods of play and interaction, the more she allows the baby to disengage and recover quietly during periods of nonplay, before initiating actively arousing play again."

Neuropsychological research now indicates that this attuned interaction—engaged play, disengagement and restful nonplay, followed by a return to play behavior—is especially helpful for brain growth and the development of cerebral circuits. This makes sense in light of the revelation that future cognitive development depends not on the cognitive stimulation of flashcards and videos, but on the attuned, dynamic and emotional interactions between parent and child. The play periods stimulate baby's central nervous system to excitation, followed by a restful period of alert inactivity in which the developing brain is able to process the stimulation and the interaction.

In this way, you, the parents, are the safety net under your baby's emotional highwire; the act of calming her down, or giving her the opportunity to calm down, will help her learn to handle ever-increasing intensity of stimulation and thus build emotional tolerance and resilience.

**WHAT TO DO:** There are two steps to maximizing your attunement ability: spontaneity and reflection. When in sync, you and baby will both experience positive emotion; when out of sync, you will see negative emotions. If much of your interactions seem to result in negative emotion, then it is time to reflect on your contribution to the equation.

In these instances, parents need to help one another discover what may be impeding the attunement process. Sometimes, on an unconscious level, it may be memories of our own childhood. For example, my friend sings nursery rhymes with a Boston accent, even though she grew up in New York, because her native Bostonian father sang them to her that way. While the "Fahmah in the Dell" will probably not throw baby into a temper tantrum, it's a good example of how our actions or parenting style may be problematic without our realizing it.

But all parents have days when they are out of sync with baby, and the new perspective is that it's not such a bad thing. In fact, it's quite valuable. "Misattunement" is not a bioneurological disaster if you can become attuned again. The process of falling out of sync and then repairing the bond actually teaches children resilience, and a sense of confidence that the world will respond to them and repair any potential hurt.

Finally, let your baby take the lead. Schore suggests we "follow baby's own spontaneous expression of himself," which lets the child know that another person, i.e., mom or dad, can understand what he is feeling, doing, and even thinking. Such experiences, says Schore, assist in the development of the prefrontal area, which controls "empathy, and therefore that which makes us most 'human.'"

**4** **THE SHAME TRANSACTION**
Toward the end of the first year, as crawling turns to walking, a shift occurs in the communication between child and parents. "Observational studies show that 12-month-olds receive more positive responses from mothers, while 18-month-olds receive more instructions and directions," says Schore. In one study, mothers of toddlers expressed a prohibition—basically telling the child "no"—approximately every nine minutes! That's likely because a mobile toddler has an uncanny knack for finding the most dangerous things to explore!

Yesterday, for example, I walked into the living room to find my daughter scribbling on the wall with a purple marker. "NO!" shot out of my mouth. She looked up at me with stunned shock, then realized what she had done. Immediately, she hung her head, about to cry. I babbled on a bit about how markers are only for paper, yada-yada and then thought, "Heck, it's washable." As I put my arm around my daughter, I segued into a suggestion for another activity: washing the wall! She brightened and raced to get the sponge. We had just concluded a "shame transaction."

**OLD THINKING:** Researchers considered all these "no's" a necessary byproduct of child safety or the socialization process. After all, we must teach children to use the potty rather than wet the bed, not to hit another child when mad, to behave properly in public. Researchers did not consider the function of shame vis-a-vis brain development. Instead, they advised trying to limit situations in which the child would feel shame.

**NEW THINKING:** It's true that you want to limit the shame situations, but they are not simply a necessary evil in order to civilize your baby. Neurobiological studies indicate that episodes of shame like the one I described can actually stimulate the development of the right hemisphere, the brain's source of creativity, emotion and sensitivity, as long as the shame period is short and followed by a recovery. In essence, it's not the experience of shame that can be damaging, but rather the inability of the parent to help the child recover from that shame.

**WHAT TO DO:** It's important to understand "the growth-facilitating importance of small doses of shame in the socialization

process of the infant," says Schore. Embarrassment (a component of shame) first emerges around 14 months, when mom's "no" results in the child lowering his head and looking down in obvious sadness. The child goes from excited (my daughter scribbling on the wall) to sudden deflation (my "NO!") back to excitement ("It's okay, let's wash the wall together"). During this rapid process, various parts of the brain get quite a workout and experience heightened connectivity, which strengthens these systems. The result is development of the orbitofrontal cortex (cognitive area) and limbic system (emotional area) and the ability for the two systems to interrelate emotional resiliency in the child and the ability to self-regulate emotions and impulse control.

What is important to remember about productive shame reactions is that there must be a quick recovery. Extended periods of shame result in a child learning to shut down, or worse, become hyperirritable, perhaps even violent. It's common sense: Just think how you feel when someone embarrasses you. If that embarrassment goes on without relief, don't you tend to either flee the situation or rail against it?

From these new research findings, it's clear that successful parenting isn't just about intuition, instinct and doing what your mother did. It's also not about pushing the alphabet, multiplication tables or violin lessons. We now believe that by seeing the newborn as a whole person—as a thinking, feeling creature who can and should participate in his own emotional and cognitive development—we can maximize the nurturing and stimulating potential of our relationship with a newborn baby.

*Joanna Lipari is pursuing a Psy.D. at Pepperdine University in Los Angeles.*

### READ MORE ABOUT IT
*The Irreducible Needs of Children: What Every Child Must Have to Grow, Learn and Flourish,* T. Berry Brazelton, M.D., and Stanley Greenspan, M.D. (Perseus Books, 2000).

*Building Healthy Minds,* Stanley Greenspan, M.D. (Perseus Books, 1999).

# A World Of Their Own

## They're spiritual, optimistic and ambitious. How teens want to shape the future.

### By Sharon Begley

THE TEMPTATION, OF COURSE, IS to seek The Teen, the one who can stand as a symbol of this generation, who exemplifies in a single, still-young life the aspirations, the values, the habits and outlook of the 22 million other Americans 13 to 19. Who, then, shall we offer up? Perhaps Vanesa Vathanasombat, 17, of Whittier, Calif., who spends her free time going to the beach and hanging at malls with friends. "You are who you hang around with," she says. "Before, parents made you who you are. Now, teens are pretty much defined by their friends. I see my mom maybe an hour a day and not at all on weekends." Or maybe Zoe Ward, 15, of Shoreline, Wash., who takes road trips with a friend (they sleep in the car) and sells her poetry on the street: "I can't decide if I want to be famous or if I want to go live in the mountains. That's what it's like for a lot of high-school kids: we don't know how to get there, what it's really going to be like." Or, finally, Marcus Ruopp, 16, of Newton, Mass., who would like to be an engineer or maybe a teacher after the Peace Corps, in order to "give back to the community."

No one teen incorporates all the attitudes and characteristics that the teachers who teach them, the parents who raise them, the researchers who study them and the kids who *are* them name as the identifying marks of this generation. In large part that is because "today's teens may have less in common with each other than those in generations past," says psychologist William Damon of Stanford University. "[Some] are absolutely on track: they're bright-eyed, genuine and ambitious. But a significant number are drifting or worse." Innumerable teens, then, will not recognize themselves in the portraits that follow. Yes, of course there are teens for whom adults are a strong presence, and teens who seldom volunteer. There are teens who are emotional wrecks, or even mentally ill. There are teens to whom "Instant Message" means Mom's telling them right away who phoned while they were out. And there are teens who belong to no clique—or "tribe." But, according to a new NEWSWEEK Poll as well as sociologists who have studied tens of thou
sands of the kids born between 1981 and 1987, those teens are the exceptions. As much as is possible when you are talking about 22 million human beings, a portrait of the millennial generation is emerging.

They were born at a time when the very culture was shifting to accommodate them—changing tables in restrooms, BABY ON BOARD signs and minivans. Yet, as a group, they lead lives that are more "adult-free" than those of previous generations. "Adolescents are not a tribe apart because *they* left *us,* as most people assume," says Patricia Hersch, author of the 1998 book "A Tribe Apart." "We left them. This generation of kids has spent more time on their own than any other in recent history."

When today's teens are not with their friends, many live in a private, adult-free world of the Web and videogames. Aminah McKinnie, 16, of Madison, Miss., attends church, loves gospel hip-hop and hopes to work in the computer industry. She doesn't "hang out," she says. "I shop on the Internet and am looking for a job on the Internet. I do homework, research, e-mail and talk to my friends on the Internet." She is not unusual. Data released last year from the Alfred P. Sloan Study of Youth and Social Development found that teens spend 9 percent of their waking hours outside school with friends. They spend 20 percent of their waking hours alone. "Teens are isolated to an extent that has never been possible before," says Stanford's Damon. "There is an ethic among adults that says, 'Kids want to be autonomous; don't get in their face.' "

This generation is strongly peer-driven. "This is much more a team-playing generation," says William Strauss, coauthor of the 1997 book "The Fourth Turning." "Boomers may be bowling alone, but Millennials are playing soccer in teams." That makes belonging so crucial that it can be a matter of life and death. In Littleton, Colo., a year ago, the two teenage shooters stood apart, alienated from the jock culture that infused Columbine High School. Yet in a landmark study of 7,000 teens, researchers led by Bar-

## Style counts

### Teen cliques are more fluid than adults think, but each has its own distinctive tribal markings, from hippie chic to body art to buttoned-down prep

# Sound and Fury

## "There's a lot of anger in my generation. You can hear it in the music. Kids are angry for a lot of reasons, but mostly because parents aren't around."

Robertino Rodriquez, 17

bara Schneider of the University of Chicago found that teen social groups are as fluid and hard to pin down as a bead of mercury. "Students often move from one group to another, and friendships change over a period of a few weeks or months," they write in "The Ambitious Generation." "Best friends are few." As a group, today's teens are also in-fused with an optimism not seen among kids in decades (it doesn't hurt to have grown up in a time of relative peace and the longest economic expansion in U.S. history). "I think a lot of adolescents now are being taught that they can make a difference," says Sophie Mazuroski, 15, of Portland, Maine. "Children of our generation want to. I am

very optimistic." Still the law of teenage angst is still on the books: 4.3 percent of ninth graders make suicide attempts serious enough to require medical treatment.

This generation of teens is more spiritual than their parents, but often less conventionally so. Many put together their own religious canon as they would a salad from a salad bar. Yet despite their faith, teens, as well as those who study them, say that "lying and cheating are standard behavior," as Trisha Sandoval, 17, of Santa Fe Springs, Calif., puts it—more so than for earlier generations. Elsewhere on the values front, teens today are less likely than those in 1992 "to get somebody pregnant, drive drunk or get into fights," says Kevin Dwyer, president of the National Association of School Psychologists. And teens, says Strauss, "had harsher opinions about the Clinton-Lewinsky scandal than any other group." Coming of age in a time of interracial marriages, many

# A Snapshot of a Generation

In the Internet age, teens seem to be coming of age ever earlier. A recent NEWSWEEK Poll explores what concerns today's youth and asks if their parents have a clue.

- **Stress:** Do teens today face more problems than their parents did as teens?

| | TEENS |
|---|---|
| More | 70% |
| Fewer | 5 |
| Same | 24 |

- **Family:** Do your parents spend enough time with you?

| | TEENS |
|---|---|
| Enough | 61% |
| Too little | 24 |
| Too much | 15 |

- 48% of teens say they use a computer almost every day at home

- 21% have looked at something on the Internet that they wouldn't want their parents to know about

- **Identity:** How much peer pressure from friends do you feel (does your teen feel) today to do the following?

| THOSE RESPONDING 'A LOT' | TEENS | PARENTS |
|---|---|---|
| Have sex | 10% | 20% |
| Grow up too fast | 16 | 34 |
| Steal or shoplift | 4 | 11 |
| Use drugs or abuse alcohol | 10 | 18 |
| Defy parents or teachers | 9 | 16 |
| Be mean to kids who are different | 11 | 14 |

If you had to choose between fitting in with friends or becoming outstanding in some way, which would you (your teen) choose?

| | TEENS | PARENTS |
|---|---|---|
| Fitting in | 26% | 43% |
| Becoming outstanding | 69 | 50 |

- **Worries:** How concerned are you about the following?

| THOSE RESPONDING 'A LOT' | TEENS | PARENTS |
|---|---|---|
| Not having enough money to buy the things you (they) want | 34% | 35% |
| The cost of your (their) college education | 54 | 68 |
| Violence in society | 59 | 82 |
| Not being sure about your (their) future job opportunities | 43 | 49 |
| Your (their) getting into trouble with drugs | 25 | 66 |
| Your (their) drinking or abusing alcohol | 26 | 64 |
| Sexual permissiveness in society | 33 | 72 |
| Sexually transmitted diseases | 58 | 75 |

- **Hostility:** Many teens these days feel a lot of anger. How angry are you?

| | TEENS |
|---|---|
| Very | 3% |
| Somewhat | 25 |
| Not too | 43 |
| Not at all | 29 |

- **Faith:** How important is religion in your life today?

| | TEENS |
|---|---|
| Very | 43% |
| Somewhat | 35 |
| Not too | 14 |
| Not at all | 8 |

- 17% of teens and 37% of parents say they worry a lot about safety at school

- 21% of teenagers polled say that most of the teens they know have already had sex

FOR THIS SPECIAL NEWSWEEK POLL, PRINCETON SURVEY RESEARCH ASSOCIATES INTERVIEWED A NATIONAL SAMPLE OF TEENS 13–19 AND 509 PARENTS OF SUCH TEENS BY TELEPHONE APRIL 20–28. THE MARGIN OF ERROR IS +/– 5 PERCENTAGE POINTS FOR PARENTS; +/– 6 FOR ALL TEENS; COPYRIGHT 2000 BY NEWSWEEK, INC.

## In Living Colors

"We don't care about skin, man. I know a lot about my heritage, about who I am. I'm more than just some black dude who is good at sports. I'm the future."

**Marcus Robinson, 17**

eschew the old notions of race; maturing at Internet speed, they are more connected than any generation. Both may bode well for tolerance. "Prejudice against homosexuals, bisexuals, African-Americans, Latinos—this is a big issue," says Kathryn Griffin, 18, of Palo Alto, Calif., who hopes to make a career in advertising or marketing. "It's insane that people have these feelings [about other people] when they don't even know them."

What do they want out of life? Schneider and coauthor David Stevenson found that today's teens "are the most occupationally and educationally ambitious generation" ever. Most plan to attend college, and many aspire to work as professionals. A majority identify "happiness" as a goal, along with love and a long and enjoyable life. But many doubt that marriage and career will deliver that, so they channel their energies more broadly. About half of teens perform community service once a month by, for instance, delivering meals to the homeless or reading to the elderly. But does their volunteer work reflect real compassion, or meeting a school requirement?

Regardless of what their terrified parents suspect, the belief that today's teens "are more sexual, rebellious and inebriated is flat-out wrong," says pediatrician Victor Strasburger of the University of New Mexico. In 1997, 48 percent of high-school students had had sexual intercourse, compared with 54 percent in 1991, according to the CDC. More are smoking (36 percent, compared with 28 percent in 1991), but the percentage who are drinking alcohol remains at 51 percent. The social surround, though, may be different now. "A lot of my friends are into drinking a lot," says Marcus Ruopp. "Kids don't see it as a big problem. It's a regular thing, not like they're rebelling. There is no pressure to drink."

Some sociologists believe that each generation assumes the societal role of the generation that is dying, as if something in the Zeitgeist whispers to the young what is being lost, what role they can fill. Those now passing away are the children of the Depression and of World War II. They were tested, and they emerged with optimism, and purpose, and a commitment to causes larger than themselves. As Trisha Sandoval puts it, "We want to accomplish something with our lives." Teens today, with their tattoos and baggy shorts, could not seem more different from their grandparents. But every generation has a chance at greatness. Let this one take its shot.

*With* PAT WINGERT *in Washington,* HOPE WHITE SCOTT *in Boston,* ANA FIGUEROA *in Los Angeles and* DEVIN GORDON, SUSANNAH MEADOWS *and* MICHAEL CRONIN *in New York*

# Live to 100? No thanks

## *Most people opt for quality, not quantity, in later years*

**BY SUSAN L. CROWLEY**

Despite stunning medical advances that can extend life, most Americans do not want to live to be 100. They fear the disabilities, impoverishment and isolation commonly thought to accompany old age.

The finding emerged in a wide-ranging AARP survey on attitudes toward longevity. When asked how long they want to live, 63 percent of the 2,032 respondents opted for fewer than 100 years.

"What this says to me," notes Constance Swank, director of research at AARP, "is that people are more interested in the quality of their lives than the length. They don't want to be encumbered by poor health and financial worries in their older years."

Survey respondents reported they would like to live to an average of about 91 years, but expect to live to 80. According to the U.S. Census Bureau, the life expectancy for a child born in 1997 is 76.5 years. A person turning 65 in 1997 could expect to live another 17.6 years.

The telephone survey, conducted from April 9 to 14 for AARP by Market Facts, Inc. of McLean, Va., also found that a huge majority of people are aware that their behavior and habits can affect how well they age.

This was "the real take-home message for me," says Terrie Wetle, deputy director of the National Institute on Aging. "It was very good news that more than 90 percent recognized that they had some control over how they age."

Harvard neuropsychologist Margery Hutter Silver, who is associate director of the New England Centenarian Study, agrees: "Just the fact of thinking you have control is going to have tremendous impact."

Over eight out of 10 respondents reported doing things to stay healthy. Seventy percent said they exercise, 33 percent watch their diets, 10 percent watch their weight and 10 percent maintain a positive attitude.

Most Americans are also optimistic that life will be better for the typical 80-year-old in 2050 and that medical advances will lead to cures for cancer, heart disease, AIDS and Alzheimer's disease.

Yet, even though they are taking steps to age well and are upbeat about the future, most people are still leery of what might befall them if they live to be 100.

That shouldn't come as a surprise, people of all ages told the Bulletin.

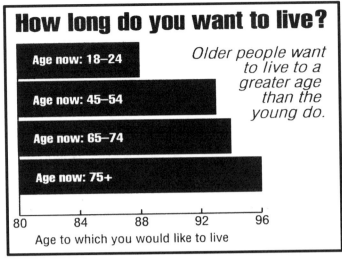

**How long do you want to live?**

Age now: 18–24

Age now: 45–54

Age now: 65–74

Age now: 75+

*Older people want to live to a greater age than the young do.*

80    84    88    92    96

Age to which you would like to live

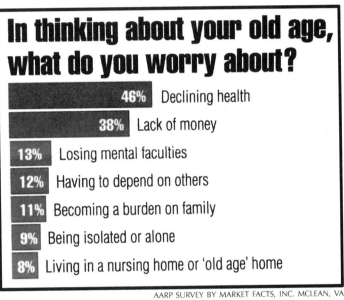

**In thinking about your old age, what do you worry about?**

46% Declining health

38% Lack of money

13% Losing mental faculties

12% Having to depend on others

11% Becoming a burden on family

9% Being isolated or alone

8% Living in a nursing home or 'old age' home

AARP SURVEY BY MARKET FACTS, INC. MCLEAN, VA.

"Our society bases its economy on young stars and young entrepreneurs," says Lynda Preble, 28, who works for a public relations firm in San Francisco. "I'm sure most people don't understand where they fit in once they are older."

"I was not surprised," says writer and publicist Susan Hartt, 57, of Baltimore. "As the saying goes, 'Old age is not for sissies.' "

Even though disability rates among the old are declining, chronic health problems and poverty are still more likely to appear in advanced age, Wetle says, and "people know that."

"I'm going to hang it up when I'm restricted to bed," say Marion Ballard, 59, a former software company owner in Bethesda, Md.

"A slow mental decline scares me the most," says Lilavati Sinclair, a 32-year-old mother in Bothell, Wash. For Peter Winkert, 47, a sales executive in Cazenovia, N.Y., "running out of income is my biggest concern."

Others express fear of being alone, burdening their families, living in a nursing home or, as one person puts it, "losing my joy and will to keep on living."

How old a person is tends to influence his or her views on age and aging. Among those ages 18 to 24, a person is "old" at 58, according to the survey, while those 65 or older think "old" starts at 75.

"I used to think I would be dead at 30," jokes one woman who just turned 30. "Now that I know I'll be around a while, I want to enjoy life as long as possible."

Not unexpectedly, older people hope and expect to live to greater ages than the young. Survey respondents 75 and older want to live to 96, but for 18- to 24-year-olds, 88 is enough.

Julie Vermillion, 24, who is a public affairs assistant in Washington, D.C.,

and Erin Laughlin, 23, a dog trainer in Sebastopol, Calif., say that living to 85 is about right.

Yet 85-year-old Lucille Runkel of Cochranton, Pa., is still in good shape and still active. "I wouldn't mind living to be 100 if I'm in good health," she says, "but I don't want to be dependent on my children."

"If I feel well enough," says lawyer Lester Nurick, 84, of Potomac, Md., "I could go on forever....but I would never put a number on it."

"Young people deal with the mythology instead of the reality of aging," says AARP's Swank. "Older people are living it, and many embrace the challenges, the joys. No one wants to be debilitated, but for many, the later years are highly satisfying. So why walk away from it?"

Older people have also witnessed the development of life-saving vaccines, drugs and surgical techniques and are more confident of continuing medical breakthroughs. "What we see here," Swank says, "is the wisdom of age."

Writer Hartt says she wouldn't mind putting up with some infirmities to achieve such wisdom. "So what was adolescence—a day at the beach?"

Lack of information helps fuel the myths of old age. For example, only 28 percent of survey respondents know that the 85-plus age group is the fastest-growing segment of the population.

And many people don't know that most Americans over 65 live independently, with fewer than 5 percent in nursing homes, adds Harvard's Silver.

Other survey highlights:

• On average, people with a college education hope to live longer (to age 92) than those with a high-school education (to 89).

• Fifty-two percent of those with a yearly household income of over $50,000 worry about poor health in old age, compared to 41 percent among those with incomes lower than $50,000.

• Those who say they are doing things to stay healthy and active expect to live to 81, while others expect to live to 76.

Given new findings about centenarians—whose numbers in the United States grew to more than 62,000 by 1998 and by some estimates could reach 1 million by 2050—aiming for the century mark is not unreasonable.

Living to 100 doesn't mean you'll be in poor health, says Silver, who is co-author with Thomas T. Perls, M.D., of "Living to 100" (Basic Books, 1999). To the contrary, centenarians are often healthier than people in their 80s.

But there's a trick, according to their book: "One must stay healthy the vast majority of one's life in order to live to 100."

Some think it's a worthy goal.

"It would be cool to live for over a century, just because of the history involved," says one 30-something. "I can't even guess what will come."

# Start the Conversation

## The MODERN MATURITY guide to end-of-life care

## The Body Speaks

Physically, dying means that "the body's various physiological systems, such as the circulatory, respiratory, and digestive systems, are no longer able to support the demands required to stay alive," says Barney Spivack, M.D., director of Geriatric Medicine for the Stamford (Connecticut) Health System. "When there is no meaningful chance for recovery, the physician should discuss realistic goals of care with the patient and family, which may include letting nature take its course. Lacking that direction," he says, "physicians differ in their perception of when enough is enough. We use our best judgment, taking into account the situation, the information available at the time, consultation with another doctor, or guidance from an ethics committee."

Without instructions from the patient or family, a doctor's obligation to a terminally ill person is to pro-

vide life-sustaining treatment. When a decision to "let nature take its course" has been made, the doctor will remove the treatment, based on the patient's needs. Early on, the patient or surrogate may choose to stop interventions such as antibiotics, dialysis, resuscitation, and defibrillation. Caregivers may want to offer food and fluids, but those can cause choking and the pooling of dangerous fluids in the lungs. A dying patient does not desire or need nourishment; without it he or she goes into a deep sleep and dies in days to weeks. A breathing machine would be the last support: It is uncomfortable for the patient, and may be disconnected when the patient or family finds that it is merely prolonging the dying process.

## The Best Defense Against Pain

Pain-management activists are fervently trying to reeducate physicians about the importance and safety of making patients comfortable. "In medical school 30 years ago, we worried a lot about creating addicts,"

# In Search of a Good Death

If we think about death at all, we say that we want to go quickly, in our sleep, or, perhaps, while fly-fishing. But in fact only 10 percent of us die suddenly. The more common process is a slow decline with episodes of organ or system failure. Most of us want to die at home; most of us won't. All of us hope to die without pain; many of us will be kept alive, in pain, beyond a time when we would choose to call a halt. Yet very few of us take steps ahead of time to spell out what kind of physical and emotional care we will want at the end.

The new movement to improve the end of life is pioneering ways to make available to each of us a good death—as we each define it. One goal of the movement is to bring death through the cultural process that childbirth has achieved; from an unconscious, solitary act in a cold hospital room to a situation in which one is buffered by pillows, pictures, music, loved ones, and the solaces of home. But as in the childbirth movement, the real goal is choice—here, to have the death you want. Much of death's sting can be averted by planning in advance, knowing the facts, and knowing what options we all have. Here, we have gathered new and relevant information to help us all make a difference for the people we are taking care of, and ultimately, for ourselves.

says Philadelphia internist Nicholas Scharff. "Now we know that addiction is not a problem: People who are in pain take pain medication as long as they need it, and then they stop." Spivack says, "We have new formulations and delivery systems, so a dying patient should never have unmet pain needs."

In 1999, the Joint Commission on Accreditation of Healthcare Organizations issued stern new guidelines about easing pain in both terminal and nonterminal patients. The movement intends to take pain seriously: to measure and treat it as the fifth vital sign in hospitals, along with blood pressure, pulse, temperature, and respiration.

The best defense against pain, says Spivack, is a combination of education and assertiveness. "Don't be afraid to speak up," he says. "If your doctor isn't listening, talk to the nurses. They see more and usually have a good sense of what's happening." Hospice workers, too, are experts on physical comfort, and a good doctor will respond to a hospice worker's recommendations. "The best situation for pain management," says Scharff, "is at home with a family caregiver being guided by a hospice program."

The downsides to pain medication are, first, that narcotics given to a fragile body may have a double effect: The drug may ease the pain, but it may cause respiratory depression and possibly death. Second, pain medication may induce grogginess or unconsciousness when a patient wants to be alert. "Most people seem to be much more willing to tolerate pain than mental confusion," says senior research scientist M. Powell Lawton, Ph.D., of the Philadelphia Geriatric Center. Dying patients may choose to be alert one day for visitors, and asleep the next to cope with pain. Studies show that when patients control their own pain medication, they use less.

## Final Symptoms

**Depression** This condition is not an inevitable part of dying but can and should be treated. In fact, untreated depression can prevent pain medications from working effectively, and antidepressant medication can help relieve pain. A dying patient should be kept in the best possible emotional state for the final stage of life. A combination of medications and psychotherapy works best to treat depression.

**Anorexia** In the last few days of life, anorexia—an unwillingness or inability to eat—often sets in. "It has a protective effect, releasing endorphins in the system and contributing to a greater feeling of well-being," says Spivack. "Force-feeding a dying patient could make him uncomfortable and cause choking."

**Dehydration** Most people want to drink little or nothing in their last days. Again, this is a protective mechanism, triggering a release of helpful endorphins.

**Drowsiness and Unarousable Sleep** In spite of a coma-like state, says Spivack, "presume that the patient hears everything that is being said in the room."

# Hospice: The Comfort Team

Hospice is really a bundle of services. It organizes a team of people to help patients and their families, most often in the patient's home but also in hospice residences, nursing homes, and hospitals:

■ Registered nurses who check medication and the patient's condition, communicate with the patient's doctor, and educate caregivers.
■ Medical services by the patient's physician and a hospice's medical director, limited to pain medication and other comfort care.
■ Medical supplies and equipment.
■ Drugs for pain relief and symptom control.
■ Home-care aides for personal care, homemakers for light housekeeping.
■ Continuous care in the home as needed on a short-term basis.
■ Trained volunteers for support services.
■ Physical, occupational, and speech therapists to help patients adapt to new disabilities.
■ Temporary hospitalization during a crisis.
■ Counselors and social workers who provide emotional and spiritual support to the patient and family.
■ Respite care—brief noncrisis hospitalization to provide relief for family caregivers for up to five days.
■ Bereavement support for the family, including counseling, referral to support groups, and periodic check-ins during the first year after the death.

**Hospice Residences** Still rare, but a growing phenomenon. They provide all these services on-site. They're for patients without family caregivers; with frail, elderly spouses; and for families who cannot provide at-home care because of other commitments. At the moment, Medicare covers only hospice services; the patient must pay for room and board. In many states Medicaid also covers hospice services (see How Much Will It Cost?). Keep in mind that not all residences are certified, bonded, or licensed; and not all are covered by Medicare.

**Getting In** A physician can recommend hospice for a patient who is terminally ill and probably has less than six months to live. The aim of hospice is to help people cope with an illness, not to cure it. All patients entering hospice waive their rights to curative treatments, though only for conditions relating to their terminal illness. "If you break a leg, of course you'll be treated for that," says Karen Woods, executive director of the Hospice Association of America. No one is forced to accept a hospice referral, and patients may leave and opt for curative care at any time. Hospice programs are listed in the Yellow Pages. For more information, see Resources.

**Agitation and Restlessness, Moaning and Groaning** The features of "terminal delirium" occur when the patient's level of consciousness is markedly decreased; there is no significant likelihood that any pain sensation can reach consciousness. Family members and other caregivers may interpret what they see as "the patient is in pain" but as these signs arise at a point very close to death, terminal delirium should be suspected.

# The Ultimate Emotional Challenge

A dying person is grieving the loss of control over life, of body image, of normal physical functions, mobility and strength, freedom and independence, security, and the illusion of immortality. He is also grieving the loss of an earthly future, and reorienting himself to an unknowable destiny.

At the same time, an emotionally healthy dying person will be trying to satisfy his survival drive by adapting to this new phase, making the most of life at the moment, calling in loved ones, examining and appreciating his own joys and accomplishments. Not all dying people are depressed; many embrace death easily.

### Facing the Fact

Doctors are usually the ones to inform a patient that he or she is dying, and the end-of-life movement is training physicians to bring empathy to that conversation in place of medspeak and time estimates. The more sensitive doctor will first ask how the patient feels things are going. "The patient may say, 'Well, I don't think I'm getting better,' and I would say, 'I think you're right,' " says internist Nicholas Scharff.

At this point, a doctor might ask if the patient wants to hear more now or later, in broad strokes or in detail. Some people will need to first process the emotional blow with tears and anger before learning about the course of their disease in the future.

"Accept and understand whatever reaction the patient has," says Roni Lang, director of the Geriatric Assessment Program for the Stamford (Connecticut) Health System, and a social worker who is a longtime veteran of such conversations. "Don't be too quick with the tissue. That sends a message that it's not okay to be upset. It's okay for the patient to be however she is."

### Getting to Acceptance

Some patients keep hoping that they will get better. Denial is one of the mind's miracles, a way to ward off painful realities until consciousness can deal with them. Denial may not be a problem for the dying person, but it can create difficulties for the family. The dying person could be leaving a lot of tough decisions, stress, and confusion behind. The classic stages of grief outlined by Elisabeth Kübler-Ross—denial, anger, bargaining, depression, and acceptance—are often used to describe post-death grieving, but were in fact delineated for the process of accepting impending loss. We now know that these states may not progress in order. "Most people oscillate between anger and sadness, embracing the prospect of death and unrealistic episodes of optimism," says Lang. Still, she says, "don't place demands on them to accept their death. This is not a time to proselytize." It is enough for the family to accept the coming loss, and if necessary, introduce the idea of an advance directive and healthcare proxy, approaching it as a "just in case" idea. When one member of the family cannot accept death, and insists that doctors do more, says Lang, "that's the worst nightmare. I would call a meeting, hear all views without interrupting, and get the conversation around to what the patient would want. You may need another person to come in, perhaps the doctor, to help 'hear' the voice of the patient."

### What Are You Afraid Of?

The most important question for doctors and caregivers to ask a dying person is, What are you afraid of? "Fear aggravates pain," says Lang, "and pain aggravates fear." Fear of pain, says Spivack, is one of the most common problems, and can be dealt with rationally. Many people do not know, for example, that pain in dying is not inevitable. Other typical fears are of being separated from loved ones, from home, from work; fear of being a burden, losing control, being dependent, and leaving things undone. Voicing fear helps lessen it, and pinpointing fear helps a caregiver know how to respond.

### How to Be With a Dying Person

Our usual instinct is to avoid everything about death, including the people moving most rapidly toward it. But, Spivack says, "In all my years of working with dying people, I've never heard one say 'I want to die alone.' " Dying people are greatly comforted by company; the benefit far outweighs the awkwardness of the visit. Lang offers these suggestions for visitors:

■ Be close. Sit at eye level, and don't be afraid to touch. Let the dying person set the pace for the conversation. Allow for silence. Your presence alone is valuable.

■ Don't contradict a patient who says he's going to die. Acceptance is okay. Allow for anger, guilt, and fear, without trying to "fix" it. Just listen and empathize.

# Survival Kit for Caregivers

A study published in the March 21, 2000, issue of **Annals of Internal Medicine** shows that caregivers of the dying are twice as likely to have depressive symptoms as the dying themselves.

No wonder. Caring for a dying parent, says social worker Roni Lang, "brings a fierce tangle of emotions. That part of us that is a child must grow up." Parallel struggles occur when caring for a spouse, a child, another relative, or a friend. Caregivers may also experience sibling rivalry, income loss, isolation, fatigue, burnout, and resentment.

To deal with these difficult stresses, Lang suggests that caregivers:

■ Set limits in advance. How far am I willing to go? What level of care is needed? Who can I get to help? Resist the temptation to let the illness always take center stage, or to be drawn into guilt-inducing conversations with people who think you should be doing more.

■ Join a caregiver support group, either disease-related like the Alzheimer's Association or Gilda's Club, or a more general support group like The Well Spouse Foundation. Ask the social services department at your hospital for advice. Telephone support and online chat rooms also exist (see Resources).

■ Acknowledge anger and express it constructively by keeping a journal or talking to an understanding friend or family member. Anger is a normal reaction to powerlessness.

■ When people offer to help, give them a specific assignment. And then, take time to do what energizes you and make a point of rewarding yourself.

■ Remember that people who are critically ill are self-absorbed. If your empathy fails you and you lose patience, make amends and forgive yourself.

■ Give the patient as much decision-making power as possible, as long as possible. Allow for talk about unfinished business. Ask: "Who can I contact for you?"

■ Encourage happy reminiscences. It's okay to laugh.

■ Never pass up the chance to express love or say good-bye. But if you don't get the chance, remember that not everything is worked through. Do the best you can.

# Taking Control Now

Sixty years ago, before the invention of dialysis, defibrillators, and ventilators, the failure of vital organs automatically meant death. There were few choices to be made to end suffering, and when there were—the fatal dose of morphine, for example— these decisions were made privately by family and doctors who knew each other well. Since the 1950s, medical technology has been capable of extending lives, but also of prolonging dying. In 1967, an organization called Choice in Dying (now the Partnership for Caring: America's Voices for the Dying; see Resources) designed the first advance directive—a document that allows you to designate under what conditions you would want life-sustaining treatment to be continued or terminated. But the idea did not gain popular understanding until 1976, when the parents of Karen Ann Quinlan won a long legal battle to disconnect her from respiratory support as she lay for months in a vegetative state. Some 75 percent of Americans are in favor of advance directives, although only 30–35 percent actually write them.

## Designing the Care You Want

There are two kinds of advance directives, and you may use one or both. A Living Will details what kind of life-sustaining treatment you want or don't want, in the event of an illness when death is imminent. A durable power of attorney for health care appoints someone to be your decision-maker if you can't speak for yourself. This person is also called a surrogate, attorney-in-fact, or health-care proxy. An advance directive such as Five Wishes covers both.

Most experts agree that a Living Will alone is not sufficient. "You don't need to write specific instructions about different kinds of life support, as you don't yet know any of the facts of your situation, and they may change," says Charles Sabatino, assistant director of the American Bar Association's Commission on Legal Problems of the Elderly.

The proxy, Sabatino says, is far more important. "It means someone you trust will find out all the options and make a decision consistent with what you would want." In most states, you may write your own advance directive, though some states require a specific form, available at hospital admitting offices or at the state department of health.

## When Should You Draw Up a Directive?

Without an advance directive, a hospital staff is legally bound to do everything to keep you alive as long as possible, until you or a family member decides otherwise. So advance directives are best written before emergency status or a terminal diagnosis. Some people write them at the same time they make a will. The process begins with discussions between you and your family and doctor. If anybody is reluctant to discuss the subject, Sabatino suggests starting the conversation with a story. "Remember what happened to Bob Jones and what his family went through? I want us to be different...." You can use existing tools—a booklet or questionnaire (see Resources)—to keep the conversation moving. Get your doctor's commitment to support your wishes. "If you're asking for something that is against your doctor's conscience" (such as prescribing a lethal dose of pain medication or removing life support at a time he considers premature), Sabatino says, "he may have an obligation to transfer you to another doctor." And make sure the person you name as surrogate agrees to act for you and understands your wishes.

### Filing, Storing, Safekeeping...

An estimated 35 percent of advance directives cannot be found when needed.

■ Give a copy to your surrogate, your doctor, your hospital, and other family members. Tell them where to find the original in the house—not in a safe deposit box where it might not be found until after death.

■ Some people carry a copy in their wallet or glove compartment of their car.

■ Be aware that if you have more than one home and you split your time in several regions of the country, you should be registering your wishes with a hospital in each region, and consider naming more than one proxy.

■ You may register your Living Will and health-care proxy online at uslivingwillregistry.com (or call 800-548-9455). The free, privately funded confidential service will instantly fax a copy to a hospital when the hospital requests one. It will also remind you to update it: You may want to choose a new surrogate, accommodate medical advances, or change your idea of when "enough is enough." M. Powell Lawton, who is doing a study on how people anticipate the terminal life stages, has discovered that "people adapt relatively well to states of poor health. The idea that life is still worth living continues to readjust itself."

### Assisted Suicide: The Reality

While advance directives allow for the termination of life-sustaining treatment, assisted suicide means supplying the patient with a prescription for life-ending medication. A doctor writes the prescription for the medication; the patient takes the fatal dose him- or herself. Physician-assisted suicide is legal only in Oregon (and under consideration in Maine) but only with rigorous preconditions. Of the approximately 30,000 people who died in Oregon in 1999, only 33 received permission to have a lethal dose of medication and only 26 of those actually died of the medication. Surrogates may request an end to life support, but to assist in a suicide puts one at risk for charges of homicide.

# Good Care: Can You Afford It?

The ordinary person is only one serious illness away from poverty," says Joanne Lynn, M.D., director of the Arlington, Virginia, Center to Improve Care of the Dying. An ethicist, hospice physician, and health-services researcher, she is one of the founding members of the end-of-life-care movement. "On the whole, hospitalization and the cost of suppressing symptoms is very easy to afford," says Lynn. Medicare and Medicaid will help cover that kind of acute medical care. But what is harder to afford is at-home medication, monitoring, daily help with eating and walking, and all the care that will go on for the rest of the patient's life.

"When people are dying," Lynn says, "an increasing proportion of their overall care does not need to be done by doctors. But when policymakers say the care is nonmedical, then it's second class, it's not important, and nobody will pay for it."

Bottom line, Medicare pays for about 57 percent of the cost of medical care for Medicare beneficiaries. Another 11 percent is paid by Medicaid, 20 percent by the patient, 10 percent from private insurance, and the rest from other sources, such as charitable organizations.

### Medi-what?

This public-plus-private network of funding sources for end-of-life care is complex, and who pays for how much of what is determined by diagnosis, age, site of care, and income. Besides the private health insurance that many of us have from our employers, other sources of funding may enter the picture when patients are terminally ill.

■ **Medicare** A federal insurance program that covers health-care services for people 65 and over, some disabled people, and those with end-stage kidney disease. Medicare Part A covers inpatient care in hospitals, nursing homes, hospice, and some home health care. For most people, the Part A premium is free. Part B covers doctor fees, tests, and other outpatient medical services. Although Part B is optional, most people choose to enroll through their local Social Security office and pay the monthly premium ($45.50). Medicare beneficiaries share in the cost of care through deductibles and co-insurance. What Medicare does not cover at all is outpatient medication, long-term nonacute care, and support services.

■ **Medicaid** A state and federally funded program that covers health-care services for people with income or assets below certain levels, which vary from state to state.

■ **Medigap** Private insurance policies covering the gaps in Medicare, such as deductibles and co-payments, and in some cases additional health-care services, medical supplies, and outpatient prescription drugs.

Many of the services not paid for by Medicare can be covered by private long-term-care insurance. About 50 percent of us over the age of 65 will need long-term care at home or in a nursing home, and this insurance is an extra bit of protection for people with major assets to protect. It pays for skilled nursing care as well as non-health services, such as help with dressing, eating, and bathing. You select a dollar amount of coverage per day (for example, $100 in a nursing home, or $50 for at-home care), and a coverage period (for example, three years—the average nursing-home stay is 2.7 years). Depending on your age and the benefits you choose, the insurance can cost anywhere from around $500 to more than $8,000 a year. People with pre-existing conditions such as Alzheimer's or MS are usually not eligible.

## How Much Will It Cost?

Where you get end-of-life care will affect the cost and who pays for it.

■ **Hospital** Dying in a hospital costs about $1,000 a day. After a $766 deductible (per benefit period), Medicare reimburses the hospital a fixed rate per day, which varies by region and diagnosis. After the first 60 days in a hospital, a patient will pay a daily deductible ($194) that goes up (to $388) after 90 days. The patient is responsible for all costs for each day beyond 150 days. Medicaid and some private insurance, either through an employer or a Medigap plan, often help cover these costs.

■ **Nursing home** About $1,000 a week. Medicare covers up to 100 days of skilled nursing care after a three-day hospitalization, and most medication costs during that time. For days 21–100, your daily co-insurance of $97 is usually covered by private insurance—if you have it. For nursing-home care not covered by Medicare, you must use your private assets, or Medicaid if your assets run out, which happens to approximately one-third of nursing-home residents. Long-term-care insurance may also cover some of the costs.

■ **Hospice care** About $100 a day for in-home care. Medicare covers hospice care to patients who have a life expectancy of less than six months. (See Hospice: The Comfort Team.) Such care may be provided at home, in a hospice facility, a hospital, or a nursing-home. Patients may be asked to pay up to $5 for each prescription and a 5 percent co-pay for in-patient respite care, which is a short hospital stay to relieve

# Five Wishes

Five Wishes is a questionnaire that guides people in making essential decisions about the care they want at the end of their life. About a million people have filled out the eight-page form in the past two years. This advance directive is legally valid in 34 states and the District of Columbia. (The other 16 require a specific state-mandated form.)

The document was designed by lawyer Jim Towey, founder of Aging With Dignity, a nonprofit organization that advocates for the needs of elders and their caregivers. Towey, who was legal counsel to Mother Teresa, visited her Home for the Dying in Calcutta in the 1980s. He was struck that in that haven in the Third World, "the dying people's hands were held, their pain was managed, and they weren't alone. In the First World, you see a lot of medical technology, but people die in pain, and alone." Towey talked to MODERN MATURITY about his directive and what it means.

**What are the five wishes?** Who do I want to make care decisions for me when I can't? What kind of medical treatment do I want toward the end? What would help me feel comfortable while I am dying? How do I want people to treat me? What do I want my loved ones to know about me and my feelings after I'm gone?

**Why is it so vital to make advance decisions now?** Medical technology has extended longevity, which is good, but it can prolong the dying process in ways that are almost cruel. Medical schools are still concentrating on curing, not caring for the dying. We can have a dignified season in our life, or die alone in pain with futile interventions. Most people only discover they have options when checking into the hospital, and often they no longer have the capacity to choose. This leaves the family members with a guessing game and, frequently, guilt.

**What's the ideal way to use this document?** First you do a little soul searching about what you want. Then discuss it with people you trust, in the living-room instead of the waiting room—before a crisis. Just say, "I want a choice about how I spend my last days," talk about your choices, and pick someone to be your health-care surrogate.

**What makes the Five Wishes directive unique?** It's easy to use and understand, not written in the language of doctors or lawyers. It also allows people to discuss comfort dignity, and forgivness, not just medical concerns. When my father filled it out, he said he wanted his favorite afghan blanket in his bed. It made a huge difference to me that, as he was dying, he had his wishes fulfilled.

For a copy of Five Wishes in English or Spanish, send a $5 check or money order to Aging With Dignity, PO Box 1661, Tallahassee, FL 32302. For more information, visit www.agingwithdignity.org.

caregivers. Medicaid covers hospice care in all but six states, even for those without Medicare.

About 60 percent of full-time employees of medium and large firms also have coverage for hospice services, but the benefits vary widely.

■ **Home care without hospice services** Medicare Part A pays the full cost of medical home health care for up to 100 visits following a hospital stay of at least three days. Medicare Part B covers home health-care visits beyond those 100 visits or without a hospital stay. To qualify, the patient must be homebound, require skilled nursing care or physical or speech therapy, be under a physician's care, and use services from a Medicare-participating home-health agency. Note that this coverage is for medical care only; hired help for personal nonmedical services, such as that often required by Alzheimer's patients, is not covered by Medicare. It is covered by Medicaid in some states.

A major financial disadvantage of dying at home without hospice is that Medicare does not cover outpatient prescription drugs, even those for pain. Medicaid does cover these drugs, but often with restrictions on their price and quantity. Private insurance can fill the gap to some extent. Long-term-care insurance may cover payments to family caregivers who have to stop work to care for a dying patient, but this type of coverage is very rare.

# Resources

## MEDICAL CARE

*For information about pain relief and symptom management:*
**Supportive Care of the Dying**
(503-215-5053; careofdying.org).

*For a comprehensive guide to living with the medical, emotional, and spiritual aspects of dying:*
**Handbook for Mortals**
by Joanne Lynn and Joan Harrold, Oxford University Press.

*For a 24-hour hotline offering counseling, pain management, downloadable advance directives, and more:*
**The Partnership for Caring**
(800-989-9455; www.partnershipforcaring.org).

## EMOTIONAL CARE

*To find mental-health counselors with an emphasis on lifespan human development and spiritual discussion:*
**American Counseling Association**
(800-347-6647; counseling.org).

*For disease-related support groups and general resources for caregivers:*

**Caregiver Survival Resources**
(caregiver911.com).

*For AARP's online caregiver support chatroom,* access **America Online** every Wednesday night, 8:30–9:30 EST
(keyword: AARP).

*Education and advocacy for family caregivers:*
**National Family Caregivers Association**
(800-896-3650; nfcacares.org).

*For the booklet,*
**Understanding the Grief Process**
(D16832, EEO143C), e-mail order with title and numbers to member@aarp.org or send postcard to AARP Fulfillment, 601 E St NW, Washington DC 20049. Please allow two to four weeks for delivery.

*To find a volunteer to help with supportive services to the frail and their caregivers:*
**National Federation of Interfaith Volunteer Caregivers** (816-931-5442; nfivc.org).

*For information on support to partners of the chronically ill and/or the disabled:*
**The Well Spouse Foundation**
(800-838-0879; www.wellspouse.org).

## LEGAL HELP

AARP members are entitled to a free half-hour of legal advice with a lawyer from **AARP's Legal Services Network.**
(800-424-3410; www.aarp.org/lsn).

For **Planning for Incapacity,** a guide to advance directives in your state, send $5 to Legal Counsel for the Elderly, Inc.,
PO Box 96474,
Washington DC 20090-6474.
Make out check to LCE Inc.

*For a* **Caring Conversations** *booklet on advance-directive discussion:*
**Midwest Bioethics Center**
(816-221-1100; midbio.org).

*For information on care at the end of life, online discussion groups, conferences:*
**Last Acts Campaign**
(800-844-7616; lastacts.org).

## HOSPICE

*To learn about end-of-life care options and grief issues through videotapes, books, newsletters, and brochures:*
**Hospice Foundation of America**
(800-854-3402; hospicefoundation.org).

*For information on hospice programs, FAQs, and general facts about hospice:*

**National Hospice and Palliative Care Organization** (800-658-8898; nhpco.org).

For **All About Hospice: A Consumer's Guide** (202-546-4759; www.hospice-america.org).

## FINANCIAL HELP

For **Organizing Your Future,** a simple guide to end-of-life financial decisions, send $5 to Legal Counsel for the Elderly, Inc., PO Box 96474, Washington DC 20090-6474. Make out check to LCE Inc.

For **Medicare and You 2000** and a **2000 Guide to Health Insurance for People With Medicare** (800-MEDICARE [633-4227]; medicare.gov).
*To find your State Agency on Aging:* **Administration on Aging,** U.S. Department of Health and Human **Services** (800-677-1116; aoa.dhhs.gov).

## GENERAL

*For information on end-of-life planning and bereavement:* (www.aarp.org/endoflife/).

*For health professionals and others who want to start conversations on end-of-life issues in their community:* Discussion Guide: On Our Own Terms: Moyers on Dying, based on the PBS series, airing September 10–13. The guide provides essays, instructions, and contacts. From PBS, www.pbs.org/onourownterms Or send a postcard request to On Our Own Terms Discussion Guide, Thirteen/WNET New York, PO Box 245, Little Falls, NJ 07424-9766.

# Unit 8

## Unit Selections

28. **The Stability of Personality: Observations and Evaluations,** Robert R. McCrae and Paul T. Costa Jr.
29. **Making Sense of Self-Esteem,** Mark R. Leary
30. **Shyness: The New Solution,** Bernardo Carducci

## Key Points to Consider

❖ What is the study of personality; what is the definition of personality? What are some of the major tenets of personality theories? Can you differentiate trait theory from humanistic theory?

❖ What do you think contributes most to our unique personalities, biology or environment? If you answered biology, what does this imply about the possibility of personality change? If you answered environment, do you think that biology plays any role in personality?

❖ Is personality stable or ever-changing across a lifetime? What are the advantages of a stable personality? What would be the advantages of an ever-changing personality? How is trait theory different from other personality theories?

❖ What is self-esteem? Do you think self-esteem comes exclusively from appraisals by others? If not, from where else does it originate? How can we raise children with high self-esteem? What are the consequences of low self-esteem?

❖ From where does the trait of shyness originate? What can shy individuals do to overcome their shyness? What role can the Internet play in helping shy individuals become more outgoing?

❖ What other traits do you think would be important to measure besides shyness? Psychologists think there are five robust traits; that is, psychologists have now identified five traits that they think describe all individuals fairly well. Do you think shyness is one of these traits? What other traits do you think are included in the Big Five, as they are known?

 **Links**   **www.dushkin.com/online/**

23. **The Personality Project**
   *http://personality-project.org/personality.html*

These sites are annotated on pages 4 and 5.

Sabrina and Sadie are identical twins. When the girls were young children, their parents tried very hard to treat them equally. Whenever Sabrina received a present, Sadie received one. Both girls attended dance school and completed early classes in ballet and tap dance. In elementary school, the twins were both placed in the same class with the same teacher. The teacher also tried to treat them the same.

In junior high school, Sadie became a tomboy. She loved to play rough-and-tumble sports with the neighborhood boys. On the other hand, Sabrina remained indoors and practiced on her piano. Sabrina was keenly interested in the domestic arts, such as sewing, needlepoint, and crochet. Sadie was more interested in reading science fiction novels, and in watching adventure programs on television.

As the twins matured, they decided it would be best to attend different colleges. Sabrina went to a small, quiet college in a rural setting, and Sadie matriculated at a large public university. Sabrina majored in English, with a specialty in poetry; Sadie switched majors several times and finally decided on a communications major.

Why, when these twins were exposed to the same early childhood environment, did their interests and paths diverge later? What makes people, even identical twins, so unique, so different from one another?

The study of individual differences is the domain of personality. The psychological study of personality has included two major thrusts. The first has focused on the search for the commonalities of human life and development. Its major question would be: How are humans, especially their personalities, affected by specific events or activities? Personality theories are based on the assumption that a given event, if it is important, will affect almost all people in a similar way, or that the processes by which events affect people are common across events and people. Most psychological research into personality variables has made this assumption. Failures to replicate a research project are often the first clues that differences in individual responses require further investigation.

While some psychologists have focused on personality-related effects that are presumed to be universal among humans, others have devoted their efforts to discovering the bases on which individuals differ in their responses to environmental events. In the beginning, this specialty was called genetic psychology, because most people assumed that individual differences resulted from differences in genetic inheritance. By the 1950s the term genetic psychology had given way to the more current term: the psychology of individual differences.

Does this mean that genetic variables are no longer the key to understanding individual differences? Not at all. For a time, psychologists took up the philosophical debate over whether genetic or environmental factors were more important in determining behaviors. Even today, behavior geneticists compute the heritability coefficients for a number of personality and behavior traits, including intelligence. This is an expression of the degree to which differences in a given trait can be attributed to differences in inherited capacity or ability. Most psychologists, however, accept the principle that both genetic and environmental determinants are important in any area of behavior. These researchers are devoting more of their efforts to discovering how the two sources of influence interact to produce the unique individual. Given the above, the focus of this unit is on personality characteristics and the differences and similarities among individuals.

What is personality? Most researchers in the area define personality as patterns of thoughts, feelings, and behaviors that persist over time and over situations, are characteristic or typical of the individual, and usually distinguish one person from another.

We first examine two theoretical approaches to personality. In the first article we take a general look at trait theory, which proposes that personality is relatively stable over a lifetime. "The Stability of Personality: Observations and Evaluations" features research on individual differences. After reviewing the pertinent literature, Robert McCrae and Paul Costa conclude that our personality characteristics do remain relatively stable across a lifetime.

Another theory of personality is humanistic theory. The humanists focus on self-concept, especially self-esteem. They do not fragment the personality into traits or smaller units as do the trait theorists. Similarly, humanistic theorists believe that people know themselves well, which is unlike the assumption in Freudian theory that we are constantly deceived by our unconscious. In "Making Sense of Self-Esteem," Mark Leary redefines self-esteem and offers a conception of it that includes evaluations from others as its antecedent. Leary continues with the notion that those with low self-esteem are bound to experience psychological disorders. High esteem, then, is important to mental health, as proposed by the humanistic theorists.

Last, we look at a specific aspect of personality. The trait we examine is shyness. In "Shyness: The New Solution," Bernardo Carducci explains that shyness is caused by social anxiety. He then elaborates upon the causes of and cures for shyness, or extreme social anxiety. One suggestion is to utilize the Internet, a place where individuals can avoid face-to-face contact and thus perhaps overcome some of their shyness.

# Personality Processes

# The Stability of Personality: Observations and Evaluations

**Robert R. McCrae and
Paul T. Costa, Jr.**

**Robert R. McCrae** is Research Psychologist and **Paul T. Costa, Jr.,** is Chief, Laboratory of Personality and Cognition, both at the Gerontology Research Center, National Institute on Aging, National Institutes of Health. Address correspondence to Robert R. McCrae, Personality, Stress and Coping Section, Gerontology Research Center, 4940 Eastern Ave., Baltimore, MD 21224.

"There is an optical illusion about every person we meet," Ralph Waldo Emerson wrote in his essay on "Experience":

> In truth, they are all creatures of given temperament, which will appear in a given character, whose boundaries they will never pass: but we look at them, they seem alive, and we presume there is impulse in them. In the moment it seems impulse; in the year, in the lifetime, it turns out to be a certain uniform tune which the revolving barrel of the music-box must play.[1]

In this brief passage, Emerson anticipated modern findings about the stability of personality and pointed out an illusion to which both laypersons and psychologists are prone. He was also perhaps the first to decry personality stability as the enemy of freedom, creativity, and growth, objecting that "temperament puts all divinity to rout." In this article, we summarize evidence in support of Emerson's observations but offer arguments against his evaluation of them.[2]

## EVIDENCE FOR THE STABILITY OF ADULT PERSONALITY

Emerson used the term temperament to refer to the basic tendencies of the individual, dispositions that we call personality traits. It is these traits, measured by such instruments as the Minnesota Multiphasic Personality Inventory and the NEO Personality Inventory, that have been investigated in a score of longitudinal studies over the past 20 years. Despite a wide variety of samples, instruments, and designs, the results of these studies have been remarkably consistent, and they are easily summarized.

1. The mean levels of personality traits change with development, but reach final adult levels at about age 30. Between 20 and 30, both men and women become somewhat less emotional and thrill-seeking and somewhat more cooperative and self-disciplined—changes we might interpret as evidence of increased maturity. After age 30, there are few and subtle changes, of which the most consistent is a small decline in activity level with advancing age. Except among individuals with dementia, stereotypes that depict older people as being withdrawn, depressed, or rigid are unfounded.
2. Individual differences in personality traits, which show at least some continuity from early childhood on, are also essentially fixed by age 30.

Stability coefficients (test-retest correlations over substantial time intervals) are typically in the range of .60 to .80, even over intervals of as long as 30 years, although there is some decline in magnitude with increasing retest interval. Given that most personality scales have short-term retest reliabilities in the range from .70 to .90, it is clear that by far the greatest part of the reliable variance (i.e., variance not due to measurement error) in personality traits is stable.

3. Stability appears to characterize all five of the major domains of personality—neuroticism, extraversion, openness to experience, agreeableness, and conscientiousness. This finding suggests that an adult's personality profile as a whole will change little over time, and studies of the stability of configural measures of personality support that view.
4. Generalizations about stability apply to virtually everyone. Men and women, healthy and sick people, blacks and whites all show the same pattern. When asked, most adults will say that their personality has not changed much in adulthood, but even those who claim to have had major changes show little objective evidence of change on repeated administrations of personality questionnaires. Important exceptions to this generalization include people suffering from dementia and certain

From *Current Directions in Psychological Science*, December 1994, pp. 173–175. © 1999 by the American Psychological Society. Reprinted by permission of Blackwell Publishers.

categories of psychiatric patients who respond to therapy, but no moderators of stability among healthy adults have yet been identified.[3]

When researchers first began to publish these conclusions, they were greeted with considerable skepticism—"I distrust the facts and the inferences" Emerson had written—and many studies were designed to test alternative hypotheses. For example, some researchers contended that consistent responses to personality questionnaires were due to memory of past responses, but retrospective studies showed that people could not accurately recall how they had previously responded even when instructed to do so. Other researchers argued that temporal consistency in self-reports merely meant that individuals had a fixed idea of themselves, a crystallized self-concept that failed to keep pace with real changes in personality. But studies using spouse and peer raters showed equally high levels of stability.[4]

The general conclusion that personality traits are stable is now widely accepted. Some researchers continue to look for change in special circumstances and populations; some attempt to account for stability by examining genetic and environmental influences on personality. Finally, others take the view that there is much more to personality than traits, and seek to trace the adult developmental course of personality perceptions or identity formation or life narratives.

These latter studies are worthwhile, because people undoubtedly do change across the life span. Marriages end in divorce, professional careers are started in mid-life, fashions and attitudes change with the times. Yet often the same traits can be seen in new guises: Intellectual curiosity merely shifts from one field to another, avid gardening replaces avid tennis, one abusive relationship is followed by another. Many of these changes are best regarded as variations on the "uniform tune" played by individuals' enduring dispositions.

## ILLUSORY ATTRIBUTIONS IN TEMPORAL PERSPECTIVE

Social and personality psychologists have debated for some time the accuracy of attributions of the causes of behavior to persons or situations. The "optical illusion" in person perception that Emerson pointed to was somewhat different. He felt that people attribute behavior to the live and spontaneous person who freely creates responses to the

situation, when in fact behavior reveals only the mechanical operation of lifeless and static temperament. We may (and we will!) take exception to this disparaging, if common, view of traits, but we must first concur with the basic observation that personality processes often appear different when viewed in longitudinal perspective: "The years teach much which the days never know."

Consider happiness. If one asks individuals why they are happy or unhappy, they are almost certain to point to environmental circumstances of the moment: a rewarding job, a difficult relationship, a threat to health, a new car. It would seem that levels of happiness ought to mirror quality of life, and that changes in circumstances would result in changes in subjective well-being. It would be easy to demonstrate this pattern in a controlled laboratory experiment: Give subjects $1,000 each and ask how they feel!

But survey researchers who have measured the objective quality of life by such indicators as wealth, education, and health find precious little association with subjective well-being, and longitudinal researchers have found surprising stability in individual differences in happiness, even among people whose life circumstances have changed markedly. The explanation is simple: People adapt to their circumstances rapidly, getting used to the bad and taking for granted the good. In the long run, happiness is largely a matter of enduring personality traits.[5] "Temper prevails over everything of time, place, and condition, and . . . fix[es] the measure of activity and of enjoyment."

A few years ago, William Swann and Craig Hill provided an ingenious demonstration of the errors to which too narrow a temporal perspective can lead. A number of experiments had shown that it was relatively easy to induce changes in the self-concept by providing self-discrepant feedback. Introverts told that they were really extraverts rated themselves higher in extraversion than they had before. Such studies supported the view that the self-concept is highly malleable, a mirror of the evaluation of the immediate environment.

Swann and Hill replicated this finding, but extended it by inviting subjects back a few days later. By that time, the effects of the manipulation had disappeared, and subjects had returned to their initial self-concepts. The implication is that any one-shot experiment may give a seriously misleading view of personality processes.[6]

The relations between coping and adaptation provide a final example. Cross-sectional studies show that individuals who use such coping mechanisms as

self-blame, wishful thinking, and hostile reactions toward other people score lower on measures of well-being than people who do not use these mechanisms. It would be easy to infer that these coping mechanisms detract from adaptation, and in fact the very people who use them admit that they are ineffective. But the correlations vanish when the effects of prior neuroticism scores are removed; an alternative interpretation of the data is thus that individuals who score high on this personality factor use poor coping strategies and also have low well-being: The association between coping and well-being may be entirely attributable to this third variable.[7]

Psychologists have long been aware of the problems of inferring causes from correlational data, but they have not recognized the pervasiveness of the bias that Emerson warned about. People tend to understand behavior and experience as the result of the immediate context, whether intrapsychic or environmental. Only by looking over time can one see the persistent effects of personality traits.

## THE EVALUATION OF STABILITY

If few findings in psychology are more robust than the stability of personality, even fewer are more unpopular. Gerontologists often see stability as an affront to their commitment to continuing adult development; psychotherapists sometimes view it as an alarming challenge to their ability to help patients;[8] humanistic psychologists and transcendental philosophers think it degrades human nature. A popular account in *The Idaho Statesman* ran under the disheartening headline "Your Personality—You're Stuck With It."

In our view, these evaluations are based on misunderstandings: At worst, stability is a mixed blessing. Those individuals who are anxious, quarrelsome, and lazy might be understandably distressed to think that they are likely to stay that way, but surely those who are imaginative, affectionate, and carefree at age 30 should be glad to hear that they will probably be imaginative, affectionate, and carefree at age 90.

Because personality is stable, life is to some extent predictable. People can make vocational and retirement choices with some confidence that their current interests and enthusiasms will not desert them. They can choose friends and mates with whom they are likely to remain compatible. They can vote on the basis of candidates' records, with some assurance that future policies will resemble past ones. They can learn which co-workers they can depend on, and which they cannot. The personal and social utility of personality stability is enormous.

But it is precisely this predictability that so offends many critics. ("I had fancied that the value of life lay in its inscrutable possibilities," Emerson complained.) These critics view traits as mechanical and static habits and believe that the stability of personality traits dooms human beings to lifeless monotony as puppets controlled by inexorable forces. This is a misunderstanding on several levels.

First, personality traits are not repetitive habits, but inherently dynamic dispositions that interact with the opportunities and challenges of the moment.[9] Antagonistic people do not yell at everyone; some people they flatter, some they scorn, some they threaten. Just as the same intelligence is applied to a lifetime of changing problems, so the same personality traits can be expressed in an infinite variety of ways, each suited to the situation.

Second, there are such things as spontaneity and impulse in human life, but they are stable traits. Individuals who are open to experience actively seek out new places to go, provocative ideas to ponder, and exotic sights, sounds, and tastes to experience. Extraverts show a different kind of spontaneity, making friends, seeking thrills, and jumping at every chance to have a good time. People who are introverted and closed to experience have more measured and monotonous lives, but this is the kind of life they choose.

Finally, personality traits are not inexorable forces that control our fate, nor are they, in psychodynamic language, ego alien. Our traits characterize us; they are our very selves;[10] we act most freely when we express our enduring dispositions. Individuals sometimes fight against their own tendencies, trying perhaps to overcome shyness or curb a bad temper. But most people acknowledge even these failings as their own, and it is well

that they do. A person's recognition of the inevitability of his or her one and only personality is a large part of what Erik Erikson called ego integrity, the culminating wisdom of a lifetime.

## Notes

1. All quotations are from "Experience," in *Essays: First and Second Series,* R.W. Emerson (Vintage, New York, 1990) (original work published 1844).

2. For recent and sometimes divergent treatments of this topic, see R.R. McCrae and P.T. Costa, Jr., *Personality in Adulthood* (Guilford, New York, 1990); D. C. Funder, R.D. Parke, C. Tomlinson-Keasey and K. Widaman, Eds., *Studying Lives Through Time: Personality and Development* (American Psychological Association, Washington, DC, 1993); T. Heatherton and J. Weinberger, *Can Personality Change?* (American Psychological Association, Washington, DC, 1994).

3. L.C. Siegler, K.A. Welsh, D.V. Dawson, G.G. Fillenbaum, N.L. Earl, E.B. Kaplan, and C.M. Clark, Ratings of personality change in patients being evaluated for memory disorders, *Alzheimer Disease and Associated Disorders, 5,* 240–250 (1991); R.M.A. Hirschfeld, G.L. Klerman, P. Clayton, M.B. Keller, P. McDonald-Scott, and B. Larkin, Assessing personality: Effects of depressive state on trait measurement, *American Journal of Psychiatry, 140,* 695–699 (1983); R.R. McCrae, Mederated analyses of longitudinal personality stability, *Journal of Personality and Social Psychology, 65,* 577–585 (1993).

4. D. Woodruff, The role of memory in personality continuity: A 25 year follow-up, *Experimental Aging Research, 9,* 31–34 (1983); P.T. Costa, Jr., and R.R. McCrae, Trait psychology comes of age, in *Nebraska Symposium on Motivation: Psychology and Aging,* T.B. Sonderegger, Ed.

(University of Nebraska Press, Lincoln, 1992).

5. P.T. Costa, Jr., and R.R. McCrae, Influence of extraversion and neuroticism on subjective well-being: Happy and unhappy people, *Journal of Personality and Social Psychology, 38,* 668–678 (1980).

6. The study is summarized in W.B. Swann, Jr., and C.A. Hill, When our identities are mistaken: Reaffirming self-conceptions through social interactions, *Journal of Personality and Social Psychology, 43,* 59–66 (1982). Dangers of single-occasion research are also discussed in J.R. Council, Context effects in personality research, *Current Directions in Psychological Science, 2,* 31–34 (1993).

7. R.R. McCrae and P.T. Costa, Jr., Personality, coping, and coping effectiveness in an adult sample, *Journal of Personality, 54,* 385–405 (1986).

8. Observations in nonpatient samples show what happens over time under typical life circumstances; they do not rule out the possibility that psychotherapeutic interventions can change personality. Whether or not such change is possible, in practice much of psychotherapy consists of helping people learn to live with their limitations, and this may be a more realistic goal than "cure" for many patients. See P.T. Costa, Jr., and R.R. McCrae, Personality stability and its implications for clinical psychology, *Clinical Psychology Review, 6,* 407–423 (1986).

9. A. Tellegen, Personality traits: Issues of definition, evidence and assessment, in *Thinking Clearly About Psychology: Essays in Honor of Paul E. Meehl,* Vol. 2, W. Grove and D. Cicchetti, Eds. (University of Minnesota Press, Minneapolis, 1991).

10. R.R. McCrae and P.T. Costa, Jr., Age, personality, and the spontaneous self-concept, *Journals of Gerontology: Social Sciences, 43,* S177–S185 (1988).

# Making Sense of Self-Esteem

## Mark R. Leary[1]

Department of Psychology, Wake Forest University, Winston-Salem, North Carolina

*Abstract*

Sociometer theory proposes that the self-esteem system evolved as a monitor of social acceptance, and that the so-called self-esteem motive functions not to maintain self-esteem per se but rather to avoid social devaluation and rejection. Cues indicating that the individual is not adequately valued and accepted by other people lower self-esteem and motivate behaviors that enhance relational evaluation. Empirical evidence regarding the self-esteem motive, the antecedents of self-esteem, the relation between low self-esteem and psychological problems, and the consequences of enhancing self-esteem is consistent with the theory.

*Keywords*

self-esteem; self; self-regard; rejection

Self-esteem has been regarded as an important construct since the earliest days of psychology. In the first psychology textbook, William James (1890) suggested that the tendency to strive to feel good about oneself is a fundamental aspect of human nature, thereby fueling a fascination—some observers would say obsession—with self-esteem that has spanned more than a century. During that time, developmental psychologists have studied the antecedents of self-esteem and its role in human development, social psychologists have devoted attention to behaviors that appear intended to maintain self-esteem, personality psychologists have examined individual differences in the trait of self-esteem, and theorists of a variety of orientations have discussed the importance of self-regard to psychological adjustment. In the past couple of decades, practicing psychologists and social engineers have suggested that high self-esteem is a remedy for many psychological and social problems.

Yet, despite more than 100 years of attention and thousands of published studies, fundamental issues regarding self-esteem remain poorly understood. Why is self-esteem important? Do people really have a need for self-esteem? Why is self-esteem so strongly determined by how people believe they are evaluated by others? Is low self-esteem associated with psychological difficulties and, if so, why? Do efforts to enhance self-esteem reduce personal and social problems as proponents of the self-esteem movement claim?

## PERSPECTIVES ON THE FUNCTION OF SELF-ESTEEM

Many writers have assumed that people seek to maintain their self-esteem because they possess an inherent "need" to feel good about themselves. However, given the apparent importance of self-esteem to psychological functioning, we must ask why self-esteem is so important and what function it might serve. Humanistic psychologists have traced high self-esteem to a congruency between a person's real and ideal selves and suggested that self-esteem signals people as to when they are behaving in self-determined, autonomous ways. Other writers have proposed that people seek high self-esteem because it facilitates goal achievement. For example, Bednar, Wells, and Peterson (1989) proposed that self-esteem is subjective feedback about the adequacy of the self. This feedback—self-esteem—is positive when the individual copes well with circumstances but negative when he or she avoids threats. In turn, self-esteem affects subsequent goal achievement; high self-esteem increases coping, and low self-esteem leads to further avoidance.

The ethological perspective (Barkow, 1980) suggests that self-esteem is an adaptation that evolved in the service of maintaining dominance in social relationships. According to this theory, human beings evolved mechanisms for monitoring dominance because dominance facilitated the acquisition of mates and other reproduction-enhancing resources. Because attention and favorable reactions from others were associated with being dominant, feelings of self-esteem became tied to social approval and deference. From this perspective, the motive to evaluate oneself positively reduces, in evolutionary terms, to the motive to enhance one's relative dominance.

One of the more controversial explanations of self-esteem is provided by terror management theory, which suggests that the function of self-esteem is to buffer people against the existential terror they experience at the prospect of their own death and annihilation (Solomon, Greenberg, & Pyszczynski, 1991). Several experiments have supported aspects of the theory, but not the strong argument that the function of the self-esteem system is to provide an emotional buffer specifically against death-related anxiety.

All of these perspectives offer insights into the nature of self-esteem, but each has conceptual and empirical difficulties (for critiques, see Leary, 1999; Leary & Baumeister, in press). In the past few years, a novel perspective—sociometer theory—has cast self-esteem in a somewhat different light as it attempts to address lingering questions about the nature of self-esteem.

## SOCIOMETER THEORY

According to sociometer theory, self-esteem is essentially a psychological meter, or gauge, that monitors the quality of people's relationships with others (Leary, 1999; Leary & Baumeister, in

From *Current Directions in Psychological Science,* February 1999, pp. 32-35. © 1999 by the American Psychological Society. Reprinted by permission of Blackwell Publishers.

press; Leary & Downs, 1995). The theory is based on the assumption that human beings possess a pervasive drive to maintain significant interpersonal relationships, a drive that evolved because early human beings who belonged to social groups were more likely to survive and reproduce than those who did not (Baumeister & Leary, 1995). Given the disastrous implications of being ostracized in the ancestral environment in which human evolution occurred, early human beings may have developed a mechanism for monitoring the degree to which other people valued and accepted them. This psychological mechanism—the *sociometer*—continuously monitors the social environment for cues regarding the degree to which the individual is being accepted versus rejected by other people.

The sociometer appears to be particularly sensitive to changes in relational evaluation—the degree to which others regard their relationship with the individual as valuable, important, or close. When evidence of low relational evaluation (particularly, a decrement in relational evaluation) is detected, the sociometer attracts the person's conscious attention to the potential threat to social acceptance and motivates him or her to deal with it. The affectively laden self-appraisals that constitute the "output" of the sociometer are what we typically call self-esteem.

Self-esteem researchers distinguish between *state self-esteem*—momentary fluctuations in a person's feelings about him- or herself—and *trait self-esteem*—the person's general appraisal of his or her value; both are aspects of the sociometer. Feelings of state self-esteem fluctuate as a function of the degree to which the person perceives others currently value their relationships with him or her. Cues that connote high relational evaluation raise state self-esteem, whereas cues that connote low relational evaluation lower state self-esteem. Trait self-esteem, in contrast, reflects the person's general sense that he or she is the sort of person who is valued and accepted by other people. Trait self-esteem may be regarded as the resting state of the sociometer in the absence of incoming information relevant to relational evaluation.

## SELF-ESTEEM AND ITS RELATIONSHIP TO BEHAVIOR

Sociometer theory provides a parsimonious explanation for much of what we know about self-esteem. Here I examine how sociometer theory answers four fundamental questions about self-esteem raised earlier.

### The Self-Esteem Motive

As noted, many psychologists have assumed that people possess a motive or need to maintain self-esteem. According to sociometer theory, the so-called self-esteem motive does not function to maintain self-esteem but rather to minimize the likelihood of rejection (or, more precisely, relational devaluation). When people behave in ways that protect or enhance their self-esteem, they are typically acting in ways that they believe will increase their relational value in others' eyes and, thus, improve their chances of social acceptance.

The sociometer perspective explains why events that are known (or potentially known) by other people have much greater effects on self-esteem than events that are known only by the individual him- or herself. If self-esteem involved only private self-judgments, as many psychologists have assumed, public events should have no greater impact on self-esteem than private ones.

### Antecedents of Self-Esteem

Previous writers have puzzled over the fact that self-esteem is so strongly tied to people's beliefs about how they are evaluated by others. If self-esteem is a *self*-evaluation, why do people judge themselves by *other* people's standards? Sociometer theory easily explains why the primary determinants of self-esteem involve the perceived reactions of other people, as well as self-judgments on dimensions that the person thinks are important to significant others. As a monitor of relational evaluation, the self-esteem system is inherently sensitive to real and potential reactions of other people.

Evidence shows that state self-esteem is strongly affected by events that have implications for the degree to which one is valued and accepted by other people (Leary, Haupt, Strausser, & Chokel, 1998; Leary, Tambor, Terdal, & Downs, 1995). The events that affect self-esteem are precisely the kinds of things that, if known by other people, would affect their evaluation and acceptance of the person (Leary, Tambor, et al., 1995). Most often, self-esteem is lowered by failure, criticism, rejection, and other events that have negative implications for relational evaluation; self-esteem rises when a person succeeds, is praised, or experiences another's love—events that are associated with relational appreciation. Even the mere possibility of rejection can lower self-esteem, a finding that

makes sense if the function of the self-esteem system is to warn the person of possible relational devaluation in time to take corrective action.

The attributes on which people's self-esteem is based are precisely the characteristics that determine the degree to which people are valued and accepted by others (Baumeister & Leary, 1995). Specifically, high trait self-esteem is associated with believing that one possesses socially desirable attributes such as competence, personal likability, and physical attractiveness. Furthermore, self-esteem is related most strongly to one's standing on attributes that one believes are valued by significant others, a finding that is also consistent with sociometer theory.

In linking self-esteem to social acceptance, sociometer theory runs counter to the humanistic assumption that self-esteem based on approval from others is false or unhealthy. On the contrary, if the function of self-esteem is to avoid social devaluation and rejection, then the system must be responsive to others' reactions. This system may lead people to do things that are not always beneficial, but it does so to protect their interpersonal relationships rather than their inner integrity.

### Low Self-Esteem and Psychological Problems

Research has shown that low self-esteem is related to a variety of psychological difficulties and personal problems, including depression, loneliness, substance abuse, teenage pregnancy, academic failure, and criminal behavior. The evidence in support of the link between low self-esteem and psychological problems has often been overstated; the relationships are weaker and more scattered than typically assumed (Mecca, Smelser, & Vasconcellos, 1989). Moreover, high self-esteem also has notable drawbacks. Even so, low self-esteem tends to be more strongly associated with psychological difficulties than high self-esteem.

From the standpoint of sociometer theory, these problems are caused not by low self-esteem but rather by a history of low relational evaluation, if not outright rejection. As a subjective gauge of relational evaluation, self-esteem may parallel these problems, but it is a coeffect rather than a cause. (In fact, contrary to the popular view that low self-esteem causes these problems, no direct evidence exists to document that self-esteem has any causal role in thought, emotion, or behavior.) Much research shows that interpersonal rejection results in emotional problems, difficulties relating with others, and maladaptive efforts to be accepted (e.g., excessive dependency, membership in deviant groups), precisely the concomitants of low self-esteem (Leary, Schreindorfer, & Haupt, 1995). In addition, many personal problems lower self-esteem because they lead other people to devalue or reject the individual.

## Consequences of Enhancing Self-Esteem

The claim that self-esteem does not cause psychological outcomes may appear to fly in the face of evidence showing that interventions that enhance self-esteem do, in fact, lead to positive psychological changes. The explanation for the beneficial effects of programs that enhance self-esteem is that these interventions change people's perceptions of the degree to which they are socially valued individuals. Self-esteem programs always include features that would be expected to increase real or perceived social acceptance; for example, these programs include components aimed at enhancing social skills and interpersonal problem solving, improving physical appearance, and increasing self-control (Leary, 1999).

## CONCLUSIONS

Sociometer theory suggests that the emphasis psychologists and the lay public have placed on self-esteem has been somewhat misplaced. Self-esteem is certainly involved in many psychological phenomena, but its role is different than has been supposed. Subjective feelings of self-esteem provide ongoing feedback regarding one's relational value vis-à-vis other people. By focusing on the monitor rather than on what the monitor measures, we have been distracted from the underlying interpersonal processes and the importance of social acceptance to human well-being.

## Recommended Reading

Baumeister, R. F. (Ed.). (1993). *Self-esteem: The puzzle of low self-regard.* New York: Plenum Press.
Colvin, C. R., & Block, J. (1994). Do positive illusions foster mental health? An examination of the Taylor and Brown formulation. *Psychological Bulletin, 116,* 3–20.
Leary, M. R. (1999). (See References)
Leary, M. R., & Downs, D. L. (1995). (See References)
Mecca, A. M., Smelser, N. J., & Vasconcellos, J. (Eds.). (1989). (See References)

## Note

1. Address correspondence to Mark Leary, Department of Psychology, Wake Forest University, Winston-Salem, NC 27109; e-mail: leary@wfu.edu.

## References

Barkow, J. (1980). Prestige and self-esteem: A biosocial interpretation. In D. R. Omark, F. F. Strayer, & D. G. Freedman (Eds.), *Dominance relations: An ethological view of human conflict and social interaction* (pp. 319–332). New York: Garland STPM Press.
Baumeister, R. F., & Leary, M. R. (1995). The need to belong: Desire for interpersonal attachments as a fundamental human motivation. *Psychological Bulletin, 117,* 497–529.
Bednar, R. L., Wells, M. G., & Peterson, S. R. (1989). *Self-esteem: Paradoxes and innovations in clinical theory and practice.* Washington, DC: American Psychological Association.
James, W. (1890). *The principles of psychology* (Vol. 1). New York: Henry Holt.
Leary, M. R. (1999). The social and psychological importance of self-esteem. In R. M. Kowalski & M. R. Leary (Eds.), *The social psychology of emotional and behavioral problems: Interfaces of social and clinical psychology* (pp. 197–221). Washington, DC: American Psychological Association.
Leary, M. R., & Baumeister, R. F. (in press). The nature and function of self-esteem: Sociometer theory. *Advances in Experimental Social Psychology.*
Leary, M. R., & Downs, D. L. (1995). Interpersonal functions of the self-esteem motive: The self-esteem system as a sociometer. In M. H. Kernis (Ed.), *Efficacy, agency, and self-esteem* (pp. 123–144). New York: Plenum Press.
Leary, M. R., Haupt, A. L., Strausser, K. S., & Chokel, J. L. (1998). Calibrating the sociometer: The relationship between interpersonal appraisals and state self-esteem. *Journal of Personality and Social Psychology, 74,* 1290–1299.
Leary, M. R., Schreindorfer, L. S., & Haupt, A. L. (1995). The role of self-esteem in emotional and behavioral problems: Why is low self-esteem dysfunctional? *Journal of Social and Clinical Psychology, 14,* 297–314.
Leary, M. R., Tambor, E. S., Terdal, S. J., & Downs, D. L. (1995). Self-esteem as an interpersonal monitor. The sociometer hypothesis. *Journal of Personality and Social Psychology, 68,* 518–530.
Mecca, A. M., Smelser, N. J., & Vasconcellos, J. (Eds.). (1989). *The social importance of self-esteem.* Berkeley: University of California Press.
Solomon, S., Greenberg, J., & Pyszczynski, T. (1991). A terror management theory of social behavior: The psychological functions of self-esteem and cultural worldviews. *Advances in Experimental Social Psychology, 24,* 93–159.

# Shyness:
# The New Solution

## The results of a recent survey are shaking up our ideas about shyness and pointing to a surprising new approach for dealing with it.

BY BERNARDO CARDUCCI, PH.D.

At the core of our existence as human beings lies a powerful drive to be with other people. There is much evidence that in the absence of human contact people fall apart physically and mentally; they experience more sickness, stress and suicide than well-connected individuals. For all too many people, however, shyness is the primary barrier to that basic need.

For more than two decades, I have been studying shyness. In 1995, in an article in PSYCHOLOGY TODAY, I, along with shyness pioneer Philip Zimbardo, Ph.D., summed up 20 years of shyness knowledge and research, concluding that rates are rising. At the same time, I ran a small survey that included five open-ended questions asking the shy to tell us about their experiences.

The thousands of responses we received have spawned a whole new generation of research and insight. In addition to the sheer volume of surveys, my colleague and I were surprised at the depth of the comments, often extending to five or 10 handwritten pages. It was as if we had turned on a spigot, allowing people to release a torrent of emotions. They understood that we were willing to listen. For that reason, perhaps, they were not at all shy about answering. This article represents the first analysis of their responses.

## The New View

*"My ex-wife picked me to marry her, so getting married wasn't a problem. I didn't want to get divorced, even though she was cheating on me, because I would be back out there trying to* socialize. *[But] I have a computer job now, and one of my strengths is that I work well alone."*

Traditionally, shyness is viewed as an intrapersonal problem, arising within certain individuals as a result of characteristics such as excessive self-consciousness, low self-esteem and anticipation of rejection. The survey responses have shown, however, that shyness is also promoted by outside forces at work in our culture, and perhaps around the globe.

In addition, our research has led us to conclude that there is nothing at all wrong with being shy. Certainly shyness can control people and make them ineffective in classroom, social and business situations. Respondents told us that they feel imprisoned by their shyness. It is this feeling that seems to be at the core of their pain. But ironically, we find that the way to break out of the prison of shyness may be to embrace it thoroughly. There are many steps the shy can take to develop satisfying relationships without violating their basic nature.

## The Cynically Shy

*"My shyness has caused major problems in my personal/ social life. I have a strong hate for most people. I also have quite a superiority complex. I see so much stupidity and ignorance in the world that I feel superior to virtually everyone out there. I'm trying [not to], but it's hard."*

Of the many voices of shy individuals we "heard" in response to our survey, one in particular emerged very clearly. Among the new patterns our analysis identified was a group I call the cynically shy. These are people who have been rejected by their peers because of their lack of social skills. They

Reprinted from *Psychology Today,* January/February 2000, pp. 38-45, 78. © 2000 by Bernardo Carducci.

# The Eight Habits of Highly Popular People

## By Hara Estroff Marano

If you were ever the last person picked for a team or asked to dance at a party, you've probably despaired that popular people are born with complete self-confidence and impeccable social skills. But over the past 20 years, a large body of research in the social sciences has established that what was once thought the province of manna or magic is now solidly our own doing—or undoing. Great relationships, whether friendships or romances, don't fall out of the heavens on a favored few. They depend on a number of very sophisticated but human-scale social skills. These skills are crucial to developing social confidence and acceptance. And it is now clear that everyone can learn them.

And they should. Recent studies illustrate that having social contact and friends, even animal ones, improves physical health. Social ties seem to impact stress hormones directly, which in turn affect almost every part of our body, including the immune system. They also improve mental health. Having large social networks can help lower stress in times of crisis, alleviate depression and provide emotional support.

Luckily, it's never too late to develop the tools of the socially confident. Research from social scientists around the world, including relationship expert John Gottman, Ph.D., and shyness authority Bernardo Carducci, Ph.D., show that the most popular people follow these steps to social success:

### 1. Schedule Your Social Life
It is impossible to hone your social skills without investing time in them. Practice makes perfect, even for the socially secure. Accordingly, the well-liked surround themselves with others, getting a rich supply of opportunities to observe interactions and to improve upon their own social behaviors.

You need to do the same. Stop turning down party invitations and start inviting people to visit you at home. Plan outings with close friends or acquaintances you'd like to know better.

### 2. Think Positive
Insecure people tend to approach others anxiously, feeling they have to prove that they're witty or interesting. But self-assured people expect that others will respond positively—despite the fact that one of the most difficult social tasks is to join an activity that is already in progress.

### 3. Engage in Social Reconnaissance
Like detectives, the socially competent are highly skilled at information gathering, always scanning the scene for important details to guide their actions. They direct their focus outward, observing others and listening actively.

Socially skilled people are tuned in to people's expression of specific emotions, sensitive to signals that convey such information as what people's interests are, whether they want to be left alone or whether there is room in an activity for another person.

To infer correctly what others must be feeling, the socially confident are also able to identify and label their own experience accurately. That is where many people, particularly men, fall short.

Good conversationalists make comments that are connected to what is said to them and to the social situation. The connectedness of their communication is, in fact, one of its most outstanding features. Aggressive people actually make more attempts to join others in conversation but are less successful at it than the socially adept because they call attention to themselves, rather than finding a way to fit into ongoing group activity. They might throw out a statement that disrupts the conversation, or respond contentiously to a question. They might blurt something about the way they feel, or shift the conversation to something of interest exclusively to themselves.

"You don't have to be interesting. You have to be interested," explains John Gottman, Ph.D., professor of psychology at the University of Washington. "That's how you have conversations."

### 4. Enter Conversations Gracefully
Timing is everything. After listening and observing on the perimeter of a group they want to join, the socially competent look for an opportunity to step in, knowing it doesn't just happen. It usually appears as a lull in the conversation.

Tuned in to the conversational or activity theme, the deft participant asks a question or elaborates on what someone else has already said. This is not the time to shift the direction of the conversation, unless it comes to a dead halt. Then it might be wise to throw out a question, perhaps something related to events of the day, and, if possible, something tangentially related to the recent discussion. The idea is to use an open-ended question that lets others participate. "Speaking of the election, what does everybody think about so-and-so's decision not to run?"

"People admire the person who is willing to take a risk and throw out a topic for conversation, but you have to make sure it has general appeal," says Bernardo Carducci, Ph.D., director of the Shyness Research Institute at Indiana University Southeast. Then you are in the desirable position of having rescued the group, which confers immediate membership and acceptance. Once the conversation gets moving, it's wise to back off talking and give others a chance. Social bores attempt to dominate a discussion. The socially confident know that the goal is to help the group have a better conversation.

### 5. Learn to Handle Failure
It is a fact of life that everyone will sometimes be rejected. Rebuffs happen even to popular people. What distinguishes the socially confident from mere mortals is their reaction to rejection. They don't attribute it to internal causes, such as their own unlikability or inability to make friends. They assume it can result from many factors—incompatibility, someone else's bad mood, a misunderstanding. And some conversations are just private.

Self-assured people become resilient, using the feedback they get to shape another go at acceptance. Studies show that when faced with failure, those who are well-liked turn a negative response into a counterproposal. They say things like, "Well, can we make a date for next week instead?" Or they move onto another group in the expectation that not every conversation is closed.

And should they reject others' bids to join with them, they do it in a polite and positive way. They invariably offer a reason or counter with an alternative idea: "I would love to talk with you later."

### 6. Take Hold of Your Emotions

Social situations are incredibly complex and dynamic. One has to pay attention to all kinds of verbal and nonverbal cues, such as facial expression and voice tone, interpret their meaning accurately, decide on the best response for the scenario, and then carry out that response—all in a matter of microseconds. No one can pay attention to or correctly interpret what is going on, let alone act skillfully, without a reasonable degree of control over their own emotional states, especially negative emotions such as anger, fear, anxiety—the emotions that usually arise in situations of conflict or uncertainty.

Recently, studies have found that people who are the most well-liked also have a firm handle on their emotions. It isn't that they internalize all their negative feelings. Instead, they shift attention away from distressing stimuli toward positive aspects of a situation. In other words, they have excellent coping skills. Otherwise, they become overly reactive to the negative emotions of others and may resort to aggression or withdraw from social contact.

### 7. Defuse Disagreements

Since conflict is inevitable, coping with confrontations is one of the most critical of social skills. It's not the degree of conflict that sinks relationships, but the ways people resolve it. Disagreements, if handled well, can help people know themselves better, improve language skills, gain valuable information and cement their relationships.

Instead of fighting fire with fire, socially confident people stop conflict from escalating; they apologize, propose a joint activity, make a peace offering of some kind, or negotiate. And sometimes they just change the subject. That doesn't mean that they yield to another's demands. Extreme submissiveness violates the equality basic to healthy relationships—and a sense of self-worth.

As people gain social competence, they try to accommodate the needs of both parties. Managing conflict without aggression requires listening, communicating—arguing, persuading—taking the perspective of others, controlling negative emotions, and problem-solving. Researchers have found that when people explain their point of view in an argument, they are in essence making a conciliatory move. That almost invariably opens the door for a partner to offer a suggestion that ends the standoff.

### 8. Laugh A Little

Humor is the single most prized social skill, the fast track to being liked—at all ages. Humor works even in threatening situations because it defuses negativity. There's no recipe for creating a sense of humor. But even in your darkest moments, try to see the lighter side of a situation.

*If you need more help, call the American Psychological Association at 1-800-964-2000 for a referral to a therapist near you. For further resources check http://www.shyness.com/.*

---

do not feel connected to others—and they are angry about it. They feel a sense of alienation. And like the so-called trench coat mafia in Littleton, Colorado, they adapt a stance of superiority as they drift away from others.

Their isolation discourages them from having a sense of empathy, and this leads them to dehumanize others and take revenge against them. This process is the same one used by the military to train young boys to kill. The difference is, the military is now in your house, on your TV, in your video games.

## Inside the Shy Mind

*"As we talked, I felt uneasy. I worried about how I looked, what I said, how I said what I said, and so forth. Her compliments made me uncomfortable."*

One of the solutions to shyness is a greater understanding of its internal dynamics. It is important to note that a critical feature of shyness is a slowness to warm up. Shy people simply require extra time to adjust to novel or stressful situations, including even everyday conversations and social gatherings.

They also need more time to master the developmental hurdles of life. The good news is that shy people eventually achieve everything that everyone else does—they date, marry, have children. The bad news is, it takes them a little longer.

An unfortunate consequence of the shy being on this delayed schedule is that they lack social support through many important life experiences. When they start dating and want to talk about first-date jitters, for example, their peers will be talking about weddings. As a result, the shy may need to take an especially active role in finding others who are in their situation. One way is to build social support by starting groups of like-minded people. Another is to seek out existing groups of shy people, perhaps via the Internet. While technology often works against the shy, it can also lend them an unexpected helping hand.

Our research reveals the fact that the shy tend to make unrealistic social comparisons. In a room full of others, their attention is usually drawn to the most socially outstanding person, the life of the party—against whom they compare themselves, unfavorably, of course. This is just a preemptive strike. Typically, they compound the negative self-appraisal by attributing their own comparatively poor performance to enduring and unchangeable internal characteristics—"I was born shy" or "I don't have the gift of gab." Such attributions only heighten self-consciousness and inhibit performance.

The shy are prone to such errors of attribution because they believe that they are always being evaluated by others. Self-consciously focused on their own shortcomings, they fail to look around and notice that most people are just like them—listeners, not social standouts. Our surveys show that 48% of people are shy. So not only are the shy not alone, they probably have plenty of company at any social function.

The No. 1 problem area for the shy is starting a relationship. Fifty-eight percent told us they have problems with introductions; they go to a party but nothing happens. Forty percent said their problem was social; they had trouble developing friendships. Only seven percent of the shy have a problem with intimacy. If you get into an intimate relationship, shyness no longer seems to be a problem. Unfortunately, it's hard to get there.

## The New Cultural Climate

It is no secret that certain technological advances—the Internet, e-mail, cell phones—are changing the conditions of the culture we live in, speeding it up and intensifying its complexity. This phenomenon, dubbed hyperculture, has trickled down to alter the nature of day-to-day interactions, with negative consequences for the shy. In this cultural climate, we lose patience quickly because we've grown accustomed to things happening faster and faster. We lose tolerance for those who need time to warm up. Those who are not quick and intense get passed by. The shy are bellwethers of this change: They are the first to feel its effects. And so it's not surprising that hyperculture is actually exacerbating shyness, in both incidence and degree.

Another effect of hyperculture is what I call identity intensity. Our society is not only getting faster, it is getting louder and brighter. It takes an increasingly powerful personality to be recognized. We see this in the emergence of shock jocks like Howard Stern and outrageous characters like Dennis Rodman. People have to call attention to themselves in ways that are more and more extreme just to be noticed at all. That, of course, puts the shy at a further disadvantage.

We are also undergoing "interpersonal disenfranchisement." Simply put, we are disconnecting from one another. Increasingly, we deal with the hyperculture cacophony by cocooning—commuting home with headphones on while working on our laptops. We go from our cubicle to the car to our gated community, maintaining contact with only a small circle of friends and family. As other people become just e-mail addresses or faceless voices at the other end of electronic transactions, it becomes easier and easier to mistreat and disrespect them. The cost of such disconnection is a day-to-day loss of civility and an increase in rudeness. And, again, the shy pay. They are the first to be excluded, bullied or treated in a hostile manner.

As we approach the limits of our ability to deal with the complexities of our lives, we begin to experience a state of anxiety. We either approach or avoid. And, indeed, we are seeing both phenomena—a polarization of behavior in which we see increases in both aggression, marked by a general loss of manners that has been widely observed, and in withdrawal, one form of which is shyness. Surveys we have conducted reliably show that over the last decade and a half, the incidence of shyness has risen from 40% to 48%.

So it is no accident that the pharmaceutical industry has chosen this cultural moment to introduce the antidepressant Paxil as a treatment for social phobia. Paxil is touted as a cure for being "allergic to people." One of the effects of hyperculture is to make people impatient for anything but a pill that instantly reduces their anxiety level.

The use of Paxil, however, operates against self-awareness. It makes shyness into a medical or psychiatric problem, which it has never been. It essentially labels as pathology what is a personality trait. I think it is a mistake for doctors to hand out a physiological remedy when we know that there are cognitive elements operating within individuals, communication difficulties existing between individuals, and major forces residing outside of individuals that are making it difficult for people to interact.

It is much easier for the shy to take a pill, doctors figure, than for them to take the time to adjust to their cautious tendencies, modify faulty social comparisons or learn to be more civil to others. The promise of Paxil does not include teaching the shy to develop the small talk skills they so desperately need.

## Strategies of the Shy

*"I have tried to overcome my shyness by being around people as much as possible and getting involved in the conversation; however, after a few seconds, I become quiet. I have a problem keeping conversation flowing."*

In our survey, we asked people what they do to cope with their shyness. What we found surprised us. The shy put a lot of effort into overcoming their shyness, but the strategies they use are largely ineffective, sometimes even counterproductive. Occasionally their solutions are potentially dangerous.

Ninety-one percent of shy respondents said they had made at least some effort to overcome their shyness. By far, the top technique they employ is forced extroversion. Sixty-seven percent of them said they make themselves go to parties, bars, dances, the mall—places that will put them in proximity to others. That is good. But unfortunately, they expect the others to do all the work, to approach them and draw them out of their isolation. Simply showing up is not enough. Not only is it ineffective, it cedes control of interactions to others.

But it exemplifies the mistaken expectations the shy often have about social life. Hand in hand with the expectation that others will approach them is their sense of perfectionism. The shy believe that anything they say has to come out perfect, sterling, supremely witty, as if everyday life is some kind of sitcom. They believe that everybody is watching and judging them—a special kind of narcissism.

> **Once the shy learn to focus more on the lives of other people, shyness no longer controls them.**

Their second most popular strategy is self-induced cognitive modification: thinking happy thoughts, or the "Stuart Smalley Effect"—remember the sketch from *Saturday Night Live?* "I'm

> # Shy people tend either to reveal information about themselves too quickly, or hold back and move too slowly.

good enough, I'm smart enough, and, doggone it, people like me." Twenty-two percent of the shy try to talk themselves into not being shy. But just talking to yourself doesn't work. You have to know how to talk to other people. And you have to be around other people. The shy seldom combine extroversion with cognitive modification.

Fifteen percent of the shy turn to self-help books and seminars, which is great. But not enough people do it.

And about 12 % of the shy turn to what I call liquid extroversion. They are a distinct population of people, who, often beginning in adolescence, ingest drugs or alcohol to deal with their shyness. They self-medicate as a social lubricant, to give them courage. And while it may remove inhibitions, it doesn't provide them with what they desperately need—actual social skills, knowledge about how to be with others. Further, drinking interferes with their cognitive functioning.

Liquid extroversion poses the great danger of overconsumption of alcohol. Indeed, we have found in separate studies that a significant proportion of problem drinkers in the general population are shy.

But "shy alcoholics" tell us they do not like having to drink to perform better; they feel uneasy and lack confidence in their true selves. They begin to believe that people will like them only if they are outgoing, not the way they really are. Interestingly, the largest program for problem drinkers, Alcoholics

Anonymous, works squarely against shy people. Whereas the shy are slow to warm up, AA asks people to stand up right away, to be highly visible, to immediately disclose highly personal information. It is my belief that there needs to be an AA for the shy, a program that takes into consideration the nature and dynamics of shyness. A meeting might, for example, begin by having a leader speak for the first 45 minutes while people get comfortable, followed by a break in which the leader is available to answer questions. That then paves the way for a general question-and-answer period.

## Cyberbonding

*"I can be anyone I want to be on the Internet and yet mostly be myself, because I know I will never meet these people I'm talking with and can close out if I get uncomfortable."*

*"I think the Internet hinders people in overcoming their shyness. You can talk to someone but you don't have to actually interact with them. You can sit in your room and not REALLY socialize."*

Another strategy of the shy is electronic extroversion. The Net is a great social facilitator. It enables people to reach out to many others and join in at their own speed, perhaps observing in a chat room before participating. Still, Internet interaction requires less effort than face-to-face interaction, so it may increase their frustration and cause difficulties in real-life situations where social skills are not only required, but born and learned.

We know that people start out using the Internet for informational purposes, then progress to use that is social in nature, such as entering chat rooms; some then progress to personal use, talking about more intimate topics and disclosing information about themselves. The danger of electronic extroversion is that anonymity makes it easy for the shy to misrepresent themselves and to deceive others, violating the trust that is the foundation of social life.

And talk about disconnecting. The irony of a World Wide Web packed with endless amounts of information is that it can also be isolating. As individuals head to their own favorite bookmarked sites, they cut out all the disagreement of the world and reinforce their own narrow perspective, potentially leading to alienation, disenfranchisement and intolerance for people who are different.

In addition, the shy are more vulnerable to instant intimacy because of their lack of social know-how. Normally, relationships progress by way of a reasonably paced flow of self-disclosure that is reciprocal in nature. A disclosure process that moves too quickly—and computer anonymity removes the stigma of getting sexu-

## SHYNESS SURVEY

- 64% of shy individuals view their shyness as a result of external factors beyond their control, such as early family experiences, overprotective parents or peer victimization.

- 24% attribute shyness to internal factors within their control, such as intrapersonal difficulties, like low self-esteem and high self-consciousness, or interpersonal difficulties, like poor social skills and dating difficulties.

- 62% experience feelings of shyness daily.

- 82% report shyness as an undesirable experience.

- **Types of Individuals who make the shy feel shy:**
  75% strangers
  71% persons of the opposite sex, in a group
  65% persons of the opposite sex, one-on-one
  56% persons of the same sex, in a group
  45% relatives, other than immediate family
  38% persons of the same sex, one-on-one
  22% their parents
  20% siblings

- 46% believe their shyness can be overcome.

- 7.2% do not believe their shyness can be overcome.

- 85% are willing to work seriously at overcoming shyness.

ally explicit—doesn't just destroy courtship; it is a reliable sign of maladjustment. Shy people tend either to reveal information about themselves too quickly, or hold back and move too slowly.

Like most cultural influences, the Internet is neither devil nor angel. It's a social tool that works in different ways, depending on how it's used.

## The Solution to Shyness

*"I was very shy as a kid. Every situation scared me if it required interacting with others. After high school and into college, I became much less shy. I consciously made each interaction an exercise in overcoming shyness. Just talking to people I didn't know, getting a part-time job, volunteering. I had always been afraid to sing in front of people, but now I sing all the time. That's a big deal to me."*

Every shy person believes that shyness is a problem located exclusively within the self. But our work suggests that the solution to shyness lies outside the self. To break free of the prison of shyness, you must stop dwelling on your own insecurities and become more aware of the people around you.

Through our survey, we have identified a group of people we call the successfully shy. Essentially, they recognize that they are shy. They develop an understanding of the nature and dynamics of shyness, its impact on the body, on cognitive processes and on behavior. And they take action based on that self-awareness. The successfully shy overcome their social anxiety by letting go of their self-consciousness, that inward focus of attention on the things they can't do well (like tell a joke). They accept that they aren't great at small talk or that they get so nervous in social situations that they can't draw on what is inside their mind. Or that they are paying so much attention to their feelings that they don't pay full attention to the person they're talking to. In place of self-consciousness, they substitute self-awareness. Rather than becoming anxious about their silence in a conversation, they plan ahead of time

to have something to say, or rehearse asking questions. They arrive early at parties to feel comfortable in their new setting. By contrast, less successful shy people arrive late in an effort to blend in.

The fact is, these are the same kinds of strategies that non-shy people employ. Many of them develop a repertoire of opening gambits for conversation. When among others, they engage in social reconnaissance—they wait to gather information about speakers and a discussion before jumping in.

The successfully shy also take steps at the transpersonal level, getting involved in the lives of others. They start small, making sure their day-to-day exchanges involve contact with other people. When they pick up a newspaper, for instance, they don't just put their money on the counter. They focus on the seller, thanking him or her for the service. This creates a social environment favorable to positive interactions. On a larger scale, I encourage volunteering. Once the shy are more outwardly focused on the lives of other people, shyness no longer controls them.

The successfully shy don't change who they are. They change the way they think and the actions they make. There is nothing wrong with being shy. In fact, I have come to believe that what our society needs is not less shyness but a little more.

---

*Bernardo Carducci, Ph.D., is the director of the Shyness Research Institute at Indiana University Southeast. His last article for* Psychology Today, *also on shyness, appeared in the December 1995 issue.*

## READ MORE ABOUT IT

*Shyness: A Bold New Approach,* Bernardo J. Carducci, Ph.D. (HarperCollins, 1999)

*The Shy Child,* Philip G. Zimbardo, Ph.D., Shirley L. Radl (ISHK Book Service, 1999)

# Unit 9

## Unit Selections

## Key Points to Consider

❖ What is lying? Do only humans lie? How can you detect whether a person is deceiving you? Is the face the only key to deception? How can computers detect a liar?

❖ What is crowding? Is crowding always deleterious? What did early research with animals demonstrate about the effects of crowding? What does newer research demonstrate? If humans can adapt to crowding, to what other environmental conditions might they be able to adapt?

❖ What is prejudice? Can you differentiate it from stereotyping? Is there any such thing as old-fashioned prejudice and modern prejudice? If so, can you provide an example of each? Is prejudice only negative; can we also have positive biases? Are most biased thoughts processed automatically? Can we overcome our prejudices if they are fairly automatic? How so? Or should we give up and let prejudice exist?

❖ What is culture? What is cultural diversity? Why is there a push in U.S. schools to teach about other cultures? How should we teach about other cultures? How might plans to teach appreciation of other cultures backfire?

 **Links** **www.dushkin.com/online/**

24. **National Clearinghouse for Alcohol and Drug Information**
    *http://www.health.org*

These sites are annotated on pages 4 and 5.

Everywhere we look there are groups of people. Your general psychology class is a group. It is what social psychologists would call a secondary group, a group which comes together for a particular, somewhat contractual reason and then disbands after its goals have been met. Other secondary groups include athletic teams, church associations, juries, committees, and so forth.

There are other types of groups, too. One other type is a primary group. A primary group has much face-to-face contact, and there is often a sense of "we-ness" (cohesiveness, as social psychologists would call it) in the group. Examples of primary groups include families, suite mates, sororities, and fraternities.

Collectives are loosely knit, large groups of people. A bleacher full of football fans would be a collective. A line of people waiting to get into a rock concert would also be a collective. As you might guess, collectives behave differently from primary and secondary groups.

Mainstream American society and any other large group that shares common rules and norms is also a group, albeit an extremely large group. While we might not always think about our society and how it shapes our behavior and our attitudes, society and culture nonetheless have a measureless influence on us. Psychologists, anthropologists, and sociologists alike are all interested in studying the effects of a culture on its members.

In this unit we will look at both positive and negative forms of social interaction. We will move from a focused form of social interaction to broader forms of social interaction, from interpersonal to group to societal processes.

In the first article, we concentrate on interpersonal relations. In "How to Spot a Liar," James Geary demonstrates how deception is a normal part of human life. In fact, he points out how even animals deceive one another. Humans are well equipped, however, to detect deception, and Geary shows us how. The face, he says, is the key to detecting lying by others.

We next move to a slightly larger social setting—groups. Groups are often placed in quarters that are too small for everyone to feel comfortable. In the article "Coping With Crowding," the authors

review early research on crowding, much of which was done with animals. The authors also report new research that demonstrates that humans and animals are capable of adapting better to environmental conditions such as crowding than was earlier believed.

The next article investigates the darker side of social relationships. One lingering societal problem in the United States is prejudice. Hate groups and white supremacy groups are active in many communities. Two prominent psychologists in the field of prejudice and stigma differentiate various forms of prejudice as well as suggest means for reducing prejudice and intergroup bias.

In the final article of this unit on social behavior, we explore the largest social issue of all—culture. There is a push in the United States to teach about other cultures. In "Merits and Perils of Teaching About Other Cultures," Walter McDougall investigates the trend of teaching about cultural diversity in public schools and universities. He suggests that some of the best-laid plans go astray and that we need to rethink how, when, and what we teach about other cultures.

# How to Spot a Liar

## With some careful observation— and a little help from new software—anyone can learn to be a lie detector

*By JAMES GEARY/London*
*With reporting by Eric Silver/Jerusalem*

"You can tell a lie but you will give yourself away. Your heart will race. Your skin will sweat . . . I will know. I am the lie detector." Thus began each episode of Lie Detector, a strange cross between a relationship counseling session and an episode of the Jerry Springer Show that ran on British daytime television last year. Against a backdrop of flashing computer screens and eerie blue light, participants—usually feuding couples but sometimes warring neighbors or aggrieved business partners—sat on a couch and were quizzed by the program's host. A frequent topic of discussion was one guest's suspicion that his or her partner had been unfaithful. The person suspected of infidelity denied it, of course, and the object of the show was to find out—through cross-examination and computer analysis—whether that person was telling the truth.

However much we may abhor it, deception comes naturally to all living things. Birds do it by feigning injury to lead hungry predators away from nesting young. Spider crabs do it by disguise: adorning themselves with strips of kelp and other debris, they pretend to be something they are not—and so escape their enemies. Nature amply rewards successful deceivers by allowing them to survive long enough to mate and reproduce. So it may come as no surprise to learn that human beings—who, according to psychologist Gerald Jellison of the University of

South California, are lied to about 200 times a day, roughly one untruth every five minutes—often deceive for exactly the same reasons: to save their own skins or to get something they can't get by other means.

But knowing how to catch deceit can be just as important a survival skill as knowing how to tell a lie and get away with it. A person able to spot falsehood quickly is unlikely to be swindled by an unscrupulous business associate or hoodwinked by a devious spouse. Luckily, nature provides more than enough clues to trap dissemblers in their own tangled webs—if you know where to look. By closely observing facial expressions, body language and tone of voice, practically anyone can recognize the telltale signs of lying. Researchers are even programming computers—like those used on Lie Detector—to get at the truth by analyzing the same physical cues available to the naked eye and ear. "With the proper training, many people can learn to reliably detect lies," says Paul Ekman, professor of psychology at the University of California, San Francisco, who has spent the past 15 years studying the secret art of deception.

In order to know what kind of lies work best, successful liars need to accurately assess other people's emotional states. Ekman's research shows that this same emotional intelligence is essential for good lie detectors, too. The emotional state to watch out for is

stress, the conflict most liars feel between the truth and what they actually say and do.

Even high-tech lie detectors don't detect lies as such; they merely detect the physical cues of emotions, which may or may not correspond to what the person being tested is saying. Polygraphs, for instance, measure respiration, heart rate and skin conductivity, which tend to increase when people are nervous—as they usually are when lying. Nervous people typically perspire, and the salts contained in perspiration conduct electricity. That's why a sudden leap in skin conductivity indicates nervousness—about getting caught, perhaps?—which might, in turn, suggest that someone is being economical with the truth. On the other hand, it might also mean that the lights in the television studio are too hot—which is one reason polygraph tests are inadmissible in court. "Good lie detectors don't rely on a single sign," Ekman says, "but interpret clusters of verbal and nonverbal clues that suggest someone might be lying."

Those clues are written all over the face. Because the musculature of the face is directly connected to the areas of the brain that process emotion, the countenance can be a window to the soul. Neurological studies even suggest that genuine emotions travel different pathways through the brain than insincere ones. If a patient paralyzed by stroke on one side of the face, for example, is asked

From *Time Europe*, March 13, 2000, pp. 44-49. © 2000 by Time Inc. Reprinted by permission.

to smile deliberately, only the mobile side of the mouth is raised. But tell that same person a funny joke, and the patient breaks into a full and spontaneous smile. Very few people—most notably, actors and politicians—are able to consciously control all of their facial expressions. Lies can often be caught when the liar's true feelings briefly leak through the mask of deception. "We don't think before we feel," Ekman says. "Expressions tend to show up on the face before we're even conscious of experiencing an emotion."

One of the most difficult facial expressions to fake—or conceal, if it is genuinely felt—is sadness. When someone is truly sad, the forehead wrinkles with grief and the inner corners of the eyebrows are pulled up. Fewer than 15% of the people Ekman tested were able to produce this eyebrow movement voluntarily. By contrast, the lowering of the eyebrows associated with an angry scowl can be replicated at will by almost everybody. "If someone claims they are sad and the inner corners of their eyebrows don't go up," Ekman says, "the sadness is probably false."

The smile, on the other hand, is one of the easiest facial expressions to counterfeit. It takes just two muscles—the zygomaticus major muscles that extend from the cheekbones to the corners of the lips—to produce a grin. But there's a catch. A genuine smile affects not only the corners of the lips but also the orbicularis oculi, the muscle around the eye that produces the distinctive "crow's-feet" associated with people who laugh a lot. A counterfeit grin can be unmasked if the lip corners go up, the eyes crinkle but the inner corners of the eyebrows are not lowered, a movement controlled by the orbicularis oculi that is difficult to fake. The absence of lowered eyebrows is one reason why false smiles look so strained and stiff.

Ekman and his colleagues have classified all the muscle movements—ranging from the thin, taut lips of fury to the arched eyebrows of surprise—that underlie the complete repertoire of human facial expressions. In addition to the nervous tics and jitters that can give liars away, Ekman discovered that fibbers often allow the truth to slip through in brief, unguarded facial expressions. Lasting no more than a quarter of a second, these fleeting glimpses of a person's true emotional state—or "microexpressions," as Ekman calls them—are reliable guides to veracity.

In a series of tests, Ekman interviewed and videotaped a group of male American college students about their opinions regarding capital punishment. Some participants were instructed to tell the truth—whether they were for or against the death penalty—and some were instructed to lie. Liars who successfully fooled the interviewer received $50. Ekman then studied the tapes to map the microexpressions of mendacity.

One student, for example, appeared calm and reasonable as he listed the reasons why the death penalty was wrong. But every time he expressed these opinions, he swiftly, almost imperceptibly, shook his head. But the movement is so subtle and quick many people don't even see it until it's pointed out to them. While his words explained the arguments against capital punishment, the quick, involuntary shudder of his head was saying loud and clear, "No, I don't believe this!" He was, in fact, lying, having been for many years a firm supporter of the death penalty.

Another student also said that he was against the death penalty. But during the interview, he spoke very slowly, paused often, and rarely looked the interrogator in the eye, instead fixing his gaze on some vague point on the floor. Speech that is too slow (or too fast), frequent hesitations, lack of direct eye contact: these are all classic symptoms of lying. But this man was telling the truth. He paused and hesitated because he was shy. After all, even honest and normally composed individuals can become flustered if they believe others suspect them of lying. His lack of eye contact could be explained by the fact that he came from Asia, where an averted gaze is often a sign of deference and respect, not deception. This scenario highlights Ekman's admonition that before branding someone a liar, you must first know that person's normal behavior patterns and discount other explanations, such as cultural differences.

Ekman has used this tape to test hundreds of subjects. His conclusion: most people are lousy lie detectors, with few individuals able to spot duplicity more than 50% of the time. But Ekman's most recent study, published last year in Psychological Science, found that four groups of people did significantly better than chance: members of the U.S. Central Intelligence Agency, other U.S. federal law enforcement officers, a handful of Los Angeles County sheriffs and a group of clinical psychologists. Reassuringly, perhaps, the federal officials performed best, accurately detecting liars 73% of the time. What makes these groups so good at lie catching? According to Ekman, it's training, experience and motivation. The jobs—and in some cases, the lives—of everyone in these groups depend on their ability to pick up deceit.

Ekman has used his findings to assist law enforcement agents—including members of the U.S. Secret Service and Federal Bureau of Investigation, Britain's Scotland Yard and the Israeli police force—in criminal investigations and antiterrorist activities. He refuses to work with politicians. "It is unlikely that judging deception from demeanor alone will ever be admissible in court," Ekman says. "But the research shows that it's possible for some people to make highly accurate judgements about lying without any special aids, such as computers."

But for those who still prefer a bit of technological assistance, there's the Verdicator—a device that, according to its 27-year-old inventor Amir Liberman, enables anyone equipped with a personal computer and a phone or microphone to catch a liar. A person's tone of voice can be just as revealing as the expression on his face. A low tone, for example, can suggest a person is lying or is stressed, while a higher pitch can mean excitement. Liberman claims the Verdicator, a $2,500 piece of software produced by Integritek Technologies in Petah Tikvah near Tel Aviv, is between 85% and 95% accurate

## THE LYIN' KING

### Four signs that may indicate deception

**1. AN EMBLEM** is a gesture with a specific meaning, like shrugging the shoulders to say, "I don't know." An emblem may be a sign of deceit if only part of the gesture is performed (a one-shoulder shrug, for example) or if it is performed in a concealed manner.

**2. MANIPULATORS** are repetitive touching motions like scratching the nose, tapping the foot or twisting the hair. They tend to increase when people are nervous, and may be an attempt to conceal incriminating facial expressions.

**3. AN ILLUSTRATOR** is a movement that emphasizes speech. Illustrators increase with emotion, so too few may indicate false feelings while too many may be an attempt to distract attention from signs of deceit on the face.

**4. MICROEXPRESSIONS** flash across the face in less than a quarter of a second—a frown, for example, that is quickly covered up by a grin. Though fleeting, they can reveal subtle clues about the true feelings that a person may wish to repress or conceal.

"With proper training, many people can learn to reliably detect lies."

"It would be an impossible world if no one lied."

*James Geary/London*
*With reporting by Eric Silver/Jerusalem.*

in determining whether the person on the other end of the line is lying, an accuracy rate better than that for traditional polygraphs. "Our software knows how to size you up," Liberman boasts.

The Verdicator delivers its results by analyzing voice fluctuations that are usually inaudible to the human ear. When a person is under stress, anxiety may cause muscle tension and reduce blood flow to the vocal cords, producing a distinctive pattern of sound waves. Liberman has catalogued these patterns and programmed the Verdicator to distinguish among tones that indicate excitement, cognitive stress—the difference between what you think and what you say—and outright deceit. Once linked to a communications device and computer, the Verdicator monitors the subtle vocal tremors of your conversational partner and displays an assessment of that person's veracity on the screen. "The system can tell how nervous you are," Liberman explains. "It builds a

psychological profile of what you feel and compares it to patterns associated with deception." And the Verdicator has one great advantage over the polygraph: the suspect doesn't need to know he's being tested. To be accurate, though, the Verdicator must pick up changes—which might indicate deceit— in a person's normal voice.

During the Monica Lewinsky scandal, Liberman demonstrated the system on President Clinton's famous disclaimer, "I did not have sexual relations with that woman." After analyzing an audio tape of the statement 100 times, the Verdicator showed that Clinton "was telling the truth," Liberman says, "but he had very high levels of cognitive stress, or 'guilt knowledge.' He didn't have sexual relations, but he did have something else."

Integritek will not name the law enforcement agencies, banks or financial institutions that are using the Verdicator. But company president Naaman Boury says that last year more than 500 Verdicators were sold in

North and South America, Australia, Asia and Europe. The Japanese firm Atlus is marketing a consumer version of the Verdicator in Asia. "We get the best results—close to 95% accuracy—in Japan," Liberman reports. "The Japanese feel very uncomfortable when lying. We get the poorest results—nearer 85% accuracy—in Russia, where people seldom seem to say what they really feel."

In moderation, lying is a normal—even necessary—part of life. "It would be an impossible world if no one lied," Ekman says. But by the same token, it would be an intolerable world if we could never tell when someone was lying. For those lies that are morally wrong and potentially harmful, would-be lie detectors can learn a lot from looking and listening very carefully. Cheating partners, snake oil salesmen and scheming politicians, beware! The truth is out there.

*James Geary/London*
*With reporting by Eric Silver/Jerusalem*

# Coping with CROWDING

*A persistent and popular view holds that high population density inevitably leads to violence. This myth, which is based on rat research, applies neither to us nor to other primates*

## by Frans B. M. de Waal, Filippo Aureli and Peter G. Judge

*FRANS B. M. DE WAAL, FILIPPO AURELI and PETER G. JUDGE share a research interest in the social relationships and behavioral strategies of nonhuman primates. Their work on aspects of this topic will appear in* Natural Conflict Resolution, *to be published by the University of California Press. De Waal, author of* Chimpanzee Politics *and* Good Natured, *worked for many years at the Arnhem zoo in the Netherlands before coming to the U.S., where he is now director of the Living Links Center at the Yerkes Regional Primate Research Center in Atlanta and professor of psychology at Emory University. Aureli is a senior lecturer in biological and earth sciences at Liverpool John Moores University in England. Judge is an assistant professor at Bloomsburg University in Pennsylvania and a research associate at Yerkes.*

In 1962 this magazine published a seminal paper by experimental psychologist John B. Calhoun entitled "Population Density and Social Pathology." The article opened dramatically with an observation by the late-18th-century English demographer Thomas Malthus that human population growth is automatically followed by increased vice and misery. Calhoun went on to note that although we know overpopulation causes disease and food shortage, we understand virtually nothing about its behavioral impact.

This reflection had inspired Calhoun to conduct a nightmarish experiment. He placed an expanding rat population in a crammed room and observed that the rats soon set about killing, sexually assaulting and, eventually, cannibalizing one another. Much of this activity happened among the occupants of a central feeding section. Despite the presence of food elsewhere in the room, the rats were irresistibly drawn to the social stimulation—even though many of them could not reach the central food dispensers. This pathological togetherness, as Calhoun described it, as well as the attendant chaos and behavioral deviancy, led him to coin the phrase "behavioral sink."

In no time, popularizers were comparing politically motivated street riots to rat packs, inner cities to behavioral sinks and urban areas to zoos. Warning that society was heading for either anarchy or dictatorship, Robert Ardrey, an American science journalist, remarked in 1970 on the voluntary nature of human crowding: "Just as Calhoun's rats freely chose to eat in the middle pens, we freely enter the city." Calhoun's views soon became a central tenet of the voluminous literature on aggression.

In extrapolating from rodents to people, however, these thinkers and writers were making a gigantic leap of faith. A look at human populations suggests why such a simple extrapolation is so problematic. Compare, for instance, per capita murder rates with the number of people per square kilometer in different nations—as we did, using data from the United Nation's *1996 Demographic Yearbook.* If things were straightforward, the two ought to vary in tandem. Instead there is no statistically meaningful relation.

But, one could argue, perhaps such a relation is obscured by variation in national income level, political organization or some other variable. Apparently not, at least for income. We divided the nations into three categories—free-market, former East Block and Third World—and did the analysis again. This time we did find one significant correlation, but it was in the other direction: it showed more violent crime in the least crowded countries of the former East Block. A similar trend existed for free-market nations, among which the U.S.

FRANS B. M. DE WAAL

RHESUS MONKEYS from three different settings show different rates of grooming—that is, of calming one another. The monkeys seem to adapt to crowded conditions by grooming more frequently. Among the males, grooming of each other and of females was more common when they lived in crowded conditions than when they lived in more spacious quarters. Among female non-kin, aggression was common and increased further with crowding but was accompanied by increased grooming, which served to reduce conflicts.

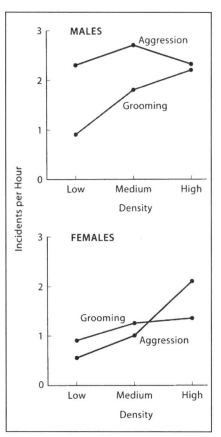

BRYAN CHRISTIE

SOURCE: Peter G. Judge and Frans B. M. de Waal

had by far the highest homicide rate despite its low overall population density. The Netherlands had a population density 13 times as high, but its homicide rate was eight times lower.

Knowing that crime is generally more common in urban areas than it is in the countryside, we factored in the proportion of each nation's population that lives in large cities and controlled for it. But this correction did nothing to bring about a positive correlation between population density and homicide. Perhaps because of the overriding effects of history and culture, the link between available space and human aggression—if it exists at all—is decidedly not clear-cut.

Even if we look at small-scale human experiments, we find no supporting evidence. Crowding of children and college students, for instance, sometimes produced irritation and mild aggression, but in general, people seemed adept at avoiding conflict. Andrew S. Baum and his co-workers in the psychiatry depart-

ment at the Uniformed Services University found that dormitory residents who shared facilities with many people spent less time socializing and kept the doors to their rooms closed more often than did students who had more space. Baum concluded that the effects of crowding are not nearly as overwhelming as originally presumed. Published in the 1980s, these and other findings began to undermine, at least in the scientific community, the idea that people and rats react in the same ways to being packed together. In modern society, people commonly assemble in large masses—during their daily commute to work or during holiday-season shopping expeditions—and most of the time they control their behavior extraordinarily well.

Calhoun's model, we must conclude, does not generally apply to human behavior. Is this because our culture and intelligence makes us unique, or is the management of crowding part of an older heritage? To answer this question, we turn to the primates.

## PRIMATES ARE NOT RATS

Primate research initially appeared to support the harrowing scenario that had been presented for rats. In the 1960s scientists reported that city-dwelling monkeys in India were more aggressive than were those living in forests. Others claimed that monkeys in zoos were excessively violent. Those monkeys were apparently ruled by terrifying bullies who dominated a social hierarchy that was considered an artifact of captivity—in other words, in the wild, peace and egalitarianism prevailed. Borrowing from the hyperbole of popularizers, one study of crowding in small captive groups of baboons even went so far as to report a "ghetto riot."

As research progressed, however, conflicting evidence accumulated. Higher population density seemed to increase aggression occasionally—but the opposite was also true. One report, for instance, described intense fighting and killing when a group of macaques were released into a corral 73 times *larger* than their previous quarters had been. Then, after two and a half years in the corral, a similar increase in aggression occurred when the monkeys were crowded back into a small pen.

Whereas the macaque study manipulated population density through environmental change, other early research did so by adding new monkeys to existing groups. Given the xenophobic nature of monkeys, these tests mainly measured their hostile attitude toward strangers, which is quite different from the effect of density. The better controlled the studies became, the less clear-cut the picture turned out to be. Increased population density led to increased aggression in only 11 of the

17 best-designed studies of the past few decades.

In the meantime, the view of wild primates was changing. They were no longer the purely peaceful, egalitarian creatures people had presumed them to be. In the 1970s field-workers began reporting sporadic but lethal violence in a wide range of species—from macaques to chimpanzees—as well as strict and well-defined hierarchies that remained stable for decades. This view of an often anxiety-filled existence was confirmed when researchers found high levels of the stress hormone cortisol in the blood of wild monkeys [see "Stress in the Wild," by Robert M. Sapolsky; SCIENTIFIC AMERICAN, JANUARY 1990.

As the view of primates became more complex, and as the rat scenario

was weakened by counterexamples, researchers began to wonder whether primates had developed a means to reduce conflict in crowded situations. We saw the first hint of this possibility in a study of the world's largest zoo colony of chimpanzees in Arnhem, the Netherlands. The apes lived on a spacious, forested island in the summer but were packed together in a heated building during the winter. Despite a 20-fold reduction in space, aggression increased only slightly. In fact, the effect of crowding was not entirely negative: friendly grooming and greetings, such as kissing and submissive bowing, increased as well.

We wondered if this conciliatory behavior mitigated tension and proposed a way to test this possibility. Without ig-

FRANS B. M. DE WAAL

CHIMPANZEES IN THE WILD have hostile territorial relations with other groups, and in captivity they are bothered by the presence of noisy neighboring chimps. By examining apes under three conditions—those living in a crowded space and able to hear their neighbors, those living in a crowded space without such worrisome sounds, and those living in isolated large compounds *(photograph below)*—we were able to measure the association between aggression, space and stress. Aggression *(photograph at left)* remained the same, but stress varied with neighbors' noise. Chimpanzees in small spaces exposed to vocalizations from other groups showed the highest levels of the stress hormone cortisol.

FRANS B. M. DE WAAL

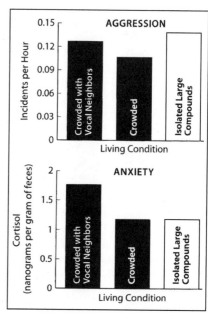

BRYAN CHRISTIE

*SOURCE: Filippo Aureli and Frans B. M. de Waal*

noring the fact that crowding increases the potential for conflict, we predicted that primates employ counterstrategies—including avoiding potential aggressors and offering appeasement or reassuring body contact. Because some of the skills involved are probably acquired, the most effective coping responses would be expected in animals who have experienced high density for a long time. Perhaps they develop a different "social culture" in the same way that people in different places have varying standards of privacy and interpersonal comfort zones. For example, studies show that white North Americans and the British keep greater distances from others during conversations than Latin Americans and Arabs do.

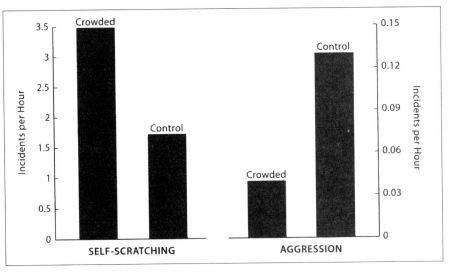

BRYAN CHRISTIE

SOURCE: Filippo Aureli and Frans B. M. de Waal

During brief periods of crowding, people often limit social interaction—a way of avoiding any conflict. Chimpanzees do the same, reducing their aggressive interactions. This doesn't mean that crowded situations do not induce anxiety. Chimpanzees packed together tend to scratch themselves more often—a sign of stress.

## COPING CULTURE

We set about finding several populations of monkeys that were of the same species but that had been living in different conditions to see if their behavior varied in discernible ways. We collected detailed data on 122 individual rhesus monkeys at three different sites in the U.S.: in relatively cramped outdoor pens at the Wisconsin primate center in Madison, in large open corrals at the Yerkes primate center in Atlanta and on Morgan Island off the coast of South Carolina. These last monkeys had approximately 2,000 times more space per individual than the highest-density groups. All three groups had lived together for many years, often for generations, and included individuals of both sexes. All the groups had also been in human care, receiving food and veterinary treatment, making them comparable in that regard as well.

Rhesus society typically consists of a number of subgroups, known as matrilines, of related females and their offspring. Females remain together for life, whereas males leave their natal group at puberty. Rhesus monkeys make a sharp distinction between kin and non-kin: by far the most friendly contact, such as grooming, takes place within the matrilines. Females of one matriline also fiercely support one another in fights against other matrilines. Because of

their strict hierarchy and pugnacious temperament, rhesus seemed to be ideal subjects. We figured that if this aggressive primate showed coping responses, our hypothesis would have withstood its most rigorous test.

Our first finding was, surprisingly, that density did not affect male aggressiveness. Adult males increasingly engaged in friendly contact under crowded conditions. They groomed females more, and likewise the females groomed the males more frequently. (Grooming is a calming behavior. In another study, we demonstrated that a monkey's heart rate slows down when it is being groomed.) Females also bared their teeth more often to the males—the rhesus way of communicating low status and appeasing potentially aggressive dominant monkeys.

Females showed a different response with other females, however. Within their own matrilines they fought more but did not change the already high level of friendly interaction. In their dealings with other matrilines, they also showed more aggression—but here it was coupled with more grooming and submissive grinning.

These findings make sense in light of the differences between kin and non-kin

relationships. Related females—such as sisters and mothers and daughters—are so strongly bonded that their relationships are unlikely to be disrupted by antagonism. Rhesus monkeys are used to managing intrafamilial conflict, cycling through fights and reconciliations, followed by comforting contact. Crowding does little to change this, except that they may have to repair frayed family ties more often. Between matrilines, on the other hand, crowding poses a serious challenge. Normally, friendly contact between matrilines is rare and antagonism common. But reduced escape opportunities make the risk of escalated conflict greater in a confined space. And our data indicated that female rhesus monkeys make a concerted effort at improving these potentially volatile relationships.

## EMOTIONS IN CHECK

In a second project, we turned our attention to chimpanzees. As our closest animal relatives, chimpanzees resemble us in appearance, psychology and cognition. Their social organization is also humanlike, with well-developed male bonding—which is rare in nature—reciprocal exchange and a long dependency of offspring on the mother. In the wild, male chimpanzees are extremely territorial, sometimes invading neighboring territories and killing enemy males. In captivity such encounters are, of course, prevented.

We collected data on more than 100 chimpanzees in various groups at the Yerkes primate center. Although some groups had only a tenth the space of others, cramped quarters had no measurable impact on aggression. In contrast to the monkeys, chimpanzees maintained their grooming and appeasement behavior—no matter the situation. If crowding did induce social tensions, our chimpanzees seemed to control them directly.

We usually do not think of animals as holding in their emotions, but chimpanzees may be different. These apes are known for deceptive behavior—for instance, they will hide hostile intentions behind a friendly face until an adversary has come within reach. In our study, emotional control was reflected in the way chimpanzees responded to the vocalizations of neighboring groups. Such noises commonly provoke hooting and charging displays, which in wild chimpanzees serve to ward off territorial intrusion.

In a confined space, however, excited reactions trigger turmoil within the group. We found that chimpanzees in the most crowded situations had a three times *lower* tendency to react to neighbors' vocalizations than chimpanzees with more space did. Chimpanzees may be smart enough to suppress responses to external stimuli if those tend to get them into trouble. Indeed, field-workers report that chimpanzee males on territorial patrol suppress all noise if being detected by their neighbors is to their disadvantage.

The inhibition of natural responses is not without cost. We know that continuous stress has the potential to suppress the immune system and therefore has important implications for health and longevity. We developed two noninvasive techniques to measure stress in our chimpanzees. One was to record the rate of self-scratching. Just as with college students who scratch their heads when faced with a tough exam question, self-scratching indicates anxiety in other primates. Our second technique was to collect fecal samples and analyze them for cortisol. Both measures showed that groups of chimpanzees who had little space and heard neighbors' vocalizations experienced more stress. Space by itself was not a negative factor, because in the absence of noisy neighbors, chimpanzees in small spaces showed the same stress level as those with a good deal of space.

So even though chimpanzees fail to show a rise in aggression when crowded, this does not necessarily mean that they are happy and relaxed. They may be working hard to maintain the peace. Given a choice, they would prefer more room. Every spring, when the chimpanzees at the Arnhem zoo hear the door to their outdoor island being opened for the first time, they fill the building with a chorus of ecstasy. They then rush outside to engage in a pandemonium in which all of the apes, young and old, embrace and kiss and thump one another excitedly on the back.

The picture is even more complex if we also consider short periods of acute crowding. This is a daily experience in human society, whether we find ourselves on a city bus or in a movie theater. During acute crowding, rhesus monkeys show a rise in mild aggression, such as threats, but not violence. Threats serve to keep others at a distance, forestalling unwanted contact. The monkeys also avoid one another and limit active social engagement, as if they are trying to stay out of trouble by lying low.

Chimpanzees take this withdrawal tactic one step further: they are actually less aggressive when briefly crowded. Again, this reflects greater emotional restraint. Their reaction is reminiscent of people on an elevator, who reduce frictions by minimizing large body movements, eye contact and loud verbalizations. We speak of the elevator effect, therefore, as a way in which both people and other primates handle the risks of temporary closeness.

Our research leads us to conclude that we come from a long lineage of social animals capable of flexibly adjusting to all kinds of conditions, including unnatural ones such as crowded pens and city streets. The adjustment may not be without cost, but it is certainly preferable to the frightening alternative predicted on the basis of rodent studies.

We should add, though, that even the behavioral sink of Calhoun's rats may not have been entirely the product of crowding. Food competition seemed to play a role as well. This possibility contains a serious warning for our own species in an ever more populous world: the doomsayers who predict that crowding will inevitably rip the social fabric may have the wrong variable in mind. We have a natural, underappreciated talent to deal with crowding, but crowding combined with scarcity of resources is something else.

## Further Information

THE HIDDEN DIMENSION. E. T. Hall. Doubleday, 1966.

CROWDING. A. Baum in *Handbook of Environmental Psychology*, Vol. 1. Edited by D. Stokols and I. Altman. Wiley, 1987.

THE MYTH OF A SIMPLE RELATION BETWEEN SPACE AND AGGRESSION IN CAPTIVE PRIMATES. F. B. M. de Waal in *Zoo Biology* supplement, Vol. 1, pages 141–148; 1989.

INHIBITION OF SOCIAL BEHAVIOR IN CHIMPANZEES UNDER HIGH-DENSITY CONDITIONS. F. Aureli and F. B. M. de Waal in *American Journal of Primatology*, Vol. 41, No. 3, pages 213–228; March 1997.

RHESUS MONKEY BEHAVIOUR UNDER DIVERSE POPULATION DENSITIES: COPING WITH LONG-TERM CROWDING. P. G. Judge and F. B. M. de Waal in *Animal Behaviour*, Vol. 54, no. 3, pages 643–662; September 1997.

# Reducing Prejudice: Combating Intergroup Biases

John F. Dovidio[1] and Samuel L. Gaertner

Department of Psychology, Colgate University, Hamilton, New York (J.F.D.), and Department of Psychology, University of Delaware, Newark, Delaware (S.L.G.)

### Abstract

Strategies for reducing prejudice may be directed at the traditional, intentional form of prejudice or at more subtle and perhaps less conscious contemporary forms. Whereas the traditional form of prejudice may be reduced by direct educational and attitude-change techniques, contemporary forms may require alternative strategies oriented toward the individual or involving intergroup contact. Individual-oriented techniques can involve leading people who possess contemporary prejudices to discover inconsistencies among their self-images, values, and behaviors such inconsistencies can arouse negative emotional states (e.g., guilt), which motivate the development of more favorable attitudes. Intergroup strategies can involve structuring intergroup contact to produce more individualized perceptions of the members of the other group, foster personalized interactions between members of the different groups, or redefine group boundaries to create more inclusive, superordinate representations of the groups. Understanding the nature and bases of prejudice can thus guide, theoretically and pragmatically, interventions that can effectively reduce both traditional and contemporary forms of prejudice.

### Keywords

attitude change; intergroup contact; prejudice; racism; social categorization

Prejudice is commonly defined as an unfair negative attitude toward a social group or a member of that group. Stereotypes, which are overgeneralizations about a group or its members that are factually incorrect and inordinately rigid, are a set of beliefs that can accompany the negative feelings associated with prejudice. Traditional approaches consider prejudice, like other attitudes, to be acquired through socialization and supported by the beliefs, attitudes, and values of friends and peer groups (see Jones, 1997). We consider the nature of traditional and contemporary forms of prejudice, particularly racial prejudice, and review a range of techniques that have been demonstrated empirically to reduce prejudice and other forms of intergroup bias. Bias can occur in many forms, and thus it has been assessed by a range of measures. These measures include standardized tests of prejudice toward another social group, stereotypes, evaluations of and feelings about the group in general, support for policies and individual actions benefiting the other group, and interaction and friendship patterns.

In part because of changing norms and the Civil Rights Act and other legislative interventions that made discrimination not simply immoral but also illegal, overt expressions of prejudice have declined significantly over the past 35 years. Contemporary forms of prejudice, however, continue to exist and affect the lives of people in subtle but significant ways (Dovidio & Gaertner, 1998; Gaertner & Dovidio, 1986). The negative feelings and beliefs that underlie contemporary forms of prejudice may be rooted in either individual processes (such as cognitive and motivational biases and socialization) or intergroup processes (such as realistic group conflict or biases associated with the mere categorization of people into in-groups and out-groups). These negative biases may occur spontaneously, automatically, and without full awareness.

Many contemporary approaches to prejudice based on race, ethnicity, or sex acknowledge the persistence of overt, intentional forms of prejudice but also consider the role of these automatic or unconscious processes[2] and the consequent indirect expressions of bias. With respect to the racial prejudice of white Americans toward blacks, for example, in contrast to "old-fashioned" racism, which is blatant, aversive racism represents a subtle, often unintentional, form of bias that characterizes many white Americans who possess strong egalitarian values and who believe that they are nonprejudiced. Aversive racists also possess negative racial feelings and beliefs (which develop through normal socialization or reflect social-categorization biases) that they are unaware of or that they try to dissociate from their nonprejudiced self-images. Because aversive racists consciously endorse egalitarian values, they will not discriminate directly and openly in ways that can be attributed to racism; however, because of their negative feelings, they will discriminate, often unintentionally, when their behavior can be justified on the basis of some factor other than race (e.g., questionable qualifications for a position). Thus, aversive racists may regularly engage in discrimination while they maintain self-images of being nonprejudiced. According to symbolic racism theory, a related perspective

From *Current Directions in Psychological Science,* August 1999, pp. 101-105. © 1999 by the American Psychological Society.

that has emphasized the role of politically conservative rather than liberal ideology (Sears, 1988), negative feelings toward blacks that whites acquire early in life persist into adulthood but are expressed indirectly and symbolically, in terms of opposition to busing or resistance to preferential treatment, rather than directly or overtly, as in support for segregation.

Contemporary expressions of bias may also reflect a dissociation between cultural stereotypes, which develop through common socialization experiences and because of repeated exposure generally become automatically activated, and individual differences in prejudicial motivations. Although whites both high and low in prejudice may be equally aware of cultural stereotypes and show similar levels of automatic activation, only those low in prejudice make a conscious attempt to prevent those negative stereotypes from influencing their behavior (Devine & Monteith, 1993).

## INDIVIDUAL PROCESSES AND PREJUDICE REDUCTION

Attempts to reduce the direct, traditional form of racial prejudice typically involve educational strategies to enhance knowledge and appreciation of other groups (e.g., multicultural education programs), emphasize norms that prejudice is wrong, and involve direct persuasive strategies (e.g., mass media appeals) or indirect attitude-change techniques that make people aware of inconsistencies in their attitudes and behaviors (Stephan & Stephan, 1984). Other techniques are aimed at changing or diluting stereotypes by presenting counter-stereotypic or nonstereotypic information about group members. Providing stereotype-disconfirming information is more effective when the information concerns a broad range of group members who are otherwise typical of their group rather than when the information concerns a single person who is not a prototypical representative of the group. In the latter case, people are likely to maintain their overall stereotype of the group while subtyping, with another stereotype, group members who disconfirm the general group stereotype (e.g., black athletes; Hewstone, 1996). The effectiveness of multicultural education programs is supported by the results of controlled intervention programs in the real world; evidence of the effectiveness of attitude- and stereotype-change approaches, and the hypothesized underlying processes, comes largely (but not exclusively) from experimental laboratory research.

Approaches for dealing with the traditional form of prejudice are generally less effective for combating the contemporary forms. With respect to contemporary racism, for example, whites already consciously endorse egalitarian, nonprejudiced views and disavow traditional stereotypes. Instead, indirect strategies that benefit from people's genuine motivation to be nonprejudiced may be more effective for reducing contemporary forms of prejudice. For example, techniques that lead people who possess contemporary prejudices to discover inconsistencies among their self-images, values, and behaviors may arouse feelings of guilt, tension about the inconsistencies, or other negative emotional states that can motivate the development of more favorable racial attitudes and produce more favorable intergroup behaviors (even nonverbal behaviors) several months later. Also, people who consciously endorse nonprejudiced attitudes, but whose behaviors may reflect racial bias, commonly experience feelings of guilt and compunction when they become aware of discrepancies between their potential behavior toward minorities (i.e., what they *would* do) and their personal standards (i.e., what they *should* do) during laboratory interventions. These emotional reactions, in turn, can motivate people to control subsequent spontaneous stereotypical responses and behave more favorably in the future (Devine & Monteith, 1993). People's conscious efforts to suppress stereotypically biased reactions can inhibit even the immediate activation of normally automatic associations, and with sufficient practice, these efforts can eliminate automatic stereotype activation over the long term.

Approaches oriented toward the individual, however, are not the only way to combat contemporary forms of prejudice. Strategies that emphasize intergroup processes, such as intergroup contact and social categorization and identity, are alternative, complementary approaches.

## INTERGROUP CONTACT

Real-world interventions, laboratory studies, and survey studies have demonstrated that intergroup contact under specified conditions (including equal status between the groups, cooperative intergroup interactions, opportunities for personal acquaintance, and supportive egalitarian norms) is a powerful technique for reducing intergroup bias and conflict (Pettigrew, 1998). Drawing on these principles, cooperative learning and "jigsaw" classroom interventions (Aronson & Patnoe, 1997) are designed

to increase interdependence between members of different groups working on a designated problem-solving task and to enhance appreciation for the resources they bring to the task. Cooperation is effective for reducing subsequent intergroup bias when the task is completed successfully, group contributions to solving the problem are seen as different or complementary, and the interaction among participants during the task is friendly, personal, and supportive.

Recent research has attempted to elucidate how the different factors of intergroup contact (e.g., cooperation, personal interaction) operate to reduce bias. Engaging in activities to achieve common, superordinate goals, for instance, changes the functional relations between groups from actual or symbolic competition to cooperation. Through psychological processes to restore cognitive balance or reduce inconsistency between actions and attitudes, attitudes toward members of the other group and toward the group as a whole may improve to be consistent with the positive nature of the interaction. Also, the rewarding properties of achieving success may become associated with members of other groups, thereby increasing attraction.

## SOCIAL CATEGORIZATION AND IDENTITY

Factors of intergroup contact, such as cooperation, may also reduce bias through reducing the salience of the intergroup boundaries, that is, through *decategorization*. According to this perspective, interaction during intergroup contact can individuate members of the out-group by revealing variability in their opinions (Wilder, 1986) or can produce interactions in which people are seen as unique individuals (personalization), with the exchange of intimate information (Brewer & Miller, 1984). Alternatively, intergroup contact may be structured to maintain but alter the nature of group boundaries, that is, to produce *recategorization*. One recategorization approach involves either creating or increasing the salience of cross cutting group memberships. Making interactants aware that members of another group are also members of one's own group when groups are defined by a different dimension can improve intergroup attitudes (Urban & Miller, 1998). Another recategorization strategy, represented by our own work on the Common In-Group Identity Model, involves interventions to change people's conceptions of groups, so that they think of membership not in terms of several different groups, but in terms of one, more inclusive group

| Conditions of Contact | Representational Mediators | Consequences |
|---|---|---|
| Intergroup Interdependence (e.g., cooperation) | *One Group* Recategorization ("We") | Cognitive Effects (e.g., stereotyping) |
| Group Differentiation (e.g., similarity) | *Two Subgroups in One Group* Recategorization ("Us+Them=We") | Affective Consequences (e.g., empathy) |
| Environmental Context (e.g., egalitarian norms) | *Two Groups* Categorization ("We/They") | |
| Pre-Contact Experience (e.g., affective priming) | *Separate Individuals* Decategorization ("Me/You") | Behavioral Effects (e.g., helping) |

FIG. 1. The Common In-Group Identity Model. In this model, elements of an intergroup contact situation (e.g., intergroup interdependence) influence cognitive representations of the groups as one superordinate group (recategorization), as two subgroups in one group (recategorization involving a dual identity), as two groups (categorization), or as separate individuals (decategorization). Recategorization and decategorization, in turn, can both reduce cognitive, affective, and behavioral biases, but in different ways. Recategorization reduces bias by extending the benefits of in-group favoritism to former out-group members. Attitudes and behavior toward these former out-group members thus become more favorable, approaching attitudes and behaviors toward in-group members. Decategorization, in contrast, reduces favoritism toward original in-group members as they become perceived as separate individuals rather than members of one's own group.

(Gaertner, Dovidio, Anastasio, Bachman, & Rust, 1993).

The Common In-Group Identity Model recognizes the central role of social categorization in reducing as well as in creating intergroup bias (Tajfel & Turner, 1979). Specifically, if members of different groups are induced to conceive of themselves more as members of a single, superordinate group rather than as members of two separate groups, attitudes toward former out-group members will become more positive through processes involving pro-in-group bias. Thus, changing the basis of categorization from race to an alternative dimension can alter who is a "we" and who is a "they," undermining a contributing force to contemporary forms of racism, such as aversive racism. The development of a superordinate identity does not always require people to abandon their previous group identities; they may possess dual identities, conceiving of themselves as belonging both to the superordinate group and to one of the original two groups included within the new, larger group. The model also recognizes that decategorization (seeing people as separate individuals) can also reduce bias. In contrast, perceptions of the groups as

different entities (we/they) maintains and reinforces bias. The Common In-Group Identity Model is presented schematically in Figure 1.

In experiments in the laboratory and in the field, and in surveys in natural settings (a multi-ethnic high school, banking mergers, and blended families), we have found evidence consistent with the Common In-Group Identity Model and the hypothesis that intergroup contact can reduce prejudice. Specifically, we have found that key aspects of intergroup contact, such as cooperation, decrease intergroup bias in part through changing cognitive representations of the groups. The development of a common ingroup identity also facilitates helping behaviors and self-disclosing interactions that can produce reciprocally positive responses and that can further reduce intergroup prejudices through other mechanisms such as personalization.

Moreover, the development of a common in-group identity does not necessarily require groups to forsake their original identities. Threats to important personal identities or the "positive distinctiveness" of one's group can, in fact, exacerbate intergroup prejudices. The development of a dual identity (two sub-

groups in one group; see Fig. 1), in which original and superordinate group memberships are simultaneously salient, is explicitly considered in the model. Even when racial or ethnic identity is strong, perceptions of a superordinate connection enhance interracial trust and acceptance. Indeed, the development of a dual identity, in terms of a bicultural or multicultural identity, not only is possible but can contribute to the social adjustment, psychological adaptation, and overall well-being of minority-group members (LaFromboise, Coleman, & Gerton, 1993). Recognizing both different and common group membership, a more complex form of a common in-group identity, may also increase the generalizability of the benefits of intergroup contact for prejudice reduction. The development of a common in-group identity contributes to more positive attitudes toward members of other groups present in the contact situation, whereas recognition of the separate group memberships provides the associative link by which these more positive attitudes may generalize to other members of the groups not directly involved in the contact situation.

## CONCLUSION

Prejudice can occur in its blatant, traditional form, or it may be rooted in unconscious and automatic negative feelings and beliefs that characterize contemporary forms. Whereas the traditional form of prejudice may be combated by using direct techniques involving attitude change and education, addressing contemporary forms requires alternative strategies. Individual-level strategies engage the genuine motivations of people to be nonprejudiced. Intergroup approaches focus on realistic group conflict or the psychological effects of categorizing people into in-groups and out-groups. The benefits of intergroup contact can occur through many routes, such as producing more individualated perceptions of out-group members and more personalized relationships. Intergroup contact can also produce more inclusive, superordinate representations of the groups, which can harness the psychological forces that contribute to intergroup bias and redirect them to improve attitudes toward people who would otherwise be recognized only as out-group members. Understanding the processes involved in the nature and development of prejudice can thus guide, both theoretically and pragmatically, interventions that can effectively reduce both traditional and contemporary forms of prejudice.

## Recommended Reading

Brewer, M. B., & Miller, N. (1996). *Intergroup relations.* Pacific Grove, CA: Brooks/Cole.

Brown, R. J. (1995). *Prejudice.* Cambridge, MA: Blackwell.

Hawley, W. D., & Jackson, A. W. (Eds.). (1995). *Toward a common destiny: Improving race and ethnic relations in America.* San Francisco: Jossey-Bass.

Landis, D., & Bhagat, R. S. (Eds.). (1996). *Handbook of intercultural training.* Thousand Oaks, CA: Sage.

Stephan, W. G., & Stephan, C. W. (1996). *Intergroup relations.* Boulder, CO: Westview Press.

**Acknowledgments**—Preparation of this article was facilitated by National Institute of Mental Health Grant MH 48721.

## Notes

1. Address correspondence to John F. Dovidio, Department of Psychology, Colgate University, Hamilton, NY 13346; e-mail: jdovidio@mail.colgate.edu.

2. For further information and a demonstration in which you can test the automaticity of your own racial attitudes using the Implicit Association Test, see Anthony Greenwald's World Wide Web site: http://weber.u.washington.edu/~agg/ (e-mail: agg@u.washington.edu).

## References

Aronson, E., & Patnoe, S. (1997). *The jigsaw classroom.* New York: Longman.

Brewer, M. B., & Miller, N. (1984). Beyond the contact hypothesis: Theoretical perspectives on desegregation. In N. Miller & M. B. Brewer (Eds.), *Groups in contact: The psychology of desegregation* (pp. 281–302). Orlando, FL: Academic Press.

Devine, P. G., & Monteith, M. J. (1993). The role of discrepancy-associated affect in prejudice reduction. In D. M. Mackie & D. L. Hamilton (Eds.), *Affect, cognition, and stereotyping: Interactive processes in intergroup perception* (pp. 317–344). Orlando, FL: Academic Press.

Dovidio, J. F., & Gaertner, S. L. (1998). On the nature of contemporary prejudice: The causes, consequences, and challenges of aversive racism. In J. Eberhardt & S. T. Fiske (Eds.), *Confronting racism: The problem and the response* (pp. 3–32). Newbury Park, CA: Sage.

Gaertner, S. L., & Dovidio, J. F. (1986). The aversive form of racism. In J. F. Dovidio & S. L. Gaertner (Eds.), *Prejudice, discrimination, and racism* (pp. 61–89). Orlando, FL: Academic Press.

Gaertner, S. L., Dovidio, J. F., Anastasio, P. A., Bachman, B. A., & Rust, M. C. (1993). The Common Ingroup Identity Model: Recategorization and the reduction of intergroup bias. In W. Stroebe & M. Hewstone (Eds.), *European review of social psychology* (Vol. 4, pp. 1–26). London: Wiley.

Hewstone, M. (1996). Contact and categorization: Social psychological interventions to change intergroup relations. In N. Macrae, M. Hewstone, & C. Stangor (Eds.), *Foundations of stereotypes and stereotyping* (pp. 323–368). New York: Guilford Press.

Jones, J. M. (1997). *Prejudice and racism* (2nd ed.). New York: McGraw-Hill.

LaFromboise, T., Coleman, H. L. K., & Gerton, J. (1993). Psychological impact of biculturalism: Evidence and theory. *Psychological Bulletin, 114,* 395–412.

Pettigrew, T. F. (1998). Intergroup Contact Theory. *Annual Review of Psychology, 49,* 65–85.

Sears, D. O. (1988). Symbolic racism. In P. A. Katz & D. A. Taylor (Eds.), *Eliminating racism: Profiles in controversy* (pp. 53–84). New York: Plenum Press.

Stephan, W. G., & Stephan, C. W. (1984). The role of ignorance in intergroup relations. In N. Miller & M. B. Brewer (Eds.), *Groups in contact: The psychology of desegregation* (pp. 229–257). Orlando, FL: Academic Press.

Tajfel, H., & Turner, J. C. (1979). An integrative theory of intergroup conflict. In W. G. Austin & S. Worchel (Eds.), *The social psychology of intergroup relations* (pp. 33–48). Monterey, CA: Brooks/Cole.

Urban, L. M., & Miller, N. (1998). A theoretical analysis of crossed categorization effects: A meta-analysis. *Journal of Personality and Social Psychology, 74,* 894–908.

Wilder, D. A. (1986). Social categorization: Implications for creation and reduction of intergroup bias. In L. Berkowitz (Ed.), *Advances in experimental social psychology* (Vol. 19, pp. 291–355). Orlando, FL: Academic Press.

# MERITS AND PERILS OF TEACHING ABOUT OTHER CULTURES

BY WALTER A. MCDOUGALL

**N**OTHING IN my experience sums up the merits and perils of studying other cultures better than an appalling week I spent at Fort Sill in February 1969. Almost all of us recent graduates from artillery school had orders for Vietnam, and so we were subjected to a week of what the army called "In-

*Walter A. McDougall, who won a Pulitzer Prize for* The Heavens and the Earth: A Political History of the Space Age, *is Alloy-Ansin Professor of International Relations and History at the University of Pennsylvania, co-director of the Foreign Policy Research Institute's (FPRI) History Academy, and the editor of* Orbis: A Journal of World Affairs.

*This article was originally published in the Fall 1999 issue of* Orbis *and is based on Professor McDougall's address to the FPRI History Institute for secondary school and junior college teachers on the theme, "Multiculturalism in World History," held in Bryn Mawr, Pa., on May 1–2, 1999. For information about future History Institutes for teachers, e-mail: FPRI@FPRI.org*

Country Orientation." A model Vietnamese fortified hamlet had been constructed there on the Oklahoma plains, and our instructor, a butter-bar lieutenant no older than I, insisted that its defenses were impregnable, as if none of us had ever heard the frequent news reports of villages overrun. We were also told what to do in case of an ambush: which is not to get pinned down, but charge right into the enemy's guns. And we learned all about the poisonous serpents and insects we could expect to encounter. In sum, far from boosting our morale and making us gung-ho, the course left us feeling utterly terrified and unprepared. But worst of all was when they herded hundreds of us into an auditorium to hear a lecture on Vietnamese culture and society. The instructor was not a scholarly expert, or a native Vietnamese, or perhaps a Green Beret who knew Vietnamese and had lived with the people. Rather, the teacher was a grizzled drill sergeant who paraphrased a manual, stumbling over his words. "Awright, you mens, listen up! You will now git orientated into Vit-mese so-ciety. Da mostly thing y'all gots to know is dat Vit-nam is a Confusion society. Dat means that ever'body is in a kind of high-arky: like the chillun obey deir parents, and the womens obey deir mens, and ever'body obeys the guv-ment. It's sorta like da army chain o' command."

I must have stopped listening, because that is all I remember. But looking back, I can imagine that orientation as a metaphor of the whole U.S. enterprise in Southeast Asia. As our current fiasco in the Balkans demonstrates anew, Americans make a habit of declaring a war, sending over massive firepower, then expressing amazement when the locals do not bend at once to our will. Only then do we finally decide that it might be a good idea to learn something about the history and culture of the people we are trying to bludgeon, help, and change. Not that a common soldier needs an advanced degree in multicultural studies, but it would help if our policymakers took time to study the world over which they profess to exercise a benevolent hegemony.

The value of studying other cultures is not something we Americans, or Westerners in general, discovered only recently, as a consequence of having our consciousness raised by the multiculturalists. Medieval Christians were fascinated by their Muslim adversaries. The Age of Exploration inspired Europeans to collect information about the strange lands they discovered, think of themselves as one civilization among many, and ask what caused the differences, as well as similarities, among cultures. The Enlightenment systematized the study of non-Western peoples, giving birth eventually to world history (Voltaire), encyclopedias (Diderot), and comparative politics (Montesquieu). In the 19th century, archaeology, cultural anthropology, comparative religion, and a new burst of European imperialism enriched the study of other civilizations, however much solipsistic Westerners took for granted the superiority of their own ways and assumed that all other peoples must inevitably follow in their path. As Walt Whitman wrote,

One thought ever at the fore
That in the Divine Ship, breasting time and space
All peoples of the globe together sail,
    sail the same voyage
Are bound to the same destination.

Today's radical multiculturalists accordingly disparage what they call Europe's "Enlightenment Project" as a campaign to explore, subdue, and study the whole world for the purpose of controlling it, exploiting it, and ultimately making it an extension of Western civilization. That is highly tendentious, but does have a measure of truth. At Amherst College in 1964, all of us freshmen were obliged to take History 1, a course that developed themes in world history rather than Western Civ, and as such was very progressive. But the themes chosen were invariably Western themes projected onto the history of other civilizations. One early block of material dealt with the conquest of Mexico by Cortes. To be sure, we were taught about pre-Columbian cultures, but whereas I remember a good deal about the Spanish side of this culture clash, literally all

I remember about the Aztec side was their belief that a hummingbird on the left was an omen of good luck—or was it bad luck? Anyway, "hummingbird-on-the-left" became a stock laugh line for Amherst students.

A later instruction block compared the Mexican, Chinese, and Young Turk revolutions of the early 20th century, a truly interesting exercise. But the theme uniting them was "paths to modernization," so it was not the essence of historic Mexican, Chinese, or Islamic culture that was at issue, but rather the struggles of those civilizations to come to grips with their backwardness and adopt Western ways. Indeed, I do not think I ever studied other cultures on their own terms—independent of Western intrusions—until my graduate years at Chicago, when I read the books of William H. McNeill, beginning with *The Rise of the West: A History of the Human Community*. To be sure, Amherst and Chicago had many professors who specialized in other cultures and offered courses on them. But those of us in mainstream fields such as European and American history were not exposed to true multicultural education in the survey courses of high school and college.

McNeill was a tireless advocate for the study of world history and other cultures long before it became fashionable. But alas, no sooner did his campaign for world history, as opposed to Western Civ surveys, begin to gain ground than the whole movement was captured by the ideological multiculturalists, Afrocentrists, ethnic lobbies, and victim groups who substituted curricula that depicted Western Civ as a story of progress for curricula that damned Western Civ as a story of plunder, rapine, imperialism, exploitation, and slavery. In other words, the focus was *still* on the West, with other cultures appearing mostly as virginal victims.

Another expression of the multicultural trend is less subjective, but anodyne, and that is the "non-Western" requirement that so many college majors, including the International Relations program I direct, impose on their students. We feel we must make a bow toward multiculturalism, so we just insist that students take one or two courses that are non-Western in focus. The implicit purpose would seem to be to sensitize students to other cultural traditions and alert them to the astonishing fact that there is a whole world out there beyond Great Neck, Long Island, and Newport Beach, California. (I recently asked an I.R. major if he had any experience traveling abroad. He proudly said yes, he had been to Cancun.) But what good does one course on sub-Saharan Africa or Ming China really achieve? It is not enough to make one really conversant in African or Chinese history, religion, and society, and it certainly tells one nothing about the variety of human cultures. Ultimately, instead of acquiring new categories to use in thinking about human nature and history, the student merely receives a smattering of knowledge that is *hors de categorie:* outside Western norms, and therefore just strange. Rather, it is like the high school athletic program that—in between major sports—schedules two days of lacrosse and handball just to let students know that those games exist.

Should we teach our students about other cultures? Absolutely! But do we succeed? I think most of us do not. First,

# Only multicultural history can teach students the ways all human beings are alike.

because few of us are qualified to teach about Islam, or India, or traditional China or Japan. We may do better than that drill sergeant, but do we risk just conveying new stereotypes to students, rather than getting beyond stereotypes? And how do we integrate non-Western material into existing courses? The recent debate over the National History Standards reveals the difficulty in doing this, even leaving aside all political controversy. The easiest way is to retain the old Western Civ chronology, but to insert flashback sections on other cultures at the moment Europeans first come into contact with them. Needless to say, that is still Eurocentric. Another way is to grant Western Civ merely an equal status, and to study each culture in turn: a month on China, a month on India, a month on Europe, and so forth. But that artificially disconnects civilizations from each other, ignoring perhaps the most powerful theme in McNeill's works, which is the cross-cultural borrowing, challenge, and response mechanism that is so often the engine of historical change.

What is more, the teacher who goes into some depth about other cultures on their own terms, clearly a good thing on the face of it, runs the risk of offending someone's self-esteem and landing in the principal's or dean's office on charges of insensitivity or even racism! But if we are going to teach about other cultures on their own terms, and not just as targets for Western imperialism, then we must stress the bad and ugly as well as the good: the oppression, slavery, and reciprocal racism and brutality among Asian and African peoples themselves. We must teach about the binding of girls' feet in China, the forced suicide of widows in India, the Islamic texts that place women somewhere above goats but below cattle, the genital mutilation of women in Africa. Now, we can try to deflect criticism by drumming into children's heads that they must not make value judgments, especially ones based, after all, on Western traditions: the Bible and the Enlightenment. But to try to be value-free about, for instance, Aztec human sacrifice, slavery in the Islamic world, or the barbaric tortures practiced by the Comanches and Apaches, is to do exactly what we all say must *not* be done with regard to the darker chapters of Western history. Thus, even as we try to explain to students why the Spanish Inquisition was set up, or how the Nazis could come to power in Germany, we quickly add that whereas we must try to understand the past on its own terms, to understand is not to forgive: *zu verstehen ist nicht zu vergeben.* So we cannot just give all other cultures a "pass" when it comes to their inhumane practices. But to condemn the "bad" in other cultures is by definition to impose a Western standard of good and bad.

Above all, to treat other cultures in isolation, to censor aspects of their history that might damage some student's self-esteem, or to refrain from making any moral judgments at all, is to cheat students of the one thing they need to learn most, and which only multicultural history can teach them: and that is the many ways in which all human beings, all cultures and civilizations, are alike. For no real toleration among peoples can exist unless they are given a reason to imagine themselves and others as "we," and not just as "we" and "they." In what ways are all people alike? They are all *Homo sapiens,* they are all conceived and born the same way, and they all face the certainty of death. They all live on the same planet and need food and shelter. They all wonder about the meaning of life, love, tragedy, and what if anything happens after they die. They have different answers to the eternal questions, and they invent different political and social forms to order their brief and toilsome time on this earth. But at bottom they are all alike. Thus, Chinese are not angels, but neither are they aliens.

I have no solution to the curricular issues, except to insist that all high school students take at least three full years of history—one being world history. Alas, in many states the trend is to cut back, not expand, history requirements. But I did hit upon a technique this semester for handling the "self-esteem" issue, which seemed to work. (At least, I have not as yet been summoned to the office of the Penn ombudsperson.) In my last lecture in the modern history survey, I asked students to recall a question that I had posed in the first lecture: not why people and societies so often do bad things, but rather why on occasion they do good things, why on occasion people have taken risks and made sacrifices in order to improve the lot of others. Evil is banal and universal. What is shocking and in need of explanation in history is the good.

Thus, I granted that European and American civilization has been imperialistic and exploitative. But so has every other civilization in history. What is unique about the West is that it invented *anti*-imperialism. I granted that the West practiced slavery. But so has every other civilization in history. What is unique about the West is that it gave rise to an anti-slavery movement. I granted that the West has waged war on a ferocious scale. But so has every other civilization at one time or another. What is unique about the West is that it tried over and over to devise international systems that might prevent war. I granted that women were in a subordinate status throughout Western history. But so were they in every other civilization. What is unique about the West is that it spawned a movement for female equality. And I granted that the West has known tyranny and indeed totalitarianism of the most brutal sort. But forms of tyranny and even genocide have appeared in all other civilizations. What is unique about the West is that it alone has declared certain human rights to be universal and tried to devise governments that expand, not crush, liberty.

What is needed to ensure that multicultural education can be a glue and not a solvent of American community is dedicated, knowledgeable, and above all honest teaching. All civilizations are worthy of celebration by dint of their being civilizations, that is, extraordinary examples of collective human invention. But all have also been horribly flawed by dint of their being human creations. If Western civilization appears to have done more nasty things in recent centuries, it is not because it is worse than others, but only because it has lately been the most powerful. What is more, the three ways in which people from all the world, while cherishing their diversity, can nevertheless identify themselves as part of a single human community are themselves gifts of Western civilization. Those unifying forces are science and technology, the Enlightenment doctrine of natural law and natural rights, and the astounding Judeo-Christian theology to the effect that all human beings are children of one and the same loving God.

Unfortunately, the radical multiculturalists denounce science and technology as an evil, masculine "discourse" that oppresses the weak, pollutes the environment, and privileges "linear thinking." They attack the "Enlightenment Project" as an ideological cover for Western cultural imperialism. And they hate the Bible for promoting patriarchy and heterosexism. In so doing, they are attempting to destroy the very principles under which toleration of diverse cultures has in fact the best chance of flowering! In so doing, the multiculturalists help to perpetuate the tragedy that Alexander Solzhenitsyn called "A World Split Apart." Asked to deliver the Harvard commencement address in 1978, Solzhenitsyn, a survivor of the Soviet gulag, shocked his audience by proclaiming that the line that divides the world does not run between communism and capitalism, or along the boundaries between nations, races, social classes, or genders. The line that splits the world apart runs straight through the middle of each human heart.

# Unit 10

## Unit Selections

35. **Mental Health Gets Noticed,** David Satcher
36. **Mental Disorders Are Not Diseases,** Thomas Szasz
37. **Depression: Beyond Serotonin,** Hara Estroff Marano
38. **The Clustering and Contagion of Suicide,** Thomas E. Joiner Jr.
39. **The Doubting Disease,** Jerome Groopman

## Key Points to Consider

❖ Do you believe that everyone has the potential for developing a mental disorder? Just how widespread is mental disorder in the United States? What circumstances lead an individual to mental illness? In general, what can be done to reduce the number of cases of mental disorder or to promote better mental health in the United States?

❖ Do you think that mental disorders are biologically or psychologically induced? If we discover that most mental disorders are caused by something physiological, do you think mental disorders will remain the purview of psychology? Why?

❖ If mental disorders are biological, do you think they might be "contagious" (caused by disease and passed from person to person)? Do you think that mental disorders are brain disorders, or do you think this is a hoax perpetrated by so-called experts on those diagnosed with mental illness? How do you think treatments might differ depending on the origin of a mental disturbance?

❖ What is depression? How widespread are depressive episodes? What causes depression? What neurotransmitters are involved in depression? What role does the nervous system play in promoting depression? What are some promising cures for this disorder?

❖ Why do individuals commit suicide? Is suicide a pervasive problem in the United States? Who is most likely to commit suicide? Is suicide contagious? What is media-inspired suicide? How does it differ from a point-cluster suicide?

❖ What is obsessive-compulsive disorder? Why is obsessive-compulsive disorder called the doubting disease? Do you have any obsessions; why and about what do you obsess? Do you have any compulsions? Do you think this is normal? What are the treatments for obsessive-compulsive disorder? What does misdiagnosis mean to the individual who is or is not truly obsessive-compulsive?

 **Links**     **www.dushkin.com/online/**

These sites are annotated on pages 4 and 5.

Jay and Harry were two brothers who owned a service station. They were the middle children of four. The other two children were sisters, the oldest of whom had married and moved out of the family home. The service station was once owned by their father who had retired and turned it over to them.

Harry and Jay had a good working relationship. Harry was the "up-front" man. Taking customer orders, accepting payments, and working with parts distributors, Harry was the individual who dealt most directly with the customers and others. Jay worked behind the scenes. While Harry made the mechanical diagnoses, Jay was the one who did the corrective work. Some of his friends thought Jay was a mechanical genius.

Preferring to spend time by himself, Jay had always been a little odd and a bit of a loner. His emotions had been more inappropriate and intense than other people's emotional states. Harry was the stalwart in the family. He was the acknowledged leader and decision maker when it came to family finances.

One day Jay did not show up for work on time. When he did, he was dressed in the most garish outfit and was laughing hysterically and talking to himself. Harry at first suspected that his brother had taken some illegal drugs. However, Jay's condition persisted. Out of concern, his family took him to the their physician who immediately sent Jay and his family to a psychiatrist. The diagnosis? Schizophrenia. Jay's uncle had also been schizophrenic. The family grimly left the psychiatrist's office. After several other appointments with the psychiatrist, they traveled to the local pharmacy to fill a prescription for antipsychotic medications that Jay would probably take the rest of his life.

What caused Jay's drastic and rather sudden change in mental health? Was Jay destined to be schizophrenic because of his family genes? Did competitiveness with his brother and the feeling that he was a less-revered family member than Harry cause Jay's descent into mental disorder? How can psychiatrists and clinical psychologists make accurate diagnoses? Once a diagnosis of mental disorder is made, can the individual ever completely recover?

These and other questions are the emphasis in this unit. Mental disorder has fascinated and, on the other hand, terrified us for centuries. At various times in our history, those who suffered from these disorders were persecuted as witches, tortured to drive out possessing spirits, punished as sinners, jailed as a danger to society, confined to insane asylums, or, at best, hospitalized for simply being too ill to care for themselves.

Today, psychologists propose that the view of mental disorders as "illnesses" has outlived its usefulness. We should think of mental disorders as either biochemical disturbances or disorders of learning in which the person develops a maladaptive pattern of behavior that is then maintained by an inappropriate environment. At the same time, we need to recognize that these reactions to stressors in the environment or to the inappropriate learning situations may be genetically preordained; some people may more easily develop the disorders than others. Serious disorders are serious problems and not just for the individual who is the patient or client. The impact of mental disorders on the family (just as for Jay's family) and friends deserves our full attention, too. Diagnosis, treatment and the implications of the disorders are covered in some of the articles in this section. Unit 11 will explore further the concept of treatment of mental disorders.

The first two articles in this unit offer a general introduction to the concept of mental disorder. In the first, "Mental Health Gets Noticed," David Satcher reveals his agenda for better mental health care in the United States. Mental disorders, he concludes, are more widespread than previously thought. Only an active policy of assisting those who need help can change the status of those with mental disorders in this country.

In the next article, renowned critic of the mental health field Thomas Szasz proposes that mental disorders are not merely brain disorders or diseases. He says that to advance this notion dilutes attempts to argue that the mental health care system does a disservice to its clients. Only when we fully understand mental disorders can we assist those who have them. Mental disorders, in fact, may well be a myth created by the health care system.

We turn next to some specific problems of mental health. Depression is one of the most common forms of mental disorder. In its severe form, depression can sometimes lead to suicide. Psychologists recently have been studying the biochemical mechanisms underlying severe depression. In "Depression: Beyond Serotonin," the author looks at the role of the central nervous system and neurotransmitters. In a companion article, "The Clustering and Contagion of Suicide," Thomas Joiner asks whether suicide is contagious. The answer is that some types of suicide are and some types are not. What the two types are and when suicide is contagious is revealed in this informative article.

The final article in this series, "The Doubting Disease," discusses a peculiar disorder that plagues some people. In obsessive-compulsive disorder, individuals are obsessed with thoughts that compel them to repeat certain related behaviors. The article describes the disorder as well as offers explanations for it.

# Psychological Disorders

# MENTAL HEALTH GETS NOTICED

## The First-Ever Surgeon General's Report on Mental Health

BY DAVID SATCHER, M.D., PH.D., UNITED STATES SURGEON GENERAL

I am pleased to issue the first-ever Surgeon General's Report on Mental Health. In doing so, I am alerting the American people that mental illness is a critical public health problem that must be addressed immediately. As a society, we assign a high priority to disease prevention and health promotion; so, too, must we ensure that mental health and the prevention of mental disorders share that priority.

Mental illness is the second leading cause of disability in major market economies such as the United States, with mental disorders collectively accounting for more than 15% of all disabilities. Mental disorders—depression, schizophrenia, eating disorders, depressive (bipolar) illness, anxiety disorders, attention deficit hyperactivity disorder and Alzheimer's disease, to name a few—are as disabling and serious as cancer and heart disease in terms of premature death and lost productivity.

Few Americans are untouched by mental illness, whether it occurs within one's family or among neighbors, co-workers or members of the community. In fact, in any one year, one in five Americans—including children, adolescents, adults and the elderly—experience a mental disorder. Unfortunately, over half of those with severe mental illness do not seek treatment. This is mostly due to some very real barriers to access, foremost among them the stigma that people attach to mental illness and the lack of parity between insurance coverage for mental health services and other health care services.

Over the past 25 years, there has been a scientific revolution in the fields of mental health and mental illness that has helped remove the stigma. The brain has emerged as the central focus for studies of mental health and mental illness, with emphasis on the activities that underlie our abilities to feel, learn, remember and, when brain activity goes awry, experience mental health problems or a mental illness. We now know that not only do the workings of the brain affect behavior, emotions and memory, but that experience, emotion and behavior also affect the workings of the brain.

As information about the brain accumulates, the challenge then becomes to apply this new knowledge to clinical practice.

Today, mental disorders can be correctly diagnosed and, for the most part, treated with medications or short-term psychotherapy, or with a combination of approaches. The single most explicit recommendation I make in my report is to seek help if you have a mental health problem or think you have symptoms of a mental disorder. It is my firm conviction

## GREG GIANNINI

I'd describe myself as a regular person. . . . Most of the time I like taking walks around my house. Before I was living in a group home out in the country and there weren't that many stores or streets to walk on. I like walking to 7-Eleven and Mr. D's fast food.

## ROSE CLARK

Sometimes I wake up so sick, but then I go to work and feel better. Being with animals makes me feel 100% better. Does that sound funny?

I love my boss. He's crazy. When he does surgery he dances, does the jitterbug. Sometimes I go into surgery with him to make sure all the animals are lying down straight and not awake. Mostly my responsibilities are taking care of the cages and general cleaning.

I've been with this program for four years. Since then I've gone back to school and gotten a job. I live in my own apartment, got two cats, and have a checking and savings account.

# "Mental health is fundamental to overall health"

that mental health is indispensable to personal well-being and balanced living. Overall quality of life is tremendously improved when a mental disorder is diagnosed early and treated appropriately.

My report presents an in-depth look at mental health services in the U.S. and at the scientific research that supports treatment interventions for people with mental disorders. Summarized briefly below, it attempts to describe trends in the mental health field; explore mental health across the human life span; examine the organization and financing of mental health services; and recommend courses of action to further improve the quality and availability of mental health services for all Americans. The report's conclusions are based on a review of more than 3,000 research articles and other materials, including first person accounts from people who have experienced mental disorders.

## A Vision for the Future

I cannot emphasize enough the principal recommendation of my report: Seek help if you think you have a mental health problem or symptoms of a mental disorder. But because stigma and substantial gaps in the accessibility to state-of-the-art mental health services keep many from seeking help, I offer the nation the following additional recommendations, which are intended to overcome some of these barriers:

- *Continue to Build the Science Base:* As scientific progress propels us into the next century, there should be a special effort to address pronounced gaps in current knowledge, including the urgent need for research relating to mental health promotion and illness prevention.
- *Overcome Stigma:* An emerging consumer and family movement has, through vigorous advocacy, sought to overcome stigma and prevent discrimination against people

with mental illness. Powerful and pervasive, stigma prevents people from acknowledging their mental health problems and disclosing them to others. To improve access to care, stigma must no longer be tolerated. Research and more effective treatments will help move this country toward care and support of the ill—and away from blame and stigma.

- *Improve Public Awareness of Effective Treatments:* Mental health treatments have improved by leaps and bounds over the past 25 years, but those treatments do no good unless people are aware they exist and seek them out. There are effective treatments for virtually every mental disorder. For more information on how to take advantage of them, call (877) 9MHEALTH.
- *Ensure the Supply of Mental Health Services and Providers:* Currently, there is a shortage of mental health professionals serving children and adolescents, elderly people with serious mental disorders and those who suffer from mental illness-related substance abuse. There is also a shortage of specialists with expertise in cognitive behavioral therapy and interpersonal therapy—two forms of psychotherapy that have proven effective for many types of mental health problems.
- *Ensure Delivery of State-of-the-Art Treatments:* A wide variety of effective, community-based services—carefully refined through years of research—exist for even the most severe mental illnesses, but they are not yet widely available in community settings. We need to ensure that mental health services are as universally accessible as other health services in the continuously changing health care delivery system. We must speed the transfer of new information from the re-

search setting into the service delivery setting.

- *Tailor Treatment to Individuals, Acknowledging Age, Gender, Race and Culture:* To be optimally effective, diagnosis and treatment of mental illness must be attentive to these factors. Patients often prefer to be treated by mental health professionals who are of the same racial and ethnic background, a fact that underscores the need to train more minorities in the mental health professions.
- *Facilitate Entry into Treatment:* Access to mental health services can be improved immediately if we enhance the abilities of primary care providers, public schools, the child welfare system and others to help people with mental health problems seek treatment. In addition, ensuring ready access to appropriate services for people with severe mental disorders promises to significantly reduce the need for involuntary care, which is sometimes required in order to prevent behavior that could be harmful to oneself or others.
- *Reduce Financial Barriers to Treatment:* Equality or parity between mental health coverage and other health coverage is an affordable and effective way to decrease the number of ill people who are not receiving proper treatment.

The U.S. system is extremely complex; it is a hybrid system that serves many people well, but often seems fragmented and inaccessible to those with the most extensive problems and fewest financial resources. Critical gaps exist between those who need services and those who receive them; only about 40% of those with severe disorders use any services at all.

Although research shows little direct evidence of problems with quality in

---

## TONY RIVERA

When I first came to the Pastimes Cafe & Antiques I told them that it reminds me of the coffee shops in Baltimore and Maryland. They laughed and we've been friends for two years. They know my name when I walk in. I used to know all their names but I only come every few weeks now and I can't remember. They make me feel comfortable, like I'm not bothering anybody.

---

## KATHY MOLYNEAUX

I didn't know I was depressed until after college. I just thought everyone felt the same way I did. I had problems sleeping, feeling down, overwhelmed, worried and not happy. My graduation from DePaul University in 1983 was a good day. After college, I worked successfully as a nurse for 13 years. I felt like I could relate to the patients because I had been there myself.

## SHERYL CAUDLE

My family at first didn't understand why I was so depressed. My dad kept asking me why couldn't I be happy?...I never thought I'd be able to work again because of my illness. I've had to quit other jobs in the past, but I don't want to quit cleaning the Roxy [a local movie theater]; I want to have an apartment someday and a job in the community. Both of these things would be special to me because it would mean I've come a long way.

## PATTI REID

I used to live in a house with my family, but I have a rare disorder that makes me think about the past. In 1992, I got this disorder and I couldn't drive my car anymore. I miss driving the most. My two big battles are smiling and taking my medications. Both of these are very hard.

mental health service programs, there are signs that programs could be better implemented, especially ones that serve children and people with serious impairment. While an array of quality monitoring and improvement methods have been developed, incentives to improve conditions lag behind incentives to reduce costs.

These inequities in insurance coverage for mental and physical health care have prompted 27 states to adopt legislation requiring parity, and compelled President Clinton to order the Federal Employees Health Benefits Program to provide parity for federal employees by the year 2001. Some localized attempts at creating parity so far have resulted in better mental health service access at negligible cost increases for managed care organizations.

Issues relating to mental health and mental illness have been overlooked or ignored in this country too often and for too long. While we cannot change the past, I am convinced that we can shape a better future.

---

*David Satcher, M.D., Ph.D., is the 16th surgeon general of the United States. He is also Assistant Secretary for Health, advising the Secretary on public health matters and directing the Office of Public Health and Science.*

PSYCHOLOGY

# Mental Disorders Are Not Diseases

## Psychiatrists and their allies have succeeded in persuading the scientific community, courts, media, and general public that mental illnesses are phenomena independent of human motivation or will.

### BY THOMAS SZASZ, M.D.

THE CORE CONCEPT of mental illness—to which the vast majority of psychiatrists and the public adhere—is that diseases of the mind are diseases of the brain. The equation of the mind with the brain and of mental disease with brain disease, supported by the authority of a large body of neuroscience literature, is used to render rational the drug treatment of mental illness and justify the demand for parity in insurance coverage for medical and mental disorders.

Reflecting the influence of these ideas, on Sept. 26, 1997, Pres. Clinton signed the Mental Health Parity Act of 1996, which took effect on Jan. 1, 1998. "This landmark law," according to the National Alliance for the Mentally Ill, "begins the process of ending the long-held practice of providing less insurance coverage for mental illnesses, or brain disorders, than is provided for equally serious physical disorders." Contrary to these views, I maintain that the mind is not the brain, that mental functions are not reducible to brain functions, and that mental diseases are not brain dis-

eases—indeed, that mental diseases are not diseases at all.

When I assert the latter, I do not imply that distressing personal experiences and deviant behaviors do not exist. Anxiety, depression, and conflict do exist—in fact, are intrinsic to the human condition—but they are not diseases in the pathological sense.

According to the *Oxford English Dictionary*, disease is "a condition of the body, or of some part or organ of the body, in which its functions are disturbed or deranged; a morbid physical condition." Diagnosis, in turn, is "the determination of the nature of a diseased condition . . . also, the opinion (formally stated) resulting from such investigation."

The core medical concept of disease is a bodily abnormality. Literally, the term "disease" denotes a demonstrable lesion of cells, tissues, or organs. Metaphorically, it may be used to denote any kind of malfunctioning of individuals, groups, economies, etc. (substance abuse, violence, unemployment, *et al.*).

The psychiatric concept of disease rests on a radical alteration of the medical defi-

nition. The mind is not a material object; hence, it can be diseased only in a metaphorical sense. In his classic, *Lectures on Clinical Psychiatry*, Emil Kraepelin—the founder of modern psychiatry—wrote: "The subject of the following course of lectures will be the Science of Psychiatry, which, as its name implies, is that of the treatment of mental disease. It is true that, in the strictest terms, we cannot speak of the mind as becoming diseased."

If we accept the idea that the diagnoses of mental illnesses refer to real diseases, we are compelled to accept them as diagnoses on a par with those of bodily diseases, albeit the criterion for what counts as a mental disease is completely different from what counts as a bodily disease. For instance, in *Psychiatric Diagnosis*, Donald Goodwin and Samuel B. Guze, two of the most respected psychiatrists in the U.S., state: "When the term 'disease' is used, this is what is meant: A disease is a cluster of symptoms and/or signs with a more or less predictable course. Symptoms are what patients tell you; signs are what you see. The cluster may be associated with physical ab-

From *USA Today Magazine,* July 2000, pp. 30-31. © 2000 by the Society for the Advancement of Education. Reprinted by permission.

normality or may not. The essential point is that it results in consultation with a physician." According to these authorities, disease is not an observable phenomenon, but a social relationship.

In contrast to Goodwin and Guze's assertion that mental illness need not be associated with physical abnormality, Allen Frances, the chief architect of the American Psychiatric Association's *Diagnostic and Statistical Manual, DSM-IV*, states: "The special features of *DSM-IV* are . . . elimination of the term 'organic mental disorder' because it incorrectly implied that other psychiatric disorders did not have a biological contribution."

Linguistic considerations help to illuminate the differences between bodily and mental disease, as well as between disease and diagnosis. We do not attribute motives to a person for having leukemia, do not say that a person has reasons for having glaucoma, and would be uttering nonsense if we asserted that diabetes has caused a person to shoot the President. However, we can and do say all of these things about a person with a mental illness. One of the most important philosophical-political features of the concept of mental illness is that, at one fell swoop, it removes motivation from action, adds it to illness, and thus destroys the very possibility of separating disease from non-disease and disease from diagnosis.

Diseases are physico-chemical phenomena or processes—for example, the abnormal metabolism of glucose (diabetes). Mental diseases are patterns of personal conduct, unwanted by the self or others. Psychopathology is diagnosed by finding behavioral, not physical, abnormalities in bodies. Disease qua psychopathology cannot be asymptomatic. Changing the official classification of mental diseases can transform non-disease into psychopathology and psychopathology into non-disease (*i.e.*, smoking from a behavioral habit into "nicotine dependence"). In short, medical diseases are *discovered* and then given a name, such as acquired immune deficiency syndrome (AIDS). Mental diseases are *invented* and then given a name, such as attention deficit disorder.

Nowadays, names routinely are given not only to somatic pathology (real or bodily diseases), but to behavioral pathology (psychopathology or mental diseases). Indeed, if we propose to treat misbehavior as a disease instead of a matter of law or social policy, we name it accordingly (for instance, "substance abuse"). Not surprisingly, we diagnose mental illnesses by finding abnormalities (unwanted behaviors) in persons, not abnormalities (lesions) in bodies. That is why forensic psychiatrists "interview" criminals called "patients" (who often do not regard themselves as patients), whereas forensic pa-

thologists examine body fluids. In the case of bodily illness, the clinical diagnosis is a hypothesis, typically confirmed or disconfirmed through an autopsy. It is not possible to die of a mental illness or to find evidence of it in organs, tissues, cells, or body fluids during an autopsy.

To summarize, anthrax is a disease that is biologically constructed and can, and does, kill its host. Attention deficit disorder, on the other hand, is socially constructed and cannot kill the patient.

If we fail or refuse to distinguish between literal and metaphorical diseases, we confuse and deceive ourselves and others not only about the differences between treatments influencing the body and those influencing the person, but about the differences between medical treatments (such as performing an appendectomy for acute appendicitis) and medical interventions (performing an abortion terminating a healthy, but unwanted pregnancy). To be sure, there is something to be gained by not distinguishing between diseases and diagnoses, complaints and lesions, and/or treatments and interventions. It permits creation of a therapeutic utopia—a medical fairyland with "miracle cures" not only for diseases, but for non-diseases as well.

## Mental diseases are behaviors

No one believes that love sickness is a disease, but nearly everyone believes that mental sickness is, and virtually no one realizes that, if this were true, it would prove the nonexistence of mental illness. If mental illnesses are brain diseases (like Parkinsonism), then they are diseases of the body, not the mind. A screwdriver may be a drink or a tool, but it would be foolish to do research in the hope of discovering that some cases of orange juice and vodka are hitherto unrecognized instances of carpenters' implements.

The contemporary American mind-set is so thoroughly psychiatrized that it is quite useless to demonstrate the logical-linguistic misconceptions inherent in the claim that "mental illness is like any other illness." Unless people are prepared to defy the combined forces of the state, science, medicine, law, and popular opinion, they must believe—or at least pretend to believe—that mental illnesses are brain diseases; scientists have identified the somatic lesions that cause such illnesses; and psychiatrists possess effective treatments for them. Conventional wisdom as well as political correctness preclude entertaining the possibility that mental illness, like spring fever, is a metaphor.

In short, psychiatrists and their allies have succeeded in persuading the scientific community, courts, media, and general public that the conditions they call mental

disorders are diseases—that is, phenomena independent of human motivation or will. Because there is no empirical evidence to back this claim (indeed, there can be none), the psychiatric profession relies on supporting it with periodically revised versions of its pseudo-scientific bible, the *American Psychiatric Association's Diagnostic and Statistical Manual of Mental Disorders*.

The official view is that these manuals list the various "mental disorders" that afflict "patients." My view is that they are rosters of officially accredited psychiatric diagnoses, constructed by task forces appointed by officers of the American Psychiatric Association. Psychiatrists thus have constructed diagnoses, pretended that the terms they coined were morally neutral descriptions of brain diseases, and few in political power have challenged their pretensions.

My argument may be put another way: The existence of John Smith's bodily disease—say, astrocytoma, a nerve tissue tumor—is discovered and empirically verified. Radiologists identify the tumor; neurosurgeons verify its presence by observing the lesion with their naked eyes; and pathologists confirm the diagnosis by examination of the tissues. In contrast, the existence of John Smith's mental disease—say, schizophrenia—is declared and socially verified. His alleged illness is identified by psychiatrists, who diagnose his behavior as schizophrenia; other psychiatrists verify its presence by committing him to a mental hospital, where he acquires the right to refuse treatment, which he exercises; and a judge confirms the diagnosis by declaring him mentally incompetent to refuse treatment.

Because the idea of mental illness combines a mistaken conceptualization (of non-disease as disease) with an immoral justification (of coercion as cure), the effect is two-pronged—it corrupts language and curtails freedom and responsibility. Because psychiatrists have power over persons denominated as patients, their descriptive statements typically function as covert prescriptions. For instance, psychiatrists may describe a man who asserts that he hears God's voice telling him to kill his wife as schizophrenic. This "diagnosis" functions as a prescription—for example, to hospitalize the patient involuntarily (lest he kill his wife) or, after he has killed her, to acquit him as not guilty by reason of insanity and again hospitalize him against his will. This coercive-tactical feature of psychiatric diagnosis is best appreciated by contrasting medical with psychiatric diagnosis. Diagnosis of bodily illness is the operative word that justifies a physician to admit to a hospital a patient who wants to be so admitted. Diagnosis of mental illness is the operative word that justifies a judge to incarcerate in a mental hospital a sex criminal who has completed his prison sentence.

So long as there are no objective, physico-chemical observations shown to be causally related to depression and schizophrenia, the claim that they are brain diseases is unsubstantiated. In the absence of such evidence, psychiatrists rest their claim that these major mental diseases are brain diseases largely on the contention that drugs keep the disease processes "under control." The absurdity of this claim lies in its own consequences.

Diabetes is kept under control by insulin. When patients stop taking their medication, the disease process flares up and kills them. Lupus is kept under control by steroids. When patients stop taking their medication, the disease process flares up and kills them.

This is not what happens when patients with serious mental diseases stop taking their medication. Depression is kept under control by antidepressants. When patients stop taking their medication, the disease process flares up, but the disease does not kill them. They kill themselves, an act psychiatrists attribute to their so-called mental illness. Schizophrenia is kept under control by anti-psychotic drugs. When patients stop taking their medication, the disease process flares up, but the disease does not kill them. They kill someone else, an act psychiatrists attribute to their supposed illness.

If we restrict the concept of treatment to a voluntary relationship between a medical practitioner and a competent client, then a coerced medical intervention imposed on persons not legally incompetent is, by definition, assault and battery, not treatment. Psychiatry is thus a systematic violation of this legal-political principle, one that is especially odious because most persons treated against their will by psychiatrists are defined as legally competent—they can vote, marry and divorce, etc. It is important to keep in mind that, in a free society, the physician's "right" to treat a person rests not on the diagnosis, but on the subject's consent to treatment.

Regardless of psychiatric diagnosis, the typical mental patient is entitled to liberty, unless convicted of a crime punishable by imprisonment. If that patient breaks the law and is convicted, then he or she ought to be punished for it as prescribed by the criminal law. In a free society, a person ought not to profit from psychiatric excuses or suffer from psychiatric coercions.

---

*Thomas Szasz is professor of psychiatry emeritus, State University of New York Health Science Center, Syracuse.*

# D E P R E S S I O N :
## BEYOND SEROTONIN

New research is challenging the assumption that the world's most common mental ailment is *just* a chemical imbalance in the brain.

BY HARA ESTROFF MARANO

Death was now a daily presence, blowing over me in cold gusts. Mysteriously and in ways that are totally remote from normal experience, the gray drizzle of horror induced by depression takes on the quality of physical pain. But it is not an immediately identifiable pain, like that of a broken limb. It may be more accurate to say that despair, owing to some evil trick played upon the sick brain by the inhabiting psyche, comes to resemble the diabolical discomfort of being imprisoned in a fiercely overheated room. And because no breeze stirs this caldron, because there is no escape from the smothering confinement, it is entirely natural that the victim begins to think ceaselessly of oblivion.

— William Styron

Melancholy is a fertile muse. No sooner had William Styron become the poet laureate of depression after describing his bout with madness in *Darkness Visible* (Random House, 1990) when all manner of confessions followed. Mike Wallace. Art Buchwald. Dick Cavett lined up to disclose their own struggles with the disabling disorder. It quickly became acceptable, even chic, to publicly confide vulnerability to depression

At the same time, the world was being made safe for depression, or at least public revelations of it, by another development, the 1988 advent of the so-called SSRIs— Prozac, Paxil and related drugs believed to specifically combat depression by beefing up serotonin and other neurotransmitters that ferry signals between nerve cells. The wild success of psychiatrist Peter D. Kramer's thoughtful *Listening to Prozac* (Viking, 1993) generated not only new respect for the effectiveness of Prozac but new appreciation of the disorder it was intended to treat. There followed hundreds of new book titles on depression, over 100 on Prozac alone, surely making it the most heralded drug on the planet. Depression chic cannot be dismissed as a passing fad because, it turns out, how the disorder is defined and popularized deeply shapes what patients are willing to do about it.

Despite the flood of Prozac prose, depression itself has remained, as Styron saw it, a mystery. One of science's cruel ironies is that it can explain bizarre rare conditions, but common afflictions like depression—Western countries' second most disabling ailment (after heart disease) and the world's fourth—elude understanding. That, however, is changing.

In the last three years, refined imaging techniques have begun providing an unprecedented look into the neurobiology of depression, showing what goes on in the brains of patients as they process positive and negative experiences. Though in its infancy, the work is already forcing a radically revised view of depression, one that prom-

ises new treatments for the future. Among the findings:

• Regarding depression as "just" a chemical imbalance wildly misconstrues the disorder. "It is not possible to explain either the disease or its treatment based solely on levels of neurotransmitters," says Yale University neurobiologist Ronald Duman, Ph.D.

The newest evidence indicates that recurrent depression is in fact a neurodegenerative disorder, disrupting the structure and function of brain cells, destroying nerve cell connections, even killing certain brain cells, and precipitating cognitive decline. At the very least, depression sets up neural roadblocks to the processing of information and keeps us from responding to life's challenges.

• Human emotions take shape in a neural circuit involving several key brain structures, including the hippocampus, the amygdala, and the prefrontal cortex. In depression, faulty circuitry fails both in generating positive feelings and inhibiting disruptive negative ones.

• Stress-related events may kick off 50% of all depression and early life stress can prime people for later depression. Ongoing research in animals and in people demonstrates that early strain can alter nerve circuits that control emotion, exaggerating later responses to stress and creating the neurochemical and behavioral changes of depression. In other words, the deeper researchers probe the brain, the more they validate the psychoanalytic view that early adverse life events can create adult psychopathology.

•Depression is not just a disorder from the neck up but a disorder involving many body systems. It both leads to heart disease in otherwise healthy adults and magnifies the deadliness of existing cardiac problems. What's more, it accelerates changes in bone mass that lead to osteoporosis. "The lifetime risk of fracture related to depression is substantial," researchers have declared in the *New England Journal of Medicine*.

•Just as nerve cell connections can be destroyed in depression, perhaps they can be rebuilt. The common denominator in effective antidepressant treatments, including electroshock, may be their ability to stimulate the sprouting of neurons in key brain regions, literally the forging of behavioral flexibility. A neurochemical pathway newly identified promises to revolutionize therapy by suggesting ways to do this better and faster.

•The adult brain has a degree of plasticity that is astonishing researchers. "The big news is the structural plasticity of the adult brain, the remodeling of neurons," says neurobiologist Bruce McEwen, Ph.D., of Rockefeller University. "The idea that there are long-lasting, even permanent, changes in structure and function that can affect the way brains process information is the most important part of what we're doing in the lab. We thought that after birth, the brain is a stable organ like a computer that just works away, and no more new nerve cells are produced. The emphasis was on chemical imbalances, as if the circuitry itself was fairly stable. All these changes—cell loss, atrophy of connections—that's very new, and still catching people by surprise."

## Uniting Mind and Brain

To understand depression we have to confront the mind/body dilemma head on. Although we often arbitrarily divide the mind from the brain and regard "mental illness" as strictly mental, mood disorders are not disembodied ailments. If depression proves anything, the mind and the brain are one. There are nerve circuits in the brain that color psychological events positively and negatively, that lead us to see rewards and pleasures or merely emptiness and hopelessness, and then to negotiate the world by engaging it or withdrawing from it.

Such nerve circuits connect widely with other brain areas and they malfunction in depression, spreading the malaise into every fiber of being. What sets the malfunction in motion may be environmental circumstances, such as childhood neglect, or an internal physical fact, such as a faulty gene controlling a brain enzyme. Or, likely, a mixture of both.

## The Natural History of Depression

Likelihood that a person will develop major depression or dysthymia in his/her life time: 6.1%

Likelihood that a person will suffer some depressive symptoms in his/her lifetime: 23.1%

Average age of first onset of major depression: 25–29

Average duration of all depressive episodes: 20 weeks

Percent of patients who recover within a year after onset of symptoms: 74%

Likelihood of a second or more episodes of major depression: 80%

Likelihood of a second or more episodes of minor depression: 100%

Median number of major depressive episodes during a patient's lifetime: 4

Percent of patients whose depression takes a chronic unremitting course: 12%

Incidence of depression in women vs men: 3.62 vs 1.98 per 1000 per year

Female: male ratio of depression incidence in cultures with low rates of alcoholism: 1:1

Rank of unipolar major depression in the world league of disabling diseases in 1990:4

Rank of unipolar major depression among disabling diseases in westernized countries: 2

Rank of depression among disabling diseases the world over, projected, in 2020:2

## Circuit Riding

Depression appears to hold the very soul hostage, with total lack of energy, disturbed sleep, loss of interest in food and sex, inability to experience pleasure, difficulty concentrating and thinking clearly, impaired short-term memory, self-blame, and inability to see alternatives. But the disorder's full-blown misery arises in just a few distinct centers in the brain. These hubs have discrete channels of communication with each other, their messages sent out over long filamentous arms extending from the cell bodies in one center to those in another.

One seminal spot in the circuitry of depression is the prefrontal cortex (PFC), the brain area just behind the forehead, which acts as the executive branch of emotions. According to Richard Davidson, Ph.D., professor of psychology and psychiatry at the University of Wisconsin, two of the PFC's most important functions are restricted to one side or the other. His studies show that the left side of the PFC is crucial to establishing and maintaining positive feelings, while the right is associated with negative ones. Depressed people appear to have a power failure of the left PFC. The failure shows up both in electrical studies of brain response and PET scans indicating decreased blood flow and metabolism. The depressed just don't activate the machinery to process positive emotions or respond to positive stimuli.

Specifically, the left PFC is instrumental in producing what Davidson calls "pre-goal attainment positive affect," what you and I call eagerness, the emotion that arises as we approach a desired goal. The depressed can't mentally hang on to goals or stay attuned to rewards. Result: lowered capacity for pleasure, lack of motivation, loss of interest.

But the left PFC doesn't just activate positive feelings. Davidson finds that it is also crucial in inhibiting negative emotion that gets in the way of focusing on positive goals. In this, the left PFC draws on its links to the amygdala, an almond-shaped structure in the center of the brain that pumps out negative feelings.

By placing subjects in a functional magnetic resonance imager to measure brain activity while showing them emotionally laden pictures—photographs of starving children, for example—Davidson has graphically confirmed what many scientists have suspected: that the amygdala scans incoming experience for emotional significance, puts a flag on negative feelings such as fear, and sends out notice of threat, information we could not survive without.

If the PFC masterminds depression by failing to activate, the amygdala controls the severity of depression by its negative output. Along with the University of Pittsburgh's Wayne C. Drevets, M.D., Davidson has found that blood flow in the amygdala is greater the more depressed a person is. Moreover, studies show that the amygdala is highly active during states of helplessness, as when people face an insoluble problem. Amygdala activity also determines how firmly a negative event is held in memory.

Ordinarily, as the left PFC turns on, it simultaneously shuts off the amygdala and dampens the flow of negative emotions from it. But among the depressed, the general failure of activation of the left PFC leaves the amygdala running unchecked, overwhelming them with dread, fear and other negative feelings.

Individuals normally differ in the degrees of neural activation of the left and right sides of the PFC in response to emotional messages. That difference may help account not only for a person's vulnerability to depression, Davidson says, but also for variations in personality. A peppy left PFC underlies extraversion, while a relatively more active right PFC is linked to inhibition and anxiety.

It isn't clear how asymmetries in prefrontal activity get established to begin with. "Although these characteristics of brain function are very stable in adults," Davidson says, "they are much less so in children." That suggests to him that activation levels of this circuit are set early in life, certainly by puberty.

One clue may be that differences in PFC activation go hand in hand with differences in brain levels of the stress-related hormone cortisol. When the left PFC is highly active, not only do people have a sunny outlook, but levels of cortisol are low. Cortisol patterns suggest that stress had a hand in there somewhere.

## No Glee Over Glia

Barely two years ago, Wayne Drevets, then at Washington University, discovered that depressed persons not only have altered PFC activity, but their prefrontal cortex is actually smaller than in the nondepressed. It is one thing to find abnormalities in the way the brains of the depressed function—but *structural* abnormalities? *Anatomical* ones?

Drevets found that depressed patients have a drastically smaller volume of a section of the left PFC that sits about two and a half inches behind the bridge of nose and is called the ventral anterior cingulate. Drevets calls it the subgenual prefrontal cortex because it sits beneath the genua, or knee, of the corpus callossum, the Continental Divide of the brain. The little site was 40% smaller in the depressed.

The subgenual cortex is vastly important: it is one of the few cortical regions connecting to the hypothalamus, a deep-brain structure that instigates the body's stress response. The subgenual cortex also helps orchestrate the body's hormonal response to stressful stimuli.

Taking their cue from Drevets' findings, colleagues at Washington University began searching for what could account for the cortical shrinkage. They examined tissue that, at autopsy, had been collected from the brains of normal individuals and those with bipolar or unipolar depression.

At a recent meeting of the Society of Neuroscience, graduate student Dost Ongur reported startling findings. He had expected to see a decrease in the number of neurons, what he calls "the business end of the brain in terms of processing information and generating actions." Instead he found a dramatic loss in the number of glia,

small cells that perform important—maybe critica—housekeeping functions for the more patrician neurons. The loss of glia was seen only in those with a family history of depression.

## Glut of Glutamate

The glia are known to nourish neurons by assuring a steady supply of glucose, their preferred food. They also protect neurons by stabilizing levels of the neurotransmitter glutamate. Glutamate is the main transmitter in the cortex that activates cells. But too much glutamate can overstimulate neurons, causing collapse of the branches by which they communicate with other cells.

The glia also play a big role in the development of the serotonin neurotransmitter system, which, everyone now knows, also functions abnormally in depression. "It could be," Drevets says, "that some defect in the neural development of the prefrontal cortex could be the initial abnormality in depression that starts a cascade of changes in other systems."

It may also be that the action of antidepressant drugs on serotonin is less important than their action on glutamate. Researchers know that one effect of antidepressants is to reduce the sensitivity of re-

ceptors in the PFC for glutamate. "Suddenly," says Drevets, "that makes sense. Agents that desensitize the frontal cortex to glutamate may be compensating for the loss of glial cells."

Of course, that still leaves the possibility that a serotonin deficit in other parts of the brain could induce other depressive symptoms. But that's exactly the point; not only is serotonin not the whole story of depression, neurotransmitters may not even be the main story.

Changes in the structure of the brain—losses of cells—are relatively permanent types of alteration. So far, there's no evidence that such changes, once they occur (and it's not clear when in the lifetime course of depression they set in) are reversed with drug or other therapy. And that may account for the propensity of depression to recur. "What's less clear," Drevets says, "is why there are periods when the illness remits, then returns."

## Nature, Nurture, Neuron

One of the most debilitating features of depression is the inability of the afflicted to see out of their rut, to imagine alternative ways of being and doing. "In depression," says Ronald Duman, associate professor of psychiatry and pharmacology

The prefrontal cortex, when activated on the left side, normally generates positive feelings and dampens flow of negativity from the amygdala.

The amygdala, center of negative emotions, informs the brain of threat. It runs unchecked in depression.

The hypothalamus, center of the stress response, is overactive in depression.

The hippocampus, center of memory, loses nerve-to-nerve links in depression.

Vincent Perez/Anatomyworks

# Skirmish or Siege?

## Depression is a chronic illness with recurring episodes. So should we deploy antidepressants battle by battle, or order them in for the long war?

### By Christina Frank

When Sheila Singleton, 45, filled her first prescription for an antidepressant, she assumed it would also be her last. "I thought OK, when the pills work and I get myself straightened out, I'll go back to taking nothing but my vitamins," she says. Seventeen years later, Singleton still pops a pill every day. During the brief intervals when she's gone off medication, or when the ones she was on stopped working, the depression returned with a vengeance.

Among the newer antidepressants, options range from SSRIs (selective serotonin reuptake inhibitors) such as Prozac, Paxil, and Zoloft, to those—Wellbutrin and Effexor, for example—that target different or combined neurotransmitters. Most satisfied patients claim they provide highly effective relief with few side effects.

But there is one notorious downside: roughly 70% of SSRI users are plagued by sexual difficulty. "It's a big problem," acknowledges Donald Klein, M.D., professor of psychiatry at Columbia University and director of research at the New York State Psychiatric Institute. "There are no hard data on how many people actually discontinue treatment due to the sexual side effects; it largely depends on how they are handled by the specific doctor. Zoloft, for example, is short-acting and can be stopped for a couple of days, restoring sexual function for that period. Adding Wellbutrin to an SSRI is another way to restore libido. But not all doctors may try these adjustments; they may just say that's the price you have to pay."

Another fly in the psychiatric salve is that these drugs have been officially approved only for short-term use—six to 12 months—yet are routinely prescribed for indefinite periods, in order to prevent future depressive episodes. It's not that the drugs are contraindicated for long-term use, it's just been impossible to conduct long-term studies. Americans move or drop out.

"So you have this disparity between the length of time for which the medications are approved and the length of time you might have to take them in order to have a good interval without depression,"

says Peter D. Kramer, M.D. "No one has really bridged that gap and figured out just what is appropriate for long-term treatment. It does seem that recurrences are prevented. On the other hand, do the medications lose their effectiveness? Are there long-term side effects? These are just not known."

What is known is that although many individual depressive episodes can be temporarily "fixed" by antidepressants, the drugs are not curative, no more than insulin cures diabetes or antihypertensives cure high blood pressure. The demon almost always returns at some point.

"We're increasingly recognizing something our European colleagues, who've been able to do longitudinal studies on depression, have known for some time: That major depression is predominantly a recurrent illness," says Fred Goodwin, M.D., professor of psychiatry at George Washington University, former director of the National Institute of Mental Health, and host of *The Infinite Mind* on National Public Radio. "Eighty percent of people who have had one episode will eventually have another one, one year or many years down the road."

So why not just stop the medication after one episode is cured and wait until the next one hits before resuming treatment? Kramer points to a phenomenon known as kindling: the more episodes you have, the worse they get—and the less stress it takes to trigger them. Anecdotal evidence also suggests that going on and off medications may increase the dose needed next time to achieve the same benefit as last time. In the long run, stopping and starting doesn't reduce overall drug exposure.

Untreated, some depressive episodes eventually resolve themselves, on average, says Goodwin, in less than a year, though there is considerable variation from person to person. What antidepressants do is speed recovery by eliminating symptoms and enhancing motivation and energy.

Klein points out that of 100 depressed patients given any antidepressant, only 66 will show improvement. However, half of these positive responses are a placebo ef-

fect. Thus, only a third of patients are truly responding to the specific drug.

In Klein's estimation, the vast majority of sufferers—85% to 90%—can find substantial relief with one or a combination of drugs within six to eight weeks, assuming they faithfully follow the prescribed drug regimen ("total compliance" in medical jargon). Most people with depression, he says, can find relief with the first or second antidepressant they try. Only about 10% to 15% of patients, unipolar and bipolar, are truly resistant to treatment.

A study of 161 outpatients, recently reported in the *Journal of the American Medical Association,* demonstrated that long-term treatment with sertraline (Zoloft) prevents recurrence of chronic severe depression. In the study, conducted for 76 weeks, 50% (42) of 84 placebo-treated patients experienced recurrence of significant depressive symptoms, versus only 26% (20) of 77 patients given sertraline.

When determining who is a candidate for long-term drug therapy (lasting more than one year), doctors consider frequency of and length of time between episodes, severity of depressive symptoms, risk of suicide as well as family history of mood disorders. One of the most debated treatment dilemmas today is how to handle the persistent low-grade depression known as chronic dysthymia: does it merit long-term medication, or medication at all? Jesse Rosenthal, M.D., chief psychopharmacologist at Beth Israel Medical Center in New York City, suggests that the personal price paid by the chronically dysthymic can be as great as that paid by people with major depression, in terms of damaged relationships, poor work performance and overall low energy.

Still, it's not as simple as just putting everyone who is depressed on long-term drug therapy. Some patients will run into so-called "poop-out"; the medications simply stop working after a while. There are no official data on the antidepressant poop-out rate, but experts estimate it at about 20%. According to Klein, poop-out is highly unlikely to occur before three or four months of treatment; after that, there is no saying whether or when it will. "Poop-out is not uncommon, but it's not the expectation" says Goodwin. "It is possible to keep taking these drugs indefinitely at the same dose and maintain the same level of relief."

Another unknown is what's behind poop-out—whether it is true pharmacologic failure or a worsening of the disease, a relapse that overrides medication. Other factors that can dent a medication's apparent effectiveness are aging (which tends to worsen or change depressive symptoms), substance abuse, a co-existing medical illness and noncompliance, a big problem.

Rajinder Judge, M.D., clinical research physician for Prozac at Eli Lilly, estimates that just 50% of patients actually take antidepressants properly. "They miss doses or just stop on their own," she says. It is not uncommon for patients to drop their medications after four months, although prevention of relapse is believed to warrant longer treatment. Some find the side effects too pesky. Others become overconfident because they feel so much better. "Once you recover," Judge explains, "you

don't want to be reminded of those dark days and the only thing reminding you is this little pill."

Whatever the cause of poop-out, it can almost always be remedied by upping (or sometimes even reducing) the dose, or changing or adding medications. Whereas older medications—so-called tricyclic antidepressants and monoamine oxidase (MAO) inhibitors—can be dangerous at high doses, amounts of the SSRIs can be doubled and then doubled again without harm, according to Peter Kramer. "Sometimes the patient ends up on a more complicated regimen to get the same effect," he says. "Or sometimes it's a matter of taking a person off one drug and reintroducing it later. One way or another, it is mostly possible to get people back to where they were."

While Kramer is a proponent of antidepressants, he also expresses some skepticism, especially where dosing and long-term side effects are concerned. "My sense is that we're giving Prozac at too high a dose. Many people can do well with 10 mg, but 20 mg to 80 mg is common. Also, there's suspicion that the SSRIs may affect memory in the long run; it's

hard to be sure because depression itself impairs memory."

And what role does good old-fashioned psychotherapy play these days? A recent mega-analysis of 595 patients with major depressive disorder, reported the *Archives of General Psychiatry,* concluded that the best treatment plan involves a combination of psychotherapy and drug therapy.

But there are many kinds of therapy and not all are equally effective. Goodwin advocates a here-and-now approach of behavioral and cognitive techniques.

Furthermore, he says, even patients prescribed medication alone need psychological attention. Knowledgeable clinicians "can miss things like poor compliance, life stresses and substance abuse that can interfere with the medicine's working."

Depression, Donald Klein asserts, is among the most medically treatable illnesses. Accepting that short-term treatment may not be a possibility for most is perhaps the next hurdle to get over. "I now know that there is no cure," says Sheila Singleton. "I will have depression for the rest of my life and I'll take medication for the rest of my life."

at Yale, "there's a loss of appropriate adaptability."

Ordinarily, the neurons of the brain have an ability to change and adapt by sprouting new dendritic spines, tiny fibrous protrusions that are the primary receiving end of connections between nerve cells. By literally opening new neural pathways, this sprouting is what allows us to learn and remember, to change our behavior, to meet new challenges, to adapt to new circumstances. Scientists call this capacity neuronal plasticity.

Duman has tracked the inside operations of nerve cells and found evidence that the depressed have a deficit in specific nerve growth factors, the substances that make possible the sprouting of new nerve cell connections. One in particular is brain-derived neurotrophic factor. BDNF strengthens synaptic connections in the hippocampus (a center of learning and memory) and enhances the growth of neurons that respond to serotonin.

Duman's studies also show, yet again, that how antidepressant agents are believed to work and what actually accounts for their effectiveness may be two different things. Long-term antidepressant treatments—including electroshock—do increase receptors for serotonin at the cell surface. But, Duman found, they also do something else inside the neuron that may be more important. They kick off a cascade

of molecular steps that winds up amplifying a neuron's own production of BDNF—and the sprouting of new connections. Moreover, they do this in parts of the brain that have been linked to depression, such as the hippocampus. The real power of antidepressants, then, may be summed in two words: neuronal plasticity.

The molecular cascade Duman has exposed opens up a whole new realm of possibilities for improving treatment of depression. It may be possible to create therapies that more directly and more strongly augment BDNF output. At the same time, the molecular pathway of BDNF production suggests new target points for a more rapid-acting treatment.

Duman's evidence that neuronal plasticity is at stake in depression fits with imaging studies showing that structural changes are taking place in the brains of the depressed. The two strands of information suggest a way that depression might originate. In a word: stress.

## New Stress on Stress

"There is elegant work showing that stress, whether environmental or social, actually changes the shape, size and number of neurons in the hippocampus," says Duman. "There are studies showing that stress decreases levels of BDNF. It's a really hot area of research just now." And right at its

epicenter is Bruce McEwen, Ph.D., director of the neurobiology lab at New York's Rockefeller University and head of a MacArthur Foundation workgroup on socioeconomic status and health.

McEwen is studying what happens in the adult brain, specifically the hippocampus, of animals undergoing repeated stress. Imaging studies have found that this area, like the prefrontal cortex and the amygdala, shrinks in people with recurrent depression. Prolonged stress, research has shown, kills hippocampal cells, precipitating cognitive decline.

McEwen himself has documented that several kinds of stress—the psychosocial stress of being a subordinate among group-living animals, the stress of being physically restrained—can cause hippocampal cells to atrophy and retract their dendrites. Others have seen the same effects in animals subjected to the stresses of social isolation and, in infancy, to deprivation of maternal care. McEwen has also found that stress can suppress nerve cell growth in a part of the hippocampus recently shown capable of renewing nerve cells in adult life. He's trying to nail down what is cause and what is effect.

"So far," McEwen says, "all we know is that atrophy of these brain structures is seen in people who have a long history of recurrent depressive illness. It may be that those changes cannot be reversed."

But they may be preventable earlier in the course of depression, by use of an appropriate drug, before repeated bouts of depression kill off brain cells. "We've begun to look at this," reports Yale's Ronald Duman. "And we have found that antidepressant treatments are in fact able to induce the genesis of neurons."

## Freud 1, Neurobiology 1

For many neurobiologists, behavioral plasticity is only half the new story on depression. The other part is the degree to which early experience can establish a lifelong pattern of brain activity. New research both in animals and in people demonstrates that stress early in life permanently sensitizes neurons and receptors throughout the central nervous system so that they perpetually overrespond to stress.

At the most recent meeting of the Society for Neuroscience, for example, psychologist Christine Heim, Ph.D., reported that sexual abuse in girls before puberty creates hyperactivity of the stress-hormone system headquartered in the brain's hypothalamus. And that likely makes them subject to depression as adults. "This is the first human study to report persistent changes in the reactivity of the hypothalamus-pituitary-adrenal axis among adult survivors of early trauma," she points out.

Heim so far has studied eight depressed women with a documented history of childhood abuse, seven women who also experienced childhood abuse but who do not have depression, and seven women who were never exposed to such early life stress and who have never been depressed. At Emory University, she tracked the chemical footprints of stress reactivity, in both brain and body, in all 22 women after applying mild stress—having them make a brief speech and do mental math in front of an audience.

Normally, when a threat to physical or psychological well-being is detected, the hypothalamus steps up production of corticotropin-releasing factor (CRF). This induces the pituitary gland to secrete ACTH, which in turn instructs the adrenal glands to pour out cortisol. Early trauma, Heim found, leads to chronic overactivation of the system. CRF, studies show, acts on various brain sites to create symptoms of depression.

All of the women who experienced early trauma reacted to the experimental stress with elevated stress hormones. The levels were highest in those with current major depression.

Such studies are leading researchers to a new model of depression, one they call the diathesis-stress model. Simply put, some inherited factor—a flawed gene for BDNF, individual differences in PFC activ-

> ## "If you're 45, in perfect health, and depressed, you're 50% to 100% more likely to have a heart attack."

ity—creates the biological vulnerability for major depression. Then some early stressful experience—such as parental neglect or physical or sexual abuse—sets up the brain to permanently overreact to environmental pressures. Then even small degrees of later stress provoke an outpouring of stress hormones, such as CRF and cortisol, throughout the brain (and body). These hormones act directly on multiple sites to produce the behavioral symptoms of depression—the vegetative state, the sleep disturbances, the cognitive dullness, the loss of pleasure. They push the amygdala into overdrive, churning out the negative emotions that steer the depression's severity and add a twist of anxiety. To boot, they magnify the effects of the neurotransmitter glutamate so that it overstimulates neurons until their dendrites collapse and shrink up.

The moral of the story: early life experience counts. Not because it creates oral fixations or such. But because it shapes wiring patterns in the brain and sets the sensitivity level of the molecular machinery behind nerve-cell operations.

## It's Not All In The Head

While disparate biological changes suggest that there are different types of depression—some arising spontaneously from within, others reflecting heightened reactivity to life events—all depression is more than an affliction from the neck up. It is a whole-body disorder.

At Columbia University, where he is professor of psychiatry, Alexander Glassman, M.D., was studying cardiac effects of antidepressant drugs when reports began to trickle in confirming what he had suspected: depression makes heart disease particularly deadly. But it wasn't clear what role cigarettes played; the depressed are apt to smoke, and smoking leads to heart disease. So Glassman teamed up with epidemiologists following more than 2,000 people for over a decade. In 1993 the group reported that, even after they controlled for smoking, depression essentially multiplies the malignity of heart disease, substantially increasing the risk of sudden death within

the next year. The report dropped an even bigger bombshell; it warned that healthy people struck by depression are more likely than people without the ailment to develop heart disease 10 years down the road. Just because they once got depressed.

"There are two things we can say without any hesitancy," says Glassman. "If you're 45, in perfect health, and depressed, you're somewhere between 50% and 100% more likely to have a heart attack than if you weren't depressed. That's big. And if you have a heart attack and then get depressed, whether you simply get some symptoms of depression or the full diagnosis, over the next 18 months you are three and a half times more likely to die. That's even bigger."

There are roughly 500,000 heart attacks a year in the U.S. And 20% of heart attack victims develop depression.

What put the head and the heart on a collision course are blood platelets, which play a key role in the ability of blood to clot. Platelets turn out to be stickier in those who are depressed. At Emory University, Dominique Musselman, M.D., has shown that the platelets of depressed people are hairtrigger responsive to activation signals, aggregating when they should be flowing.

A decade ago, the thinking was that heart attacks occurred when cholesterol-laden plaques formed on coronary artery walls and, over time, grew large enough to block blood flow in the artery. Today it's known that heart attacks occur only when a crack develops in the artery lining that covers the slow-growing plaque. Then platelets are suddenly drawn to the site, where they adhere to the exposed artery wall and rope in even more platelets. Clotting occurs within minutes, choking off blood flow to the heart.

## Bones of Contention

The somatic changes of psychological depression go bone deep. Literally. The hormonal abnormalities that mark the disorder, particularly elevated body levels of cortisol, also rob the skeleton of calcium. The result: osteoporosis on a speeded schedule.

Researchers at the National Institutes of Health have found that depressed premenopausal women develop bones as porous as those of postmenopausal women. And the leaching of bone mineral persists, despite treatment with antidepressants. Led by David Michaelson, M.D., the team reported that bone mineral density was, on average, 6% lower in the spine among 24 depressed women than among 24 controls. And in the hip, it was 10% to 14% lower among the depressed—decrements that set women up for hip fractures.

"Once lost," Michaelson observes, "bone density is difficult to regain." It takes

> How antidepressants are said to work and what actually accounts for their effectiveness may be two different things.

years, plus a modicum of physical activity and a calcium-rich diet. But it probably never returns to normal in depression, since the disorder tends to recur—and depressed people tend to be physically inactive and eat poorly.

It's not that chronic depression doesn't create a huge psychological burden. But it's becoming increasingly clear, says Columbia's Glassman, that "depression is an illness with very real and dangerous physical concomitants."

## Sick, Not Sad?

The new corporeality of "mental" illness is perhaps most daringly embodied in the work of Bruce Charlton, M.D., a research psychiatrist in the department of psychology at the University of Newcastle in England. Depression, Charlton provocatively contends, doesn't just have physical concomitants; it is wholly a physical disorder, one that is misinterpreted by the brain. Sickness is read as sadness.

The low mood is a secondary response, a product of physical malaise, the same malaise—the lack of energy, slowed movement, lack of pleasurable appetites (including sex), inability to concentrate—one gets when, say, the flu strikes. "The trouble with malaise is that you don't necessarily know you've got it, and you blame yourself for your condition of low performance," he says. But it is the body's way of withdrawing (think of a wounded animal) to conserve energy and minimize risk, an "evolved pattern of behavior" mediated by the immune system. "Major depressive dis-

order," he says, "is sickness behavior inappropriately activated and sustained."

Charlton subscribes to the model of emotions put forth by the University of Iowa's Antonio Damasio, M.D., that feelings are the brain's representation of what's going on in the body. But, he says, sadness and happiness are "catch-all names given to aversive and gratifying states, end products of more primary emotions."

Still, the prevailing body state, the malaise, colors all incoming perceptions and stamps them "aversive" as they are encoded in memory. Recall, then, summons up malaise, as does thinking about the future. To the extent the malaise continues, patients are stuck, unable to even imagine anything that makes them feel motivated and energetic. Bleakness! Despair! Depression!

In this view, antidepressants, notably the tricyclics, possibly Prozac, work to the degree that they are analgesics! "Antidepressants do not make people happy," Charlton insists. They treat the state of unpleasantness. "Their effect on mood is no more remarkable than the fact that it is easier to be happy without a headache."

Charlton joins a rising chorus in disputing the way antidepressants are said to work. British psychiatrist David Healy, a card-carrying psychopharmacologist, contends in his book *The Antidepressant Era* (Harvard, 1998) that these agents are falsely presented as specific to depression. And the idea that depression is a single specific disorder was created largely by drug companies with a product—antidepressants—to sell. He argues that depression is even more than a disorder of the whole body; it's a disorder of the whole person, existential or social distress marked by unhappiness and hopelessness. It is cast into physical symptoms precisely because they have been made fashionable, sanctioned and publicized by today's medical-industrial complex.

## Flexibility Regained

Whatever pathways depression takes through the brain and the body, it is still experienced by sufferers as a disorder of the whole person, which is why its pain has always been so hard to locate. As a re-

sult, how depression is seen by psychologists and psychiatrists, how they explain it to you and me, and how patients understand their own disorder—all influence what symptoms patients complain of. And what they are willing to do about them.

Fashions in thinking about depression make a difference to recovery. "We have looked at clients' theories of why they are depressed," reports psychologist Michael Addis, Ph.D., of Clark University, "Their theories are predictive of the outcome of treatment."

What is available to clients as explanation is the very stuff psychologists and psychiatrists talk about. The culture has become both more psychological-minded and more biological-minded. As a result, Addis has heard clients say things like, "My doctor said this is a chemical imbalance, so why are you talking to me about doing pleasurable activities?" He admonishes professionals: "We don't know what our theories mean to individuals. We say 'chemical imbalance.' A patient thinks, 'I'm damned.' Our theories are not neutral."

Which is why Peter Kramer, who prescribes both psychotherapy and drug therapy, ponders "which is the umbrella concept?" Is the brain a biological organ and psychotherapy another way to influence the brain? This is the view that psychiatry is moving towards. Or is drug therapy an adjunct to psychotherapy? "This is my model," he says. "Medication is one way of helping patients broaden their perspective." In other words, it's a way to restore what makes people most human—our remarkable capacity to adapt to life's ever changing demands.

> "Medication is one way of helping patients broaden their perspective," says psychiatrist Peter Kramer.

# The Clustering and Contagion of Suicide

Thomas E. Joiner, Jr.[1]
Department of Psychology, Florida State University, Tallahassee, Florida

## Abstract

Two general types of suicide cluster have been discussed in the literature; roughly, these can be classified as mass clusters and point clusters. Mass clusters are media related, and the evidence for them is equivocal; point clusters are local phenomena, and these do appear to occur. Contagion has not been conceptually well developed nor empirically well supported as an explanation for suicide clusters. An alternative explanation for why suicides sometimes cluster is articulated: People who are vulnerable to suicide may cluster well before the occurrence of any overt suicidal stimulus, and when they experience severe negative events, including but not limited to the suicidal behavior of one member of the cluster, all members of the cluster are at increased risk for suicidality (a risk that may be offset by good social support).

## Keywords

suicide clusters; suicide contagion

The phenomena of attempted and completed suicide are troubling and mysterious enough in themselves; the possibility that suicide is socially contagious, even more so. This article considers whether suicide clusters exist, and if so, whether "contagion" processes can account for them.

There is a potentially important distinction between the terms suicide cluster and suicide contagion. A cluster refers to the factual occurrence of two or more completed or attempted suicides that are nonrandomly "bunched" in space or time (e.g., a series of suicide attempts in the same high school or a series of completed suicides in response to the suicide of a celebrity). The term cluster implies nothing about *why* the cluster came to be, only *that* it came to be. By contrast, contagion refers to a possible explanation (as I argue later, a fairly vague explanation) of *why* a cluster developed. Clusters (of a sort) appear to occur, but the status of contagion as the reason for such occurrences is more equivocal.

## CLUSTERS—OF A SORT— APPEAR TO OCCUR

Given that attempted and completed suicides are relatively rare, and given that they tend to be more or less evenly distributed in space and time (e.g., suicides occur at roughly the same rate in various regions of the United States and occur at roughly the same rate regardless of the day of the week or the month), it is statistically unlikely that suicides would cluster by chance alone. Yet cluster they do, at least under some circumstances. (Such clustering is often termed the "Werther effect," after a fictional character of Goethe's whose suicide purportedly inspired actual suicides in 18th-century Europe.) Two general types of suicide cluster have been discussed in the literature: mass clusters and point clusters. Mass clusters are media related; point clusters, local.

### Point Clusters

Point clusters occur locally, involving victims who are relatively contiguous in both space and time. The prototypical setting is institutional (i.e., a school or a hospital). Probably the best documented example was reported by Brent and his colleagues (Brent, Kerr, Goldstein, & Bozigar, 1989). In a high school of approximately 1,500 students, 2 students committed suicide within 4 days. During an 18-day span that included the 2 completed suicides, 7 other students attempted suicide and an additional 23 reported having suicidal thoughts. It is important to note, though, that Brent and his colleagues found that 75% of the members of the cluster had at least one major psychiatric disorder, which had existed before the students' exposure to the suicides (i.e., they were vulnerable to begin with). Also, victims' close friends appeared to develop suicidal symptoms more readily than students who were less close to victims. In other words, social contiguity was an important factor.

Haw (1994) described a point cluster of 14 suicides within a 1-year period among patients of a London psychiatric unit. Thirteen of the 14 patients suffered from severe, chronic mental illness (e.g., schizophrenia), and most had ongoing therapeutic contact with the psychiatric unit. The author reported that the point cluster's occurrence may have stemmed from patients' valid perceptions that the future of the hospital was uncertain and that their access to medical staff was decreasing and ultimately threatened. Several other point clusters have also been described (see, e.g., Gould, Wallenstein, & Davidson, 1989).

### When Point Clusters Do Not Occur

Given that suicidality runs in families, and that the suicide of a family member is an enormously traumatic event, one might imagine that point clusters would be particularly likely within a given family (e.g., the suicide of one family member might be followed closely by the suicide of another family member). However, within-family point clusters appear to be very rare. (Although certainly at least one has occurred, I could find no documented case in the literature. It is possible, however, that they are underreported or underpublicized.) Point clusters also appear not to occur within groupings beyond the institutional (e.g., at the level of a large community; cf. Chiu, 1988)—except, that is, in the (possible) case of mass clusters.

### Mass Clusters

Unlike point cluster, mass clusters are media-related phenomena. They are grouped more in time than in space, and are purportedly in response to the publicizing of actual or fictional suicides. Phillips and his colleagues have examined the possible relation of suicide-related media events and the rate of subsequent suicides (see, e.g., Phillips & Carstensen, 1986, 1988). These researchers have argued that the suicide rate in the population increases in the days after descriptions of suicides appear in televised news reports and in newspapers. Indeed, in many of these studies, the suicide rate did appear to rise after a publicized suicide, although the effect did not always occur, and it appeared to be primarily applicable to adolescent suicide. Interestingly, these researchers also found that accidents, such as motor vehicle fatalities, may increase in the days following a publicized suicide, apparently because many such accidents are actually intentional suicides.

However, a study by Kessler, Downey, Milavsky, and Stipp (1988) cast doubt on the conclusion that mass clusters exist. Examining adolescent suicides from 1973 to 1984, the authors found no reliable relation between suicide-related newscasts and the subsequent adolescent suicide rate. Similarly, these researchers obtained no evidence that the number of teenagers viewing the newscasts (as determined by Neilsen ratings) was correlated with the number of adolescent suicides.

In the case of fictional portrayals of suicide (e.g., a television movie in which a character commits suicide), the evidence indicates, at most, a weak effect. Schmidtke and Haefner (1988) studied responses to a serial, broadcast twice in Germany, showing the railway suicide of a young man. After each broadcast, according to these researchers, railway suicides among young men (but not among other groups) increased sharply. However, several other researchers have conducted similar studies and concluded

that there was no relation between fictionalized accounts of suicide and the subsequent suicide rate, for adolescents in particular (Phillips & Paight, 1987; Simkin, Hawton, Whitehead, & Fagg, 1995), as well as for people in general (Berman, 1988).

## CLUSTERING DOES NOT CONTAGION MAKE

If suicide clusters exist (and it appears that point clusters do, although mass clusters may not), contagion—the social, or interpersonal, transmission of suicidality from one victim to another—may or may not be involved. With regard to an array of unfortunate events (e.g., disasters, accidents, even illnesses), it is easy to imagine that there would be point clusters of victims without contagion of any sort. For example, the victims of the Chernobyl nuclear disaster were point-clustered, not because of any type of contagion between victims, but because of victims' simultaneous exposure to radiation. Even cases of mass suicide, the victims of which are point-clustered, are best viewed as instances of mass delusion (e.g., Heaven's Gate) or of a combination of delusion and coercion (e.g., Jonestown), rather than of contagion. In cases such as Chernobyl and even Jonestown, the point clustering of victims may be seen as due to the simultaneous effects of some pernicious, external influence, such as radiation, on a preexisting, socially contiguous group of people, such as those working at or living near the Chernobyl plant.

In disease, the agent of contagion (e.g., some microbial pathogen) is specified, and its mechanism of action delineated. By contrast, no persuasive agent or mechanism of suicide contagion has been articulated. Indeed, with one exception, the very definition of suicide contagion has been so vague as to defy analysis. The one exception is behavioral imitation, which, although clearly defined, lacks explanatory power (e.g., in a school, what determines who, among all the students, imitates a suicide?).

## A SPECULATION REGARDING POINT-CLUSTERED SUICIDES

I suggest that the concepts of imitation or contagion may not be needed to explain point-clustered suicides. Rather, four sets of findings, taken together, indicate an alternative view. First, severe negative life events are risk factors for suicidality (and the suicidal behavior of a friend or peer qualifies as one of a large array of severe negative life events).

Second, good social support (e.g., healthy family functioning) buffers people against developing suicidal symptoms. Third, there exists an array of person-based risk factors for suicidality (e.g., personality disorder or other psychiatric disorder). Fourth, people form relationships *assortatively*—that is, people who possess similar qualities or problems, including suicide risk factors, may be more likely to form relationships with one another. Therefore, it is possible that people who are vulnerable to suicide may cluster well before the occurrence of any overt suicidal stimulus (i.e., suicide point clusters may be, in a sense, prearranged), and when they experience severe negative events, including but not limited to the suicidal behavior of one member of the cluster, all members of the cluster are at increased risk for suicidality (a risk that may be offset by good social support).

Consider, the example, the point cluster described by Haw (1994), in which victims were assortatively related on the basis of, at least in part, shared suicide risk factors (e.g., the chronic mental illness that brought them all to the same psychiatric unit). Vulnerable people were brought together (through contact with the agency), were exposed to severe stress (potential for dissolution of the agency; lack of access to important caregivers; for some, suicides of peers), and may not have been well buffered by good social support (the chronically mentally ill often have low social support; a main source of support may have been the agency, which was threatened).

Or consider the example of point clusters within high schools. In this case, the assortative relationships—the prearrangement of clusters—may occur in one or both of two ways. First, because they have mutual interests, compatible qualities, or similar problems (including vulnerability to and experience of psychopathology), vulnerable adolescents may gravitate toward one another. A point cluster reported by Robbins and Conroy (1983) demonstrates this possibility. In this cluster, two adolescent suicides were followed by five attempts (all five teenagers were subsequently admitted to the hospital) and one hospital admission for having suicidal thoughts. Of the six hospitalized teens, all had regularly socialized with each other, and all visited each other during their hospitalizations. Second, having social contact (for whatever reason, assortative or not) with an adolescent who completes or attempts suicide appears to lower the threshold at which a teen becomes suicidal (Brent et al., 1989). The mere occurrence, then, of suicidality in one adolescent may automatically arrange a potential cluster.

Although the empirical facts on point clusters are limited, they appear to be consistent with my speculation that severe negative life events, person-based risk, social contiguity (perhaps as a function of assortative relationships), and lack of buffering by social support, taken together, explain the phenomenon. In an effort to provide further empirical support for this view, I conducted an analogue study among college roommates. College roommates provide an interesting "natural laboratory" for studying issues involving assortative relationships, because in many large universities, a sizable proportion of roommates are randomly assigned to each other (by the university housing agency) and the rest assortatively choose to room with each other. I predicted that suicidality levels would be more similar among roommates who chose to room together than among those randomly paired together. Moreover, I predicted that suicidality levels would be particularly consonant among pairs who both chose one another and, by their own reports, had been experiencing negative life events that affected both of them. Results supported the view that prearranged point clusters (in this case, arranged by people choosing to live together) would share suicide-related features (in this case, symptoms), and that clustered suicidality was particularly likely in those prearranged clusters that had been affected by negative life events. It must be emphasized that this study was an analogue study, and that, in general, students' levels of suicidality were quite low, making the generalization to attempted or completed suicide questionable. The results, however, converge with those from reports on actual point clusters to make the explanation offered here, at the least, a candidate for further study.

## ADDRESSING POTENTIAL CRITICISMS OF THIS EXPLANATION

### Why Don't Point Clusters Happen All the Time?

According to my speculation about why point clusters develop, at least two concepts are key to understanding why they are relatively rare. First, my explanation involves the joint operation of several phenomena that themselves are infrequent in occurrence. Severe negative events, high person-based risk, suicidality itself, and low social support—all jointly operating ingredients of

my explanation—are relatively rare; their confluence is even more so. Second, even given the confluence of these factors, attempted or completed suicides represent an extreme and severe psychopathology, the threshold for which is presumably quite high. Thus, even when life events are severely negative, person-based risk is high, and social support is low, the threshold may not be reached.

### Why Don't Point Clusters Occur Within Families?

Because suicidality and suicide risk run in families, because the suicide of a family member is arguably the most severe of negative events, and because family members are socially contiguous, families would appear to be likely sources for point-clustered suicides. Apparently, however, they are not. This may be because of the protective action of social support. Social support is, in general, pervasive (indeed, the need to belong has been proposed as a fundamental human motive; Baumeister & Leary, 1995), and it is intensified for families in mourning. Increased social support thus may offset families' risk for additional suicides among family members.

## CONCLUSIONS

The evidence for mass clusters is weak or equivocal, whereas point clusters appear to occur. But clustering does not contagion make. By implication at least, suicide clusters often have been explained as analogous to miniepidemics of contagious illness. I have suggested, however, that a more apt analogy is disasters or industrial accidents, in which simultaneous exposure to some external, pernicious agent (e.g., radiation) is the mechanism of action, a mechanism that is particularly harmful to already vulnerable people. Point-clustered suicides may occur similarly: Contiguous people, if exposed to noxious stimuli (e.g., a severe negative life event, such as the suicide of a peer), and if vulnerable but unprotected (by social support), may simultaneously develop suicidal symptoms.

### Recommended Reading

Brent, D. A., Kerr, M. M., Goldstein, C., & Bozigar, J. (1989). (See References)
Gould, M. S., Wallenstein, S., & Davidson, L. (1989). (See References)

Kessler, R. C., Downey, G., Milavsky, J. R., & Stipp, H. (1988). (See References)

### Note

1. Address correspondence to Thomas Joiner, Department of Psychology, Florida State University, Tallahassee, FL 32306-1270; e-mail: joiner@psy.fsu.edu.

### References

Baumeister, R. F., & Leary, M. R. (1995). The need to belong: Desire for interpersonal attachments as a fundamental human motivation. *Psychological Bulletin, 117,* 497–529.

Berman, A. L. (1988). Fictional depiction of suicide in television films and imitation effects. *American Journal of Psychiatry, 145,* 982–986.

Brent, D. A., Kerr, M. M., Goldstein, C., & Bozigar, J. (1989). An outbreak of suicide and suicidal behavior in a high school. *Journal of the American Academy of Child & Adolescent Psychiatry, 28,* 918–924.

Chiu, L. P. (1988). Do weather, day of the week, and address affect the rate of attempted suicide in Hong Kong? *Social Psychiatry & Psychiatric Epidemiology, 23,* 229–235.

Gould, M. S., Wallenstein, S., & Davidson, L. (1989). Suicide clusters: A critical review. *Suicide & Life-Threatening Behavior, 19,* 17–29.

Haw, C. M. (1994). A cluster of suicides at a London psychiatric unit. *Suicide & Life-Threatening Behavior, 24,* 256–266.

Kessler, R. C., Downey, G., Milavsky, J. R., & Stipp, H. (1988). Clustering of teenage suicides after television news stories about suicides: A reconsideration. *American Journal of Psychiatry, 145,* 1379–1383.

Phillips, D. P., & Carstensen, L. L. (1986). Clustering of teenage suicides after television news stories about suicide. *New England Journal of Medicine, 315,* 685–689.

Phillips, D. P., & Carstensen, L. L. (1988). The effect of suicide stories on various demographic groups, 1968–1985. *Suicide & Life-Threatening Behavior, 18,* 100–114.

Phillips, D. P., & Paight, D. J. (1987). The impact of televised movies about suicide: A replicative study. *New England Journal of Medicine, 317,* 809–811.

Robbins, D., & Conroy, R. C. (1983). A cluster of adolescent suicide attempts: Is suicide contagious? *Journal of Adolescent Health Care, 3,* 253–255.

Schmidtke, A., & Haefner, H. (1988). The Werther effect after television films: New evidence for an old hypothesis. *Psychological Medicine, 18,* 665–676.

Simkin, S., Hawton, K., Whitehead, L., & Fagg, J. (1995). Media influence on parasuicide: A study of the effects of a television drama portrayal of paracetamol self-poisoning. *British Journal of Psychiatry, 167,* 754–759.

# THE DOUBTING DISEASE

## *When is obsession a sickness?*

**BY JEROME GROOPMAN**

On a snowy Sunday in winter, I attended a conference in Cambridge, Massachusetts. The participants included a wide variety of scientists: molecular biologists, organic chemists, computer programmers, virologists, clinical researchers, and statisticians. Afterward, a small group of us went to dinner at a local restaurant. During the meal, the conversation turned to schooling.

"I transferred my eight-year-old out of public school last year," a chemist told the group. "The teacher wouldn't accommodate him. My kid is like me. When he has a problem to solve, he attacks it until it's done perfectly. He completely blocks out the world and won't let go. The teacher insisted that he couldn't spend more than the allotted time on a task. When my son wouldn't stop, the teacher concluded that he had a behavior disorder."

This anecdote provoked a startlingly sympathetic response around the table: most of us, it turned out, identified with the chemist's son. A biologist known for deciphering, atom by atom, the three-dimensional structure of complex proteins declared, "I bet I qualify for what psychiatrists call obsessive-compulsive disorder. When I'm reviewing lab data, and especially when I'm

ready to send out a scientific paper, I keep thinking something is wrong. I become intensely anxious. I'll stay up all night reworking every graph and equation. I'm unable to get the thought out of my head that there's a mistake. Then I find myself checking other kinds of things. I'll go blocks away from the house and turn back to make sure the doors are locked, even though I know they are." He turned to the chemist. "I'm not sure what would have happened if I had had your son's teacher."

What did it mean, I wondered as I left the restaurant, that a group of prominent scientists showed at least some traits associated with a clinical disorder during periods of high anxiety? More and more American children are being diagnosed and medicated every year, and at younger and younger ages. If my colleagues and I were in school now, would we be considered abnormal?

Current estimates hold that more than two per cent of the United States population—nearly seven million people—have or have had obsessive-compulsive disorder (O.C.D.). The American Psychiatric Association classifies all known

mental disorders in its Diagnostic and Statistical Manual, or D.S.M. Obsessive-compulsive disorder, which usually manifests itself in adolescence, is characterized by recurrent, time-consuming obsessions or compulsions that are severe enough to cause marked distress or significant impairment. Furthermore, the person recognizes that his obsessions or compulsions are excessive or unreasonable. "Obsessions" are defined in the D.S.M. as persistent thoughts, impulses, or images that are experienced as intrusive, anxiety-producing, and inappropriate.

A person with such obsessions usually tries to ignore them, or to defuse them with some other thoughts or actions: this attempt defines a compulsion. You're obsessed with the thought that you didn't turn off the stove; you compulsively check to make sure it's off. (The French call O.C.D. "the doubting disease.") Other well-recognized compulsions are hand-washing, counting, or repeating special words. In its extreme form, people afflicted with O.C.D. are virtual prisoners of their compulsions—exhausted, ashamed, alienated from others. Certainly, nobody at the restaurant would have qualified for the diagnosis. Our obsessions tended to be temporary, and connected to a productive activity, like solving an equation. We may describe ourselves as "obsessive," but our obsessions don't control us.

Although there is little information about the biological roots of the disorder—some have speculated that it can follow strep infections—recent studies indicate that people with O.C.D. have distinctive neurological circuitry. These differences are most pronounced in the limbic lobe, the caudate nucleus, and the orbital frontal cortex, the areas of the brain which participate in anxiety and automatic responses. Sophisticated brain scans show that when a potentially distressing scenario is confronted by a person without O.C.D., the brain activity in these areas barely registers on the screen; in a person with O.C.D., however, there is an intense and prolonged firing of neurons, and the scans light up like a Christmas tree. The Cambridge conference left me wondering whether scientists and other driven, detail-oriented professionals could also have distinctive neurological circuitry. Or are these mildly obsessive-compulsive people more likely to be attracted to these fields?

The next day, I found myself taking another look at the familiar environment of my laboratory. In the lab—where many scientists spend ten to twelve hours each day, six to seven days a week—everything is tightly controlled. Tedious tasks demand absolute concentration, because a single error can wreck months of work. During our lab's weekly meeting, every detail of every experiment is intensely scrutinized and challenged as we search for those hidden, threatening mistakes. In this the natural habitat of the obsessive-compulsive?

Speaking with a score of fellow-scientists throughout the week, I elicited anecdote after anecdote of mildly obsessive-compulsive behavior. One researcher said that when she approaches the lab to prepare for a particularly important experiment, she counts to herself and taps the wall as she walks down the corridor. Another "prefers" prime numbers, and counts to three or to seven before analyzing a sequence of DNA. A third told me that, during the month before her grant proposals are due, she repeatedly returns home to check the stove in her apartment, even though she knows that it is turned off.

I also looked for survey studies on personality traits of scientists, or of children and adolescents who pursue careers in high technology. I searched for published articles in the National Library of Medicine, a repository of clinical literature; I checked listings of hundreds of popular books on Internet booksellers. Nothing specifically addressed the issue. I decided that it was time to seek professional help.

What is a disorder, anyway?" the psychologist Jane Holmes Bernstein asked me rhetorically, in an animated English accent. Holmes Bernstein is the director of the neuropsychology program at Boston's Children's Hospital, and she is an expert at behavioral assessments of children. Like most scientists, she has a healthy skepticism toward her own field: "I decided early in the game that I needed to be hit with the full battery of neuropsychiatric tests that I give to kids—that it wasn't fair unless I experienced them." One day, when she was testing a child who had been referred to her for certain learning difficulties at school, she realized that he tested exactly as she herself had. "I asked myself, 'Why am I on my side of the desk?' In my environment, I function at a high level, where it plays out adaptively."

Holmes Bernstein argues that personality and behaviors can't be considered separately from the particular worlds in which people live; for that reason, she de-emphasizes labels and focusses instead on the relationship between behavior and environment. "Many psychiatrists and psychologists fit kids into diagnostic boxes," she asserted. "This thinking begins in medical school. There is distinctive, intrinsic organic pathology, the patient put into a box labelled 'diabetes' or 'H.I.V.' But those boxes are not built for behavior, because behavior is influenced so strongly by its interaction with environment."

She suggested that O.C.D. is a response to excess arousal—arousal in this instance meaning a neurological response to environmental stimuli. "The O.C.D. neurological circuits in the limbic system are set higher for certain stimuli and can respond faster," Holmes Bernstein said. She pointed to recent studies at Indiana University which show that, under certain conditions, people with O.C.D. make associations between neutral as well as aversive stimuli more quickly than people without O.C.D.

Holmes Bernstein believes that both this high state of arousal and the anxiety it produces may have evolutionary roots. In a prehistoric environment, those with the ability to focus and lock onto stimuli—particularly onto threatening elements in the environment—could have been better suited to escape the dangers of predators and treacherous terrain. But only to a point. "An adaptive mechanism can always become non-adaptive," Holmes Bernstein said.

"This argument about the precise definition of O.C.D. is not just semantic, because it is the D.S.M. that dictates treatments," she went on. "Left to itself, the human animal accepts a wide range of behavior. O.C.D. becomes as much an issue of managing load in a high-stimulus environment as it is a specific neurological disorder."

After leaving Holmes Bernstein, I got in touch with Anthony Rao, a clinical psychologist who has a large community-based practice in child and adolescent psychology in the Boston area. Rao's specialty is behavioral therapy, and he regularly sees children like the chemist's son, who are brought by their parents or referred by teachers. He feels that he is constantly battling against misguided attempts to diagnose children and provide generic remedies. "There is too much pathologizing of people's behaviors," he said. "In the educational system, it's one size fits all. Teachers run to labels, like A.D.D."—attention-deficit disorder—"or O.C.D., and even tell parents their children need to start taking medication." Even among preschoolers, as a recent *Journal of the American Medical Association* study showed, there has been a sharp rise in the use of psychiatric medications, not only for A.D.D. but also for putative anxiety and depression.

What drives all this, Rao believes, is the free-floating anxiety that parents—often successful members of the middle and upper class—foist on their children. In the instability of today's global economy, they fear that any deviation from the norm may cripple their child's future. He also believes that the currently fashionable psychiatric model—the idea that the problem is "a chemical disease of the brain"—is overly simplistic and even dangerous. These days, psychiatrists primarily treat O.C.D. with selective serotonin re-uptake inhibitors, like Prozac and Luvox, which alleviate not only its symptoms but also the anxiety and depression that often accompany it. But Rao pointed out that no one knows precisely what the long-term effects of these drugs on children will be—"especially when they are given daily for years." This approach, he contends, is treating the brain as if it were a bad kidney, when it's a far more complex organ, one which modifies itself continually.

Rao was careful to stipulate that he does not categorically oppose medication. A child or an adolescent with O.C.D. who can't leave the house, or who can't sleep because he needs to repeatedly check under the bed, may greatly benefit from drugs.

The problem is with the larger universe of kids who are summarily labelled "abnormal" and medicated. In March, the White House expressed alarm at this trend, and the National Institute of Mental Health called for new studies to assess the safety and efficacy of psychoactive drug therapy for young children.

"It's a different world in psychiatry now, with managed care," Rao went on. "In order for a psychiatrist to get paid, he needs to give you a D.S.M. diagnosis." Rao described a scenario that he often hears from clients about visits to psychiatrists: "Do you have worries? Do you have compulsive acts? Do you realize they are bothersome? Yes, yes, yes. Then it's boom-boom-boom, here's a prescription. You have O.C.D." Rao believes that the D.S.M. label resonates in the child's mind and among family members and friends in pejorative and embarrassing ways. "Your brain is your soul," Rao said fiercely. "You're telling a kid that there is something wrong with who he fundamentally is."

Rao thinks that this excess pathologizing of people's problems is strongly driven by economics: beyond the imperatives of managed care, there is a burgeoning pharmaceutical industry that reaps huge profits from psychotropic medications. Researchers have obvious incentives to conduct drug trials that will encourage the Food and Drug Administration to approve a medication for a specific D.S.M.-defined disorder. Rao, on the other hand, attempts to temper his patients' anxieties and to redirect the compulsive behavior into more productive channels.

Rao told me about a recent case of a thirteen-year-old girl whom we'll call Jan, a gifted pianist and a straight-A student. During the past year, her performance at school had plummeted. When she began to exhibit obsessive-compulsive behavior, her parents took her to a psychiatrist, who prescribed O.C.D. medication. The drugs were of little benefit, and friends and teachers began to

treat her as though she were seriously disturbed.

The family came to Rao for a second opinion. He learned that she was haunted by thoughts of serious harm coming to her parents. To try to suppress these terrifying thoughts, she had developed a ritual of walking forward in precisely measured steps and then retracing these exact steps backward. She realized this was not rational, but she thought that walking backward would somehow undo the horrific visions of her parents in danger.

"I told her that we all have terrifying thoughts, and that it doesn't mean you are crazy," Rao said. "And I explained that her precision and analytical abilities had become diverted to these irrational interior thoughts. We worked to redirect this ability outward—back to music and to math."

The girl was weaned off medication and underwent behavioral therapy, focussing on the very thoughts that she found so disturbing. When her anxiety reached its apex, Rao coached her to wait a few moments before retreating to her ritual. This process was repeated, each time increasing the delay between the disturbing thoughts and the walking compulsion. Eventually, the debilitating cycle was broken. Now, when Jan feels anxious, she practices the technique that Rao taught her. Her school work is again outstanding, and she continues to play the piano. Some studies show that such behavioral therapy can be as effective as medication in overcoming obsessions and compulsions.

On the other hand, Rao pointed out, distress is an unavoidable dimension of human experience. "Struggle over suffering and pain is necessary for development," he said. "If you ignore this, or try to medicate it away, then a person doesn't develop skills to deal with life."

In order to better understand a different point of view, I sought out Dr. Joseph Biederman in his office at the Massachusetts General Hospital. He is a professor of psychiatry at Harvard and chief of the joint program in pediatric psychopharmacology at Massachusetts General and McLean Hospital.

Biederman rejects the contention of behavioral psychologists like Anthony Rao that children and adolescents are overdiagnosed because of the exigencies of H.M.O.s or the incentives of drug companies. Nor does he think that overzealous teachers are to blame. "The schools are not failing when they insist that a child cannot endlessly obsess over some task," he said. "That's the response of a classically narcissistic parent—the child is an extension of himself, and it's the environment that must change."

Biederman also finds this response to O.C.D. naïve. "These are disruptions of normal brain functions—the diseased limbic loops are organic, not philosophical. It's a pathological state." It was not to be confused with, say, the behavior of a basketball player who mumbles things to himself before a free throw, or a pitcher who wears a special undershirt on the mound. "That's primitive, magical thinking that doesn't really interfere with functioning." Biederman illustrated his point by likening O.C.D. to high blood pressure or high cholesterol: there are well-defined limits beyond which disease occurs.

"As a doctor, you see a patient with high cholesterol, and you tell him to lose weight, exercise, restrict his fat intake. Rarely can anyone do this," he said. So a doctor will prescribe medication. "Do you want to walk from Boston to New York City, or take a plane? Behavioral therapy is the most laborious form of treatment—it's walking. Medication gets you there quickly." He went on, "What we need is a screwdriver for the brain, in order to fine-tune the lim-

bic circuit just enough so that it works efficiently and doesn't get stuck."

But isn't that measurement of efficiency a highly subjective one? "Even minor illness deserves aggressive treatment," Dr. Biederman replied. "Treat early, at the first sign, when a person is still functional. Those early indicators are what I call kindling—you want to intervene when the fire is just beginning, not let it spread." After all, what he and the psychologists had in common, he said, was the goal of alleviating pain. "These people with O.C.D. are suffering, experiencing distress, in a state of hyperarousal. Without drugs, they can't enjoy life."

I also spoke to Dr. Judith Rapoport, the chief of child psychiatry at the National Institute of Mental Health, in Bethesda, Maryland. Dr. Rapoport, who helped bring O.C.D. to the public's attention eleven years ago with her book "The Boy Who Couldn't Stop Washing," emphasized that exact terms should be used in any discussion of the disorder. "I see the kids whose lives are wrecked by intrusive thoughts and uncontrolled compulsions," she said. "The D.S.M. criteria are carefully constructed around degree of function.

"Your scientist friends are not the kind of people referred to me," Rapoport went on. She believes that these scientists more closely resemble an alternative D.S.M. diagnosis, obsessive-compulsive personality disorder (O.C.P.D.). The D.S.M. criteria here emphasize excessive devotion to work and perfectionism. A person with O.C.P.D. relentlessly engages in work, to the exclusion of social pleasures.

Other experts in the field believe that the lines are more difficult to draw. Dr. John Ratey and Catherine Johnson, in their 1997 book,

"Shadow Syndromes," argue that many obsessive people do not clearly fit D.S.M. criteria for O.C.D. or O.C.P.D. Further, of all the shadow syndromes, "mild obsessive-compulsive disorder is perhaps the one constellation of mood and thought society cannot do without." What links the compulsions is the fear of shame upon failing in public—the scientist who emerges from his laboratory to present his data, the pianist at each recital in the concert hall. "This is the intersection of shadow syndrome and normalcy," Ratey and Johnson argue. "Obsession can drive ambition—and when it does, obsession becomes a useful quality to possess."

Late one evening, I called Laurence Lasky, a nationally renowned molecular biologist, to discuss my findings with him. I was not surprised to find that he was still in his lab at Genentech, a biotechnology company in the Bay Area. Lasky agreed that laboratory researchers, himself included, exhibit traits that are distributed toward the far end of the bell-shaped curve of obsessions and compulsions. "As an adolescent, I had this compulsive habit of tapping and drumming on tables, walls, my books," he told me. "It drove my mother crazy. I needed to do it to burn off my anxiety. As I grew older, it went away." Lasky still lives with anxiety, but he said that there is a huge payoff from all this tension.

"There is nothing like making a discovery—the feeling of seeing something in the laboratory for the first time," Lasky said. "But no good scientist I know is ever completely satisfied. What does a Nobel laureate do when he wins? He tries to win again. If you're not first, and you're not right, you're nowhere." I asked Lasky if he would want to be medicated for his anxiety. Absolutely not, he replied. "Who says advancing science has anything to do with being happy?"

# Unit 11

## Unit Selections

## Key Points to Consider

❖ What varieties of psychotherapy are available? Does psychotherapy work? Are laypersons effective therapists? Is professional assistance for psychological problems always necessary? Can people successfully change themselves? When is professional help needed? What can be changed successfully? What problems seem immune to change?

❖ Is mental disorder widespread in the United States? What can be done to promote mental health? What can be done to assist those with mental disorders?

❖ How can you "think like a shrink"? What "rules of thumb" do psychologists use for determining a client's mental health status? How can you utilize these rules? Can you think of other rules that are not included in the article "Think Like a Shrink"?

❖ What types of medications are now available for use by people with psychological disorders? Do you think these and other drugs make our society too drug-dependent? What would you prefer, psychotherapy or medication? How is psychopharmacologic research conducted? What are the criticisms of such research?

❖ How does clinical depression differ from the everyday blues we sometimes experience? What are some of the treatments for severe depression? What is Prozac? How does Prozac work? What are some of its side effects and disadvantages? If you were a psychiatrist, would your first line of treatment for depression be Prozac? Why or why not?

❖ What is schizophrenia? Why is schizophrenia hard to treat? Do you think schizophrenia is a brain disorder, as some claim? What are some of the older treatments for schizophrenia? How can we reverse our trend of treating schizophrenia and instead focus on patients' recovery? Why would we want to focus on recovery? What role do patients' rights play in the recovery process?

 **Links** **www.dushkin.com/online/**

These sites are annotated on pages 4 and 5.

Have you ever had the nightmare that you are trapped in a dark, dismal place? No one will let you out. Your pleas for freedom go unanswered and, in fact, are suppressed or ignored by domineering authority figures around you. You keep begging for mercy but to no avail. What a nightmare! You are fortunate to awake in your normal bedroom and to the realities of your daily life. For the mentally ill, the nightmare of institutionalization, where individuals can be held against their will in what are sometimes terribly dreary, restrictive surroundings, is a reality. Have you ever wondered what would happen if we took perfectly normal individuals and institutionalized them? In one well-known and remarkable study, that is exactly what happened.

In 1973, eight people, including a pediatrician, a psychiatrist and some psychologists, presented themselves to psychiatric hospitals. Each claimed that he or she was hearing voices. The voices, they reported, seemed unclear but appeared to be saying "empty" or "thud." Each of these individuals was admitted to a mental hospital, and most were diagnosed as being schizophrenic. Upon admission, the fake patients gave truthful information and thereafter acted like their usual, normal selves.

Their hospital stays lasted anywhere from 7 to 52 days. The nurses, doctors, psychologists, and other staff members treated them as if they really were schizophrenic and never saw through their trickery. Some of the real patients in the hospital did recognize, however, that the pseudopatients were perfectly normal. Upon discharge almost all of the pseudopatients received the diagnosis of "schizophrenic in remission," meaning that they were still clearly construed as schizophrenic; they just were not exhibiting any of the symptoms at the time.

What does this study demonstrate about mental illness? Is true mental illness readily detectable? If we can't always detect mental disorders, the more professionally accepted term for mental illness, how can we treat them? What treatments are available and which work better for various diagnoses? The treatment of mental disorders is a challenge. The array of available treatments is ever increasing and can be downright bewildering—and not just to the patient or client! In order to demystify and simplify your understanding of various treatments, we will look at them in this unit.

We commence with two general articles on treatment. In the first, renowned psychologist Martin Seligman discusses what we can hope to accomplish if we attempt reform. Some individuals have successfully shed weight, overcome anxiety and phobias, or quit smoking either by themselves or with professional assistance. Seligman takes a realistic look at what can and cannot be successfully changed in "What You Can Change and What You Cannot Change."

In the next article, "Think Like a Shrink," Emanuel Rosen reviews the criteria psychologists utilize to determine the mental health status of an individual. The main point is that we, too, can use these same guidelines to determine the mental health standing of others and ourselves. Rosen also reveals how psychotherapy seems to function, by reducing defensiveness.

Depression afflicts many of us. Some individuals suffer from chronic and intense depression, known as clinical depression. The third article, "The Quest for a Cure," not only details the symptoms of depression but also provides a good discussion of the possible treatments for severe depression. In particular, the revolutionary drug, Prozac, is showcased.

The final article of this unit and of the book investigates treatments for schizophrenia. Schizophrenia is a psychosis that causes more profound disturbance than the disorders discussed previously. In this article, old treatment methods are criticized, and Patrick McGuire claims that a newer and better method would be to focus on recovery rather than on treatment. With recovery, schizophrenics can lead more fulfilling lives. The importance of patients' rights in their own recovery cannot be underestimated.

# What You Can Change & What You Cannot Change

**There are things we can change about ourselves and things we cannot. Concentrate your energy on what is possible—too much time has been wasted.**

## Martin E. P. Seligman, Ph.D.

This is the age of psychotherapy and the age of self-improvement. Millions are struggling to change: We diet, we jog, we meditate. We adopt new modes of thought to counteract our depressions. We practice relaxation to curtail stress. We exercise to expand our memory and to quadruple our reading speed. We adopt draconian regimens to give up smoking. We raise our little boys and girls to androgyny. We come out of the closet and we try to become heterosexual. We seek to lose our taste for alcohol. We seek more meaning in life. We try to extend our life span.

Sometimes it works. But distressingly often, self-improvement and psychotherapy fail. The cost is enormous. We think we are worthless. We feel guilty and ashamed. We believe we have no willpower and that we are failures. We give up trying to change.

On the other hand, this is not only the age of self-improvement and therapy, but also the age of biological psychiatry. The human genome will be nearly mapped be-fore the millennium is over. The brain systems underlying sex, hearing, memory, left-handedness, and sadness are now known. Psychoactive drugs quiet our fears, relieve our blues, bring us bliss, dampen our mania, and dissolve our delusions more effectively than we can on our own.

Our very personality—our intelligence and musical talent, even our religiousness, our conscience (or its absence), our politics, and our exuberance—turns out to be more the product of our genes than almost anyone would have believed a decade ago. The underlying message of the age of biological psychiatry is that our biology frequently makes changing, in spite of all our efforts, impossible.

But the view that all is genetic and biochemical and therefore unchangeable is also very often wrong. Many people surpass their IQs, fail to "respond" to drugs, make sweeping changes in their lives, live on when their cancer is "terminal," or defy the hormones and brain circuitry that "dictate" lust, femininity, or memory loss.

The ideologies of biological psychiatry and self-improvement are obviously colliding. Nevertheless, a resolution is apparent. There are some things about ourselves that can be changed, others that cannot, and some that can be changed only with extreme difficulty.

What can we succeed in changing about ourselves? What can we not? When can we overcome our biology? And when is our biology our destiny?

I want to provide an understanding of what you can and what you can't change about yourself so that you can concentrate your limited time and energy on what is possible. So much time has been wasted. So much needless frustration has been endured. So much of therapy, so much of child rearing, so much of self-improving, and even some of the great social movements in our century have come to nothing because they tried to change the unchangeable. Too often we have wrongly thought we were weak-willed failures, when the changes we wanted to make in ourselves

From *Psychology Today*, May/June 1994, pp. 34–41, 70, 72–74, 84. Excerpted from *What You Can Change and What You Can't* by Martin E. P. Seligman. © 1993 by Martin E. P. Seligman. Reprinted by permission of Alfred A. Knopf, Inc.

## So much child rearing, therapy, and self-improvement have come to nothing.

were just not possible. But all this effort was necessary: Because there have been so many failures, we are now able to see the boundaries of the unchangeable; this in turn allows us to see clearly for the first time the boundaries of what *is* changeable.

With this knowledge, we can use our precious time to make the many rewarding changes that are possible. We can live with less self-reproach and less remorse. We can live with greater confidence. This knowledge is a new understanding of who we are and where we are going.

### CATASTROPHIC THINKING: PANIC

S. J. Rachman, one of the world's leading clinical researchers and one of the founders of behavior therapy, was on the phone. He was proposing that I be the "discussant" at a conference about panic disorder sponsored by the National Institute of Mental Health (NIMH).

"Why even bother, Jack?" I responded. "Everyone knows that panic is biological and that the only thing that works is drugs."

"Don't refuse so quickly, Marty. There is a breakthrough you haven't yet heard about."

Breakthrough was a word I had never heard Jack use before.

"What's the breakthrough?" I asked.

"If you come, you can find out."

So I went.

I had known about and seen panic patients for many years, and had read the literature with mounting excitement during the 1980s. I knew that panic disorder is a frightening condition that consists of recurrent attacks, each much worse than anything experienced before. Without prior warning, you feel as if you are going to die. Here is a typical case history:

*The first time Celia had a panic attack, she was working at McDonald's. It was two days before her 20th birthday. As she was handing a customer a Big Mac, she had the worst experience of her life. The earth seemed to open up beneath her. Her heart began to pound, she felt she was smothering, and she was sure she was going to have a heart attack and die. After about 20 minutes of terror, the panic subsided. Trembling, she got in her car, raced home and barely left the house for the next three months.*

*Since then, Celia has had about three attacks a month. She does not know when they are coming. She always thinks she is going to die.*

Panic attacks are not subtle, and you need no quiz to find out if you or someone you love has them. As many as five percent of American adults probably do. The defining feature of the disorder is simple: recurrent awful attacks of panic that come out of the blue, last for a few minutes, and then subside. The attacks consist of chest pains, sweating, nausea, dizziness, choking, smothering, or trembling. They are accompanied by feelings of overwhelming dread and thoughts that you are having a heart attack, that you are losing control, or that you are going crazy.

### THE BIOLOGY OF PANIC

There are four questions that bear on whether a mental problem is primarily "biological" as opposed to "psychological":

- Can it be induced biologically?
- Is it genetically heritable?
- Are specific brain functions involved?
- Does a drug relieve it?

*Inducing panic.* Panic attacks can be created by a biological agent. For example, patients who have a history of panic attacks are hooked up to an intravenous line. Sodium lactate, a chemical that normally produces rapid, shallow breathing and heart palpitations, is slowly infused into their bloodstream. Within a few minutes, about 60 to 90 percent of these patients have a panic attack. Normal controls—subjects with no history of panic—rarely have attacks when infused with lactate.

*Genetics of panic.* There may be some heritability of panic. If one of two identical twins has panic attacks, 31 percent of the cotwins also have them. But if one of two fraternal twins has panic attacks, none of the cotwins are so afflicted.

*Panic and the brain.* The brains of people with panic disorders look somewhat unusual upon close scrutiny. Their neurochemistry shows abnormalities in the system that turns on, then dampens, fear. In addition, the PET scan (positron-emission tomography), a technique that looks at how much blood and oxygen different parts of the brain use, shows that patients who panic from the infusion of lactate have

## We are now able to see the boundaries of the unchangeable.

### What Can We Change?

When we survey all the problems, personality types, patterns of behavior, and the weak influence of childhood on adult life, we see a puzzling array of how much change occurs. From the things that are easiest to those that are the most difficult, this rough array emerges:

| Panic | Curable |
|---|---|
| Specific Phobias | Almost Curable |
| Sexual Dysfunctions | Marked Relief |
| Social Phobia | Moderate Relief |
| Agoraphobia | Moderate Relief |
| Depression | Moderate Relief |
| Sex Role Change | Moderate Relief |
| Obsessive-Compulsive Disorder | Moderate Mild Relief |
| Sexual Preferences | Moderate Mild Change |
| Anger | Mild Moderate Relief |
| Everyday Anxiety | Mild Moderate Relief |
| Alcoholism | Mild Relief |
| Overweight | Temporary Change |
| Posttraumatic Stress Disorder (PTSD) | Marginal Relief |
| Sexual Orientation | Probably Unchangeable |
| Sexual Identity | Unchangeable |

higher blood flow and oxygen use in relevant parts of their brain than patients who don't panic.

*Drugs.* Two kinds of drugs relieve panic: tricyclic antidepressants and the anti-anxiety drug Xanax, and both work better than placebos. Panic attacks are dampened, and sometimes even eliminated. General anxiety and depression also decrease.

Since these four questions had already been answered "yes" when Jack Rachman called, I thought the issue had already been settled. Panic disorder was simply a biological illness, a disease of the body that could be relieved only by drugs.

A few months later I was in Bethesda, Maryland, listening once again to the same four lines of biological evidence. An inconspicuous figure in a brown suit sat hunched over the table. At the first break, Jack introduced me to him—David Clark, a young psychologist from Oxford. Soon after, Clark began his address.

"Consider, if you will, an alternative theory, a cognitive theory." He reminded all of us that almost all panickers believe that they are going to die during an attack. Most commonly, they believe that they are having heart attacks. Perhaps, Clark suggested, this is more than just a mere symptom. Perhaps it is the root cause. Panic may simply be the *catastrophic misinterpretation of bodily sensations*.

For example, when you panic, your heart starts to race. You notice this, and you see it as a possible heart attack. This makes you very anxious, which means that your heart pounds more. You now notice that your heart is *really* pounding. You are now *sure* it's a heart attack. This terrifies you, and you break into a sweat, feel nauseated, short of breath—all symptoms of terror, but for you, they're confirmation of a heart attack. A full-blown panic attack is under way, and at the root of it is your misinterpretation of the symptoms of anxiety as symptoms of impending death.

I was listening closely now as Clark argued that an obvious sign of a disorder, easily dismissed as a symptom, is the disorder itself. If he was right, this was a historic occasion. All Clark had done so far, however, was to show that the four lines of evidence for a biological view of panic could fit equally well with a misinterpretation view. But Clark soon told us about a series of experiments he and his colleague Paul Salkovskis had done at Oxford.

First, they compared panic patients with patients who had other anxiety disorders and with normals. All the subjects read the following sentences aloud, but the last word was presented blurred. For example:

*dying*
If I had palpitations, I could be
*excited*

*choking*
If I were breathless, I could be
*unfit*

When the sentences were about bodily sensations, the panic patients, but no one else, saw the catastrophic endings fastest. This showed that panic patients possess the habit of thinking Clark had postulated.

Next, Clark and his colleagues asked if activating this habit with words would induce panic. All the subjects read a series of word pairs aloud. When panic patients

## Self-Analysis Questionnaire

**Is your life dominated by anxiety? Read each statement and then mark the appropriate number to indicate how you generally feel. There are no right or wrong answers.**

1. I am a steady person.

| Almost never | Sometimes | Often | Almost always |
|---|---|---|---|
| 4 | 3 | 2 | 1 |

2. I am satisfied with myself.

| Almost never | Sometimes | Often | Almost always |
|---|---|---|---|
| 4 | 3 | 2 | 1 |

3. I feel nervous and restless.

| Almost never | Sometimes | Often | Almost always |
|---|---|---|---|
| 1 | 2 | 3 | 4 |

4. I wish I could be as happy as others seem to be.

| Almost never | Sometimes | Often | Almost always |
|---|---|---|---|
| 1 | 2 | 3 | 4 |

5. I feel like a failure.

| Almost never | Sometimes | Often | Almost always |
|---|---|---|---|
| 1 | 2 | 3 | 4 |

6. I get in a state of tension and turmoil as I think over my recent concerns and interests.

| Almost never | Sometimes | Often | Almost always |
|---|---|---|---|
| 1 | 2 | 3 | 4 |

7. I feel secure.

| Almost never | Sometimes | Often | Almost always |
|---|---|---|---|
| 4 | 3 | 2 | 1 |

8. I have self-confidence.

| Almost never | Sometimes | Often | Almost always |
|---|---|---|---|
| 4 | 3 | 2 | 1 |

9. I feel inadequate.

| Almost never | Sometimes | Often | Almost always |
|---|---|---|---|
| 1 | 2 | 3 | 4 |

10. I worry too much over something that does not matter.

| Almost never | Sometimes | Often | Almost always |
|---|---|---|---|
| 1 | 2 | 3 | 4 |

**To score, simply add up the numbers under your answers. Notice that some of the rows of numbers go up and others go down. The higher your total, the more the trait of anxiety dominates your life. If your score was:**

10–11, you are in the lowest 10 percent of anxiety.

13–14, you are in the lowest quarter.

16–17, your anxiety level is about average.

19–20, your anxiety level is around the 75th percentile.

22–24 (and you are male) your anxiety level is around the 90th percentile.

24–26 (and you are female) your anxiety level is around the 90th percentile.

25 (and you are male) your anxiety level is at the 95th percentile.

27 (and you are female) your anxiety level is at the 95th percentile.

Should you try to change your anxiety level? Here are my rules of thumb:

- If your score is at the 90th percentile or above, you can probably improve the quality of your life by lowering your general anxiety level—regardless of paralysis and irrationality.
- If your score is at the 75th percentile or above, and you feel that anxiety is either paralyzing you or that it is unfounded, you should probably try to lower your general anxiety level.
- If your score is 18 or above, and you feel that anxiety is unfounded and paralyzing, you should probably try to lower your general anxiety level.

got to "breathlessness-suffocation" and "palpitations-dying," 75 percent suffered a full-blown panic attack right there in the laboratory. No normal people had panic attacks, no recovered panic patients (I'll tell you more in a moment about how they got better) had attacks, and only 17 percent of other anxious patients had attacks.

The final thing Clark told us was the "breakthrough" that Rachman had promised.

---

## Issues of the soul can barely be changed by psychotherapy or drugs.

---

"We have developed and tested a rather novel therapy for panic," Clark continued in his understated, disarming way. He explained that if catastrophic misinterpretations of bodily sensation are the cause of a panic attack, then changing the tendency to misinterpret should cure the disorder. His new therapy was straightforward and brief:

Patients are told that panic results when they mistake normal symptoms of mounting anxiety for symptoms of heart attack, going crazy, or dying. Anxiety itself, they are informed, produces shortness of breath, chest pain, and sweating. Once they misinterpret these normal bodily sensations as an imminent heart attack, their symptoms become even more pronounced because the misinterpretation changes their anxiety into terror. A vicious circle culminates in a full-blown panic attack.

Patients are taught to reinterpret the symptoms realistically as mere anxiety symptoms. Then they are given practice right in the office, breathing rapidly into a paper bag. This causes a buildup of carbon dioxide and shortness of breath, mimicking the sensations that provoke a panic attack. The therapist points out that the symptoms the patient is experiencing—shortness of breath and heart racing—are harmless, simply the result of overbreathing, not a sign of a heart attack. The patient learns to interpret the symptoms correctly.

"This simple therapy appears to be a cure," Clark told us. "Ninety to 100 percent of the patients are panic free at the end of therapy. One year later, only one person had had another panic attack."

This, indeed, was a breakthrough: a simple, brief psychotherapy with no side effects showing a 90-percent cure rate of a disorder that a decade ago was thought to be incurable. In a controlled study of 64 patients comparing cognitive therapy to drugs to relaxation to no treatment, Clark and his colleagues found that cognitive therapy is markedly better than drugs or relaxation, both of which are better than nothing. Such a high cure rate is unprecedented.

How does cognitive therapy for panic compare with drugs? It is more effective and less dangerous. Both the antidepressants and Xanax produce marked reduction in panic in most patients, but drugs must be taken forever; once the drug is stopped, panic rebounds to where it was before therapy began for perhaps half the patients. The drugs also sometimes have severe side effects, including drowsiness, lethargy, pregnancy complications, and addictions.

After this bombshell, my own "discussion" was an anticlimax. I did make one point that Clark took to heart. "Creating a cognitive therapy that works, even one that works as well as this apparently does, is not enough to show that the *cause* of panic is cognitive." I was niggling. "The biological theory doesn't deny that some other therapy might work well on panic. It merely claims that panic is caused at the bottom by some biochemical problem."

---

## Anxiety scans your life for imperfections. When it finds one, it won't let go.

---

Two years later, Clark carried out a crucial experiment that tested the biological theory against the cognitive theory. He gave the usual lactate infusion to 10 panic patients, and nine of them panicked. He did the same thing with another 10 patients, but added special instructions to allay the misinterpretation of the sensations. He simply told them: "Lactate is a natural bodily substance that produces sensations similar to exercise or alcohol. It is normal to experience intense sensations during infusion, but these do not indicate an adverse reaction." Only three out of the 10 panicked. This confirmed the theory crucially.

The therapy works very well, as it did for Celia, whose story has a happy ending. She first tried Xanax, which reduced the intensity and the frequency of her panic attacks. But she was too drowsy to work and she was still having about one attack every six weeks. She was then referred to Audrey, a cognitive therapist who explained that Celia was misinterpreting her heart racing and shortness of breath as symptoms of a heart attack, that they were actually just symptoms of mounting anxiety, nothing more harmful. Audrey taught Celia progressive relaxation, and then she demonstrated the harmlessness of Celia's symptoms of overbreathing. Celia then relaxed in the presence of the symptoms and found that they gradually subsided. After several more practice sessions, therapy terminated. Celia has gone two years without another panic attack.

### EVERYDAY ANXIETY

Attend to your tongue—right now. What is it doing? Mine is swishing around near my lower right molars. It has just found a minute fragment of last night's popcorn (debris from *Terminator 2*). Like a dog at a bone, it is worrying the firmly wedged flake.

Attend to your hand—right now. What's it up to? My left hand is boring in on an itch it discovered under my earlobe.

Your tongue and your hands have, for the most part, a life of their own. You can bring them under voluntary control by consciously calling them out of their "default" mode to carry out your commands: "Pick up the phone" or "Stop picking that pimple." But most of the time they are on their own. They are seeking out small imperfections. They scan your entire mouth and skin surface, probing for anything going wrong. They are marvelous, nonstop grooming devices. They, not the more fashionable immune system, are your first line of defense against invaders.

Anxiety is your mental tongue. Its default mode is to search for what may be about to go wrong. It continually, and without your conscious consent, scans your life—yes, even when you are asleep, in dreams and nightmares. It reviews your work, your love, your play—until it finds an imperfection. When it finds one, it worries it. It tries to pull it out from its hiding place, where it is wedged inconspicuously under some rock. It will not let go. If the imperfection is threatening enough, anxiety calls your attention to it by making you uncomfortable. If you do not act, it yells more insistently—disturbing your sleep and your appetite.

You can reduce daily, mild anxiety. You can numb it with alcohol, Valium, or marijuana. You can take the edge off with meditation or progressive relaxation. You can beat it down by becoming more conscious of the automatic thoughts of danger that trigger anxiety and then disputing them effectively.

But do not overlook what your anxiety is trying to do for you. In return for the pain it brings, it prevents larger ordeals by making you aware of their possibility and goading you into planning for and forestalling them. It may even help you avoid them altogether. Think of your anxiety as the "low oil" light flashing on the dashboard of your car. Disconnect it and you will be less distracted and more comfortable for a while. But this may cost you a burned-up engine. Our *dysphoria*, or bad feeling, should, some of the time, be tolerated, attended to, even cherished.

## GUIDELINES FOR WHEN TO TRY TO CHANGE ANXIETY

Some of our everyday anxiety, depression, and anger go beyond their useful function. Most adaptive traits fall along a normal spectrum of distribution, and the capacity for internal bad weather for everyone some of the time means that some of us may have terrible weather all of the time. In general, when the hurt is pointless and recurrent—when, for example, anxiety insists we formulate a plan but no plan will work—it is time to take action to relieve the hurt. There are three hallmarks indicating that anxiety has become a burden that wants relieving:

First, is it *irrational*?

We must calibrate our bad weather inside against the real weather outside. Is what you are anxious about out of proportion to the reality of the danger? Here are some examples that may help you answer this question. All of the following are not irrational:

- A fire fighter trying to smother a raging oil well burning in Kuwait repeatedly wakes up at four in the morning because of flaming terror dreams.
- A mother of three smells perfume on her husband's shirts and, consumed by jealousy, broods about his infidelity, reviewing the list of possible women over and over.
- A student who had failed two of his midterm exams finds, as finals approach, that he can't get to sleep for worrying. He has diarrhea most of the time.

The only good thing that can be said about such fears is that they are well-founded.

In contrast, all of the following are irrational, out of proportion to the danger:

- An elderly man, having been in a fender bender, broods about travel and will no longer take cars, trains, or airplanes.
- An eight-year-old child, his parents having been through an ugly divorce, wets his bed at night. He is haunted with visions of his bedroom ceiling collapsing on him.
- A housewife who has an MBA and who accumulated a decade of experience as a financial vice president before her twins were born is sure her job search

will be fruitless. She delays preparing her résumés for a month.

The second hallmark of anxiety out of control is *paralysis*. Anxiety intends action: Plan, rehearse, look into shadows for lurking dangers, change your life. When anxiety becomes strong, it is unproductive; no problem-solving occurs. And when anxiety is extreme, it paralyzes you. Has your anxiety crossed this line? Some examples:

- A woman finds herself housebound because she fears that if she goes out, she will be bitten by a cat.
- A salesman broods about the next customer hanging up on him and makes no more cold calls.
- A writer, afraid of the next rejection slip, stops writing.

---

'Dieting below your natural weight is a necessary condition for bulimia. Returning to your natural weight will cure it.'

---

The final hallmark is *intensity*. Is your life dominated by anxiety? Dr. Charles Spielberger, one of the world's foremost testers of emotion, has developed well-validated scales for calibrating how severe anxiety is. To find out how anxious *you* are, use the self-analysis questionnaire.

## LOWERING YOUR EVERYDAY ANXIETY

Everyday anxiety level is not a category to which psychologists have devoted a great deal of attention. Enough research has been done, however, for me to recommend two techniques that quite reliably lower everyday anxiety levels. Both techniques are cumulative, rather than one-shot fixes. They require 20 to 40 minutes a day of your valuable time.

The first is *progressive relaxation*, done once or, better, twice a day for at least 10 minutes. In this technique, you tighten and then turn off each of the major muscle groups of your body until you are wholly flaccid. It is not easy to be highly anxious when your body feels like Jell-O. More formally, relaxation engages a response system that competes with anxious arousal.

The second technique is regular *meditation*. Transcendental meditation ™ is one

useful, widely available version of this. You can ignore the cosmology in which it is packaged if you wish, and treat it simply as the beneficial technique it is. Twice a day for 20 minutes, in a quiet setting, you close your eyes and repeat a *mantra* (a syllable whose "sonic properties are known") to yourself. Meditation works by blocking thoughts that produce anxiety. It complements relaxation, which blocks the motor components of anxiety but leaves the anxious thoughts untouched.

Done regularly, meditation usually induces a peaceful state of mind. Anxiety at other times of the day wanes, and hyperarousal from bad events is dampened. Done religiously, TM probably works better than relaxation alone.

There's also a quick fix. The minor tranquilizers—Valium, Dalmane, Librium, and their cousins—relieve everyday anxiety. So does alcohol. The advantage of all these is that they work within minutes and require no discipline to use. Their disadvantages outweigh their advantages, however. The minor tranquilizers make you fuzzy and somewhat uncoordinated as they work (a not uncommon side effect is an automobile accident). Tranquilizers soon lose their effect when taken regularly, and they are habit-forming—probably addictive. Alcohol, in addition, produces gross cognitive and motor disability in lockstep with its anxiety relief. Taken regularly over long periods, deadly damage to liver and brain ensue.

If you crave quick and temporary relief from acute anxiety, either alcohol or minor tranquilizers, taken in small amounts and only occasionally, will do the job. They are, however, a distant second-best to progressive relaxation and meditation, which are each worth trying before you seek out psychotherapy or in conjunction with therapy. Unlike tranquilizers and alcohol, neither of these techniques is likely to do you any harm.

Weigh your everyday anxiety. If it is not intense, or if it is moderate and not irrational or paralyzing, act now to reduce it. In spite of its deep evolutionary roots, intense everyday anxiety is often changeable. Meditation and progressive relaxation practiced regularly can change it forever.

## DIETING: A WAIST IS A TERRIBLE THING TO MIND

I have been watching my weight and restricting my intake—except for an occasional binge like this—since I was 20. I weighed about 175 pounds then, maybe 15 pounds over my official "ideal" weight. I weigh 199 pounds now, 30 years later, about 25 pounds over the ideal. I have tried about a dozen regimes—fasting, the Beverly Hills Diet, no carbohydrates, Metrecal for lunch, 1,200 calories a day, low fat, no lunch, no starches, skipping every other dinner. I lost 10 or 15 pounds on each in about a month. The pounds always came back, though, and I have gained a net of about a pound a year—inexorably.

This is the most consistent failure in my life. It's also a failure I can't just put out of mind. I have spent the last few years reading the scientific literature, not the parade of best-selling diet books or the flood of women's magazine articles on the latest way to slim down. The scientific findings look clear to me, but there is not yet a consensus. I am going to go out on a limb, because I see so many signs all pointing in one direction. What I have concluded will, I believe, soon be the consensus of the scientists. The conclusions surprise me. They will probably surprise you, too, and they may change your life.

Here is what the picture looks like to me:

- Dieting doesn't work.
- Dieting may make overweight worse, not better.
- Dieting may be bad for health.
- Dieting may cause eating disorders—including bulimia and anorexia.

## ARE YOU OVERWEIGHT?

Are you above the ideal weight for your sex, height, and age? If so, you are "overweight." What does this really mean? Ideal weight is arrived at simply. Four million people, now dead, who were insured by the major American life-insurance companies, were once weighed and had their height measured. At what weight on average do people of a given height turn out to live longest? That weight is called ideal. Anything wrong with that?

You bet. The real use of a weight table, and the reason your doctor takes it seriously, is that an ideal weight implies that, on average, if you slim down to yours, you will live longer. This is the crucial claim. Lighter people indeed live longer, on average, than heavier people, but how much longer is hotly debated.

But the crucial claim is unsound because weight (at any given height) has a normal distribution, *normal* both in a statistical sense and in the biological sense. In the biological sense, couch potatoes who overeat and never exercise can legitimately be called overweight, but the buxom, "heavy-boned" slow people deemed overweight by the ideal table are at their natural and healthiest weight. If you are a 155-pound woman and 64 inches in height, for example, you are "overweight" by around 15 pounds. This means nothing more than that the average 140-pound, 64-inch-tall woman lives somewhat longer than the average 155-pound woman of your height. It

does not follow that if you slim down to 125 pounds, *you* will stand any better chance of living longer.

In spite of the insouciance with which dieting advice is dispensed, no one has properly investigated the question of whether slimming down to "ideal" weight produces longer life. The proper study would compare the longevity of people who are at their ideal weight without dieting to people who achieve their ideal weight by dieting. Without this study the common medical advice to diet down to your ideal weight is simply unfounded.

This is not a quibble; there is evidence that dieting damages your health and that this damage may shorten your life.

## MYTHS OF OVERWEIGHT

The advice to diet down to your ideal weight to live longer is one myth of overweight. Here are some others:

- *Overweight people overeat.* Wrong. Nineteen out of 20 studies show that obese people consume no more calories each day than nonobese people. Telling a fat person that if she would change her eating habits and eat "normally" she would lose weight is a lie. To lose weight and stay there, she will need to eat excruciatingly less than a normal person, probably for the rest of her life.
- *Overweight people have an overweight personality.* Wrong. Extensive research on personality and fatness has proved little. Obese people do not differ in any major personality style from nonobese people.
- *Physical inactivity is a major cause of obesity.* Probably not. Fat people are indeed less active than thin people, but the inactivity is probably caused more by the fatness than the other way around.
- *Overweight shows a lack of willpower.* This is the granddaddy of all the myths. Fatness is seen as shameful because we hold people responsible for their weight. Being overweight equates with being a weak-willed slob. We believe this primarily because we have seen people decide to lose weight and do so in a matter of weeks.

But almost everyone returns to the old weight after shedding pounds. Your body has a natural weight that it defends vigorously against dieting. The more diets tried, the harder the body works to defeat the next diet. Weight is in large part genetic. All this gives the lie to the "weak-willed" interpretations of overweight. More accurately, dieting is the conscious will of the

individual against a more vigilant opponent: the species' biological defense against starvation. The body can't tell the difference between self-imposed starvation and actual famine, so it defends its weight by refusing to release fat, by lowering its metabolism, and by demanding food. The harder the creature tries not to eat, the more vigorous the defenses become.

## BULIMIA AND NATURAL WEIGHT

A concept that makes sense of your body's vigorous defense against weight loss is *natural weight.* When your body screams "I'm hungry," makes you lethargic, stores fat, craves sweets and renders them more delicious than ever, and makes you obsessed with food, what it is defending is your natural weight. It is signaling that you have dropped into a range it will not accept. Natural weight prevents you from gaining too much weight or losing too much. When you eat too much for too long, the opposite defenses are activated and make long-term weight gain difficult.

There is also a strong genetic contribution to your natural weight. Identical twins reared apart weigh almost the same throughout their lives. When identical twins are overfed, they gain weight and add fat in lockstep and in the same places. The fatness or thinness of adopted children resembles their biological parents—particularly their mother—very closely but does not at all resemble their adoptive parents. This suggests that you have a genetically given natural weight that your body wants to maintain.

The idea of natural weight may help cure the new disorder that is sweeping young America. Hundreds of thousands of young women have contracted it. It consists of bouts of binge eating and purging alternating with days of undereating. These young women are usually normal in weight or a bit on the thin side, but they are terrified of becoming fat. So they diet. They exercise. They take laxatives by the cup. They gorge. Then they vomit and take more laxatives. This malady is called *bulimia nervosa* (bulimia, for short).

Therapists are puzzled by bulimia, its causes, and treatment. Debate rages about whether it is an equivalent of depression, or an expression of a thwarted desire for control, or a symbolic rejection of the feminine role. Almost every psychotherapy has been tried. Antidepressants and other drugs have been administered with some effect but little success has been reported.

I don't think that bulimia is mysterious, and I think that it will be curable. I believe that bulimia is caused by dieting. The bulimic goes on a diet, and her body attempts to defend its natural weight. With repeated dieting, this defense becomes more vigorous. Her body is in massive revolt—insistently demanding food, storing fat, craving sweets, and lowering metabolism. Periodically, these biological defenses will overcome her extraordinary willpower (and extraordinary it must be to even approach an ideal weight, say, 20 pounds lighter than her natural weight). She will then binge. Horrified by what this will do to her figure, she vomits and takes laxatives to purge calories. Thus, bulimia is a natural consequence of self-starvation to lose weight in the midst of abundant food.

The therapist's task is to get the patient to stop dieting and become comfortable with her natural weight. He should first convince the patient that her binge eating is caused by her body's reaction to her diet. Then he must confront her with a question: Which is more important, staying thin or getting rid of bulimia? By stopping the diet, he will tell her, she can get rid of the uncontrollable binge-purge cycle. Her body will now settle at her natural weight, and she need not worry that she will balloon beyond that point. For some patients, therapy will end there because they would rather be bulimic than "loathsomely fat." For these patients, the central issue—ideal weight versus natural weight—can now at least become the focus of therapy. For others, defying the social and sexual pressure to be thin will be possible, dieting will be abandoned, weight will be gained, and bulimia should end quickly.

These are the central moves of the cognitive-behavioral treatment of bulimia. There are more than a dozen outcome studies of this approach, and the results are good. There is about 60 percent reduction in binging and purging (about the same as with antidepressant drugs). But unlike drugs, there is little relapse after treatment. Attitudes toward weight and shape relax, and dieting withers.

Of course, the dieting theory cannot fully explain bulimia. Many people who diet don't become bulimic; some can avoid it because their natural weight is close to their ideal weight, and therefore the diet they adopt does not starve them. In addition, bulimics are often depressed, since binging-purging leads to self-loathing. Depression may worsen bulimia by making it easier to give in to temptation. Further, dieting may just be another symptom of bulimia, not a cause. Other factors aside, I can speculate that dieting below your natural weight is a necessary condition for bulimia, and that returning to your natural weight and accepting that weight will cure bulimia.

## OVERWEIGHT VS. DIETING: THE HEALTH DAMAGE

Being heavy carries some health risk. There is no definite answer to how much,

because there is a swamp of inconsistent findings. But even if you could just wish pounds away, never to return, it is not certain you should. Being somewhat above your "ideal" weight may actually be your healthiest natural condition, best for your particular constitution and your particular metabolism. Of course you can diet, but the odds are overwhelming that most of the weight will return, and that you will have to diet again and again. From a health and mortality perspective, should you? *There is, probably, a serious health risk from losing weight and regaining it.*

In one study, more than five thousand men and women from Framingham, Massachusetts, were observed for 32 years. People whose weight fluctuated over the years had 30 to 100 percent greater risk of death from heart disease than people whose weight was stable. When corrected for smoking, exercise, cholesterol level, and blood pressure, the findings became more convincing, suggesting that weight fluctuation (the primary cause of which is presumably dieting) may itself increase the risk of heart disease.

If this result is replicated, and if dieting is shown to be the primary cause of weight cycling, it will convince me that you should not diet to reduce your risk of heart disease.

## DEPRESSION AND DIETING

Depression is yet another cost of dieting, because two root causes of depression are failure and helplessness. Dieting sets you up for failure. Because the goal of slimming down to your ideal weight pits your fallible willpower against untiring biological defenses, you will often fail. At first you will lose weight and feel pretty good about it. Any depression you had about your figure will disappear. Ultimately, however, you will probably not reach your goal; and then you will be dismayed as the pounds return. Every time you look in the mirror or vacillate over a white chocolate mousse, you will be reminded of your failure, which in turn brings depression.

On the other hand, if you are one of the fortunate few who can keep the weight from coming back, you will probably have to stay on an unsatisfying low-calorie diet for the rest of your life. A side effect of prolonged malnutrition is depression. Either way you are more vulnerable to it.

If you scan the list of cultures that have a thin ideal for women, you will be struck by something fascinating. All thin-ideal cultures also have eating disorders. They also have roughly twice as much depression in women as in men. (Women diet twice as much as men. The best estimate is that 13 percent of adult men and 25 percent of adult women are now on a diet.) The cultures without the thin ideal have no eating disor-

ders, and the amount of depression in women and men in these cultures is the same. This suggests that around the world, the thin ideal and dieting not only cause eating disorders, but they may also cause women to be more depressed than men.

## THE BOTTOM LINE

I have been dieting off and on for 30 years because I want to be more attractive, healthier, and more in control. How do these goals stack up against the facts?

*Attractiveness.* If your attractiveness is a high-enough priority to convince you to diet, keep three drawbacks in mind. First, the attractiveness you gain will be temporary. All the weight you lose and maybe more will likely come back in a few years. This will depress you. Then you will have to lose it again and it will be harder the second time. Or you will have to resign yourself to being less attractive. Second, when women choose the silhouette figure they want to achieve, it turns out to be thinner than the silhouette that men label most attractive. Third, you may well become bulimic particularly if your natural weight is substantially more than your ideal weight. On balance, if short-term attractiveness is your overriding goal, diet. But be prepared for the costs.

*Health.* No one has ever shown that losing weight will increase my longevity. On balance, the health goal does not warrant dieting.

*Control.* For many people, getting to an ideal weight and staying there is just as biologically impossible as going with much less sleep. This fact tells me not to diet, and defuses my feeling of shame. My bottom line is clear: I am not going to diet anymore.

## DEPTH AND CHANGE: THE THEORY

Clearly, we have not yet developed drugs or psychotherapies that can change all the problems, personality types, and patterns of behavior in adult life. But I believe that success and failure stems from something other than inadequate treatment. Rather, it stems from the depth of the problem.

We all have experience of psychological states of different depths. For example, if you ask someone, out of the blue, to answer quickly, "Who are you?" they will usually tell you—roughly in this order—their name, their sex, their profession, whether they have children, and their religion or race. Underlying this is a continuum of depth from surface to soul—with all manner of psychic material in between.

I believe that issues of the soul can barely be changed by psychotherapy or by drugs. Problems and behavior patterns somewhere between soul and surface can be changed somewhat. Surface problems can be changed easily, even cured. What is changeable, by therapy or drugs, I speculate, varies with the depth of the problem.

My theory says that it does not matter *when* problems, habits, and personality are acquired; their depth derives only from their biology, their evidence, and their power. Some childhood traits, for example, are deep and unchangeable but not because they were learned early and therefore have a privileged place.

Rather, those traits that resist change do so either because they are evolutionarily prepared or because they acquire great power by virtue of becoming the framework around which later learning crystallizes. In this way, the theory of depth carries the optimistic message that we are not prisoners of our past.

When you have understood this message, you will never look at your life in the same way again. Right now there are a number of things that you do not like about yourself and that you want to change: your short fuse, your waistline, your shyness, your drinking, your glumness. You have decided to change, but you do not know what you should work on first. Formerly you would have probably selected the one that hurts the most. Now you will also ask yourself which attempt is most likely to repay your efforts and which is most likely to lead to further frustration. Now you know your shyness and your anger are much more likely to change than your drinking, which you now know is more likely to change than your waistline.

Some of what does change is under your control, and some is not. You can best prepare yourself to change by learning as much as you can about what you can change and how to make those changes. Like all true education, learning about change is not easy; harder yet is surrendering some of our hopes. It is certainly not my purpose to destroy your optimism about change. But it is also not my purpose to assure everybody they can change in every way. My purpose is to instill a new, warranted optimism about the parts of your life you can change and so help you focus your limited time, money, and effort on making actual what is truly within your reach.

Life is a long period of change. What you have been able to change and what has resisted your highest resolve might seem chaotic to you: for some of what you are never changes no matter how hard you try, and other aspects change readily. My hope is that this essay has been the beginning of wisdom about the difference.

Yes, you too can see through the defenses people hide behind. To guide you, just consult the handy primer below. Put together by psychiatrist Emanuel H. Rosen, it distills years of Freudian analytical training into a few simple principles that make sense of our psyches.

# THINK LIKE A SHRINK

I have always thought it horribly unfortunate that there is such a tremendous gap between psychiatry and popular culture. Psychiatrists are regularly vilified in entertainment, media, and common thought, and our patients are regularly stigmatized. Indeed, I've yet to see a single movie that accurately portrays what we do. From *Silence of the Lambs* to *The Prince of Tides,* we shrinks have a reputation as crazy unbalanced people who can read people's minds. Even the hit comedy *The Santa Clause* made us out to be bimbos.

To some degree, we've gotten just what we deserve. We've allowed ourselves to become, in the public mind at least, mere pill-pushers and to have our uncommon sense dismissed as having zero significance when, in fact, it applies to every moment of every person's life. It is our failure to educate our patients and the general public about the deeper principles of human functioning that have left us so isolated from our communities.

Most patients come to psychiatrists because they recognize that, to some degree, their perceptions contain some distortions. These are usually defensive. For example, a 40-year-old woman may begin her first session with a psychiatrist complaining of a "biological depression" and demanding Prozac. By the end of the hour, however, she may acknowledge that her husband's 10-year refusal to have sex may have as much to do with her unhappy mood.

In my practice, I've engaged in a kind of educational psychotherapy, explaining simply to patients what they are doing and why they are doing it. The result has been not only remarkably effective but catalytic in speeding up the process of psychotherapy. The same approach can help the general pub-

> **W**e all play to a hidden audience—Mom and Dad—inside our heads. Especially to Mom, whose nurturing is vital to our self-esteem—though it's not politically correct to say so.

lic delve beneath social images and better understand the deeper struggles of the people around them, and of themselves as well.

Ideas and principles can be introduced directly without the jargon psychiatrists normally hide behind in professional discussions. Doing this in a compassionate and empathic way could lead to a broadening of the vocabulary of the general public and bring about a wider acceptance of certain basic psychological truths.

The core of what we do as psychotherapists is strip away people's protective strategies. If you understand these defensive strategies and the core issues people tend to defend themselves against, you can see through people and, to a lesser extent, yourself.

Here, then, are some general principles to help you think like a shrink. Master them and you will—in some cases dramatically—increase your understanding of the world around you. You *can* see through people. *You* can read their minds.

### 1.

**If you want to know how emotionally healthy someone is, look only at their intimate relationships.**

Good-looking, athletic, charismatic, confident, rich, or intelligent people are not always emotionally healthy. For example, chronologically they may be adults, but emotionally, they may be two-year-olds. You will not really be able to make any kind of accurate, in-depth assessment of people until you learn to distinguish their superficial physical qualities from meaningful emotional ones. There are at least three key things you want to know:

• Most importantly how long-lived and committed are their current intimate relationships?

• Secondly, how much negative conflict do they experience in their work environments and how long have they held their current jobs?

• Finally what was their childhood experience like in their family of origin? Or, in plain English, did they get along with their family?

### 2.

How you feel about yourself (your self-esteem) is significantly determined by how nurturing your mother, father, and siblings were to you when you were growing

Reprinted from *Psychology Today*, September/October 1998, pp. 54-59. © 1998 by Emanuel H. Rosen. Reprinted by permission.

up—especially your mother, though it is not politically correct to say so.

It is not that mothers are to blame for all of a patient's problems. It is simply that stable healthy mothering is a strong buffer against a tremendous amount of pathology.

### 3.

**How you relate to intimate people is always based on how you related to your family when you were growing up.**

Basically, we all keep our families with us forever. We keep them in our heads. For the rest of our lives, we will have tendencies to either take on the roles of our childhood selves or those of our parents. Examine carefully your relationships with your family. It will tell you a lot about who you are.

### 4.

**We all play to a hidden audience—Mom and Dad—inside our heads.**

You often see people do strange things in their interpersonal interactions. "Where did *that* come from," you often ask. It came from a hidden screenplay that was written in that person's head.

Ostensibly he's reacting to you, but in his head, he's reacting to his mother. In fact, the less he remembers of his childhood, the more he is going to act out with you. This leads nicely to. . . .

### 5.

**People who say they "don't remember" their childhood are usually emotionally troubled.**

Physically healthy individuals who can't recall their youth have frequently endured some painful experiences that their minds are blocking out. As a result, they really don't know who they are. They have what we psychiatrists call a diminished sense of identity.

### 6.

**Victims like to be aggressors sometimes, and aggressors are often reconstituted victims.**

People actually may become more actively aggressive when they feel forced into a passive position.

### 7.

**Yes, Virginia, there is an "unconscious" or "non-conscious" mind, and it basically determines your life, everything from what job you choose to whom you marry.**

All the feelings that you had about yourself, your parents, and family are buried in this "unconscious mind." Also buried here are some very deep fears which will be touched on below

The more aware you are of your unconscious mind, the more freedom you will have.

### 8.

**Sex is critical, no matter what anyone says.**

Sex has become passé as an important explanatory factor of human behavior. Nowadays, it is more politically correct to emphasize the role of feelings, thoughts, and emotions than the role of sex. Nonetheless, sexual functioning and sexual history *do* tell you a tremendous amount about what people are really like.

### 9.

**Whenever you have two men, or two women, in a room, you have homosexual tension.**

It is a core truth that all people have both heterosexual and homosexual drives. What varies is how you deal with those drives. Just because you have a homosexual impulse or idea has absolutely nothing to do with your sexual orientation. You are defined by your sexual *behavior*, not your sexual *impulses*.

The people in our society who are most against homosexuality are the people who are most uncomfortable with their own homosexual impulses. These impulses are banished from their conscious awareness.

### 10.

**Yes, children do want to be sexual with the opposite sex parent at some point in their young lives, often between the ages of four and six.**

Just about everyone is grossed out at the thought of their parents having sex. This is because there is a significant resistance against one's own memory of sexual feelings towards one's parents.

It does not mean, however, that you have to remember your sexual impulses towards a parent to be emotionally healthy. In fact, one of the most common issues an adult has to deal with is the incomplete repression of this core conflict.

### 11.

**There is indeed such a thing as castration anxiety.**

In fact, it's the most frightening core fear that people have. It's probably not only evolutionary adaptive, but emotionally important.

### 12.

**Women do not have nearly as much penis envy as men do.**

Men are all deep down very preoccupied with their penis. Concerns usually revolve around how big it is, how long, how thick, and how deep it goes.

This is an important issue that will likely never be researched because it makes everyone way too uncomfortable to talk about. There is more mythology on this subject than the Greeks ever wrote.

### 13.

**The Oedipus complex is what keeps psychiatrists in business.**

Though lay people tend to think only of the complex's sexual aspects, it really boils down to competition. It's commonly about being bigger, richer, more powerful, a winner or a loser. The feelings surrounding it are universal—and intense.

Getting through the various stages of psychological development—oral, anal, and Oedipal—can be summarized as teach-

> **M**en have much more penis envy than do women. They're all very preoccupied with their penis—how big it is, how long, how thick, and how deep it goes.

ing you three key things:

- To feel stable and secure, to depend on people reasonably

- To feel in control

- To feel able to compete successfully and to feel like a man or a woman.

### 14.

**People are basically the same underneath it all; that is, they all want to satisfy similar deeper needs and quell identical underlying fears.**

In general, people all seem to want money, power, and admiration. They want sexual gratification. They want to, as the Bible notes of Judah and Israel, "sit under their vine and fig tree and have none make them afraid." They want to feel secure. They want to feel loved.

Related to this principle: money and intelligence do not protect you. It is only emotional health that keeps you on an even keel; your feelings about yourself and your intimate stable relationships are the only ballast that matters in life.

> **O**ur best defense is a good offense. When people act in an egotistical fashion, their underlying feeling is that they are "dick-less" or impotent.

### 15.

**People often act exactly the opposite of the way they feel, especially when they are unhealthy.**

Or: the best defense is a good offense. When people act egotistical, their underlying feeling is that they are "dick-less" or impotent.

### 16.

**More on defenses . . .**

Here is human nature in a nutshell. My favorite line from the movie *The Big Chill* is voiced by the character played by Jeff Goldblum. "Where would you be, where would any of us be, without a good rationalization? Try to live without a rationalization; I bet you couldn't do it."

**We distort reality both outside and in our minds in order to survive.** Distortions of our inner world are common. *Regression*, one of the most intriguing defenses, can be particularly illuminating to acknowledge; it means acting like a kid to avoid the real world.

"Outside" distortions can get us in very serious trouble.

*Denial* can be fatal whether it involves alcohol abuse or a herd of charging elephants.

*Devaluing*, or, in simple terms, throwing the baby out with the bath water, comes in handy when we want to insult somebody. But it can be detrimental—for example, causing us to miss a lecturer's important points because we consider the teacher to be a "total jerk."

*Idealizing*, or putting people on a pedestal, can be hurtful—say when you realize your ex-Navy Seal stockbroker has been churning your brokerage account.

*Projecting* feelings onto others is a common defensive distortion. Guilt is a painful feeling, so sometimes we may see other people as angry at us rather than feel guilty ourselves. "I know that you are angry that I forgot your birthday" you say. "Don't deny it."

Finally *splitting* our view of the world into good guys and bad guys is a distortion, even if it makes for a great western.

### 17.

**To be successful in the highly competitive American business marketplace requires** a personality ethos that will destroy your intimate relationships.

At this point, you are probably experiencing some confusion. After all, I've been saying that it is unhealthy to be striving continuously to compensate for feelings of inferiority or impotency Yet most people know that it is in fact the strivers who achieve enormous power and success in the world around them.

In order to be emotionally healthy, however, it is necessary for these "winners" to leave their work personalities at the door of their homes and become their natural selves once they cross the threshold. It is absolutely essential that the driven, rushed, acquisitive capitalist ethos not enter into the realm of intimate relationships.

CEOs of corporations and doctors are particularly at risk for this type of contamination of their family life. People who have the best of both worlds—career and relationships—are those who realize that success in the workplace does not make up for lack of success at home.

### 18.

**How well people deal with death is usually identical to how well they have dealt with life.**

### 19.

**How people relate to you in everyday life can tell you a lot about their deeper issues, even in a very short time.**

You can tell a tremendous amount about somebody's emotional stability and character by the way they say goodbye to you. People who cling or drag out good-byes often have deep-seated issues with separation. Of course, we all have issues with separation; it's a matter of degree. Those of us from loving stable backgrounds carry around a warm fuzzy teddy bear of sorts that helps us cope with saying good-bye and being alone. Without this security blanket of loving memories, being alone or saying good-bye can be hell.

A stranger who tells you his entire life's story on the first interview even if you are a psychiatrist, is also probably emotionally unhealthy because there is no boundary between that person and you—and there should be. After all, you are a stranger to that person.

### 20.

**Listen with your third ear.**

One of my mentors at Duke University Medical Center once defined the "third ear" as follows: "While you're listening to what a patient is saying, with your third ear listen to why they are saying it." Psychiatrists listen in a unique way. A family practitioner examines your ears with an otoscope. A psychiatrist examines your feelings with himself as the tool.

When you are interacting with another person, if you notice yourself feeling a certain way the odds are that your companion is somehow intending you to feel that way. You have to be emotionally stable to accurately use yourself as the examining tool.

When you become adept at identifying what you are feeling, the next step is to

> **S**trangers who blurt out their entire life story at a first meeting, even if it's with a psychiatrist, are likely to be troubled. They have no "boundary"— and they should.

determine why. There are usually two reasons. Number one, it may be because you are resonating with what the person is feeling. A second possibility is that you are being subtly provoked to play a complementary emotional role in a scene that has an often hidden script.

The process of using one's own heart as a "scope" is hard work. The fancy term for this process is "counter-transference."

### 21.

**Behind every fear, there is a wish.**

Wishes that are often consciously unacceptable can be expressed more easily as "fears." Related to this principle is the maxim: "Beware unsolicited denials." A common example is the seemingly spontaneous statement, "1 don't really care at all about money!" Hold on to your wallet.

# THE QUEST FOR A CURE

## BY MARK NICHOLS

Every few weeks, several teenage girls arrive at Halifax's Queen Elizabeth II Health Sciences Centre to take part in a study that may someday ease the crippling misery of depression. For two nights, the girls, a different group each time, bunk down in a sleep laboratory with tiny electrodes attached to their heads. Through the night, electronic equipment monitors their brain activity as they pass through the various stages of sleep, including the periods of rapid eye movement (REM) when dreaming occurs. Half of the roughly 80 girls who will take part in the study have no family history of depression. The others do—their mothers have had major depression and researchers know that these girls have a 30 percent chance of being victims, too. Dr. Stan Kutcher, a Dalhousie University psychiatrist who is involved in the study, wants to see whether a feature of sleep in depressed adults—they reach the REM stage faster than others—shows up in the kids. If it does, doctors for the first time would have a way of predicting depression and starting treatment early. Kutcher has been working with troubled youngsters most of his life. "It's a tremendous feeling to be able to help kids get better," he says. "It's a privilege to be let into their lives."

A pioneer in studying and treating adolescent depression, Kutcher is part of an army of medical researchers whose efforts are bringing new drugs, new therapies and new ways of thinking to bear in the war on the debilitating disorder. One of the biggest breakthroughs came in capsule form when Indianapolis's Eli Lilly and Co.

introduced a product called Prozac almost 10 years ago. The first of a new class of drugs that can alleviate depression without the same nasty side effects of many older antidepressants, it profoundly improved the quality of life for millions of people. Thanks to Prozac and drugs like it, says Dr. Sid Kennedy, head of the mood disorders program at Toronto's Clarke Institute of Psychiatry, "depressed people are able to live normal, productive lives in a way that wouldn't have been possible 10 years ago."

Now, drugs that are potentially even better are undergoing tests, while researchers study the intricate universe of the brain in search of clues that could someday banish depression entirely. "Things are really moving quickly," says Dr. Trevor Young, a neuroscientist at McMaster University in Hamilton. "They're really getting close to understanding the biochemical changes that occur in depressed brains."

And doctors are coming closer to the time when they may be able to start treatment, in some cases, even before depression takes hold. After the Dalhousie researchers finish their current series of tests early next year, they will keep track of their young subjects for five years to see whether their REM sleep patterns pinpoint which of them will become depressed. If they do, then doctors in the future may be able to test children from families with a history of depression, and identify potential victims. One possibility, says Kutcher, would be to begin treating those children with antidepressants even before the

## New drugs and therapies join the battle against depression

first bout of depression occurred—in the hope that it never will.

Underpinning the new wave of research is a quiet revolution that has transformed thinking about depression over the past two decades. As recently as in the 1960s, when Sigmund Freud's psychoanalytic philosophy was still pervasive, depression and most other forms of mental illness were regarded as the consequences of emotional turmoil in childhood. Now, scientists have clear evidence that inherited flaws in the brain's biochemistry are to blame for many mental problems, including manic-depressive illness—with its violent swings between depressive lows and manic highs—and, according to some experts, recurring severe depression. Beyond that, many experts think that damaging events in childhood-sexual or physical abuse, poisoned parental relationships and other blows to the child's psyche—may cause depression later by disrupting development of crucial chemical pathways in the brain. "Losses early in life," says Dr. Jane Garland, director of the mood and anxiety clinic at the British Columbia Children's Hospital in Vancouver, "can raise the brain's level of stress hormones that are associated with depression."

When the dark curtain of depression descends, today's victims have access to quick and effective treatment. Short-term "talk therapies" now in use can help haul a patient out of depression in as little as four months—as opposed to years on a psychoanalyst's couch. The purpose of such therapy, says Dr. Marie Corral, a psychiatrist at the British Columbia Women's Hospital in Vancouver, is "to deal with the skewed thinking that develops when a person has been depressed for a long time." The most widely used methods: interpersonal therapy, which focuses on specific people-related problems, and cognitive therapy, which tries to counter the feelings of worthlessness and hopelessness that plague depressed people. "We try to show the patient that much of this thinking may be unfounded," says Zindel Segal, a Toronto psychologist.

But along with the new approaches to dealing with depression, a treatment introduced nearly 60 years ago that has earned a grim public image—electroconvulsive therapy (ECT)—is still a mainstay. Popularly known as shock treatment, it remains "one of our most potent forms of therapy" for severely depressed patients who do not respond to other treatment, says Dr. David Goldbloom, chief of staff at Toronto's Clarke Institute. ECT is routinely used every year on thousands of depressed Canadians, including older patients who cannot tolerate some of the side-effects of drug therapies.

ECT's bad reputation owes much to the 1975 movie *One Flew over the Cuckoo's Nest,* in which staff members of a mental institution punish a rebellious patient, played by Jack Nicholson, with repeated ECT sessions. Patients *did* endure painful ordeals in the early days of ECT when larger electrical shocks were used to induce a limb-shaking seizure in unanesthetized patients. Electroconvulsive

treatment is gentler now. Doctors administer a muscle relaxant and a general anesthetic before subjecting the patient's brain to the amount of current needed to light a 60-watt bulb for one second.

ECT's aftereffects can include painful headaches lasting half an hour or so, and some memory loss. ECT does its job, they add, by altering the brain's electrical and chemical activity. The therapy has some bitter opponents, who claim that it can cause lasting memory loss and impair other brain functions, such as concentration. "ECT damages people's brains—that's really the whole point of it," says Wendy Funk, a 41-year-old Cranbrook, B.C., housewife. Funk says that after receiving electroconvulsive therapy for depression in 1989 and 1990, she lost virtually all memory—she could not recall even her own name or that she was married and had two children.

Meanwhile, for the approximately 70 per cent of patients who respond to them, Prozac and the family of drugs it spawned—Paxil, Zoloft, Luvox and Serzone—are making life far more bearable. Collectively, the drugs are known as SSRIs (for selective serotonin reuptake inhibitors) because they increase the brain's supply of the chemical messenger serotonin. The SSRIs have foes: the Internet bristles with accusations that the drugs can cause panic attacks, aggressive behavior and suicidal tendencies. But most doctors have nothing but praise for the drugs. It's not that they are better than their predecessors at relieving depression—most physicians say they are not.

But SSRIs are easier to live with than some older antidepressants, which often caused dry mouth, daytime sleepiness, constipation, vision problems and other unpleasant side effects. "The SSRIs are better tolerated," says Dr. Russell Joffe, dean of health sciences at McMaster University, "and it is much harder to overdose on them than the older drugs"—a vital consideration in treating people who may be at risk from suicide. The SSRIs can have side effects of their own, including insomnia and a diminished interest in sex that sometimes persuade patients to stop taking them. "You just don't get sexually aroused," says Giselle, a 41-year-old Manitoba resident who requested anonymity. "There's just nothing there."

Another problem with the SSRIs is that patients usually have to take them for three weeks or more before they start to work. The reason: when an SSRI increases the flow of serotonin in the brain, the thermostat-like mechanism that normally controls the flow of the chemical shuts down—and then takes three to six weeks to adapt and allow serotonin to flow again. "If you have a severely depressed patient who may be thinking about suicide," says Dr. Pierre Blier, a professor of psychiatry at Montreal's McGill University, "telling him he may have to wait that long for relief isn't good enough."

After studying the problem exhaustively, Blier and another McGill psychiatrist, Dr. Claude deMontigny, proposed in 1993 that the SSRIs would probably take effect more rapidly if used in conjunction with another drug that could block the brain mechanism causing the delay. Such a drug, a hypertension medication called Pindolol, existed. And the following year, a Spanish physician tried the combination—and found that it worked. Since then, studies have shown that the Pindolol-SSRI combination can cut the waiting time for SSRIs to take effect to about 10 days. Working with that knowledge, several major drug companies now are trying to develop a new generation of fast-acting SSRIs.

Meanwhile, efforts to lay bare the roots of depression are being pursued by a number of Canadian research teams:

• While most antidepressants concentrate on two of the brain's chemical messengers—serotonin and noradrenaline—a research team at the University of Alberta in Edmonton headed by neurochemist Glen Baker is studying a substance called GABA. Another of the brain's neurotransmitters, GABA appears to play a role in quelling the panic attacks that often accompany depression. GABA (for gamma-aminobutyric acid) seems to work in the brain by preventing selected nerve cells from sending signals down the line. To find out more, Baker's team is

tify which defective chemical pathways make that happen. "Once we know more about these things," says Young, "we may be able to correct the problems with drugs."

• In Toronto, a Clarke Institute team co-headed by psychiatrists Sid Kennedy and Franco Vaccarino is using high-tech imaging equipment to look at brain functioning before and after treatment with antidepressants. Images produced by a PET scan machine show that, in depressed people, some parts of the brain's pre-frontal region—an area associated with emotion—are less active than normal. Surprisingly, when antidepressant drugs start acting on the brain, those areas be come even *less* active. Kennedy thinks that may be because in depression, the brain deliberately dampens down pre-frontal activity to cope with high levels of stress, and antidepressants may help the process by reducing activity even further. Kennedy hopes next to study brains in people who had remained well on antidepressants for at least a year, and thinks "we may find that by then activity in the pre-frontal areas has returned to something normal"—meaning that the brain's overstressed condition has been corrected.

# Most doctors praise the Prozac-like drugs

studying the action of two older antidepressants that are used to treat panic, imipramine and phenelzine. They want to find out whether the drugs work by increasing GABA activity in the brain. A possible payoff: a new class of drugs that could some day stem panic by boosting the flow of GABA in the brain.

• At McMaster, Young's team is focusing on manic-depressive illness in an effort to discover which brain chemicals are involved. One approach to the puzzle involves dosing rats—which have many of the same genes as humans—with antidepressants or mood stabilizers and examining tissue samples to see which genes are activated. Eventually, Young hopes to learn more about the signalling process inside the brain that can go awry and lead to depression or mania. He also wants to iden-

The best antidepressants can banish depression—but they do not necessarily protect patients from relapses. Susan Boning, who organizes volunteer services for the Society for Depression and Manic Depression of Manitoba at its Winnipeg headquarters, had been taking Prozac for two years when she felt her mood "dipping" last March. Her condition worsened to the point where she made what she calls "a suicidal gesture" by drinking half a bottle of rum and passing out on her living-room floor. Boning, 37, has stopped taking Prozac and has turned to three other drugs, including Serzone. Boning's experience, like countless others, shows that while medical science is making rapid progress in treating depression, for many in the remorseless grip of the disease it is still not fast enough.

# NEW HOPE FOR PEOPLE WITH

# SCHIZOPHRENIA

**A growing number of psychologists say recovery is possible with psychosocial rehabilitation.**

## BY PATRICK A. McGUIRE
*Monitor staff*

Early last year, when Ronald F. Levant, EdD, sought out colleagues to support an APA miniconvention on serious mental illness, he told a group of fellow psychologists how recovery from a major disorder such as schizophrenia was not only possible, it was happening regularly.

"Recovery from schizophrenia?" a colleague snorted. "Have you lost your mind, too?"

Levant, APA's recording secretary and dean of the Center for Psychological Studies at Nova Southeastern University, was eventually able to rally support for the miniconvention, held last year in Boston. But he still cringes at the sound of that laugh.

"I know psychologists who think that way about schizophrenia," he says. "I don't think they're up to speed. They don't know the literature. They haven't talked to consumers. Frankly, they are using models that are out of date."

*The artwork featured in this article was created by people with schizophrenia.*

The old treatment models, he notes, viewed patients as hopeless cases who needed to be stabilized with hospitalization, and then maintained with medications. The heavy, tranquilizing effects of those drugs made management of patients easier, although they only masked the disease. And, many now acknowledge, they caused serious side effects, including the familiar facial disfiguration known widely in the 1960s and '70s as "the Thorazine look."

"The old clinicians used to write about 'burned out schizophrenics,' like the burned out shell of a person," says psychologist Courtenay M. Harding, PhD, a professor of psychiatry at the University of Colorado. "But given half a chance, people can significantly improve or even recover."

In fact, among a small but growing core of psychologists—many of them, like Harding and Levant, members of an APA task force on serious mental illness—the concept of recovery, with its many definitions, is emerging as a new paradigm for schizophrenia treatment.

Psychologists are not only challenging the dire predictions of the past, they are finding new career paths as planners, teachers, counselors, managers, researchers, even public policy advocates. Many even see the schizophrenia field, once nearly barren of psychologists, as a promising market niche.

## INTEGRATING SERVICES

At the heart of the recovery movement is the idea that instead of focusing on the disease or pathological aspect of schizophrenia—as does the medical model—emphasis is placed on the potential for growth in the individual. That potential is then developed by integrating medical, psychological and social interventions.

Recovery, however, does not necessarily mean cure. Traditionally, the medical model of treatment has defined a "good outcome" from schizophrenia only in terms of a total cessation of symptoms, with no further hospitalization. Many who em-

From *Monitor on Psychology*, February 2000, pp. 24-28. © 2000 by the American Psychological Association. Reprinted by permission.

brace the recovery paradigm feel those criteria are irrelevant.

"I define recovery as the development of new meaning and purpose as one grows beyond the catastrophe of mental illness," says William A. Anthony, PhD, executive director of Boston University's Center for Psychiatric Rehabilitation. "I think the literature on long-term studies . . .shows people do get past mental illness. My feeling is you can have episodic symptoms and still believe and feel you're recovering."

But even within the recovery movement, there are differing definitions of the term. Harding, for example, bases her view of recovery strictly on positive outcome research "findings," and not on the ongoing "process."

"In my definition there appears to be a recalibration of the brain to fully function again," she says. "I define recovery as reconstituted social and work behaviors, no need for meds, no symptoms, no need for compensation." Harding defines "significant improvement" as "someone who has recovered all but one of those areas."

Even with these differences, two key precepts of recovery have to do with a patient's right to play a hands-on role in getting well, and the need for the system to acknowledge that each patient is different and has different needs. That is unlike the old system, says Harding, where patients

---

"A very large group of consumers has achieved remarkable recovery. They are people who, in spite of ongoing symptoms, have carved out a life. They have goals, they make choices, they improve their situation with the right type of interventions."

*Robert D. Coursey*
*University of Maryland*

---

were treated with a "one-size-fits-all" approach, and if they didn't immediately get well, they were deemed forever chronic.

From past to present, experts have agreed on the general symptoms of schizophrenia—the hearing of voices, delusions, hallucinations, disorganized speech, confused thinking—but their efforts to trace its etiology have been stymied by the many forms the disease takes.

"Schizophrenia is a very loose concept," says Robert D. Coursey, PhD, a professor of psychology at the University of Maryland. "I once figured out that you could get 27 different profiles of people with schizophrenia using the Diagnostic and Statistical Manual-IV (DSM-IV)."

Today, an estimated 2.5 million Americans are diagnosed with schizophrenia. The National Institutes of Health says the total costs of the illness approach $30 billion to $65 billion annually. Nearly a quarter of all mental illness costs combined are connected to schizophrenia, with two-thirds of its treatment costs borne by government.

On the human side, the statistics are equally grim: One of every 10 young males with schizophrenia commits suicide.

At the most optimistic of times, the traditional treatment paradigm conceded that perhaps 10 percent to 20 percent of those with schizophrenia might achieve recovery. But proponents of the recovery movement point to data that shows as high as 68 percent rate of recovery and significant improvement.

Best known under the name psychosocial rehabilitation, the recovery philosophy is practiced in about 4,000 dedicated programs across the country, says Ruth Hughes, PhD, president of the International Association of Psychosocial Rehabilitation Services (IAPRS). Each provides patients with work and social skills training, education about their disease and why medications are important, symptom management, and often, therapy for dealing with the trauma of having schizophrenia.

They intervene in the acute stage of the disease by providing a nonthreatening place to go for symptom relief and crisis intervention, but they also work with those who have had schizophrenia for years, and haven't gotten well in other types of treatment. What makes these programs different from past treatments is the focus on a patient's potential, rather than the disease, and the closely coordinated integration of services across disciplines.

Oriented toward the practical, psychosocial rehabilitation teaches a patient how to access resources—such as health services and housing availability—and regain independent functioning. It also provides programs of enrichment or self-development, even basic support such as housing and food.

Another important tool in recovery, says Henry Tomes, PhD, APA's executive director for the public interest, is the psychosocial clubhouse. These are places, usually funded with local mental health funds and private donations, that focus primarily on teaching skills "that will lead people to live independently," says Tomes. "The primary goal is to allow people to work at competitive jobs."

Actual treatment for schizophrenia, he says, is obtained in other psychosocial programs outside the clubhouse.

All in all, says Coursey at Maryland, "A very large group of consumers has achieved remarkable recovery. They are people who, in spite of ongoing symptoms, have carved out a life. They have goals, they make choices, they improve their situation with the right type of interventions."

One of them is Ronald Bassman, PhD. Diagnosed with schizophrenia as a young man, he recovered, earned his doctorate and is now involved in patient empowerment programs in the New York State Office of Mental Health.

"It's miraculous how people come back," he says. "If you talk to someone who is doing better, he or she will tell you that someone—a friend, a family member, a pastor, a therapist—reached out with warmth and

"The old clinicians used to write about 'burned out schizophrenics,' like the burned out shell of a person. What we've discovered is that, given half a chance, people can significantly improve or even recover."

*Courtenay M. Harding*
*University of Colorado*

gentleness and kindness. This is not what is typically done in the mental health system."

To counter that, many former patients and their families have organized themselves as formidable advocates, calling themselves consumers, ex-patients and survivors. Their demand to be recognized as individuals who deserve a voice in their treatment is captured in the slogan "Nothing about us, without us."

In fact, their complaints have made them the significant factor in changing the system, say experts—and also in pointing up the failure of psychology to play a leadership role.

## WHERE ARE THE PSYCHOLOGISTS?

"Psychology as a field has not focused its training and teaching in the area of serious mental illness," says Anthony, in Boston. "This is a message that consumers have been bringing to us but we haven't been listening."

Too many psychologists, say Anthony and others, remain unaware of the new hope, and have shown little interest in working in schizophrenia.

"There is no one out there teaching patients how to cope with stressing voices," says Patricia Deegan, an ex-patient who is now director of training at the National Empowerment Center in Lawrence, Mass. "Or how

*"PARANOIA"*   by Issa Ibrahim

to avoid or get out of the delusional vortexes of thought that you slide into. I think psychologists are a decade behind."

In fact, say survivors like Bassman and Deegan, valuable testimony from patients themselves is often dismissed.

"People say 'Oh, you were misdiagnosed,'" says Bassman. "Otherwise, you couldn't be where you are now.' I mean, that's an impossible circular argument."

Sadly, says Anthony Lehman, MD, a psychiatrist at the University of Maryland School of Medicine, "There is still a lot of mistrust in the professional community about patient self-reports. We just think 'Those people are crazy and they can't provide a valid assessment of what's going on in their lives.' I think we tend to discount people."

But it's not just the treatment system that has a blind spot.

According to Hughes at IAPRS, perhaps only one in 10 of the people who need psychosocial care for schizophrenia is getting it. A big reason for that, she says, is the reluctance of insurance companies to pay for anything but traditional treatment—

which usually means medications alone.

"Most of those with schizophrenia are getting a maintenance approach that is not doing them a service," adds Lehman. "The evidence is that most people get fairly minimal treatment."

"What's really sad," says Harding, "is that [psychologists] could be really strong players in treatment and we're not."

Harding is best known for performing two of the longest longitudinal studies of schizophrenia outcomes in the United States. Her 1987 findings, viewed today by many as the centerpiece of the recovery movement, were the first empirical shots fired against the one-size-fits-all theory of that time.

## MODEL STUDY

Harding's research centered on a cohort of patients from the Vermont State Hospital, released between 1955 and 1960 in a state-funded, early model bio-psycho-social rehabilitation program. This was one of the first "deinstitutionalization" programs that emptied state hospitals across the country from the 1950s into the 1970s. Most relied solely on ex-patients taking powerful new psychotropic drugs to keep them stable on the outside.

The 269 patients chosen for the Vermont model study, however, were classic back ward cases—those diagnosed with chronic schizophrenia and deemed unable to survive outside.

Their 10-year rehabilitation program (1955–1965) relied on a team of caregivers including psychiatrists, a psychologist, a nurse, sociologists and a vocational counselor to maintain a continuity of care for the ex-patients. The team found community housing and provided vocational clinics that led to jobs, education and social supports, individualized treatment planning, as well as social skills training.

About two-thirds of the ex-patients did well, says Harding. When the model program ended, the cohort of ex-patients was already connected with natural community supports. Many of their original caregivers even checked in with them on a volunteer basis.

Harding entered the picture in the 1980s when she and her colleagues tracked down and interviewed all but seven of the original 269 patients—an average of 32 years after their first admission to the hospital.

"My clinical assessors and I were quite skeptical about finding any kind of recovery," she says, "because we'd all been trained in the old model. As a former psychiatric nurse on an inpatient unit, it sure didn't look like to me that anyone could get better."

Her methodology included a recalibration of the original diagnosis of each patient, using the current (1980) volume of the DSM-III. Its definition of schizophrenia was more restrictive than the volume published by the American Psychiatric Association in 1952. Those who interviewed the patients for Harding were blind to everything in the records, and the record abstracter was blind as to current outcome.

Not only did the rediagnoses of schizophrenia hold to the narrower definitions, Harding's study in *The American Journal of Psychiatry* (Vol. 144, No. 6, p. 718–735) showed that 62 percent to 68 percent of those former back ward patients showed no signs at all of schizophrenia. "They just didn't have them anymore."

But why? Harding suspected the psychosocial treatment program had made the difference, and got funding to conduct a comparison study to determine if that was true. She spent eight years looking for a similar cohort of patients and, with the help of colleague Michael DeSisto, PhD, as well as the Maine director of mental health, found a near-perfect match in the Augusta State Hospital in Maine.

"We matched each patient in Vermont to an Augusta patient," she says. "We matched everything. The age, the diagnosis, gender and the length of hospitalization. We matched the catchment areas on health and census data and all the protocols. We used DSM-III to do a rediagnosis on them. And matched the treatment era of the mid-1950s."

Only one thing did not match. In the years after their release, the ex-patients from Maine had not received any rehabilitation or systematic follow-up. The results: A significant improvement and recovery rate of 48 percent.

The Vermonters, says Harding, showed fewer symptoms, many more of them were working, and they showed much better community adjustment.

It dawned on her then that the Maine system and the Vermont system at the time were driven by very different treatment strategies.

"The Vermont model was self-sufficiency, rehabilitation and community integration," she recalls. "The Maine model was meds, maintenance and stabilization."

Even so, why did Vermont's strategy work better than Maine's? The answer reflects an intriguing aspect of the recovery movement: No one is quite sure why.

## TURNING POINTS

For instance, at Maryland, Coursey and his graduate students have conducted numerous interviews with people who have recovered from schizophrenia, asking them the same 'why' questions. Many describe critical turning points.

They said the most important element "had been finding a safe, decent place to live, rather than being out on the streets," he says. "And a lot of these people in our studies had a mentor. Someone they trusted, who cared."

But why did that help?

UNTITLED    by Judy Binder

"I think the 'why' is not that well understood," he says. "[Ex-patients] can describe what are the major elements, and we can see how they differ from those patients who give up. But what happened to make it happen is not always clear."

Even Anthony in Boston is not more specific.

"All of the interventions work in the context of a recovery vision," he says. "They each have their own particular goals. And combined together, they mysteriously help people recover."

Harding is more definite.

"The brain is the most plastic organ we have in interaction with the environment," she says. "Maybe what we are looking at is the neuroplasticity of the brain that is very slowly correcting the problem on its own, in interaction with the environment."

Does that mean people with schizophrenia will spontaneously recover at some point? Harding only smiles at the question, but notes that all of those in her Maine and Vermont studies who had fully recovered, had long since stopped taking medications.

What they had in common was that they were out of the hospital, she says, "and had someone who believed

> "We see many patients who have improved substantially from their baseline diagnosis. Many patients emerge from the acute phase and stabilize, and then steadily improve."
>
> *Nancy Andreasen*
> *University of Iowa*

in them, someone who had told them they had a chance to get better."

## HIGH RATES OF RECOVERY

Harding's Vermont study was an immediate sensation because, while even skeptics agreed that from 10 percent to 20 percent of those with schizophrenia might recover, no one in the United States had ever suggested such a high rate of recovery, and in such a long-term study.

Also, Harding's results did not agree with the American Psychiatric Association's DSM-III, which explicitly said the prognosis for schizophrenia was uniformly poor.

"She was one of the researchers who dispelled many myths about long-term chronicity in mental illness," says Anthony, in Boston.

Harding cites nine other longitudinal studies like hers, conducted in Asia and Europe. Three of those were conducted before her 1987 study, but had been ignored by American researchers. Each of the nine studies reported an average of 50 percent or higher recovery rates. Hers was the only long-term pair of studies to be matched, and, say colleagues, were so expensive and time consuming that few others can afford to attempt a replication.

## SELF-FULFILLING PROPHECIES

Some, though, even in the medical community, are conducting more lim-

ited versions. Nancy Andreasen, MD, PhD, of the University of Iowa, for example is just beginning to pull together the results of a longitudinal study, tracking patients with schizophrenia over 10 years.

"We see many patients who have improved substantially from their baseline diagnosis," she says. "Many patients emerge from the acute phase and stabilize, and then steadily improve."

Andreasen, a psychiatrist known for her research into the biological basis of human behavior in people with schizophrenia, agrees that the medical model is not the total answer to the question of treatment.

"INSIDE MY HEAD"    by Catherine Broger

"Nobody believes more strongly than I that [treatment] should include psychological support and a decent effort to do psychosocial rehab," she says.

"Many of us feel that when you tell people their disease is lifelong, you may be creating self-fulfilling prophecies. There is empirical data accumulating that indicates the dire prognosis of schizophrenia we once had may not be so dire in many cases."

And, she adds, she and her colleagues in medicine and psychology "don't really know, scientifically, what the outcome is of schizophrenia in the era we live in—where patients are cared for in the community and treated with medications that have fewer side effects. We haven't really touched the surface of what we can do with psychosocial or cognitive rehabilitation. We need more of those programs."

True, says Levant at Nova Southeastern, but rehabilitation is only half the battle.

"The other half is advocacy," he says. "We need to change the system. If it is possible to rehabilitate two-thirds of patients, why aren't we?

That's the sad aspect of story. If people think of [people with schizophrenia] as hopeless, they won't be motivated to put money into them."

### FURTHER READING

- Anthony, William A. Recovery from mental illness: The guiding vision of the mental health service system in the 1990s. *Psychosocial Rehabilitation Journal,* Vol. 16, No. 4, p. 11–23 (1993).
- Coursey, Robert D., Alford, Joe, and Safarjan, Bill. Significant advances in understanding and treating serious mental illness. *Professional Psychology: Research and Practice,* Vol. 28, No. 3, p. 205–216 (1997).
- Frese, Frederick J., and Davis, Wendy Walker. The consumer-survivor movement, recovery and consumer-professionals. *Professional Psychology: Research and Practice,* Vol. 28, No. 3, p. 243–245 (1997).
- Lenzenweger, Mark F., and Dworkin, Robert H., eds. "Origins and Development of Schizophrenia (APA Books, 1998).

Glossary

*This glossary of psychology terms is included to provide you with a convenient and ready reference as you encounter general terms in your study of psychology and personal growth and behavior that are unfamiliar or require a review. It is not intended to be comprehensive, but taken together with the many definitions included in the articles themselves, it should prove to be quite useful.*

**abnormal behavior** Behavior that contributes to maladaptiveness, is considered deviant by the culture, or that leads to personal psychological distress.

**absolute threshold** The minimum amount of physical energy required to produce a sensation.

**accommodation** Process in cognitive development; involves altering or reorganizing the mental picture to make room for a new experience or idea.

**acculturation** The process of becoming part of a new cultural environment.

**acetylcholine** A neurotransmitter involved in memory.

**achievement drive** The need to attain self-esteem, success, or status. Society's expectations strongly influence the achievement motive.

**achievement style** The way people behave in achievement situations; achievement styles include the direct, instrumental, and relational styles.

**acquired immune deficiency syndrome (AIDS)** A fatal disease of the immune system.

**acquisition** In conditioning, forming associations in first learning a task.

**actor-observer bias** Tendency to attribute the behavior of other people to internal causes and our own behavior to external causes.

**acupuncture** Oriental practice involving the insertion of needles into the body to control pain.

**adaptation** The process of responding to changes in the environment by altering responses to keep a person's behavior appropriate to environmental demands.

**adjustment** How we react to stress; some change that we make in response to the demands placed upon us.

**adrenal glands** Endocrine glands involved in stress and energy regulation.

**adrenaline** A hormone produced by the adrenal glands that is involved in physiological arousal; adrenaline is also called epinephrine.

**affective flattening** Individuals with schizophrenia who do not exhibit any emotional arousal.

**aggression** Behavior intended to harm a member of the same or another species.

**agoraphobia** Anxiety disorder in which an individual is excessively afraid of places or situations from which it would be difficult or embarrassing to escape.

**alarm reaction** The first stage of Hans Selye's general adaptation syndrome. The alarm reaction is the immediate response to stress; adrenaline is released and digestion slows. The alarm reaction prepares the body for an emergency.

**all-or-none law** The principle that states that a neuron only fires when a stimulus is above a certain minimum strength (threshold), and when it fires, it does so at full strength.

**alogia** Individuals with schizophrenia that show a reduction in speech.

**alpha** Brain-wave activity that indicates that a person is relaxed and resting quietly; 8–12 Hz.

**altered state of consciousness (ASC)** A state of consciousness in which there is a redirection of attention, a change in the aspects of the world that occupy a person's thoughts, and a change in the stimuli to which a person responds.

**ambivalent attachment** Type of infant-parent attachment in which the infant seeks contact but resists once the contact is made.

**amphetamine** A strong stimulant; increases arousal of the central nervous system.

**amygdala** A part of the limbic system involved in fear, aggression, and other social behaviors.

**anal stage** Psychosexual stage during which, according to Sigmund Freud, the child experiences the first restrictions on his or her impulses.

**analytical psychology** The personality theory of Carl Jung.

**anorexia nervosa** Eating disorder in which an individual becomes severely underweight because of self-imposed restrictions on eating.

**antisocial personality disorder** Personality disorder in which individuals who engage in antisocial behavior experience no guilt or anxiety about their actions; sometimes called sociopathy or psychopathy.

**anxiety disorder** Fairly long-lasting disruption of a person's ability to deal with stress; often accompanied by feelings of fear and apprehension.

**applied psychology** The area of psychology that is most immediately concerned with helping to solve practical problems; includes clinical and counseling psychology as well as industrial, environmental, and legal psychology.

**approach-approach conflict** Occurs when we are attracted to two equally desirable goals that are incompatible.

**approach-avoidance conflict** When we are faced with a single goal that has positive and negative aspects.

**aptitude test** Any test designed to predict what a person with the proper training can accomplish in the future.

**archetypes** In Carl Jung's personality theory, unconscious universal ideas shared by all humans.

**arousal theory** Theory that focuses on the energy (arousal) aspect of motivation; it states that we are motivated to initiate behaviors that help to regulate overall arousal level.

**asocial phase** Phase in attachment development in which the neonate does not distinguish people from objects.

**assertiveness training** Training that helps individuals stand up for their rights while not denying rights of other people.

**assimilation** Process in cognitive development; occurs when something new is taken into the child's mental picture.

**associationism** A theory of learning suggesting that once two stimuli are presented together, one of them will remind a person of the other. Ideas are learned by association with sensory experiences and are not innate.

**attachment** Process in which the individual shows behaviors that promote proximity with a specific object or person.

**attention** Process of focusing on particular stimuli in the environment.

**attention deficit disorder** Hyperactivity; inability to concentrate.

**attitude** Learned disposition that actively guides us toward specific behaviors; attitudes consist of feelings, beliefs, and behavioral tendencies.

**attribution** The cognitive process of determining the motives of someone's behavior, and whether they are internal or external.

**autism** A personality disorder in which a child does not respond socially to people.

**autokinetic effect** Perception of movement of a stationary spot of light in a darkened room.

**autonomic nervous system** The part of the peripheral nervous system that carries messages from the central nervous system to the endocrine glands, the smooth muscles controlling the heart, and the primarily involuntary muscles controlling internal processes; includes the sympathetic and parasympathetic nervous systems.

**aversion therapy** A counterconditioning therapy in which unwanted responses are paired with unpleasant consequences.

**avoidance conditioning** Learning situation in which a subject avoids a stimulus by learning to respond appropriately before the stimulus begins.

**avoidant attachment** Type of infant-parent attachment in which the infant avoids the parent.

**avolition** Individuals with schizophrenia who lack motivation to follow through on an activity.

**backward conditioning** A procedure in classical conditioning in which the US is presented and terminated before the termination of the CS; very ineffective procedure.

**basic research** Research conducted to obtain information for its own sake.

**behavior** Anything you do or think, including various bodily reactions. Behavior includes physical and mental responses.

**behavior genetics** How genes influence behavior.

**behavior modification** Another term for behavior therapy; the modification of behavior through psychological techniques; often the application of conditioning principles to alter behavior.

**behaviorism** The school of thought founded by John Watson; it studied only observable behavior.

**belongingness and love needs** Third level of motives in Maslow's hierarchy; includes love and affection, friends, and social contact.

**biological motives** Motives that have a definite physiological basis and are biologically necessary for survival of the individual or species.

**biological response system** Systems of the body that are important in behavioral responding; includes the senses, muscles, endocrine system, and the nervous system.

**biological therapy** Treatment of behavior problems through biological techniques; major biological therapies include drug therapy, psychosurgery, and electroconvulsive therapy.

**bipolar disorder** Mood disorder characterized by extreme mood swings from sad depression to joyful mania; sometimes called manic-depression.

**blinding technique** In an experiment, a control for bias in which the assignment of a subject to the experimental or control group is unknown to the subject or experimenter or both (a double-blind experiment).

**body dysmorphic disorder** Somatoform disorder characterized by a preoccupation with an imaginary defect in the physical appearance of a physically healthy person.

**body language** Communication through position and movement of the body.

**bottom-up processing** The psychoanalytic process of understanding communication by listening to words, then interpreting phrases, and finally understanding ideas.

**brief psychodynamic therapy** A therapy developed for individuals with strong egos to resolve a core conflict.

**bulimia nervosa** Eating disorder in which an individual eats large amounts of calorie-rich food in a short time and then purges the food by vomiting or using laxatives.

**bystander effect** Phenomenon in an emergency situation in which a person is more likely to help when alone than when in a group of people.

**California Psychological Inventory (CPI)** An objective personality test used to study normal populations.

**Cannon-Bard theory of emotion** Theory of emotion that states that the emotional feeling and the physiological arousal occur at the same time.

**cardinal traits** In Gordon Allport's personality theory, the traits of an individual that are so dominant that they are expressed in everything the person does; few people possess cardinal traits.

**catatonic schizophrenia** A type of schizophrenia that is characterized by periods of complete immobility and the apparent absence of will to move or speak.

**causal attribution** Process of determining whether a person's behavior is due to internal or external motives.

**central nervous system** The part of the human nervous system that interprets and stores messages from the sense organs, decides what behavior to exhibit, and sends appropriate messages to the muscles and glands; includes the brain and spinal cord.

**central tendency** In statistics, measures of central tendency give a number that represents the entire group or sample.

**central traits** In Gordon Allport's personality theory, the traits of an individual that form the core of the personality; they are developed through experience.

**cerebellum** The part of the hindbrain that is involved in balance and muscle coordination.

**cerebral cortex** The outermost layer of the cerebrum of the brain where higher mental functions occur. The cerebral cortex is divided into sections, or lobes, which control various activities.

**cerebrum (cerebral hemisphere)** Largest part of the forebrain involved in cognitive functions; the cerebrum consists of two hemispheres connected by the corpus callosum.

**chromosome** Bodies in the cell nucleus that contain the genes.

**chunking** Process of combining stimuli in order to increase memory capacity.

**classical conditioning** The form of learning in which a stimulus is associated with another stimulus that causes a particular response. Sometimes called Pavlovian conditioning or respondent conditioning.

**clinical psychology** Subfield in which psychologists assess psychological problems and treat people with behavior problems using psychological techniques (called psychotherapy).

**cognition** Mental processes, such as perception, attention, memory, language, thinking, and problem solving; cognition involves the acquisition, storage, retrieval, and utilization of knowledge.

**cognitive behavior therapy** A form of behavior therapy that identifies self-defeating attitudes and thoughts in a subject, and then helps the subject to replace these with positive, supportive thoughts.

**cognitive development** Changes over time in mental processes such as thinking, memory, language, and problem solving.

**cognitive dissonance** Leon Festinger's theory of attitude change that states that, when people hold two psychologically inconsistent ideas, they experience tension that forces them to reconcile the conflicting ideas.

**cognitive expectancy** The condition in which an individual learns that certain behaviors lead to particular goals; cognitive expectancy motivates the individual to exhibit goal-directed behaviors.

**cognitive learning** Type of learning that theorizes that the learner utilizes cognitive structures in memory to make decisions about behaviors.

**cognitive psychology** The area of psychology that includes the study of mental activities involved in perception, memory, language, thought, and problem solving.

**cognitive restructuring** The modification of the client's thoughts and perceptions that are contributing to his or her maladjustments.

**cognitive therapy** Therapy developed by Aaron Beck in which an individual's negative, self-defeating thoughts are restructured in a positive way.

**cognitive-motivational-relational theory of emotion** A theory of emotion proposed by Richard Lazarus that includes cognitive appraisal, motivational goals, and relationships between an individual and the environment.

**collective unconscious** Carl Jung's representation of the thoughts shared by all humans.

**collectivistic cultures** Cultures in which the greatest emphasis is on the loyalty of each individual to the group.

**comparative psychology** Subfield in which experimental psychologists study and compare the behavior of different species of animals.

**compulsions** Rituals performed excessively such as checking doors or washing hands to reduce anxiety.

**concept formation (concept learning)** The development of the ability to respond to common features of categories of objects or events.

**concrete operations period** Stage in cognitive development, from 7 to 11 years, in which the child's ability to solve problems with reasoning greatly increases.

**conditioned response (CR)** The response or behavior that occurs when the conditioned stimulus is presented (after the CS has been associated with the US).

**conditioned stimulus (CS)** An originally neutral stimulus that is associated with an unconditioned stimulus and takes on the latter's capability of eliciting a particular reaction.

**conditioned taste aversion (CTA)** An aversion to particular tastes associated with stomach distress; usually considered a unique form of classical conditioning because of the extremely long interstimulus intervals involved.

**conditioning** A term applied to two types of learning (classical and operant). Conditioning refers to the scientific aspect of the type of learning.

**conflict** Situation that occurs when we experience incompatible demands or desires; the outcome when one individual or group perceives that another individual or group has caused or will cause harm.

**conformity** Type of social influence in which an individual changes his or her behavior to fit social norms or expectations.

**connectionism** Recent approach to problem solving; the development of neural connections allows us to think and solve problems.

**conscientiousness** The dimension in the five-factor personality theory that includes traits such as practical, cautious, serious, reliable, careful, and ambitious; also called dependability.

**conscious** Being aware of experiencing sensations, thoughts, and feelings at any given point in time.

**conscious mind** In Sigmund Freud's psychoanalytic theory of personality, the part of personality that we are aware of in everyday life.

**consciousness** The processing of information at various levels of awareness; state in which a person is aware of sensations, thoughts, and feelings.

**consensus** In causal attribution, the extent to which other people react as the subject does in a particular situation.

**conservation** The ability to recognize that something stays the same even if it takes on a different form; Piaget tested conservation of mass, number, length, and volume.

**consistency** In causal attribution, the extent to which the subject always behaves in the same way in a situation.

**consolidation** The biological neural process of making memories permanent; possibly short-term memory is electrically coded and long-term memory is chemically coded.

**contingency model** A theory that specific types of situations need particular types of leaders.

**continuum of preparedness** Martin Seligman's proposal that animals are biologically prepared to learn certain responses more readily than they are prepared to learn others.

**control group** Subjects in an experiment who do not receive the independent variable; the control group determines the effectiveness of the independent variable.

**conventional morality** Level II in Lawrence Kohlberg's theory, in which moral reasoning is based on conformity and social standards.

**convergence** Binocular depth cue in which we detect distance by interpreting the kinesthetic sensations produced by the muscles of the eyeballs.

**conversion disorder** Somatoform disorder in which a person displays obvious disturbance in the nervous system without a physical basis for the problem.

**correlation** Statistical technique to determine the degree of relationship that exists between two variables.

**counterconditioning** A behavior therapy in which an unwanted response is replaced by conditioning a new response that is incompatible with it.

**creativity** A process of coming up with new or unusual responses to familiar circumstances.

**critical period hypothesis** Period of time during development in which particular learning or experiences normally occur; if learning does not occur, the individual has a difficult time learning it later.

**culture-bound** The idea that a test's usefulness is limited to the culture in which it was written and utilized.

**cumulative response curve** Graphed curve that results when responses for a subject are added to one another over time; if subjects respond once every 5 minutes, they will have a cumulative response curve value of 12 after an hour.

**curiosity motive** Motive that causes the individual to seek out a certain amount of novelty.

**cyclothymia disorder** A moderately severe problem with numerous periods of hypomanic episodes and depressive symptoms.

**death instinct** (also called Thanatos) Freud's term for an instinct that is destructive to the individual or species; aggression is a major expression of death instinct.

**decay** Theory of forgetting in which sensory impressions leave memory traces that fade away with time.

**defense mechanisms** Psychological techniques to help protect ourselves from stress and anxiety, to resolve conflicts, and to preserve our self-esteem.

**delayed conditioning** A procedure in classical conditioning in which the presentation of the CS precedes the onset of the US and the termination of the CS is delayed until the US is presented; most effective procedure.

**delusion** The holding of obviously false beliefs; for example, imagining someone is trying to kill you.

**dependent variable** In psychology, the behavior or response that is measured; it is dependent on the independent variable.

**depersonalization disorder** Dissociative disorder in which the individual escapes from his or her own personality by believing that he or she does not exist or that his or her environment is not real.

**depolarization** Any change in which the internal electrical charge becomes more positive.

**depression** A temporary emotional state that normal individuals experience or a persistent state that may be considered a psychological disorder. Characterized by sadness and low self-esteem.

**descriptive statistics** Techniques that help summarize large amounts of data information.

**developmental psychology** Study of physical and mental growth and behavioral changes in individuals from conception to death.

***Diagnostic and Statistic Manual of Mental Disorders (DSM)*** Published by the American Psychiatric Association in 1952, and revised in 1968, 1980, 1987, and 1994, this manual was provided to develop a set of diagnoses of abnormal behavior patterns.

**diffusion of responsibility** Finding that groups tend to inhibit helping behavior; responsibility is shared equally by members of the group so that no one individual feels a strong commitment.

**disorganized schizophrenia** A type of schizophrenia that is characterized by a severe personality disintegration; the individual often displays bizarre behavior.

**displacement** Defense mechanism by which the individual directs his or her aggression or hostility toward a person or object other than the one it should be directed toward; in Freud's dream theory, the process of reassigning emotional feelings from one object to another one.

**dissociative disorder** Psychological disorder that involves a disturbance in the memory, consciousness, or identity of an individual; types include multiple personality disorder, depersonalization disorder, psychogenic amnesia, and psychogenic fugue.

**dissociative fugue** Individuals who have lost their memory, relocated to a new geographical area, and started a new life as someone else.

**dissociative identity disorder (multiple personality disorder)** Dissociative disorder in which several personalities are present in the same individual.

**distinctiveness** In causal attribution, the extent to which the subject reacts the same way in other situations.

**Down syndrome** Form of mental retardation caused by having three number 21 chromosomes (trisomy 21).

**dream analysis** Psychoanalytic technique in which a patient's dreams are reviewed and analyzed to discover true feelings.

**drive** Motivational concept used to describe the internal forces that push an organism toward a goal; sometimes identified as psychological arousal arising from a physiological need.

**dyssomnia** Sleep disorder in which the chief symptom is a disturbance in the amount and quality of sleep; they include insomnia and hypersomnia.

**dysthymic disorder** Mood disorder in which the person suffers moderate depression much of the time for at least two years.

**ego** Sigmund Freud's term for an individual's sense of reality.

**egocentric** Seeing the world only from your perspective.

**eidetic imagery** Photographic memory; ability to recall great detail accurately after briefly viewing something.

**Electra complex** The Freudian idea that the young girl feels inferior to boys because she lacks a penis.

**electroconvulsive therapy (ECT)** A type of biological therapy in which electricity is applied to the brain in order to relieve severe depression.

**emotion** A response to a stimulus that involves physiological arousal, subjective feeling, cognitive interpretation, and overt behavior.

**empiricism** The view that behavior is learned through experience.

**encoding** The process of putting information into the memory system.

**encounter group** As in a sensitivity training group, a therapy where people become aware of themselves in meeting others.

**endorphins** Several neuropeptides that function as neurotransmitters. The opiate-like endorphins are involved in pain, reinforcement, and memory.

**engineering psychology** Area of psychology that is concerned with how work is performed, design of equipment, and work environment; also called human factors psychology.

**engram** The physical memory trace or neural circuit that holds memory; also called memory trace.

**episodic memory** Highest memory system; includes information about personal experiences.

**Eros** Sigmund Freud's term for an instinct that helps the individual or species survive; also called life instinct.

**esteem needs** Fourth level of motives in Abraham Maslow's hierarchy; includes high evaluation of oneself, self-respect, self-esteem, and respect of others.

**eustress** Stress that results from pleasant and satisfying experiences; earning a high grade or achieving success produces eustress.

**excitement phase** First phase in the human sexual response cycle; the beginning of sexual arousal.

**experimental group** Subjects in an experiment who receive the independent variable.

**experimental psychology** Subfield in which psychologists research the fundamental causes of behavior. Many experimental psychologists conduct experiments in basic research.

**experimenter bias** Source of potential error in an experiment from the action or expectancy of the experimenter; might influence the experimental results in ways that mask the true outcome.

**external locus of control** In Julian Rotter's personality theory, the perception that reinforcement is independent of a person's behavior.

**extraversion** The dimension in the five-factor personality theory that includes traits such as sociability, talkativeness, boldness, fun-lovingness, adventurousness, and assertiveness; also called surgency. The personality concept of Carl Jung in which the personal energy of the individual is directed externally.

**factor analysis** A statistical procedure used to determine the relationship among variables.

**false memories** Memories believed to be real, but the events never occurred.

**fast mapping** A process by which children can utilize a word after a single exposure.

**fetal alcohol syndrome (FAS)** Condition in which defects in the newborn child are caused by the mother's excessive alcohol intake.

**five-factor model of personality tracts** A trait theory of personality that includes the factors of extraversion, agreeableness, conscientiousness, emotional stability, and openness.

**fixed action pattern (FAP)** Unlearned, inherited, stereotyped behaviors that are shown by all members of a species; term used in ethology.

**fixed interval (FI) schedule** Schedule of reinforcement where the subject receives reinforcement for a correct response given after a specified time interval.

**fixed ratio (FR) schedule** Schedule of reinforcement in which the subject is reinforced after a certain number of responses.

**flashbulb memory** Memory of an event that is so important that significant details are vividly remembered for life.

**forgetting** In memory, not being able to retrieve the original learning. The part of the original learning that cannot be retrieved is said to be forgotten.

**formal operations period** Period in cognitive development; at 11 years, the adolescent begins abstract thinking and reasoning. This period continues throughout the rest of life.

**free association** Psychoanalytic technique in which the patient says everything that comes to mind.

**free recall** A verbal learning procedure in which the order of presentation of the stimuli is varied and the subject can learn the items in any order.

**frequency theory of hearing** Theory of hearing that states that the frequency of vibrations at the basilar membrane determines the frequency of firing of neurons carrying impulses to the brain.

**frustration** A cause of stress that results from the blocking of a person's goal-oriented behavior.

**frustration-drive theory of aggression** Theory of aggression that states that it is caused by frustration.

**functionalism** School of thought that studied the functional value of consciousness and behavior.

**fundamental attribution error** Attribution bias in which people overestimate the role of internal disposition and underestimate the role of external situation.

**gate-control theory of pain** Theory of pain that proposes that there is a gate that allows pain impulses to travel from the spinal cord to the brain.

**gender-identity disorder (GID)** Incongruence between assigned sex and gender identity.

**gender-identity/role** Term that incorporates gender identity (the private perception of one's sex) and gender role (the public expression of one's gender identity).

**gene** The basic unit of heredity; the gene is composed of deoxyribonucleic acid (DNA).

**general adaptation syndrome (GAS)** Hans Selye's theory of how the body responds to stress over time. GAS includes alarm reaction, resistance, and exhaustion.

**generalized anxiety disorder** Anxiety disorder in which the individual lives in a state of constant severe tension, continuous fear, and apprehension.

**genetics** The study of heredity; genetics is the science of discovering how traits are passed along generations.

**genotype** The complete set of genes inherited by an individual from his or her parents.

**Gestalt psychology** A school of thought that studied whole or complete perceptions.

**Gestalt therapy** Insight therapy designed to help people become more aware of themselves in the here and now and to take responsibility for their own actions.

**grandiose delusion** Distortion of reality; one's belief that he or she is extremely important or powerful.

**group therapy** Treatment of several patients at the same time.

**groupthink** When group members are so committed to, and optimistic about, the group that they feel it is invulnerable; they become so concerned with maintaining consensus that criticism is muted.

**growth** The normal quantitative changes that occur in the physical and psychological aspects of a healthy child with the passage of time.

**GSR (galvanic skin response)** A measure of autonomic nervous system activity; a slight electric current is passed over the skin, and the more nervous a subject is, the easier the current will flow.

**hallucinations** A sensory impression reported when no external stimulus exists to justify the report; often hallucinations are a symptom of mental illness.

**hallucinogens** Psychedelic drugs that result in hallucinations at high doses, and other effects on behavior and perception in mild doses.

**halo effect** The finding that once we form a general impression of someone, we tend to interpret additional information about the person in a consistent manner.

**haptic** Relating to or based on the sense of touch. Also, a predilection for the sense of touch.

**Hawthorne effect** The finding that behavior can be influenced just by participation in a research study.

**health psychology** Field of psychology that studies psychological influences on people's health, including how they stay healthy, why they become ill, and how their behavior relates to their state of health.

**heuristic** Problem-solving strategy; a person tests solutions most likely to be correct.

**hierarchy of needs** Abraham Maslow's list of motives in humans, arranged from the biological to the uniquely human.

**higher order conditioning** Learning to make associations with stimuli that have been learned previously.

**hippocampus** Brain structure in the limbic system that is important in learning and memory.

**homeostasis** The state of equilibrium that maintains a balance in the internal body environment.

**hormones** Chemicals produced by the endocrine glands that regulate activity of certain bodily processes.

**humanistic psychology** Psychological school of thought that believes that people are unique beings who cannot be broken down into parts.

**hyperphagia** Disorder in which the individual continues to eat until he or she is obese; can be caused by damage to ventromedial hypothalamus.

**hypersomnia** Sleep disorder in which an individual falls asleep at inappropriate times; narcolepsy is a form of hypersomnia.

**hypnosis** Altered state of consciousness characterized by heightened suggestibility.

**hypochondriasis** Somatoform disorder in which the individual is obsessed with fears of having a serious medical disease.

**hypothalamus** Part of the brain's limbic system; involved in motivational behaviors, including eating, drinking, and sex.

**hypothesis** In the scientific method, an educated guess or prediction about future observable events.

**iconic memory** Visual information that is encoded into the sensory memory store.

**id** Sigmund Freud's representation of the basic instinctual drives; the id always seeks pleasure.

**identification** The process in which children adopt the attitudes, values, and behaviors of their parents.

**identity diffusion** In Marcia's adolescent identity theory, the status of individuals who have failed to make a commitment to values and roles.

**illusion** An incorrect perception that occurs when sensation is distorted.

**imitation** The copying of another's behavior; learned through the process of observation.

**impression formation** Developing an evaluation of another person from your perceptions; first, or initial, impressions are often very important.

**imprinting** A form of early learning in which birds follow a moving stimulus (often the mother); may be similar to attachment in mammals.

**independent variable** The condition in an experiment that is controlled and manipulated by the experimenter; it is a stimulus that will cause a response.

**indiscriminate attachment phase** Stage of attachment in which babies prefer humans to nonhumans, but do not discriminate among individual people.

**individuation** Carl Jung's concept of the process leading to the unification of all parts of the personality.

**inferential statistics** Techniques that help researchers make generalizations about a finding based on a limited number of subjects.

**inferiority complex** Adler's personality concept that states that because children are dependent on adults and cannot meet the standards set for themselves they feel inferior.

**inhibition** Restraint of an impulse, desire, activity, or drive.

**insight** A sudden grasping of the means necessary to achieve a goal; important in the Gestalt approach to problem solving.

**insight therapy** Therapy based on the assumption that behavior is abnormal because people do not adequately understand the motivation causing their behavior.

**instinct** Highly stereotyped behavior common to all members of a species that often appears in virtually complete form in the absence of any obvious opportunities to learn it.

**instrumental conditioning** Operant conditioning.

**intelligence** Capacity to learn and behave adaptively.

**intelligence quotient (IQ)** An index of a person's performance on an intelligence test relative to others in the culture; ratio of a person's mental age to chronological age.

**interference** Theory of forgetting in which information that was learned before (proactive interference) or after (retroactive interference) causes the learner to be unable to remember the material of interest.

**internal locus of control** In Rotter's personality theory, the perception that reinforcement is contingent upon behavior.

**interstimulus interval** Time interval between two stimuli; in classical conditioning, it is the elapsed time between the CS and the US.

**intrinsic motivation** Motivation inside the individual; we do something because we receive satisfaction from it.

**introspection** Method in which a subject gives a self-report of his or her immediate experience.

**introversion** The personality concept of Carl Jung in which the personal energy of the individual is directed inward; characterized by introspection, seriousness, inhibition, and restraint.

**James-Lange theory of emotion** Theory of emotion that states that the physiological arousal and behavior come before the subjective experience of an emotion.

**just noticeable difference (JND)** Difference threshold: minimum amount of energy required to produce a difference in sensation.

**kinesthesis** The sense of bodily movement.

**labeling of arousal** Experiments suggest that an individual experiencing physical arousal that cannot be explained will interpret those feelings in terms of the situation she or he is in and will use environmental and contextual cues.

**language acquisition device (LAD)** Hypothesized biological structure that accounts for the relative ease of acquiring language, according to Noam Chomsky.

**latent dream content** In Sigmund Freud's dream theory, the true thoughts in the unconsciousness; the true meaning of the dream.

**latent learning** Learning that occurs when an individual acquires knowledge of something but does not show it until motivated to do so.

**law of effect** Edward Thorndike's law that if a response produces satisfaction it will be repeated; reinforcement.

**learned helplessness** Condition in which a person learns that his or her behavior has no effect on his or her environment; when an individual gives up and stops trying.

**learned social motives** Social motives that are learned; include achievement and affiliation.

**learning** The relatively permanent change in behavior or behavioral ability of an individual that occurs as a result of experience.

**learning styles** The preferences students have for learning; theories of learning styles include personality differences, styles of information processing, and instructional preferences.

**life instinct** (also called Eros) Sigmund Freud's term for an instinct that helps the individual or species survive; sex is the major expression of life instinct.

**life structure** In Daniel Levinson's theory of adult personality development, the underlying pattern of an individual's life at any particular time; seasonal cycles include preadulthood, early adulthood, middle adulthood, and late adulthood.

**linguistic relativity hypothesis** Proposal that the perception of reality differs according to the language of the observer.

**locus of control** Julian Rotter's theory in which a person's beliefs about reinforcement are classified as internal or external.

**long-term memory** The permanent memory where rehearsed information is stored.

**love** An emotion characterized by knowing, liking, and becoming intimate with someone.

**low-ball procedure** The compliance technique of presenting an attractive proposal to someone and then switching it to a more unattractive proposal.

**magic number 7** The finding that most people can remember about seven items of information for a short time (in short-term memory).

**magnetic resonance imaging (MRI)** A method of studying brain activity using magnetic field imaging.

**major depressive disorder** Severe mood disorder in which a person experiences one or more major depressive episodes; sometimes referred to simply as depression.

**maladjustment** Condition that occurs when a person utilizes inappropriate abilities to respond to demands placed upon him or her.

**manic depressive reaction** A form of mental illness marked by alternations of extreme phases of elation (manic phase) and depression.

**manifest dream content** In Sigmund Freud's dream theory, what is remembered about a dream upon waking; a disguised representation of the unconscious wishes.

**massed practice** Learning as much material as possible in long continuous stretches.

**maturation** The genetically controlled process of growth that results in orderly changes in behavior.

**mean** The arithmetic average, in which the sum of scores is divided by the number of scores.

**median** The middle score in a group of scores that are arranged from lowest to highest.

**meditation** The practice of some form of relaxed concentration while ignoring other sensory stimuli.

**memory** The process of storing information so that it can be retrieved and used later.

**memory attributes** The critical features of an event that are used when the experience is encoded or retrieved.

**mental age** The age level on which a person is capable of performing; used in determining intelligence.

**mental set** Condition in which a person's thinking becomes so standardized that he or she approaches new problems in fixed ways.

**Minnesota Multiphasic Personality Inventory (MMPI-2)** An objective personality test that was originally devised to identify personality disorders.

**mnemonic technique** Method of improving memory by combining and relating chunks of information.

**modeling** A process of learning by imitation in a therapeutic situation.

**mood disorder** Psychological disorder in which a person experiences a severe disruption in mood or emotional balance.

**moral development** Development of individuals as they adopt their society's standards of right and wrong; development of awareness of ethical behavior.

**motivated forgetting (repression)** Theory that suggests that people want to forget unpleasant events.

**motivation** The forces that initiate and direct behavior, and the variables that determine the intensity and persistence of the behavior.

**motivator needs** In Federick Herzberg's theory, the factors that lead to job satisfaction; they include responsibility, the nature of the work, advancement, and recognition.

**motive** Anything that arouses the individual and directs his or her behavior toward some goal. Three categories of motives include biological, stimulus, and learned social.

**Müller-Lyer illusion** A well-known illusion, in which two horizontal lines have end lines either going in or out; the line with the end lines going in appears longer.

**multiple approach-avoidance conflict** Conflict that occurs when an individual has two or more goals, both of which have positive and negative aspects.

**multiple attachment phase** Later attachment stage in which the baby begins to form attachments to people other than the primary caretaker.

**multiple intelligences** Howard Gardner's theory that there exists several different kinds of intelligence.

**Myers-Briggs Type Indicator (MBTI)** Objective personality test based on Carl Jung's type theory.

**narcotic analgesics** Drugs that have an effect on the body similar to morphine; these relieve pain and suppress coughing.

**naturalistic observation** Research method in which behavior of people or animals in their normal environment is accurately recorded.

**Necker cube** A visual illusion. The Necker cube is a drawing of a cube designed so that it is difficult to determine which side is toward you.

**negative reinforcement** Removing something unpleasant to increase the probability that the preceding behavior will be repeated.

**NEO Personality Inventory (NEO-PI)** An objective personality test developed by Paul Costa Jr. and Robert McCrae to measure the five major factors in personality; consists of 181 questions.

**neodissociation theory** Idea that consciousness can be split into several streams of thought that are partially independent of each other.

**neuron** A specialized cell that functions to conduct messages throughout the body.

**neurosis** A Freudian term that was used to describe abnormal behavior caused by anxiety; it has been eliminated from *DSM-IV*.

**neutral stimulus** A stimulus that does not cause the response of interest; the individual may show some response to the stimulus but not the associated behavior.

**norm** A sample of scores representative of a population.

**normal curve** When scores of a large number of random cases are plotted on a graph, they often fall into a bell-shaped curve; as many cases on the curve are above the mean as below it.

**observational learning** In social learning theory, learning by observing someone else behave; people observe and imitate in learning socialization.

**obsessions** Fears that involve the inability to control impulses.

**obsessive compulsive disorder** Anxiety disorder in which the individual has repetitive thoughts (obsessions) that lead to constant urges (compulsions) to engage in meaningless rituals.

**object permanence** The ability to realize that objects continue to exist even if we can no longer see them.

**Oedipus complex** The Freudian idea that the young boy has sexual feelings for his mother and is jealous of his father and must identify with his father to resolve the conflict.

**olfaction** The smell sense.

**openness** The dimension in the five-factor personality theory that includes traits such as imagination, creativity, perception, knowledge, artistic ability, curiosity, and analytical ability; also called culture or intellect.

**operant conditioning** Form of learning in which behavior followed by reinforcement (satisfaction) increases in frequency.

**opponent-process theory** Theory that when one emotion is experienced, the other is suppressed.

**optimum level of arousal** Motivation theory that states that the individual will seek a level of arousal that is comfortable.

**organic mental disorders** Psychological disorders that involve physical damage to the nervous system; can be caused by disease or by an accident.

**organizational psychology** Area of industrial psychology that focuses on worker attitudes and motivation; derived primarily from personality and social psychology.

**orgasm** The climax of intense sexual excitement; release from building sexual tension, usually accompanied by ejaculation in men.

**paired-associate learning** A verbal learning procedure in which the subject is presented with a series of pairs of items to be remembered.

**panic disorder** Anxiety disorder characterized by the occurrence of specific periods of intense fear.

**paranoid schizophrenia** A type of schizophrenia in which the individual often has delusions of grandeur and persecution, thinking that someone is out to get him or her.

**partial reinforcement** Any schedule of reinforcement in which reinforcement follows only some of the correct responses.

**partial reinforcement effect** The finding that partial reinforcement produces a response that takes longer to extinguish than continuous reinforcement.

**pattern recognition** Memory process in which information attended to is compared with information already permanently stored in memory.

**Pavlovian conditioning** A bond or association between a neutral stimulus and a response; this type of learning is called classical conditioning.

**perception** The active process in which the sensory information that is carried through the nervous system to the brain is organized and interpreted; the interpretation of sensation.

**persecutory delusion** A delusion in which the individual has a distortion of reality; the belief that other people are out to get one.

**person perception** The process of using the information we gather in forming impressions of people to make evaluations of others.

**personal unconscious** Carl Jung's representation of the individual's repressed thoughts and memories.

**personality disorder** Psychological disorder in which there are problems in the basic personality structure of the individual.

**phantom-limb pain** Phenomenon in which people who have lost an arm or leg feel pain in the missing limb.

**phobias** Acute excessive fears of specific situations or objects that have no convincing basis in reality.

**physiological needs** First level of motives in Abraham Maslow's hierarchy; includes the biological needs of hunger, thirst, sex, exercise, and rest.

**placebo** An inert or inactive substance given to control subjects to test for bias effects.

**plateau phase** Second phase in the human sexual response cycle, during which the physiological arousal becomes more intense.

**pleasure principle** In Freudian theory, the idea that the instinctual drives of the id unconsciously and impulsively seek immediate pleasure.

**positive reinforcement** Presenting a subject something pleasant to increase the probability that the preceding behavior will be repeated.

**postconventional morality** Level III in Lawrence Kohlberg's theory, in which moral reasoning is based on personal standards and beliefs; highest level of moral thinking.

**posttraumatic stress disorder (PTSD)** Condition that can occur when a person experiences a severely distressing event; characterized by constant memories of the event, avoidance of anything associated with it, and general arousal.

**Prägnanz (law of)** Gestalt psychology law that states that people have a tendency to group stimuli according to rules, and that people do this whenever possible.

**preconscious mind** In Sigmund Freud's psychoanalytic theory of personality, the part of personality that contains information that we have learned but that we are not thinking about at the present time.

**preconventional morality** Level I of Lawrence Kohlberg's theory, in which moral reasoning is largely due to the expectation of rewards and punishments.

**prejudice** An unjustified fixed, usually negative, way of thinking about a person or object.

**Premack principle** Principle that states that, of any two responses, the one that is more likely to occur can be used to reinforce the response that is less likely to occur.

**preoperational thought period** Period in cognitive development; from two to seven years, the period during which the child learns to represent the environment with objects and symbols.

**primacy effect** Phenomenon where items are remembered because they come at the beginning of a list.

**primary appraisal** Activity of determining whether a new stimulus event is positive, neutral, or negative; first step in appraisal of stress.

**primary narcissism** A Freudian term that refers to the oral phase before the ego has developed; the individual constantly seeks pleasure.

**primary reinforcement** Reinforcement that is effective without having been associated with other reinforcers; sometimes called unconditioned reinforcement.

**probability (p)** In inferential statistics, the likelihood that the difference between the experimental and control groups is due to the independent variable.

**procedural memory** The most basic type of long-term memory; involves the formation of associations between stimuli and responses.

**projection** Defense mechanism in which a person attributes his or her unacceptable characteristics or motives to others rather than himself or herself.

**projective personality test** A personality test that presents ambiguous stimuli to which subjects are expected to respond with projections of their own personality.

**proximity** Closeness in time and space. In perception, it is the Gestalt perceptual principle in which stimuli next to one another are included together.

**psyche** According to Carl Jung, the thoughts and feelings (conscious and unconscious) of an individual.

**psychoactive drug** A drug that produces changes in behavior and cognition through modification of conscious awareness.

**psychoanalysis** The school of thought founded by Sigmund Freud that stressed unconscious motivation. In therapy, a patient's unconscious motivation is intensively explored in order to bring repressed conflicts up to consciousness; psychoanalysis usually takes a long time to accomplish.

**psychobiology** (also called biological psychology or physiological psychology) The subfield of experimental psychology concerned with the influence of heredity and the biological response systems on behavior.

**psychogenic amnesia** A dissociative disorder in which an individual loses his or her sense of identity.

**psychogenic fugue** A dissociative disorder in which an individual loses his or her sense of identity and goes to a new geographic location, forgetting all of the unpleasant emotions connected with the old life.

**psychographics** A technique used in consumer psychology to identify the attitudes of buyers and their preferences for particular products.

**psycholinguistics** The psychological study of how people convert the sounds of a language into meaningful symbols that can be used to communicate with others.

**psychological dependence** Situation in which a person craves a drug even though it is not biologically needed by the body.

**psychological disorder** A diagnosis of abnormal behavior; syndrome of abnormal adjustment, classified in *DSM*.

**psychological types** Carl Jung's term for different personality profiles; Jung combined two attitudes and four functions to produce eight psychological types.

**psychopharmacology** Study of effects of psychoactive drugs on behavior.

**psychophysics** An area of psychology in which researchers compare the physical energy of a stimulus with the sensation reported.

**psychosexual stages** Sigmund Freud's theoretical stages in personality development.

**psychosomatic disorders** A variety of body reactions that are closely related to psychological events.

**psychotherapy** Treatment of behavioral disorders through psychological techniques; major psychotherapies include insight therapy, behavior therapy, and group therapy.

**psychotic disorders** The more severe categories of abnormal behavior.

**puberty** Sexual maturation; the time at which the individual is able to perform sexually and to reproduce.

**punishment** Any event that decreases the likelihood that the behavior preceding it will be repeated.

**quantitative trait loci (QTLs)** Genes that collectively contribute to a trait for high intelligence.

**rational-emotive therapy** A cognitive behavior modification technique in which a person is taught to identify irrational, self-defeating beliefs and then to overcome them.

**reaction formation** Defense mechanism in which a person masks an unconsciously distressing or unacceptable trait by assuming an opposite attitude or behavior pattern.

**reality principle** In Freudian theory, the idea that the drives of the ego try to find socially acceptable ways to gratify the id.

**reciprocal determinism** The concept proposed by Albert Bandura that the behavior, the individual, and the situation interact and influence each other.

**reciprocal inhibition** Concept of Joseph Wolpe that states that it is possible to break the bond between anxiety-provoking stimuli and responses manifesting anxiety by facing those stimuli in a state antagonistic to anxiety.

**reflex** An automatic movement that occurs in direct response to a stimulus.

**regression** Defense mechanism in which a person retreats to an earlier, more immature form of behavior.

**reinforcement** Any event that increases the probability that the behavior that precedes it will be repeated; also called a reinforcer; similar to a reward.

**reinforcement therapy** A behavior therapy in which reinforcement is used to modify behavior. Techniques in reinforcement therapy include shaping, extinction, and token economy.

**releaser (sign stimulus)** Specific environmental cues that stimulate a stereotyped behavior to occur; releasers cause fixed action patterns.

**repression** Defense mechanism in which painful memories and unacceptable thoughts and motives are conveniently forgotten so that they will not have to be dealt with.

**residual schizophrenia** Type of schizophrenia in which the individual currently does not have symptoms but has had a schizophrenic episode in the past.

**resistance** Psychoanalytic term used when a patient avoids a painful area of conflict.

**resolution phase** The last phase in the human sexual response cycle; the time after orgasm when the body gradually returns to the unaroused state.

**Restricted Environmental Stimulation Technique (REST)** Research technique in which environmental stimuli available to an individual are reduced drastically; formerly called sensory deprivation.

**retroactive interference** Interference caused by information learned after the material of interest.

**retrograde amnesia** Forgetting information recently learned because of a disruptive stimulus such as an electric shock.

**reversible figure** In perception, a situation in which the figure and ground seem to reverse themselves; an illusion in which objects alternate as the main figure.

**risky-shift** The tendency for groups to make riskier decisions than individuals.

**Rorschach Inkblot Test** A projective personality test in which subjects are asked to discuss what they see in cards containing blots of ink.

**safety needs** Second level of motives in Abraham Maslow's hierarchy; includes security, stability, dependency, protection, freedom from fear and anxiety, and the need for structure and order.

**Schachter-Singer theory of emotion** Theory of emotion that states that we interpret our arousal according to our environment and label our emotions accordingly.

**scheme** A unit of knowledge that the person possesses; used in Jean Piaget's cognitive development theory.

**schizophrenia** Severe psychotic disorder that is characterized by disruptions in thinking, perception, and emotion.

**scientific method** An attitude and procedure that scientists use to conduct research. The steps include stating the problem, forming the hypothesis, collecting the information, evaluating the information, and drawing conclusions.

**secondary appraisal** In appraisal of stress, this is the evaluation that an individual's abilities and resources are sufficient to meet the demands of a stressful event.

**secondary reinforcement** Reinforcement that is effective only after it has been associated with a primary reinforcer; also called conditioned reinforcement.

**secondary traits** In Gordon Allport's personality theory, the less important situation-specific traits that help round out personality; they include attitudes, skills, and behavior patterns.

**secure attachment** Type of infant-parent attachment in which the infant actively seeks contact with the parent.

**self-actualization** A humanistic term describing the state in which all of an individual's capacities are developed fully. Fifth and highest level of motives in Abraham Maslow's hierarchy, this level, the realization of one's potential, is rarely reached.

**self-efficacy** An individual's sense of self-worth and success in adjusting to the world.

**self-evaluation maintenance model (SEM)** Tesser's theory of how we maintain a positive self-image despite the success of others close to us.

**self-handicapping strategy** A strategy that people use to prepare for failure; people behave in ways that produce obstacles to success so that when they do fail they can place the blame on the obstacle.

**self-serving bias** An attribution bias in which an individual attributes success to his or her own behavior and failure to external environmental causes.

**semantic memory** Type of long-term memory that can use cognitive activities, such as everyday knowledge.

**sensation** The passive process in which stimuli are received by sense receptors and transformed into neural impulses that can be carried through the nervous system; first stage in becoming aware of environment.

**sensitivity training group (T-group)** Therapy group that has the goal of making participants more aware of themselves and their ideas.

**sensorimotor period** Period in cognitive development; the first two years, during which the infant learns to coordinate sensory experiences with motor activities.

**sensory adaptation** Tendency of the sense organs to adjust to continuous stimulation by reducing their functioning; a stimulus that once caused sensation and no longer does.

**sensory deprivation** Situation in which normal environmental sensory stimuli available to an individual are reduced drastically; also called REST (Restricted Environmental Stimulation Technique).

**serial learning** A verbal learning procedure in which the stimuli are always presented in the same order, and the subject has to learn them in the order in which they are presented.

**sex roles** The set of behaviors and attitudes that are determined to be appropriate for one sex or the other in a society.

**shaping** In operant conditioning, the gradual process of reinforcing behaviors that get closer to some final desired behavior. Shaping is also called successive approximation.

**signal detection theory** Research approach in which the subject's behavior in detecting a threshold is treated as a form of decision making.

**similarity** Gestalt principle in which similar stimuli are perceived as a unit.

**simple phobia** Excessive irrational fear that does not fall into other specific categories, such as fear of dogs, insects, snakes, or closed-in places.

**simultaneous conditioning** A procedure in classical conditioning in which the CS and US are presented at exactly the same time.

***Sixteen Personality Factor Questionnaire (16PF)*** Raymond Cattell's personality test to measure source traits.

**Skinner box** B. F. Skinner's animal cage with a lever that triggers reinforcement for a subject.

**sleep terror disorder (pavor nocturnus)** Nonrapid-eye-movement (NREM) sleep disorder in which the person (usually a child) wakes up screaming and terrified, but cannot recall why.

**sleepwalking (somnambulism)** NREM sleep disorder in which the person walks in his or her sleep.

**social cognition** The process of understanding other people and ourselves by forming and utilizing information about the social world.

**social cognitive theory** Albert Bandura's approach to personality that proposes that individuals use observation, imitation, and cognition to develop personality.

**social comparison** Theory proposed by Leon Festinger that we tend to compare our behavior to others to ensure that we are conforming.

**social exchange theory** Theory of interpersonal relationships that states that people evaluate the costs and rewards of their relationships and act accordingly.

**social facilitation** Phenomenon in which the presence of others increases dominant behavior patterns in an individual; Richard Zajonc's theory states that the presence of others enhances the emission of the dominant response of the individual.

**social influence** Influence designed to change the attitudes or behavior of other people; includes conformity, compliance, and obedience.

**social learning theory** An approach to social psychology that emphasizes observation and modeling; states that reinforcement is involved in motivation rather than in learning, and proposes that aggression is a form of learned behavior.

**social phobia** Excessive irrational fear and embarrassment when interacting with other people. Social phobias may include fear of assertive behavior, fear of making mistakes, or fear of public speaking.

**social psychology** The study of how an individual's behavior, thoughts, and feelings are influenced by other people.

**sociobiology** Study of the genetic basis of social behavior.

**sociocultural** Emphasizes the importance of culture, gender, and ethnicity in how we think, feel, and act.

**somatic nervous system** The part of the peripheral nervous system that carries messages from the sense organs and relays information that directs the voluntary movements of the skeletal muscles.

**somatization disorder** Somatoform disorder in which a person has medical complaints without physical cause.

**somatoform disorders** Psychological disorders characterized by physical symptoms for which there are no obvious physical causes.

**specific attachment phase** Stage at about six months of age, in which the baby becomes attached to a specific person.

**split-brain research** Popular name for Roger Sperry's research on the syndrome of hemisphere deconnection; research on individuals with the corpus callosum severed. Normal functioning breaks down in split-brain subjects when different information is presented to each hemisphere.

**SQ5R** A technique to improve learning and memory. Components include survey, question, read, record, recite, review, and reflect.

**stage of exhaustion** Third stage in Hans Selye's general adaptation syndrome. As the body continues to resist stress, it depletes its energy resources and the person becomes exhausted.

**stage of resistance** Second stage in Hans Selye's general adaptation syndrome. When stress is prolonged, the body builds some resistance to the effects of stress.

**standardization** The process of obtaining a representative sample of scores in the population so that a particular score can be interpreted correctly.

*Stanford-Binet Intelligence Scale* An intelligence test first revised by Lewis Terman at Stanford University in 1916; still a popular test used today.

**state-dependent learning** Situation in which what is learned in one state can only be remembered when the person is in that state of mind.

**statistically significant** In inferential statistics, a finding that the independent variable did influence greatly the outcome of the experimental and control group.

**stereotype** An exaggerated and rigid mental image of a particular class of persons or objects.

**stimulus** A unit of the environment that causes a response in an individual; a physical or chemical agent acting on an appropriate sense receptor.

**stimulus discrimination** Responding to relevant stimuli.

**stimulus generalization** Responding to stimuli similar to the stimulus that had caused the response.

**stimulus motives** Motivating factors that are internal and unlearned, but do not appear to have a physiological basis; stimulus motives cause an individual to seek out sensory stimulation through interaction with the environment.

**stimulus trace** The perceptual persistence of a stimulus after it is no longer present.

**strange situation procedure** A measure of attachment developed by Mary Ainsworth that consists of eight phases during which the infant is increasingly stressed.

**stress** Anything that produces demands on us to adjust and threatens our well-being.

*Strong Interest Inventory* An objective personality test that compares people's personalities to groups that achieve success in certain occupations.

**structuralism** First school of thought in psychology; it studied conscious experience to discover the structure of the mind.

**subject bias** Source of potential error in an experiment from the action or expectancy of a subject; a subject might influence the experimental results in ways that mask the true outcome.

**subjective organization** Long-term memory procedures in which the individual provides a personal method of organizing information to be memorized.

**sublimation** Defense mechanism; a person redirects his or her socially undesirable urges into socially acceptable behavior.

**successive approximation** Shaping; in operant conditioning, the gradual process of reinforcing behaviors that get closer to some final desired behavior.

**sudden infant death syndrome (SIDS)** Situation in which a seemingly healthy infant dies suddenly in its sleep; also called crib death.

**superego** Sigmund Freud's representation of conscience.

**surface traits** In Raymond Cattell's personality theory, the observable characteristics of a person's behavior and personality.

**symbolization** In Sigmund Freud's dream theory, the process of converting the latent content of a dream into manifest symbols.

**systematic desensitization** Application of counterconditioning, in which the individual overcomes anxiety by learning to relax in the presence of stimuli that had once made him or her unbearably nervous.

**task-oriented coping** Adjustment responses in which the person evaluates a stressful situation objectively and then formulates a plan with which to solve the problem.

**test of significance** An inferential statistical technique used to determine whether the difference in scores between the experimental and control groups is really due to the effects of the independent variable or to random chance. If the probability of an outcome is extremely low, we say that outcome is significant.

**Thanatos** Sigmund Freud's term for a destructive instinct such as aggression; also called death instinct.

*Thematic Apperception Test (TAT)* Projective personality test in which subjects are shown pictures of people in everyday settings; subjects must make up a story about the people portrayed.

**theory of social impact** Latané's theory of social behavior; it states that each member of a group shares the responsibility equally.

**Theory X** Douglas McGregor's theory that states that the worker dislikes work and must be forced to do it.

**Theory Y** Douglas McGregor's theory that states that work is natural and can be a source of satisfaction, and, when it is, the worker can be highly committed and motivated.

**therapy** In psychology, the treatment of behavior problems; two major types of therapy include psychotherapy and biological therapy.

**time and motion studies** In engineering psychology, studies that analyze the time it takes to perform an action and the movements that go into the action.

**tip-of-the-tongue phenomenon** A phenomenon in which the closer a person comes to recalling something, the more accurately he or she can remember details, such as the number of syllables or letters.

**token economy** A behavior therapy in which desired behaviors are reinforced immediately with tokens that can be exchanged at a later time for desired rewards, such as food or recreational privileges.

**trace conditioning** A procedure in classical conditioning in which the CS is a discrete event that is presented and terminated before the US is presented.

**trait** A distinctive and stable attribute in people.

**trait anxiety** Anxiety that is long-lasting; a relatively stable personality characteristic.

**transference** Psychoanalytic term used when a patient projects his feelings onto the therapist.

**transsexualism** A condition in which a person feels trapped in the body of the wrong sex.

**trial and error learning** Trying various behaviors in a situation until the solution is found.

**triangular theory of love** Robert Sternberg's theory that states that love consists of intimacy, passion, and decision/commitment.

**triarchic theory of intelligence** Robert Sternberg's theory of intelligence that states that it consists of three parts: componential, experiential, and contextual subtheories.

**Type-A behavior** Behavior shown by a particular type of individual; a personality pattern of behavior that can lead to stress and heart disease.

**unconditional positive regard** Part of Carl Rogers's personality theory; occurs when we accept someone regardless of what he or she does or says.

**unconditioned response (UR)** An automatic reaction elicited by a stimulus.

**unconditioned stimulus (US)** Any stimulus that elicits an automatic or reflexive reaction in an individual; it does not have to be learned in the present situation.

**unconscious mind** In Sigmund Freud's psychoanalytic theory of personality, the part of personality that is unavailable to us; Freud suggests that instincts and unpleasant memories are stored in the unconscious mind.

**undifferentiated schizophrenia** Type of schizophrenia that does not fit into any particular category, or fits into more than one category.

**validity** The degree to which you actually measure what you intend to measure.

**variability** In statistics, variability measures the range of the scores.

**variable interval (VI) schedule** Schedule of reinforcement in which the subject is reinforced for the first response given after a certain time interval, with the interval being different for each trial.

**variable ratio (VR) schedule** Schedule of reinforcement in which the subject is given reinforcement after a varying number of responses; the number of responses required for reinforcement is different for every trial.

**vestibular sense** Sense that helps us keep our balance.

**visuo-spatial sketch pad** Responsible for visual images involved in geographical orientation and spatial task.

**vulnerability-stress model** Theory of schizophrenia that states that some people have a biological tendency to develop schizophrenia if they are stressed enough by their environment.

**Weber's Law** Ernst Weber's law that states that the difference threshold depends on the ratio of the intensity of one stimulus to another rather than on an absolute difference.

**Wechsler Adult Intelligence Scale (WAIS)** An intelligence test for adults, first published by David Wechsler in 1955; it contains verbal and performance subscales.

**Wechsler Intelligence Scale for Children (WISC-III)** Similar to the Wechsler Adult Intelligence Scale, except that it is designed for children ages 6 through 16, and helps diagnose certain childhood disorders, such as dyslexia and other learning disabilities.

**Wechsler Preschool and Primary Scale of Intelligence (WPPSI-R)** Designed for children between the ages of 4 and 7; helps diagnose certain childhood disorders, such as dyslexia and other learning disabilities.

**withdrawal** Unpleasant physical reactions that a drug-dependent user experiences when he or she stops taking the drug.

**within-subject experiment** An experimental design in which each subject is given all treatments, including the control condition; subjects serve in both experimental and control groups.

**working memory** The memory store, with a capacity of about 7 items and enduring for up to 30 seconds, that handles current information.

**Yerkes-Dodson Law** Popular idea that performance is best when arousal is at a medium level.

## Sources for the Glossary:

*The majority of terms in this glossary are from Psychology: A ConnecText 4th Edition, Terry F. Pettijohn. ©1999 Dushkin/ McGraw-Hill, Guilford, CT 06437. The remaining terms were developed by the Annual Editions staff.*

# Test Your Knowledge Form

We encourage you to photocopy and use this page as a tool to assess how the articles in **Annual Editions** expand on the information in your textbook. By reflecting on the articles you will gain enhanced text information. You can also access this useful form on a product's book support Web site at **http://www.dushkin.com/ online/.**

NAME: _____     DATE: _____

TITLE AND NUMBER OF ARTICLE: _____

BRIEFLY STATE THE MAIN IDEA OF THIS ARTICLE: _____

LIST THREE IMPORTANT FACTS THAT THE AUTHOR USES TO SUPPORT THE MAIN IDEA:




WHAT INFORMATION OR IDEAS DISCUSSED IN THIS ARTICLE ARE ALSO DISCUSSED IN YOUR TEXTBOOK OR OTHER READINGS THAT YOU HAVE DONE? LIST THE TEXTBOOK CHAPTERS AND PAGE NUMBERS:




LIST ANY EXAMPLES OF BIAS OR FAULTY REASONING THAT YOU FOUND IN THE ARTICLE:




LIST ANY NEW TERMS/CONCEPTS THAT WERE DISCUSSED IN THE ARTICLE, AND WRITE A SHORT DEFINITION:

ANNUAL EDITIONS revisions depend on two major opinion sources: one is our Advisory Board, listed in the front of this volume, which works with us in scanning the thousands of articles published in the public press each year; the other is you—the person actually using the book. Please help us and the users of the next edition by completing the prepaid article rating form on this page and returning it to us. Thank you for your help!

# ANNUAL EDITIONS: Psychology 01/02

## ARTICLE RATING FORM

Here is an opportunity for you to have direct input into the next revision of this volume. We would like you to rate each of the 43 articles listed below, using the following scale:

**1. Excellent: should definitely be retained**
**2. Above average: should probably be retained**
**3. Below average: should probably be deleted**
**4. Poor: should definitely be deleted**

Your ratings will play a vital part in the next revision. So please mail this prepaid form to us just as soon as you complete it. Thanks for your help!

## RATING | ARTICLE

1. Science and Pseudoscience
2. Research in the Psychological Laboratory: Truth or Triviality?
3. Psychology's Tangled Web: Deceptive Methods May Backfire on Behavioral Researchers
4. The End of Nature Versus Nurture
5. Decoding the Human Body
6. The Future of the Brain
7. The Senses
8. Vision: A Window on Consciousness
9. Noise: A Rising Racket Threatens Our Hearing and Our Quality of Life. Why Isn't That Message Being Heard?
10. Is There a Sixth Sense?
11. Learning Begins Even Before Babies Are Born, Scientists Show
12. Different Strokes for Different Folks?
13. What Constitutes "Appropriate" Punishment?
14. Lots of Action in the Memory Game
15. Speak, Memory
16. Smart Genes?
17. Who Owns Intelligence?
18. Can Animals Think?
19. The Gold Medal Mind
20. Why We're Fat: Gender and Age Matter More Than You May Realize
21. What's in a Face?

## RATING | ARTICLE

22. Emotional Intelligence: Do You Have It?
23. Fetal Psychology
24. Four Things You Need to Know About Raising Baby
25. A World of Their Own
26. Live to 100? No Thanks
27. Start the Conversation
28. The Stability of Personality: Observations and Evaluations
29. Making Sense of Self-Esteem
30. Shyness: The New Solution
31. How to Spot a Liar
32. Coping With Crowding
33. Reducing Prejudice: Combating Intergroup Biases
34. Merits and Perils of Teaching About Other Cultures
35. Mental Health Gets Noticed
36. Mental Disorders Are Not Diseases
37. Depression: Beyond Serotonin
38. The Clustering and Contagion of Suicide
39. The Doubting Disease
40. What You Can Change and What You Cannot Change
41. Think Like a Shrink
42. The Quest for a Cure
43. New Hope for People With Schizophrenia

(Continued on next page)

We Want Your Advice

**ANNUAL EDITIONS: PSYCHOLOGY 01/02**

# BUSINESS REPLY MAIL
FIRST-CLASS MAIL  PERMIT NO. 84  GUILFORD CT

POSTAGE WILL BE PAID BY ADDRESSEE

**McGraw-Hill/Dushkin**
**530 Old Whitfield Street**
**Guilford, CT 06437-9989**

IIIₒₒₒIIₒₒIₒₒIₒIIIₒₒIIIₒₒIIₒIₒIₒIIₒIₒIIₒIₒ

---

## ABOUT YOU

Name _____  Date _____

Are you a teacher? ☐  A student? ☐
Your school's name _____

Department _____

Address _____  City _____  State ____  Zip ____

School telephone # _____

## YOUR COMMENTS ARE IMPORTANT TO US !

Please fill in the following information:
For which course did you use this book?
_____

Did you use a text with this *ANNUAL EDITION*?  ☐ yes  ☐ no
What was the title of the text?
_____

What are your general reactions to the *Annual Editions* concept?
_____

Have you read any particular articles recently that you think should be included in the next edition?
_____

Are there any articles you feel should be replaced in the next edition? Why?
_____

Are there any World Wide Web sites you feel should be included in the next edition? Please annotate.
_____

May we contact you for editorial input?  ☐ yes  ☐ no
May we quote your comments?  ☐ yes  ☐ no